San Francisco
AND THE BAY AREA

Barry Parr
Photography by Michael Yamashita
and Kerrick James

COMPASS AMERICAN GUIDES
An Imprint of Fodor's Travel Publications, Inc.

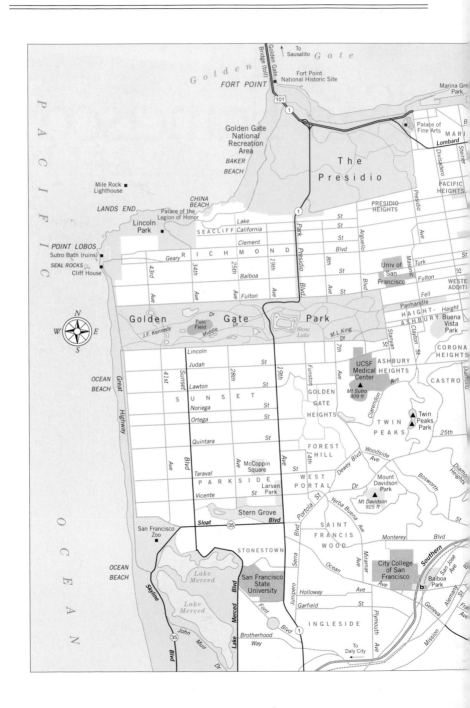

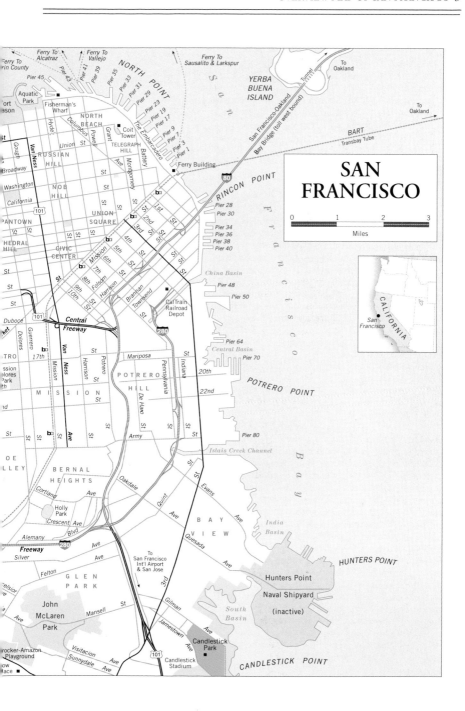

Ferry To Alcatraz
Ferry To Marin County
Ferry To Vallejo
Ferry To Sausalito & Larkspur
To Oakland
To Oakland

NORTH POINT

YERBA BUENA ISLAND

San Francisco-Oakland Bay Bridge (toll west bound)
Tunnel

BART
Transbay Tube

Pier 45
Pier 43
Pier 41
Pier 39
Pier 35
Pier 33
Pier 31
Pier 29
Pier 23
Pier 19
Pier 17
Pier 9
Pier 7
Pier 3
Pier 1

Aquatic Park
Fort Mason
Fisherman's Wharf

Hyde
Columbus
Powell
Grant
Union St

NORTH BEACH
Coit Tower
TELEGRAPH HILL

RUSSIAN HILL
Gough
Van Ness
Broadway
Washington
California

The Embarcadero
Battery
Montgomery
Ave

Ferry Building

NOB HILL

RINCON POINT

80

SAN FRANCISCO

0   1   2   3
Miles

Pier 28
Pier 30

UNION SQUARE
CATHEDRAL HILL
101

Mission
1st St
2nd St
3rd St
4th St

Pier 34
Pier 36
Pier 38
Pier 40

CIVIC CENTER
5th St
6th St
7th St
8th St
9th St
10th St
Folsom
Harrison
Brannan
Townsend

China Basin
Pier 48
Pier 50

San Francisco Bay

CALIFORNIA
San Francisco

Duboce
101
Central Freeway
280

CalTrain Railroad Depot

Pier 64
Central Basin
Pier 70

Duboce
Guerrero
Dolores
17th

Van Ness
Mission
Harrison
Potrero
St
Mariposa
Pennsylvania
Indiana

20th
POTRERO POINT

TRO
Mission
Dolores
Park

MISSION
Potrero
HILL
De Haro St
22nd

St
St
St
St
Army

Pier 80

Islais Creek Channel

Bay

OE
VALLEY

BERNAL HEIGHTS
Cortland
Ave

Oakdale
Quint
Evans
Ave

Holly Park
Crescent Ave

BAY VIEW
Quesada
Ave

India Basin

Alemany
Freeway
Silver
280

Blvd
Ave
Ave

To San Francisco Int'l Airport & San Jose

3rd

HUNTERS POINT

Hunters Point Naval Shipyard
(inactive)

Felton
excelsior
Ave

GLEN PARK

Gilman

South Basin

John McLaren Park
Mansell St
Jamestown
Ave

Candlestick Park

Crocker-Amazon Playground
low place

Visitacion
Sunnydale Ave
101

Candlestick Stadium

CANDLESTICK POINT

San Francisco and the Bay Area

Copyright © 1996 Fodor's Travel Publications, Inc.
Maps Copyright © 1996 Fodor's Travel Publications, Inc.

Fourth Edition
LIBRARY OF CONGRESS CATALOGING-IN-PUBLICATION DATA
Parr, Barry, 1955 -
    San Francisco and the Bay Area/Barry Parr: photography by Michael Yamashita. —4th ed.
    p. cm. — (Compass American guides)
    Includes bibliographical references (p.) and index.
    ISBN 1-878867-92-X
    1. San Francisco (Calif.)—Guidebooks. 2. San Francisco Bay Area (Calif.)—Guidebooks.
    I. Yamashita, Michael S. I. Title. III. Series: Compass American guides (Series)
F869.S33P378 1996   96-18643
917.94'60453—dc20   CIP

Editors: Deke Castleman, Julia Dillon   Designers: Christopher Burt, David Hurst
Managing Editor: Kit Duane   Photo Editor: Christopher Burt
Map Design: Mark Stroud, Moon Street Cartography

Compass American Guides, 5332 College Ave., Suite 201, Oakland, CA 94618
Production House: Twin Age Ltd., Hong Kong   Printed in Hong Kong
10 9 8 7 6 5 4 3 2 1

ACKNOWLEDGMENTS

Thanks are due to my fourth edition editor, **Julia Dillon,** for her insider's advice, perseverance, and first-hand contributions to the book, and especially for her splendidly insightful and entertaining "RESTAURANTS" chapter. Kudos also to **Chris Burt** for his skillful design. I am also grateful to Managing Editor **Kit Duane** for her encouragements over the years. I salute **Mike Yamashita** and **Kerrick James,** photographers par excellence, and **Deke Castleman,** whose articulate, friendly editorial guidance brought the first edition to light. Thanks to **Jim Pire** for the maps on pp. 276 and 282; to **Mark Stroud** for the city and Bay Area maps; and to **Alex Alford** for the illustration on page 9. Thanks to **John Doerper** for his expertise on the Wine Country, and to **Debi Dunn** for last minute indexing.
    Unless otherwise stated, all photography is by Michael Yamashita. The photographs on pp. 5, 15, 62 are used courtesy of Wells Fargo Bank; p. 27 courtesy of California State Library; pp. 16, 24, 39, 43 by permission of the Oakland Museum; pp. 71, 31, 36, 41, 44, 49, 64, 162 courtesy of the San Francisco Library; p. 226 courtesy of Oakland History Center, Oakland Public Library. "A Supermarket in California" by Allen Ginsberg from *Allen Ginsberg Collected Poems 1947-1980,* © 1984 by Allen Ginsberg is reprinted by permission of Harper & Row, Publishers, Inc. "Home, Home, Home" by Lawrence Ferlinghetti, from *Endless Life: Selected Poems,* © 1981 by Lawrence Ferlinghetti, is reprinted by permission of New Directions Books. "Taking the Plunge" from *Tales of the City* © 1978 by Armistead Maupin reprinted by permission of HarperCollins, Inc. The satellite image of San Francisco and other parts of the world can be purchased from Spaceshots, Inc., 33950 Barnby Rd., Acton, CA 93510; (800) 272-2779.

To my parents, Harold and Loraine,
who introduced me to my subject.

C O N T E N T S

Literary Extracts

Maps

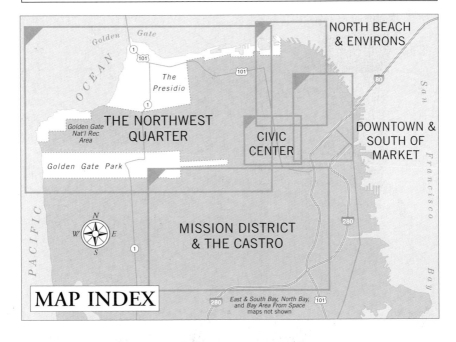

NORTH BEACH & ENVIRONS

THE NORTHWEST QUARTER

CIVIC CENTER

DOWNTOWN & SOUTH OF MARKET

MISSION DISTRICT & THE CASTRO

MAP INDEX

East & South Bay, North Bay, and Bay Area From Space maps not shown

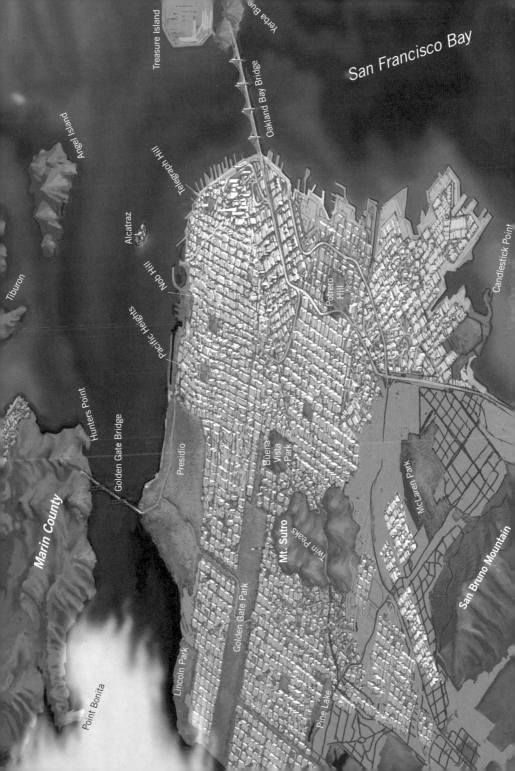

P R E F A C E

GUIDEBOOKS EMPHASIZE WHAT INTERESTS THEIR WRITERS. So it should be asked here, what interests the writer of this guide?

In brief, most everything. The morning's first cappuccino, and the evening's last espresso. Hash browns in a Haight Street diner. Fog horns, lamenting, from Clement Street at night. The engine room of the liberty ship *Jeremiah O'Brien,* pounding under a full head of steam. Bagging a cheap Bierce or Sterling in a used-book store, and cracking it open on the N-Judah, a hundred-some-odd rattling feet beneath Buena Vista Park. Taking the kids to visit the crocs at the Academy of Sciences, or coaxing them down the murky steps of the rock tomb at the Rosicrucian Egyptian Museum. Burritos and a Pacifico Clara at La Imperial, cushioned in the hearty clamor of a dinner time crowd. Cézanne, in silence, at the de Young. An aria hauntingly floating upon the glittering air of the War Memorial Opera House; or better yet, over the fast-disappearing tortellini at Ratto's. The oily reek of the Cable Car Barn, the whir of the cable pulleys, the frantic clang of bells. Starched tablecloths and blunt waiters at an old city grill.

Christmas shopping at Union Square. The salty tang on the air at the Hyde Street Pier. The warm lights of Sausalito, seen from the deck of the homeward ferry. The view from Diamond Heights. The ivy covered stones and musty caves of the Buena Vista wine cellars. The softness of the path beneath enormous redwoods. A German beer at Schroeder's at noon, and at five, an Anchor Steam at Vesuvio's. . . .

I could go on and on. In fact, I do.

Certainly if I had to organize these and all my other interests in order of preference, the book would run differently. Instead, I list them geographically, as befits a guidebook, starting with San Francisco, and proceeding on to day trips around the Bay Area. In the "RESTAURANTS," "HOTELS & INNS," AND "PRACTICALITIES" chapters you will find some names and addresses of a recommended hotels, restaurants, museums, and tour companies; they are by no means the only good ones. And since I cannot know or even like everything, in "RECOMMENDED READING" I've suggested a few of the many wonderful books which cover ground that I have lightly tread.

OVERVIEW

DOWNTOWN

San Francisco's high-rise **Financial District** meets the bay along the curving **Embarcadero**, stretching from **Jackson Square** to **Market Street. South of Market,** or SOMA, embraces a rich mixture of old warehouses, high-tech new buildings, and trendy art spaces. **Union Square** hums by day with shoppers and by night with theater-goers. Beyond lies **Civic Center,** where government offices—as well as the main library and the magnificent halls of ballet, symphony, and opera companies—gather in a stately cluster around City Hall.

NABOBS, SOJOURNERS, BOHEMIANS

Nob Hill, once the domain of the rich and powerful, is today an elite retreat of stately hotels. **Chinatown** clings from its eastern slopes, while **Russian Hill** rises on its north. Between Russian and **Telegraph hills,** the longtime Italian (and onetime Beatnik) enclave of **North Beach** remains a lively quarter of cafes and nightlife. Rolling north, North Beach meets the bay at **Fisherman's Wharf,** where tourists are the major catch.

CULTIVATED QUARTER

The northwest quarter offers culture and lovely patches of green. Fort Mason, the Exploratorium, and the Palace of Fine Arts frame the **Marina District**, with picturesque **Union Street** on its south. Standing guard is the **Presidio,** the woodsy old army headquarters. South across aristocratic Presidio Heights stretches elegant upper **Fillmore Street,** followed by **Japantown.** The residential

Richmond District, hedged in on its north by **Lincoln Park,** on its south by **Golden Gate Park,** and on its west by **Ocean Beach.** Haight Street still waters in the lee of the **Panhandle.**

UNDISCOVERED HALF
San Francisco's southern half, cut by the
lofty ridge of **Twin Peaks**, contains the quiet
Sunset District, as well as the largely Latino
Mission District, with its growing artistic
and nightlife. Clustered around Twin Peaks
are the attractive **Castro**, the nation's largest
gay neighborhood, and the well-kept Victorians of **Noe Valley**. Further south, **Bernal
Heights** and **Potrero Hill** enjoy their incog-
nito status as neighborly residential havens seldom bothered by outsiders.

THE EAST BAY
Oakland is known for its refurbished old business
district and the waterfront's **Jack London Square**.
Brainy and eccentric **Berkeley** centers around the
beautiful campus of the **University of California**,
where visitors come to see the museums, architecture, and antics of student life.

THE SOUTH BAY
The Peninsula stretches south from San Francisco
to **San Jose**, known as the capital of thriving **Silicon
Valley**, including **Palo Alto's Stanford University**.
The Peninsula's coastal side is a different world of
smaller towns, foggy beaches, and rocky cliffs.

THE NORTH BAY
Marin County captivates locals and
tourists alike with charming towns like
Sausalito and alluring parklands including **Point Reyes** and the **Muir Woods**.
The beautiful hills and valleys of **Napa**
and **Sonoma counties** are world famous
as the **Wine Country**, and also shelter
many historical and literary associations.

*Photos on page 12 and at top of page 13 by Kerrick James;
photos in center and at bottom of page 13 by Michael Yamashita.*

INTRODUCTION

LIKE MANY GREAT CITIES, San Francisco was built on a harbor. And like many hardscrabble, tinpot, boom-and-bust towns scattered through the Wild West, she was also slapped down in a rush on barren hills; worse yet, on hills stranded at the tip of a long, foggy peninsula. To these two accidents of history San Francisco owes both her prosperity and her character.

It's hard to conceive of a worse place to build a *serious* city. Maybe not quite as ridiculous as Venice, sinking in the sea, or Timbuktu, stranded by a roving river in the sandy wastes. But those are has-beens, museum pieces forsaken by the type of supercharged entrepreneurs who built them. San Francisco, for better or worse, still remains a dynamic, world-class city.

Still, as thoughtful San Franciscans sometimes admit, maybe the comparison to Venice is not all that far off. The wharfs and factories have long declined, and tourism has become San Francisco's biggest growth industry. That's a hard lump to take for a city that was once the undisputed Queen of the West.

From her Gold Rush birth till the rise of other regional capitals at the turn of the century, San Francisco set the standards of American civilization west of the Mississippi. Culturally and economically, she stood at the center of a vast sphere of influence reaching east to the Rockies, north to Alaska, and south and west to however far American ambitions might be carried by its traders and soldiers of fortune.

From Tombstone to the Klondike, when frontier capitalists sought to sink a mine or corner a market, they bankrolled it in San Francisco. Along the Yukon, when miners craved news of the outside world, they'd part with gold for a Frisco paper. When the Modocs went to war and almost won, it was San Francisco who received the summons for help, and later, the beaten warriors themselves, ferried in chains to Alcatraz. From San Francisco sailed the fleets that seized the Philippines, and likewise, rolled the whiskey and oysters that kept times flush in Virginia City. And in return, whole mountains of silver ore and gold from a thousand godforsaken sagebrush towns were mined, crushed, refined, and shipped, as a matter of course, to San Francisco.

Good or bad, those times have passed. Much of what she was, she is no longer. But to her credit, San Francisco has weathered the loss of stature gracefully. Even now her citizens lay plans to recapture a starring role in the coming Pacific Rim century.

Say what you will about the new wealth and influence of upstart Los Angeles (and most northern Californians can contrive a few choice epithets), San Francisco remains a city of extraordinary presence. Small she may be, but she can part a path through throngs of larger cities with the cast of her eye alone. In her time, she has drunk champagne from a slipper and gone barefoot, dined on both the gristle and the tenderloin, embraced the noblest ideals of humankind, and packed more red-eyed mornings, tragedy, laughter, and waywardness than many a town three and four times her age.

"There are just three big cities in the United States that are *story* cities," observed the novelist Frank Norris. "New York, of course, New Orleans, and best of the lot, San Francisco."

And what great stories they are. Just *look* at the company she's kept—bohemians, frontiersmen, merchants, poets, prostitutes, big spenders, bridge builders, lovers, lunatics, bankers, sailors, bums, rapscallions. . . . Ask any one of them, "What is San Francisco like?" and each would describe a place unlike any other.

A tent "city" sprang up on Telegraph Hill during the gold rush.

San Francisco sporting goods, ca. 1850.

To the ancient Ohlones, she was a cold, foggy shore on the fringe of paradise. To the conquistadores, grinding northward with cross and sword, she was the dire end of banishment, a wilderness of salvageable souls.

To enterprising Yankees, San Francisco will always be the instant city, miraculously begat on barren hills by hordes from every nation: the city of tents and mud, of gold and Comstock silver, alternately burning and rising, each time more stately, to the Grand Finale of 1906 when, from utter destruction, she triumphed phoenix-like from the ashes. This is the city of nabobs in gilded mansions, of cable cars and grand hotels, of gamblers and dance hall girls and the big, bad Barbary Coast; of Mark Twain swapping jokes at the Exchange Saloon, of six-shooters and sawdust-covered floors; of Clark Gable grinning, cigar in teeth, and Jeanette Mac-Donald belting out her song as the city burns around her.

And then there is the real city of rusty plumbing and moldy closets: the working stiff, the unions, the firetrap slums, the shipyards, the great strikes and greater civil engineering projects, the steel bridges, the WPA murals in Coit Tower. This is the city of the Mooney trial, greasy-spoon lunch counters, crowded steam vents, and Salvation Army bands playing street corners South of Market.

For every mother's son and daughter, San Francisco is a gathering of immigrants, each with their separate festivals and foods, and each sampling freely from their neighbors—Chinatown, Russian Richmond, Little Italy, Hunters Point, Little Osaka, and the Mexican, German, Irish, and Samoan settlements of the sprawling Mission District. It's a feast of exotic smells and flavors, of cappuccino in small cafes, sourdough French bread, local wine, Dungeness crab, fortune cookies, chop suey, pasta, cioppino, and Joe's Special. Where else can you dine on Ukranian *golubtzy* to the sound of foghorns, or pick the remnants of Mongolian lamb from your teeth to the accompaniment of an Oktoberfest accordion band?

To the sailor Frisco was a fabled port of call, a town of honky-tonks, tattoo parlors, topless joints, Anchor Steam beer, and monumental Saturday night drunks; a city of blurred Monday mornings, slowly clearing; of sea gulls, white caps, and uniforms, a crisp flag whipping in a clean wind.

Then there's Sam Spade's turf. Hard-boiled, tender at the core. Fedora pulled low, cigarette on lip, dame on elbow. Al Capone doing hard time on The Rock. Crack dealers menacing the Projects. She can be one tough babe.

Yet, always over the next hill lies romantic San Francisco, that "cool, grey City of Love," where couples haunt the stairways, gazing out over a blue bay, flecked with white, gracefully trimmed with gossamer bridges. . . .

Then it's 6 A.M. and the bridges are jammed with commuters bound for Wall Street West—corporate hq, bankers' clubs, bustling clerks, martini lunches, rising steel towers, migraine headaches. Duck left, and you're in the West Coast bastion of progressive idealism: the city of John Muir, the Sierra Club, the Gay Rights Movement, Free Speech, holistic health, and raised consciousness; but also the radical chic, dead-end divisive politics and the cults and movements that continue to repel a fascinated Middle America. The United Nations was born in San Francisco; so were Jonestown and the Symbionese Liberation Army.

Nor let us forget the pipe-dream of Bohemia, where every generation finds and loses a new Latin Quarter. Gone are the artists and their cage birds from the shacks of Telegraph Hill; gone the poets from Papa Coppa's; faded the beatniks, with their wine and jazz; and gone, too, the flower children from a street called Love. Only their stories live on . . . .

More than an accumulation of wood, steel, glass, and brick, San Francisco is a collection of people and their stories. Some are new. Some have been told and embellished for generations. Some are ugly. Some are stranger than fiction. Let the historians dicker which is which; to the traveler who seeks to know San Francisco, they are all of interest.

Taking the Plunge

*M*ary Ann Singleton was twenty-five years old when she saw San Francisco for the first time.

She came to the city alone for an eight-day vacation. On the fifth night, she drank three Irish coffees at the Buena Vista, realized that her Mood Ring was blue, and decided to phone her mother in Cleveland.

"Hi, Mom. It's me."

"Oh, darling. Your daddy and I were just talking about you. There was this crazy man on 'McMillan and Wife' who was strangling all these secretaries, and I just couldn't help thinking . . . "

"Mom . . . "

"I know. Just crazy ol' Mom, worrying herself sick over nothing. But you never can tell about those things. Look at that poor Patty Hearst, locked up in that closet with all those awful . . . "

"Mom . . . long distance."

"Oh . . . yes. You must be having a grand time."

"God . . . you wouldn't believe it! The people here are so friendly I feel like I've . . . "

"Have you been to the Top of the Mark like I told you?"

"Not yet."

"Well, don't you dare miss that! You know, your daddy took me there when he got back from the South Pacific. I remember he slipped the bandleader five dollars, so we could dance to 'Moonlight Serenade,' and I spilled Tom Collins all over his beautiful white Navy . . . "

"Mom, I want you to do me a favor."

"Of course, darling. Just listen to me. Oh . . . before I forget it, I ran into Mr. Lassiter yesterday at the Ridgemont Mall, and he said the office is just falling apart with you gone. They don't get many good secretaries at Lassiter Fertilizers."

"Mom, that's sort of why I called."

"Yes, darling?"

"I want you to call Mr. Lassiter and tell him I won't be in on Monday morning."

"Oh . . . Mary Ann, I'm not sure you should ask for an extension on your vacation."

"It's not an extension, Mom."

"Well, then why . . . ?"

"I'm not coming home, Mom."

Silence. Then, dimly in the distance, a television voice began to tell Mary Ann's father about the temporary relief of hemorrhoids. Finally her mother spoke: "Don't be silly, darling."

—Armistead Maupin, *Tales of the City,* 1978

SAN FRANCISCO'S STORY

SAN FRANCISCO SITS WITH REASONABLE STABILITY on the southern shore of the Golden Gate, surrounded on three sides by seawater. To the west is the Pacific Ocean, perennially chilled by strong Alaskan currents, even on the hottest days, and torn by rough seas murderous to swimmers, and all too often inhospitable to ships. To the east is San Francisco Bay, deep, protected, and so surpassing a harbor that it has been called by many the finest in the world. The two are joined by the Golden Gate, a narrow passage three miles long and a mile wide, which cuts San Francisco off from the northern part of the state.

The famous hills of San Francisco and the Bay Area are part of the Coast Ranges, which run north and south along almost the entire California coast. Their formidable barrier shields the inland valleys from the fogs and winds that plague San Francisco, making a summer hothouse of the interior. East of the Coast Ranges sprawls the fertile Central Valley, the nation's largest fruit and vegetable garden, and east of that, the longest block of granite in the world, the Sierra Nevada range. The rivers of the Sierra Nevada, cherished now for their precious water as they once were for their gold, pour down into the Central Valley, gathering into the Sacramento and San Joaquin rivers. Flowing from the north and south, respectively, these two rivers join in the delta east of Carquinez Straits, where they enter San Francisco Bay and are carried off by strong currents through the Golden Gate. In millennia past, these rivers gouged out the Gate and emptied into the sea some distance beyond. When the oceans rose at the end of the last Ice Age, the canyon and the valley behind were flooded, creating the inland bay of San Francisco.

Of the forces that shaped San Francisco, and which shape her still, the one most likely to concern residents and visitors in any given lifetime is the process of tectonic movement, better known as earthquakes. California's longest and most famous earthquake fault, the San Andreas, runs 650 miles up the coast of California, slipping into the sea just south of San Francisco, and emerging on land again to the north, at Point Reyes. The plate to the west of the San Andreas moves north at an average speed of two inches per year. When pressure builds at a sticking point, and then suddenly breaks loose, the surrounding earth slips and shakes. Earthquakes are an unavoidable feature of the San Francisco Bay Area. The

PETALUMA

Rodgers Creek Fault

Hayward Fault

Budoell Mt Fault

Green Valley Fault

Antioch Fault

VALLEJO

Grizzly Bay

San Pablo Bay

Sacramento

Honker Bay

Concord Fault

River

POINT SAN PEDRO

CONCORD

MT. TAMALPAIS

BRIONES HILLS

SAN PABLO RIDGE

HAYWARD

MOUNT DIABLO

ANGEL ISLAND

ALCATRAZ ISLAND

BERKELEY

LAS TRAMPAS RIDGE

Calaveras

YERBA BUENA ISLAND

POINT BONITA

OAKLAND

POINT LOBOS

SAN FRANCISCO

San Francisco Bay

LIVERMORE

CANDLESTICK POINT

San Francisco earthquake epicenter, 1906

SUNOL RIDGE

HAYWARD

POINT SAN PEDRO

Seal Cove

San Gregorio Fault

ANDREAS

COYOTE POINT

FAULT

Fault

MONTARA MOUNTAIN

Pacific Ocean

Bay

FREMONT

N

W   E

S

SANTA

PALO ALTO

BAY AREA & NATURAL FEATURES

SAN JOSE

CRUZ

Sargent-Berrocal Fault

Major Fault

Concealed or Inferred Fault

BUTANO RIDGE

MOUNTAINS

FAULT

0   5   10

Copyright: Spaceshots, Inc. Miles

famous quake of 1906 was by no means the first—nor will the powerful shaker of 1989 be the last.

■ THE FIRST INHABITANTS

Unlike the desolate, windswept, and inhospitable site of San Francisco itself, the Bay Area counties to the south, east, and north have always shown a natural hospitality to residents. When people first began crossing the Bering Straits from Asia some 20,000–36,000 years ago, the Bay Area was brimming with all the requirements of life. The gentle climate and rich patchwork of woodland, marsh, oak savannah, and upland habitats nurtured an abundance of seabirds, shellfish, ducks, antelope, deer, bear, elk, otter, fox, and rabbit, as well as edible grasses, roots, and acorns. The region also supported a human population of about 10,000 people, who built some 30 or 40 permanent villages around the bay and south to Big Sur. The San Francisco Bay Area was the most densely populated region on the continent north of Mexico, but the site of San Francisco itself attracted few residents.

Based on language groupings, anthropologists identify the native people north of the Golden Gate as the Coast Miwok, while the dominant group throughout the rest of the Bay Area is known by the Spanish names of Ohlone, or Costanoan. In fact, each Ohlone sub-tribe considered itself independent and unique, separated from its neighbors by dialect and customs, despite regular trade and intermarriage. They shared a common dependence on shellfish, as is attested by the 450 gigantic piles of cast-off shells still found around the bay, most spectacularly at Coyote Hills in southern Alameda County. During summer they migrated inland to hunt game and collect acorns to make their mush and bread. Several thousand years of this stable cycle produced a gentle, musical, unwarlike culture that did not keep records of its own past. For an Ohlone to discuss the dead was taboo. Merely making mention of a dead relative in the Ohlone culture was an impropriety equal to cursing one in Western or Asian cultures. Perhaps that is why, after thousands of years on the shores of the bay, their annihilation passed so quietly.

Legends of California flittered about the taverns and libraries of Europe for years before anyone actually came for a look. Recent discoveries of ancient coins and stone anchors suggest that Chinese ships possibly visited the California coast centuries before Columbus blundered into the Caribbean. The first *documented* visit by a foreigner to northern California, however, was made by the Portuguese explorer, João Cabrilho, who sailed up the coast in 1542, somehow missing the Golden Gate. Thirty-seven years later, in 1579, the English privateer Sir Francis Drake, while on an extended mission to harass the Spanish galleons and seize their treasures, made a landing somewhere in the Bay Area. Drake apparently also missed the narrow entrance to the Golden Gate in the fog. His chronicler's description of their anchorage leads most historians to place it at what is now called Drakes Bay, below Point Reyes. Pausing several weeks to repair his ships, Drake claimed the land for Queen Elizabeth I of England and christened it Nova Albion, inscribing his claim on a brass plate. The plate, or a convincing forgery, was found in 1933, and is now on display at the University of California in Berkeley.

■ THE HISPANICS

Another two hundred years passed before a European saw San Francisco Bay. While searching for Monterey Bay, glowingly described almost two centuries earlier by an earlier explorer, Sebastían Vizcaíno, a Spanish scouting party under the command of Gaspar de Portolá stumbled on San Francisco Bay in 1769, having overshot their true mark. Realizing that *this* couldn't possible be Monterey Bay, the soldierly Portolá stuck to his orders, and retraced his steps south.

The task of colonizing this amazing new discovery was assigned to a determined soldier, Juan Bautista de Anza. With his lieutenant, Jose Moraga, a Franciscan priest named Francisco Palóu, and a party of 34 pioneer families, Anza set out on foot from Sonora, Mexico. After a grueling desert march, they arrived at the tip of the peninsula on June 27, 1776 (seven days before another landmark date on the opposite side of the continent). There they took possession for Spain by founding a fortress, the Presidio, on a strategic hill overlooking the Golden Gate, and a church a mile south on a small lake that they named in honor of Our Lady of Sorrows (Nuestra Señora de los Dolores). The adobe church that Father Palóu built on the site, the first of five missions around the bay, was dedicated to Saint Francis of Assisi. In time, the lake's name stuck as the popular name for Mission Dolores, while the great bay itself acquired the Mission's official name, San Francisco.

The Ohlones greeted the newcomers with amazement. Many believed them to be gods—a reason, perhaps, why they succumbed so readily to the new order. The Spanish in California were decidedly more interested in the native peoples *as subjects* than were the English settlers on the Atlantic shore. Their stated purpose was to convert the natives to Christianity, to save their souls while teaching them enough farming, husbandry, and industry to create a self-perpetuating rural society in California. The plan was disastrous. For people accustomed to the subtler pace of seasonal migrations, mission life was hellish. The natives lived in barracks, segregated by sex, and did forced labor. Many ran away, only to be caught, returned, and punished by soldiers. New diseases decimated them. The death rate quickly surpassed the birth rate. Then, in 1821, Mexico broke away from Spain, and the new government secularized the missions. Order, harsh as it was, broke down. The missions decayed. Hopelessly lost from their old ways of life, the Ohlones starved in their homeland. Some drifted off to work the ranches, others to roam in homeless bands that were hunted down and killed. As a people, the Ohlone never recovered. Five thousand Indians, over half the population of the Bay Area before the Spanish arrived, lie buried in unmarked graves at Mission Dolores, Our Lady of Sorrows.

In the wake of sword and cross, Spanish (and later Mexican) civilian families, like Noé, Bernal, Moraga, and Vallejo, settled on vast government land grants, where they built cattle ranches and ruled as benevolent feudal lords. Like the Ohlones before them, the new *Californios* discovered that life in bounteous California could be very sweet indeed. Their ranches produced all that they needed, including an annual cash "crop" of hides, which they sold to passing ships for a good profit. Among the most ambitious of the rancho chieftains was a Swiss, Augustus Sutter, who built a fort to secure his vast empire near the spot where the American River empties into the Sacramento River—today the site of California's state capital, Sacramento.

Ironically, the hide trade destroyed the ranchers' isolation by bringing foreign ships to San Francisco in slowly increasing numbers. The Western world was in an expansive mood. The Pacific was opening up, and San Francisco Bay made a splendid anchorage for a Pacific empire. Mexico lacked the power to enforce her claim. As early as 1812, the Russians established Fort Ross, ostensibly as a hunting station, 60 miles north of San Francisco. French and English ships were investigating. When the Yankee sailor-turned-writer Richard Henry Dana described his 1835 visit to the bay in *Two Years Before the Mast*, Americans pricked up their ears. Expansionists among them were particularly intrigued to learn that a small, mostly Yankee settlement was already established above a cove on the eastern side of the San Francisco peninsula.

■ THE YANKEES

American and English ships had long preferred Yerba Buena
Cove to the traditional Spanish anchorage off the Presidio,
because it was better sheltered. In the year of Dana's visit,
an Anglo sailor named William Richardson
built a house there, laying out a street
and a village plaza. Being married
to the Presidio *commandante*'s
daughter, Richardson settled
with official blessing. Others
followed, and the settlement
became known as Yerba
Buena.

With classic entrepreneurial
spirit, Yerba Buena found a need
and filled it, in this case, with a ship's
chandler and a couple of grog shops. But it was
enough. On the verge of the cataclysmic 1840s, the
three sprigs on which San Francisco would bloom
had sprouted. Each was separated by an hour's
walk from the others. Two—the Mission Dolores
and the Presidio—were fast declining, but the third, the
wretched, flea-bitten, sand-blown, largely Yankee village

Spanish armor.

of Yerba Buena, was preparing to take up the torch. Richardson's street, Calle de la
Fundación (Foundation Street), would one day become Grant Avenue, and the
dusty village plaza would become Portsmouth Plaza.

The American presence in California grew in the 1840s as increasing numbers
of immigrants cut south from the Oregon Trail. The Mexican governor com-
plained uselessly about the "hoards of Yankee emigrants whose progress we cannot
arrest." America was expanding. "Manifest Destiny!" was the cry justifying west-
ward migration, settlement, and war. In 1846, the United States annexed Texas
and invaded Mexico. U.S. Senator Daniel Webster's dexterous tongue was claiming
that San Francisco Bay alone was worth 10 Texases.

The climax came that same year. A party of bombastic Yankees in Sonoma,

California, prodded on by a meddlesome American soldier of fortune named Captain John C. Frémont, raised a flag with a picture of a bear on it, and declared independence from Mexico. The California Republic lasted less than a month. On July 9, 1846, a party of American marines and sailors from the warship *Portsmouth*, under command of Captain John Montgomery, seized the plaza at Yerba Buena and ran the Stars and Stripes up a pole. The Presidio, staffed by 12 Mexican soldiers and a sergeant, surrendered peacefully. Yerba Buena was now American territory.

Big changes came quickly to Yerba Buena. Most propitiously, the citizens changed the town's name to San Francisco. Boosters argued that by taking the name of the famous bay, their town would grow famous by association and, more to the point, attract shipping away from any other bayside ports. It was a shrewd move of enormous consequences. In keeping with their grand hopes, San Francisco's first elected administrator hired an Irish sailor, Jasper O'Farrell, to draw up a street plan for the town.

Even more ambitious plans were being laid by an enterprising newcomer named Sam Brannan, who had arrived at the head of a party of Mormons shortly after the American seizure. Some have called Brannan San Francisco's founding

SAILING WITH DANA

*W*e sailed down this magnificent bay with a light wind, the tide, which was running out, carrying us at the rate of four or five knots. It was a fine day; the first of entire sunshine we had had for more than a month. We passed directly under the high cliff on which the presidio is built, and stood into the middle of the bay, from whence we could see small bays making up into the interior, large and beautifully wooded islands, and the mouths of several small rivers. If California ever becomes a prosperous country, this bay will be the center of its prosperity. The abundance of wood and water; the extreme fertility of its shores; the excellence of its climate, which is as near to being perfect as any in the world; and its facilities for navigation, affording the best anchoring grounds in the whole western coast of America,—all fit it for a place of great importance.

—Richard Henry Dana, *Two Years Before the Mast*, 1840

father. Others dismiss him as an opportunist or even a charlatan. Still, by hook or crook, Brannan managed to push to the head of nearly every scheme of improvement in San Francisco over the next booming decade. Brannan quickly broke with the Salt Lake church, and became San Francisco's leading booster. He delivered San Francisco's first English sermon, performed its first non-Catholic marriage, founded its first newspaper *(The California Star)*, helped establish the first school, and built stores both in San Francisco and at Sutter's Fort. Yet Sam Brannan's greatest coup came in 1848, after Sutter's foreman, James Marshall, discovered gold in the American River. Fearful of the awful turmoil that the discovery would bring to his rancho, Sutter sought advice from Brannan, begging his confidence. Brannan offered solace. By most accounts, he then quickly bought up waterfront lots and placed orders to stock his stores in Sacramento and San Francisco with food, dry goods, and digging tools. The next week found him in San Francisco with a bottle of the glittering metal, shouting "Gold! Gold from the American River!"

As a lesson in history and shrewd business practices, let it not be forgotten that of the thousands of gold seekers who rushed into California in the ensuing madness, a few struck it rich. But it was Sam Brannan who became San Francisco's first millionaire.

■ THE GOLD RUSH

The California Gold Rush is arguably the most extraordinary event to ever befall an American city in peacetime. At the beginning of 1848, the year that gold was discovered, San Francisco was a backwater of some 800 souls. Within a few months, its population was approaching 25,000, and its postal service handling an estimated million letters a year. By 1852, despite having been practically burnt to the ground on six occasions, San Francisco was the fourth largest entrepôt in the United States. By 1860, 14 years after Montgomery had seized the sleepy village, it was a metropolis of 56,000, poised to underwrite a large portion of Union expenses in the Civil War.

In time, California's rich land and climate undoubtedly would have attracted floods of immigrants, but the Gold Rush telescoped a half century of growth into half a year. Within weeks, the news that had electrified California and Mexico was spreading like a shipboard plague to the Eastern seaboard, the Midwest, South America, Asia, Europe, and Australia. Within months, about 90,000 men (and a very few women) struck out for California. (Another 150,000 would arrive before the rush ended in 1852.) Thousands of Americans commenced walking west, and thousands more set sail around Cape Horn or to the Isthmus of Panama. Packed ships sailed from Central and South America, the Sandwich Islands (Hawaii), China, and every seaport of Europe. The lucky ones who arrived in 1848 got first crack at the gold, but the bulk who arrived in 1849 earned the eternal sobriquet of *forty-niners*.

Most of those who came by ship landed in San Francisco, the first convenient anchorage within the Golden Gate. Other rival settlements on San Francisco Bay, particularly Benicia, were closer to the mines, but most of the argonauts were ignorant of California geography, and San Francisco *was* the famous name. On landing, many asked the way to the Mother Lode in the Sierra Nevada as though it were just up the street. Finding that a long overland journey still awaited them, they stopped to buy supplies and make plans. A tent city sprang up to house and serve them. As crews deserted to join the rush, abandoned ships were winched ashore (or the shore built out to them) for use as storehouses and hotels. Demand for nearly everything ran rampant, and supplies were perpetually being hoarded or

Miners in 1852 wash the gold from their diggings in a "long tom."

liquidated by speculators. Prices for basic commodities (food, cots, picks, shovels) rocketed to heights that won't be seen again, if we're lucky, until well into the twenty-first century—yet they sold briskly enough in 1849.

Overnight, San Francisco became the most cosmopolitan city on Earth. Although Americans comprised about half the population from 1847 to 1860, the other half was a mixture of British subjects, with the Irish in the lead, and considerable minorities of Chinese, Hispanics, continental Europeans, and Hawaiians. Most of the Hispanics came from Mexico and Chile, while Germany, France, Switzerland, Poland, Sweden, Belgium, and Italy supplied most of the Continentals. In 1860, 10 percent of San Francisco was non-white, mostly Chinese.

The ratio between the sexes was downright alarming. In 1847, men outnumbered women two to one. Things worsened drastically by 1849, when the ratio jumped to ten to one. The relative lack of women remained a serious problem in San Francisco throughout most of the century, no doubt adding fire to the Barbary Coast, the city's notorious red-light district.

San Francisco's was a youthful population, liberally sprinkled with professionals and educated gentlemen. Most had come with every intention of returning home just as soon as they made their millions. For the majority, that day never came. Surface gold was picked clean by 1849, and the deeper placers, painstakingly washed through pans and cradles, wore thin by 1852. Gold mining was becoming a corporate enterprise, better suited to companies that could raise the capital to bore tunnels or invest in expensive hydraulic mining equipment. The independent forty-niner was an anachronism. A handful went home rich. Many more departed poor. Others fanned out through the West in search of another bonanza. Solvent or broke, thousands more made their way to San Francisco.

California gold played fickle with the forty-niners, but it had not eluded San Francisco. In 1853, some tents still crowded the hillsides, but a substantial city of wood and brick had taken root. Fires roared through the city regularly. Heinrich Schliemann, the German archaeologist, was roused from his Portsmouth Square Hotel bed by the huge fire of May 4, 1851, which burned a quarter of the city. He fled up Telegraph Hill in time to catch a "frightful but sublime view" of "the roaring of the storm, the cracking of the gunpowder, the cracking of the falling stonewalls, the cries of the people and the wonderful spectacle of an immense city burning. . . ." San Francisco rebuilt, only to burn again on November 9, 1852.

San Francisco rebuilt again. Aside from a permanent population well exceeding

Benicia's old state capitol recalls its fleeting year of glory (1853–54).

30,000 people, the city now supported a lending library, scores of warehouses, theaters, eateries, hotels, brothels, a dozen newspapers, a handful of churches, and hundreds of saloons and gambling halls. New piers and landfill pushed out where Yerba Buena Cove once was, burying the old harbor along with the ships anchored therein. Forty square blocks of downtown were built on the landfill. Stockton Street, on the hill above, was the fashionable residential avenue. A new residential quarter reached south of Market to soon-to-be-fashionable Rincon Hill. Hispanic and Mediterranean settlers were already transforming Telegraph Hill and North Beach into a "Latin quarter." The Chinese had dispersed throughout the city, but their main settlement was forming along Sacramento Street. Another village of Chinese fishermen stood at the foot of Rincon Hill, in the shadow of today's Bay Bridge. Pacific Street, along the base of Telegraph Hill, was taking in some rough Australian characters, who called themselves the Sydney Ducks; in time, "Sydneytown" would reach full bloom as the notorious Barbary Coast.

A city full of frisky young gents can get a bit wild. Duels were fought in the crowded streets. Gangs of criminals robbed, extorted, and terrorized, sometimes setting fires and looting. The Chilean settlement on Telegraph Hill was a frequent target of hooligans like the Hounds, a gang of New Yorkers and Australians. The law was slow and the citizens impatient. In 1849, and again in 1851, Sam Brannan harangued the city's established community into taking justice into their own hands. The first incident ended with exile for six Hounds, but the mob settled for nothing less than lynching the second time around.

Vigilantism struck again in May 1856, after the righteous editor of the *Evening Bulletin*, James King of William, was gunned down by a shady city councilman who resented the *Bulletin's* charges of corruption. Thousands of citizens rallied around a new Committee of Vigilance, seizing the councilman, James Casey, and lynching him and a cohort, a gambler named Charles Cora. Taking up quarters in a sand-bagged building on Sacramento Street, nicknamed Fort Gunnybags, the committee set about striking terror in the criminal populace with torchlight parades and more lynchings. It finally disbanded on July 29, leaving its supporters and condemners both claiming victory, and the criminal element temporarily cowed.

Manic times breed eccentric characters, and San Francisco has bred more than a few from its earliest days. There was James Lick, the fabulous millionaire who was so tight that he wore cast-off clothes, until he repented toward the end of his life and gave his fortune away. Then there was William Walker, the adventurer who tried to make himself dictator of Nicaragua, only to die before a Honduran firing squad. And there was "Honest" Harry Meiggs, the beloved city booster who funded large and generous civic improvement schemes with borrowed cash, and skipped town hours before the bubble burst. The most fantastic eccentric of all, however, was Emperor Norton.

Joshua A. Norton came to San Francisco from London in 1849. He became a merchant, reinvested his profits in land, and prospered. In 1854, he set plans to corner the rice market, pouring all his resources into the scheme. Unfortunately for him, a rice ship sailed through the Golden Gate while he still held his hoard, and prices plummeted. Norton went bankrupt and disappeared. Then one day, several months later, he reappeared on Montgomery Street in military costume with epaulets, plumed hat and a cane. Stopping by the offices of the *San Francisco Bulletin,* he announced that he was henceforth to be known as Norton I, Emperor of the United States and Protector of Mexico.

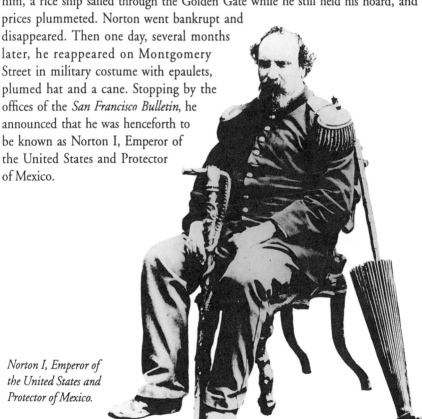

Norton I, Emperor of the United States and Protector of Mexico.

Short, slight, bearded, with clear, fierce eyes and a proud mien, Emperor Norton set about seriously to rule his empire. San Francisco, tongue in cheek, decided to play along. A printer agreed to print the Emperor's currency, and merchants agreed to honor it. The Emperor dined gratis wherever he pleased, and restaurateurs vied for the publicity of his patronage. It was said that no theater opened a performance between 1855 and 1880 without reserving free first-night seats for the Emperor and his faithful dogs, Lazarus and Bummer. Another seat was kept for him in the Sacramento legislature, which he addressed in earnest on occasion. When his uniform became ragged, he appeared before the Board of Supervisors, who amended the city charter so that he would receive an allowance for as long as he lived. In short, the city kept up its end of the madman's charade for almost 30 years, and he in turn never wore out his welcome. In fact, he took some pains to govern conscientiously. His directive to erect a tree for children at Christmas on Union Square is honored to this day. It was said that he attended both Christian and Jewish services to encourage religious harmony, and that he once diffused an anti-Chinese riot by standing at the front and reciting the Lord's Prayer till the combatants put down their fists and departed in shame. When he died in 1880, thousands from every quarter of the city came to bury him with all the pomp and dignity befitting his rank.

■ BOOM TIMES, AND BUST

As the 1850s drew to an end, the spontaneous energy that animated Gold Rush San Francisco lost torque. The economy slowed, men drifted home or took up wage-paying jobs, and society began to stabilize. Californians worried over the recession, but also began to explore other golden opportunities that were awaiting them in farming, industry, and government corruption. By the late 1850s, San Francisco had weathered its first depression and was settling into a pattern of civic and commercial growth typical of most other American cities. Little did anyone expect that San Francisco was in for another big boom.

In 1859, some California drifters stumbled on a fabulous vein of silver in the desert mountains east of the Sierra Nevada. A new rush was on. Rough-and-tumble Virginia City sprang preposterously up on the steep, dry mountainside of Mount Davidson in Washoe, soon to be the new state of Nevada. Unlike the California Gold Rush of a decade earlier, the Comstock Lode, as it came to be known, was a game unsuited to stalwart independents. Capital, heavy equipment, engineers, and organized manpower were needed to run the expensive operation of extracting, crushing, and refining the ore. Experienced San Francisco mining companies responded with a speed and know-how that drove individual prospectors, literally, into the ground. San Francisco had a good return on investment. The Comstock Lode proved to be the world's richest silver deposit. The better part of two decades was needed to exhaust its bounty.

As Virginia City grew into a factory town, where shifts worked round the clock in grim conditions, San Francisco grew fabulously rich. In short time, a new breed of millionaire, the "Bonanza Kings," was staking out gilded mansions on Nob Hill and showering patronage on the plenteous new diversions that mushroomed up to serve them. But San Francisco's benefits did not stop at Nob Hill and luxurious French restaurants. Comstock silver stimulated general prosperity, creating jobs and optimism for the city at large. William C. Ralston, an early Comstock developer and partner in the Bank of California, lent his fortune and stature to many civic projects, including factories, mills, streets, theaters, office buildings, Golden Gate Park, and the largest, most princely hotel of its day, the Palace (see page 70). His contributions and boosterism inspired some to hail him as "the man who built San Francisco."

These colorful times were fortunately well described to us by a host of San Francisco's writers. Bret Harte was among the first to receive national recognition for his heart-tugging stories of the Gold Rush. His cloying sentimentality, which proved popular in the East (and West), was counteracted by the misanthropic genius, Ambrose Bierce, whose "Devil's Dictionary" is a classic of American cynicism. They were backed by a host of lesser lights: South Seas enthusiast Charles Stoddard and the eccentric frontier poet, Joaquin Miller, as well as the doyen of California poets and scribblers, Ina Coolbrith, loved by many, beloved by all. Most famous of all, and perhaps most characteristic of San Francisco despite the fact that he lived there for less than three years, was Mark Twain. His rambling, humorous, satirical voice *was* the voice of San Francisco's better half—tolerant and curious, appreciative of the finer things, debunking pomposity, comfortably American. Robert Louis Stevenson and Rudyard Kipling passed through town and left their marks, as did Oscar Wilde, in the 1880s. A new generation—George Sterling, Frank Norris, Gertrude Atherton, and Jack London—would rise before the century ended.

The 1860s in San Francisco was an era of robust new confidence. Californians rode out the Civil War in the Union camp with little sacrifice of life and, incidentally,

The extravagant tastes and wealth of Victorian San Francisco decorate the city's architecture. James Lick imported the Conservatory of Flowers (left), now in Golden Gate Park, for his private garden. The "Painted Ladies" on Alamo Square (top) are oft-cited (and photographed) examples of Victorian architecture, which is known for its fanciful ornamentation. (top and above photos, Kerrick James)

profits intact. Now they were ready to take on the world. They were betting heavily on a new transcontinental railway that was pushing across the Sierra Nevada toward the East, financed by a Congress anxious to tie California (with its gold) and Nevada (with its silver) closer to the Union. Californians saw their isolation from the rest of the country as a barrier to development. It took a month to send a letter east by Panama steamer, and 20 to 24 days by Butterfield Stage. The Pony Express had done it in nine days to Saint Joseph, Missouri, but that enterprise went bankrupt after only 18 months, in 1861. The completion of the first transcontinental telegraph line improved communications, but Californians were betting that the railroad would bring a big boon to the state's economy.

The Central Pacific Railway was the pet project of an engineer named Theodore Judah, who personally surveyed the difficult route across the precipitous Sierra Nevada mountains. He sold his idea to four Sacramento businessmen, who found the government incentive of free land and cheap loans quite irresistible. The Big Four, as they came to be known, pushed the railroad into reality, joining up with the westward-bound Union Pacific at Promontory Point, Utah, in 1869. For their troubles, they reaped vast fortunes and created the most powerful political machine in California, the Southern Pacific Railway. They all built palaces on Nob Hill, where their names—Leland Stanford, Charles Crocker, Collis Huntington, and Mark Hopkins—are today enshrined in some of the finest hotels in San Francisco.

San Franciscans celebrated the transcontinental railroad's completion with characteristic abandon, ignoring the dire predictions of a remarkable economist, Henry George, who wrote

Nob Hill mansions embodied their masters' wealth, power, and ostentatiousness.

in a San Francisco magazine that the railroad would enrich few and impoverish many. He claimed that completion of the line would flood California with cheap manufactured goods from the eastern states, ruining California's fledgling industrial base, while the ranks of the unemployed would swell with terminated railroad workers from all over the west. He was right.

Like everyone else, William Ralston had banked heavily on the transcontinental railway. But when the boom turned to bust, Ralston was caught overextended to the tune of five million dollars. With characteristic attention to smooth business form, he closed the doors of his bank and tendered his formal resignation. That afternoon, he drowned in San Francisco Bay.

The working classes chose another course. The unemployed rose in anger against the rich railroad men and, most tragically, against the thousands of Chinese workers who had been released from the railroad, and on whom they blamed the loss of American jobs. The depression of the 1870s heralded probably the bleakest era in San Francisco's history.

■ THE CHINESE

The largest ethnic group in the city today, and one of the most influential since the beginning of the Gold Rush, the Chinese played an enormously important part in the opening of the West, California in particular. The first Chinese arrived in San Francisco in 1848, and by the following year there were about 300. They were welcomed with curiosity. Their merchants contributed to the material comfort of the rustic city, and American forty-niners readily learned to enjoy Chinese food and festivals.

The era of good feeling lasted only as long as easy gold. When the placers wore thin, laws were passed to restrict foreign competition, and sometimes enforced with violence. Even when forced to work only abandoned claims, most Chinese miners succeeded through persistent toil and lower expectations—after all, an ounce of gold went a lot further in China, where most intended to return, than it did in America. This determination to return to China encouraged few Cantonese miners to learn English or to assimilate, which reinforced their segregation.

Chinese laborers helped to build the dikes along the Sacramento River, and to plant orchards and vineyards in the fertile California valleys. They pioneered California's fisheries, and were instrumental in developing textile manufacturing, leather-working, cigar-making, and other industries. They were highly valued in construction; in fact, San Francisco's first stone structure, the Parrott Building, was quarried in China and assembled by Chinese builders (who, incidentally, staged San Francisco's first labor strike). Their most celebrated job, however, was with the transcontinental railway, when 10,000 Chinese joined other teams in laying the tracks across the formidable Sierra Nevada range. The Chinese proved strong and brave rail men, who tackled dangerous jobs with fortitude, and set records for laying track. When the job was done and the workers released from contract, thousands drifted to San Francisco, raising the ranks of the unemployed.

The depression of the 1870s hit San Francisco hard. California factories found competition from the east coast too much to bear. Bankruptcies put hundreds out of work, sowing militancy among the unemployed. Many tycoons bolstered their profits by hiring Chinese workers at lower wages—which still exceeded what they could earn in China. These practices spurned bitter resentment against the industrialists, but the Chinese were an easier target. With encouragement from sand-lot fire-eaters, hooligans bullied them. Riotous mobs stormed Chinatown, both in San Francisco and other Western towns, destroying property, and all too often committing murder. Labor organizers used the power of the vote to push politicians to

Though it has moved more than once and now occupies a modern building, the Kong Chow Temple is said by some to be the oldest Chinese temple in the United States.

pass laws, like the Exclusion Act, to harass the Chinese, and ultimately to end Chinese immigration. The Chinese could not vote; the efforts of their organizations to fight these laws in court came to naught.

To understand what happened next, it helps to understand how Chinatown was organized.

Chinatown was, and in some respects still is, a village within a city. Partly in response to outside prejudice, but also out of inclination to live in a familiar society, Chinese emigrants during the nineteenth century built Chinatowns wherever they settled. There were many throughout the American West, but San Francisco's was the largest. In violent times its population swelled with refugees.

Most Chinese who came to America in the nineteenth century joined a *tong*, or social organization, based on their place of origin. A cross between a labor guild and an insurance company, tongs negotiated contracts for members, and provided protection and support in return for dues. Rivalry between different tongs, carried over from regional rivalries on the Chinese mainland, sometimes resulted in violence.

To control tong rivalry, Chinese merchants formed a federation of representatives of six of the largest tongs, called The Six Companies. (Membership later expanded to seven, but the name remained the same.) With occasional involvement by the Consul General of China, who had an office in San Francisco, the Six Companies managed Chinatown's public affairs, including its official relations with the outside community.

Until toppled in 1911, the Manchu government forced all Chinese males to wear queues.

The Six Companies was a paternalistic organization. It took care of such matters as arbitrating disputes, issuing exit certificates to persons who could prove they had paid their debts, caring for the sick, and dispensing charity. The Six Companies' leadership also protested, unsuccessfully, against importing prostitutes from China. Unfortunately, their purpose was completely misunderstood by the non-Chinese public, who confused them with the fighting tongs, and charged them with violence and duplicity. Ironically, had the public backed the Six Companies, they probably could have prevented the era of Chinatown lawlessness called the tong wars.

The failure of the Six Companies to halt the tong wars was a direct result of anti-Chinese legislation—the Geary Act of 1892, which declared that all Chinese had to carry identity papers or face deportation. The Six Companies opposed the law by advising Chinese not to comply, while levying a small sum from members to hire lawyers to fight it in court. Although many of the best lawyers of the day insisted that the act was unconstitutional, it passed and was enforced. When the first Chinese were arrested for not carrying proper documentation, the Six Companies suffered a monumental loss of prestige. Underworld leaders moved fast to take advantage of the vacuum, strengthening individual tongs at the expense of the federation. Rival interests of different tongs quickly crossed, and rivalry quickly turned to violence.

The tongs fought over control of gambling and prostitution—diversions quite popular in the bachelor societies fossilized by the Exclusion Act. Extortion grew rampant, and the gangsters enforced their dictates with professional gunmen, known to police and later Hollywood films as highbinders, or hachetmen. The law-abiding majority of Chinatown, caught between an unsympathetic American public and lethal terrorism from within, suffered tremendously.

The tong wars were a reign of terror, and yet one that most non-Chinese followed only as a curiosity in the morning newspapers. It's only fair to note, however, that many non-Chinese rose to their defense. Many policemen genuinely served to protect the community, despite language barriers and widespread, often justified, mistrust of police. Working with English-speaking (and extremely brave, considering the risks) merchants, dedicated officers managed to bring some of the criminals to justice, but others were freed by corrupt lawyers and courts, returning to Chinatown swearing vengeance on their betrayers. Religious groups like the Methodists and the Presbyterians joined the fray.

Probably the most flamboyant crusader against the tong-controlled prostitution trade was a woman of splendidly ferocious character by the name of Donaldina

*Children were
a rare sight in
Chinatown
until relatively
recent years.*

Cameron. The spearhead of a Presbyterian mission force to rescue Chinese prostitutes, she swooped into her work with gargantuan energy. She was assisted in this
war by a band of equally courageous (and even less well-known) agents and associates from Chinatown, who lived willingly under constant, deadly threat—for
though gangsters were hesitant to harm a white woman (and to suffer the full
force of U.S. law tumbling down on their heads), they worried considerably less
about assassinating a fellow Chinese. It was said that Donaldina Cameron knew
every rooftop and passageway of Chinatown, and was a veritable devil at hunting
down hidden bagnios, which she physically stormed with the backup of her iron-
hearted comrades and a police contingent. Even more importantly, she followed
up on arrests with court battles. As her reputation grew, escaping prostitutes
sought her refuge, often with the help of merchants or young lovers, who took
grave risks, and sometimes paid with their lives. To this day, this extraordinary
woman is still remembered as Lo Ma (Old Mother) in Chinatown.

   Donaldina Cameron helped drive the tongs into retreat, but two other phenomena really struck the killing blows. One was the 1906 earthquake, which initiated a complete rebuilding of Chinatown and the reestablishment of the Six Companies' prestige. The other, and most important, cause was the Americanization of
the Chinese, which ended the hold that the tongs had over the community.

■ THE EARTHQUAKE AND FIRE

The years before 1906—especially the era of Mayor Eugene Schmitz and his grafting king-maker, Abe Ruef—were the most perniciously corrupt that the city ever knew. The Gilded Age, as it was known, pampered millionaires on Nob Hill while the labor movement boiled under pressure in the tenements south of Market. The middle classes built rows of wooden Victorians on hills far removed from the strife of Chinatown and the Barbary Coast, while confident downtown businesses expanded ever upward in daring new "skyscrapers." The port, bolstered by new business in the Philippines following the 1898 Spanish-American War, was booming. Ferries steamed between the new Ferry Building and the growing suburbs of Oakland and Marin County. Cable cars and streetcars linked distant neighborhoods of the city, pushing its boundaries to the Western Addition, the Mission District, and beyond. Theaters played to lively houses, and the higher-class red-light district, the Tenderloin, waxed complacent under semi-official protection. In Golden Gate Park, the citizenry gathered in their Sunday best to stroll, picnic, and race fast coaches. San Francisco was *the* metropolis of the Pacific, the largest, finest, most powerful American city west of Chicago.

On the morning of April 18, 1906, San Francisco's 400,000 citizens were jolted awake by a quake now estimated at 8.25 on the Richter Scale. Chimneys crashed through roofs, gas and water mains broke all over town, and fissures opened in landfill streets. Surveying damage in the better residential districts, San Franciscans were relieved to see that the city had been spared calamity. Except for the flimsy tenements south of Market Street, the wooden Victorian neighborhoods had withstood the quake with only minor damage.

Downtown, however, received a worse shock. City Hall crumbled into rubble, a victim of the scams and shortcuts taken by scoundrelly politicians and their contractors. The Central Emergency Hospital also fell, burying doctors, nurses, and patients. Considering the severity of the quake, loss of life was small, yet devastating, in that one of the victims was Fire Chief Dennis Sullivan. More than any man in the city, Sullivan might have checked the disaster that followed.

Fifty-two fires broke out that morning. The fire department fought desperately, but with water mains broken and the fire chief dying, the flames spread unchecked. Racing through the tinderbox tenements south of Market, firestorms engulfed the Palace Hotel, torched the skyscrapers, leaped over Market, and roared into the Financial District.

The lofty esteem that old-time San Franciscans held for their fire fighters is eloquently illustrated in this splendid helmet of bygone days. San Francisco, which always has been and still is predominantly a city of wood, burned to the ground on more than one occasion, despite the often heroic deeds of the fire department. Separate fire companies used to compete for the glory of being the first on the scene of a blaze, and San Franciscans followed the exploits of their neighborhood companies in much the same way as modern citizens support their local sport teams.

The fire of 1906 burned so hot that it melted metal, fused dishes (left), and according to one story, actually incinerated a collection of diamonds stored in a South of Market safe.

TWAIN MEETS HIS FIRST EARTHQUAKE

A month afterward I enjoyed my first earthquake. It was one which was long called the "great" earthquake, and is doubtless so distinguished till this day. It was just after noon, on a bright October day. I was coming down Third Street. The only objects in motion anywhere in sight in that thickly built and populous quarter, were a man in a buggy behind me, and a street car wending slowly up the cross street. Otherwise, all was solitude and a Sabbath stillness. As I turned the corner, around a frame house, there was a great rattle and jar, and it occurred to me that here was an item!—no doubt a fight in that house. Before I could turn and seek the door, there came a really terrific shock; the ground seemed to roll under me in waves, interrupted by a violent joggling up and down, and there was a heavy grinding noise as of brick houses rubbing together . . .

The "curiosities" of the earthquake were simply endless. Gentlemen and ladies who were sick, or were taking a siesta, or had dissipated till a late hour and were making up lost sleep, thronged into the public streets in all sorts of queer apparel, and some without any at all. One woman who had been washing a naked child, ran down the street holding it by the ankles as if it were a dressed turkey. Prominent citizens who were supposed to keep the Sabbath strictly, rushed out of saloons in their shirt-sleeves, with billiard cues in their hands. Dozens of men with necks swathed in napkins, rushed from barber-shops, lathered to the eyes or with one cheek clean shaved and the other still bearing a hairy stubble. . . . A lady sitting in her rocking and quaking parlor, saw the wall part at the ceiling, open and shut twice, like a mouth, and then drop the end of a brick on the floor like a tooth. She was a woman easily disgusted with foolishness, and she arose and went out of there. One lady who was coming down stairs was astonished to see a bronze Hercules lean forward on its pedestal as if to strike her with its club. They both reached the bottom of the flight at the same time—the woman insensible from the fright. . . .

—Mark Twain, description of the 1865 earthquake from *Roughing It*, 1872

The fire of 1906 destroyed far more buildings than the earthquake.

As thousands of refugees streamed to makeshift shelters in the parks and Presidio, others escaped by ferry to Oakland and Marin County. The army took over law and order in the city, with orders to kill looters on sight. Seven, in fact, were shot, one accidentally. Army dynamiters blasted through old neighborhoods in a clumsy attempt to clear firebreaks. By night, Oaklanders stared in horror at the burning city across the bay.

The flames burned for four days, destroying the downtown districts, Chinatown, North Beach, Russian Hill, Telegraph Hill, Nob Hill, and parts of the Mission District. It was finally contained at wide Van Ness by dynamiting the mansions along the eastern curb. The docks, protected by seawater sprayed by fireboats, survived, as did tiny pockets along the crests of Russian and Telegraph hills, and in the Barbary Coast. The Old Mint likewise survived to assume the role of the city's bank in the days ahead.

In all, 674 persons were listed as killed or missing. Three quarters of the city's residences and businesses burned, including almost the entire city center. More than half the city's population were homeless, with property loss estimated at $350 million. Nonetheless, San Franciscans remained remarkably upbeat. Survivors reported an almost holiday atmosphere in some tent cities. Relief funds poured in from around the country and many foreign countries. Japan sent the largest donation (a favor that San Francisco returned in the 1923 Tokyo quake).

Reconstruction started almost immediately. While government officials debated the merits of rebuilding on a newer, Paris-inspired street plan, merchants and homeowners went to work. Gutted buildings, like the Fairmont Hotel and the Merchants' Exchange, were quickly restored. Chinatown rose on its old site. South of Market districts started building vital new factories and warehouses. One after another, new theaters opened. Electric streetcars were installed, replacing cable car lines.

The citizens also took the opportunity to procure themselves a new government. Abe Ruef pleaded guilty to extortion, and was sentenced to 14 years in San Quentin Prison. Ex-Mayor Schmitz himself was awarded five years in exchange for 27 counts of graft and bribery; on appeal, however, his conviction was overturned. In 1912, with the city back on its feet, San Francisco found a mayor after its own heart in "Sunny Jim" Rolph. Mayor Rolph presided over construction of a brand new Civic Center and world's fair, the Panama Pacific International Exposition of 1915. Officially a celebration of the opening of the Panama Canal, the fair was San Francisco's boast to the world that it had recovered from 1906 with flying colors.

■ GROWTH OF THE MODERN CITY

After its amazing recovery from the devastation of 1906 and its hugely successful party in 1915, San Francisco began to win acclaim as "the city that knows how." Few cities have ever deserved the "can-do" reputation more than San Francisco during the first half of the twentieth century. Girding itself with a new sea wall, it bored tunnels through its hills to run its new electric streetcars. New streets terraced up its steep hills, and whole tracts rose in the sandy wastes of the Richmond and Sunset districts. Stimulating the growth of new towns and farms in California, its banks led San Francisco to international stature as a financial center. In 1934 the city, entirely with local funding, dammed the canyon of Hetch Hetchy, 150 miles east in the Sierra Nevada, and linked it by aqueduct to the new reservoirs on the Peninsula. The following year, it commenced the first scheduled air service to the Orient, Pan Am's *China Clipper*.

Most amazingly, in the midst of the Great Depression, it confidently set out to build three of the biggest public works projects ever undertaken. The largest bridge in the world, the Oakland Bay Bridge, opened in 1936, followed five months later by the formidable link across the Golden Gate, then the planet's longest span. In 1939, the city completed construction of the largest man-made island in the world, Treasure Island, which was appropriated (before being turned over to the Navy) for a new world's fair, the Golden Gate International Exposition.

When labor and capital were not working together to conquer San Francisco's natural barriers, they were often wrestling with the social barriers between them. Labor's demands for better pay and an eight-hour work day were justified, but its methods and influence were sometimes pernicious. The Workingman's Party, during the bitter years of the late nineteenth century, was a leading instigator of anti-Chinese protest. The Union Labor Party had put Schmitz in office. Still, they were no worse than the robber barons of the Gilded Age, who damned the public while raking in millions.

Labor unrest continued into the new century. San Francisco restaurant workers, teamsters, and machinists went on strike in 1901, and railway workers followed in 1906. Laundry workers sought eight-hour days in 1907, and streetcar drivers walked off soon after. Tensions reached a climax on July 22, 1916, when Mayor Rolph organized a Preparedness Day Parade in anticipation of American entry into World War I. Many unionists blasted involvement in the war as a working-class burden and a diversion from domestic problems. In short, threats were made, and when a pipe bomb exploded along the parade route, killing 10 and injuring others, the unions were blamed. Two union militants, Tom Mooney and Warren Billings, were arrested, charged, and convicted—without sufficient evidence. For the next two decades they languished in prison, international symbols of labor's struggle, until the pair were released (and Mooney pardoned) in 1939.

The largest strike action in American history was the San Francisco longshoremen's walkout of May 1930. When strikebreakers tried to force the lines, two people were killed and scores injured in the ensuing riots. The union fought back with a call for a general strike, which closed down the city for four days, inspiring solidarity among other Bay Area communities. It ended with the longshoremen winning their demands.

The Great Depression ended early in San Francisco, thanks in part to the injection of jobs and money by the bridge construction projects. World War II brought even greater growth—embittered, of course, by bloody losses in Europe and the Pacific—as local shipyards cranked up to battle speed. One and a half million troops embarked for the Pacific theater from San Francisco, and the city watched anxiously as the Army built bunkers and batteries in anticipation of a Japanese invasion. Fortunately they were never needed. The big guns were obsolete before the war ended.

The war brought compounded tragedy to San Francisco's citizens of Japanese ancestry. Like other mainland issei, nisei, and sansei (first, second, and third generations of Japanese Americans), the San Francisco community was evacuated wholesale and imprisoned in camps. Despite the humiliation of their incarceration, more than 33,000 Japanese Americans (about a third of the total number detained) volunteered for military service. California's contingent, the 100th Battalion, had so many casualties in Europe that it was known as the Purple Heart Battalion. Joined with the Japanese-American 442nd Regiment from Hawaii, they fought through seven major campaigns, sustaining withering losses, and finished the war as the most heavily decorated regiment in American history. General "Vinegar Joe" Stilwell, who slogged through some of the bitterest fighting of World War II, bristled with feisty indignation when he spoke of the Japanese-American persecution and sacrifice: "They bought an awful hunk of America with their blood . . . you're damn right those nisei boys have a place in the American heart, now and forever. We cannot allow a single injustice to be done to the nisei without defeating the purpose for which we fought."

A vaulting triumph of human ingenuity: the Golden Gate Bridge.

■ NEW DIRECTIONS

The war brought great changes to San Francisco. The city's work force more than doubled as thousands of workers manned (and womanned) the wartime industries. Household economies and social patterns altered permanently as more women became breadwinners. The influx of new residents continued after the war ended. Suburban communities took the brunt of this new growth, unprecedented since the Gold Rush, as prosperous groups like the Italians (who were the dominant ethnic group in San Francisco for much of this century) and Irish started moving out in larger numbers.

The following decades also saw increased immigration from Asia and Latin America. A new atmosphere of tolerance had emerged from the war, fostered by American prosperity. Reformed immigration laws and overseas unrest, including the Chinese revolution of 1949, and the Korean and Vietnam wars, boosted the numbers of Asian immigrants. Many prospered. Chinese Americans replaced Italian Americans as San Francisco's largest ethnic group in the 1980s.

Ironically, as burgeoning numbers of Chinese immigrants increasingly replace the American-born and European populations in many parts of North Beach, the Richmond, the Sunset, and other districts throughout the city, San Franciscans in greater numbers (including Asian Americans) are, more than a century after the anti-Chinese Geary Act, again expressing exasperation with Chinese immigration. (In fact, among many San Franciscans, Chinese immigrants are rapidly overtaking white males as the scapegoat *du jour* for the city's ills.) These newcomers' children will probably embrace Americanization as wholeheartedly as their forebears, but in a city with such a large immigrant population, some clash of cultures is to be expected.

Other ethnic groups have yet to realize their dreams. Thousands of African Americans from the South, arriving to work in the shipyards during World War II, settled in Hunters Point and the Western Addition. When the war ended and the yards closed or scaled down operations, many were unable to find work in the civil sector. Hunters Point and the Western Addition sank into localized depressions, deteriorating into slums. Though San Franciscans had learned to embrace Chinatown as a cultural (and tourist-industry) asset, they condemned these new inner-city ghettos as an embarrassing blight. During the 1950s and 1960s, clumsy government renovation efforts destroyed whole sectors of Victorian housing. Many

Today, the Golden Gate Bridge is admired both as an awesome accomplishment, as well as an elegant addendum to the Bay Area's natural beauty. (Kerrick James)

of the poorly managed and inadequately policed government projects that replaced them would slide into drug-driven violence during the 1970s and 1980s,
problems that have grown to epidemic proportions in the 1990s. San Franciscans
were shaken to realize that their city was not immune from what they considered
Eastern "rust belt" urban problems.

Looking at it from the outside, however, San Francisco of the 1950s and 1960s
seemed to offer an urbane, unspoiled, and exciting alternative to the problem-
plagued cities of the American Northeast. The beatniks and hippies were only the
most visible heralds of San Francisco's growing reputation as a haven from the established mores and constraints of Middle America. San Francisco's tolerance of
alternative thinking appealed to the American gay community and other groups
whose views on health, conservation, the arts, society, religion, and politics ran
counter to the established grain. This mix of new ideas and people brought new
dynamism to city life. Middle America, however, called it madness.

Changes do not come without turmoil. Since the 1960s, cults, fads, and weird
events have spawned on San Francisco's Bay like caddis flies. One of the strangest
episodes was the February 1974 kidnapping of Patty Hearst, a wealthy local newspaper publisher's daughter, by a radical group called the Symbionese Liberation
Army (SLA). Patty soon announced that she had joined up with her abductors for
the revolution, leading the fbi on a violent trail of robbery and fiery death to her
capture in San Francisco more than a year later. An even more bizarre episode
transpired in November 1978, when a transplanted San Francisco group called the
People's Temple, led by Jim Jones, committed mass suicide in the jungles of
Guyana. That same month, a city ex-Supervisor named Dan White, whose request for reinstatement had been rejected by Mayor George Moscone, assassinated
the mayor and gay supervisor Harvey Milk, right in City Hall.

The decade of the '80s saw a rise in special-interest groups and single-issue
politicians with no knack or desire for compromise, rendering the city's government incapable of clear consensus. Large-scale public works projects, like Yerba
Buena Gardens and plans for the city's new ballpark, bogged down for years in political debate. While demonstrations, litigation, and ceaseless dickering continue
to clog the city's arteries, thoughtful San Franciscans are wondering if "the city
that knows how" has lost its know-how. Indeed, the port is virtually dead to commercial shipping. Most industries have moved out. Even large corporations, com-

plaining of high rents and anti-business attitudes in San Francisco, are retreating to the suburbs-and out of state. The AIDS epidemic drains millions of dollars from the local economy, and smothers thousands with a haunting fear. In the 1990s, the federal government slammed the Bay Area with the largest block of military base closures in the country, including San Francisco's Presidio and Treasure Island. For many thousands of long-time Bay Area residents, the economic recession of the early 1990s was another in a long series of frustrations: these years also saw the greatest out-migration of Californians in history, mostly to Nevada, Texas, the Mountain States, and the Pacific Northwest.

The middle of the decade, however, has brought a resurgence of city institutions, a fantastic new library, refurbished neighborhoods, and grandiose plans for expanding old museums and building a new ballpark at China Basin. Under new leadership, the city may indeed be regaining some of its old drive and direction.

Despite the widely publicized problems of earthquake, homelessness, urban blight, shrinking tax revenues, and juvenile crime—problems, of course, that aren't unique to San Francisco—the City by the Bay remains one of the world's most beautiful and cosmopolitan cities. The arts are lively, the shopping districts crowded, the restaurants at the forefront of culinary innovation.

Culturally, the city is as vibrant as ever it has been. And perhaps most hopefully, a new generation of immigrants is setting down roots, revitalizing old neighborhoods, raising their children, and developing the skills and attitudes to fuel a new renaissance in San Francisco.

D O W N T O W N

SAN FRANCISCANS DIVIDE THEIR CITY INTO TWO ESTATES: the residential neighborhoods, and downtown. The two, according to common perception, are locked in eternal conflict. To local politicians, downtown interests serve big business, conservatives, and suburbanite commuters, while the neighborhoods represent liberal politics, the socially and environmentally conscious, and minority views. There's a good deal of truth in this, as there is in most grossly oversimplified generalizations.

Downtown is San Francisco's interface with the rest of the world. Every working day, some 225,000 people from the burbs (suburbs, exurbs) jam the bridges, trains, MUNI, BART, ferries, streets, and sidewalks—not to mention parking lots—in a Herculean effort to staff the offices and drive the wheels of international commerce. And needless to say, every evening finds them strangling the highways and skyways in a frantic rush to go home again. Fortunately for San Francisco, they don't take the keys with them. The lights of the grand hotels, shops, fine restaurants and bars continue to blaze long after the offices close down for the night, catering in part to the thousands of San Franciscans who also *live* downtown.

In a city renowned for spectacular entrances, there's none more exhilarating than the high road from Oakland across the Bay Bridge, when, rising from the water, San Francisco bursts into view, an urbane, stunning, civilized vision of hills and towers.

San Francisco's Financial District, a Pacific Rim dynamo and one of four ranking centers of American finance, was built to a compact, walkable scale. All the key financial touchstones—banks, brokers, exchanges, law offices, clubs, retailers, toney watering holes—are within ready walking distance from one another, nor do pedestrians have to contend with the city's infamously steep hills. The Financial District rose on land filled in where Yerba Buena Cove once lapped at the feet of Rincon, Telegraph, Nob, and Russian hills. Hundreds of Gold Rush ships abandoned here in 1849 still lie at anchor today, beneath the streets and foundations of America's Wall Street West.

The Financial District's most potent concentration is the intersection of Montgomery and California. Raked by honking horns and pounding jackhammers, the district shows up best during business hours, when frantic bike messengers in tribal

Financial District towers now dominate the old hills of San Francisco. (Kerrick James)

regalia ride breakneck through the bustling streets, and the bistros and restaurants buzz with big-money deals.

On the bay at the foot of Market Street stands the **Ferry Building**, for many years the gateway to the city. Completed in 1903, it survived the 1906 holocaust through heroic effort of fire-boat crews, and went on to become the second busiest transport terminal in the world, after London's Charing Cross Railway Station. Up to 50 million passengers every year crossed the gangways of 170 daily ferries binding San Francisco to the American "mainland." All that ended with the opening of the Bay Bridge in 1937. Today, the Ferry Building is a shadow of its former preeminence. Its once-beckoning wings have been converted to offices. On the pier, a lifelike statue of Mahatma Gandhi, symbol of peaceful resistance and founder of the Indian state, is frozen in vigorous stride. A few ferries from Marin County, Oakland, and Alameda now dock here.

From either side of the Ferry Building spreads further testimony to the past glories, and present languor, of San Francisco's port. The docks and wharfs along Embarcadero, a wide road built atop a sea wall stretching six miles from China Basin in the south to Fisherman's Wharf in the north, once roared and clanged with people and ships at work. Freighters, schooners, steamers, passenger liners, merchantmen, ferries, junks, square riggers, fishing boats, destroyers, and whaling barks have all, in their respective times, crowded these docks, where longshoremen and sailors labored hard and raised hell in the nearby saloons, chophouses, and flophouses. Virtually all are gone now, lost to the "mainland" ports of Oakland and Long Beach. Palm trees now line the new Embarcadero, which has been redesigned to channel auto traffic tidily below the ground level. Empty docks north of the Ferry Building have been converted to more sedate usages, mostly as offices and restaurants. One distinct improvement over all this upscale commercialization was the conversion of **Pier Seven,** the city's longest wharf, into a public promenade bedecked with genteel benches and lampposts, utilitarian fish-gutting sinks, and stirring views of bridge, bay, hill, and tower. From the Ferry Building south to beyond the Bay Bridge, the wharves have been razed, affording spectacular views of bridge and harbor that no doubt compensate for the high cost of living in the fancy new housing developments that fan out south of the bridge.

The Financial District meets the Ferry Building at **Justin Herman Plaza,** where banks of steps and *al fresco* tables gather a bustling lunch-time crowd of brown-baggers and business suits. The plaza's focal point is the **Vaillancourt Fountain,** a gargantuan work of public art that provokes strong passions of love and hate. Those who love it find it dynamic and hugely inviting on hot days. At least one wag, who presumably weighs in on the denigrators' side, has likened it to something left by a gargantuan dog with square bowels. Its designer, Mr. Vaillancourt, gave San Francisco another example of his talents in 1987, when a musician from the rock group U2 vented his artistic expression with spray paint across the fountain. Hearing of the vandalism, Vaillancourt caught a flight from Montreal to San Francisco in time to repay the group in kind across their concert stage.

Behind and above Justin Herman Plaza sprawls **Embarcadero Center**, an urbane oasis of landscaped walkways, bridges, patios, and courtyards linking four high-rise office buildings. The 31st floor of Embarcadero 1 is open to the public as an observation platform, the highest view from a downtown building that can be had without buying a drink or getting a job.

Pedestrian overpasses span north to **Maritime Plaza**, part of the Golden Gateway Redevelopment Project, an upmarket, high-rise, residential district built around open courts, fountains, and **Sydney Walton Park**, an islet of countryside in the midst of a city. Of the many fine shops, restaurants, and hotels catering to a largely corporate clientele, the showpiece is the **Hyatt Regency Hotel**, with its spectacular atrium, dripping with vines from the open-sided corridors lofting 17 stories above. (The Guinness Museum of World Records claims this as the world's largest hotel lobby!) The nucleus of the atrium is a four-story sculptured ball by Charles Perry, set amidst a rippling creek and lush trees. A piano bar and weekly tea dancing keep the music flowing. Glass elevators glide silently up and down the walls and through the ceiling to the Equinox, a revolving cocktail lounge suspended in the midst of glittering towers.

Just outside the Hyatt's front door, where California intersects Market, the California Street cable car begins its run from **Robert Frost Plaza** to Van Ness Avenue. Frost, the beloved New England poet, was in fact a native son of San Francisco. Though he moved away while still a boy, Frost never forgot the city of his childhood, and wrote fondly:

Such was life in the Golden Gate:
Gold dusted all we drank and ate,
And I was one of the children told,
We all must eat our peck of gold.

Gazing beyond passing cable cars as they climb up Nob Hill, you can spot the curving eaves of Chinatown. Those who bypass the cable car in favor of walking can explore the heart of the Financial District. Reminders of San Francisco's days as queen of the Wild West can still be found amidst the far more overwhelming symbols of the booming present. Along flag-bedecked California Street, the best monuments of post-modernist architecture blend sky-scraping power with touches of humanity. The round tower at **101 California**, designed by Philip Johnson and John Burgee, sports an Italianate plaza with flower-filled urns and a greenhouse lobby. **California Center**, a massive building straddling handsome shopping arcades, houses the spectacular Mandarin Oriental Hotel in its crown—twin towers linked by sensational glass "skybridges," guaranteed to knock the toupee off anyone suffering from vertigo.

With all due respect to Wyatt Earp and Bat Masterson, it was California Street, and especially the blocks intersecting with Montgomery, that *really* won the West. Behind these mild-mannered facades whir the financial dynamos that powered the growth of mines, farms, towns, factories, and transport arteries of the emerging West, driving the frontier farther and farther east, till it finally died of exhaustion in the barren wilds of the Rocky Mountains.

The Bank of California, oldest banking corporation in the state, maintains its 1908 headquarters in the shadow of its present headquarters tower, at 400 California Street. This was the bank of William Ralston, who bankrolled one of the Comstock's greatest bonanzas. The basement vault lodges the **Museum of the Money of the American West**, a tidy little collection of gold nuggets, minting paraphernalia and mementos of the Comstock. Most intriguing are the pistols used in the notorious duel between California Chief Justice David S. Terry and U.S. Senator David Broderick. Judge Terry was a Southerner and supporter of slavery, Senator Broderick an ardent Union man. Neither got along politically or personally, and their bandied insults finally resulted in a challenge and acceptance. They met at Lake Merced on the morning of September 15, 1859, with seconds and a party of 80 witnesses. Judge Terry supplied the pistols. On the toss of a coin, he also won first choice. Such details might have stayed mere footnotes of history had not the gun presented to Senator Broderick misfired. Judge Terry immediately returned fire, and plugged Broderick in the chest. Broderick died a martyr, Terry was hissed as a villain, and pro-Union sympathies soared in California. Take a close look at those pistols; 13 decades ago, there were many who'd have envied you the chance.

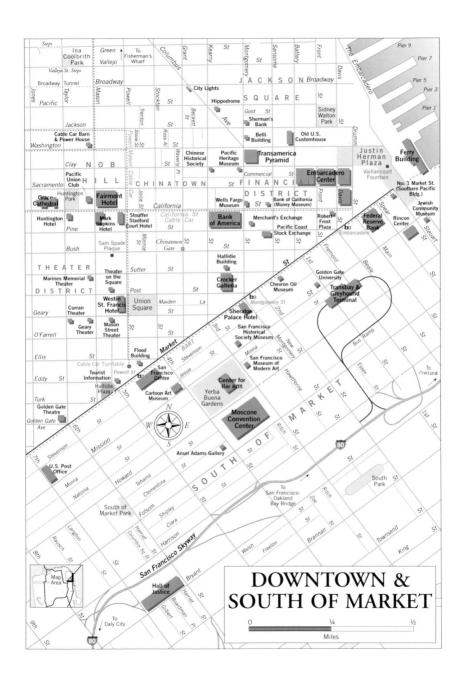

DOWNTOWN &
SOUTH OF MARKET

0 ¼ ½

Miles

Headquarters of two other banks with starring roles in American history, Wells Fargo and Bank of America, are also nearby. The massive, 52-story **Bank of America Building** at California and Kearny was built in 1969 for what was then the largest bank in the world. With a workday population of more than 5,000 people, this building alone would make a sizable burg in many a state. After 3 P.M., when the top-floor Bankers Club transforms into the Carnelian Room, it offers some of the best views of the city open to the general public. On the plaza below, the large, hard, fist-like sculpture of black marble is known by financial district clerks as *The Banker's Heart*. (Its real name is *Transcendence*, by Masayuki Nagari.) To be fair, the father of the B of A was a warmhearted man. Born in San Jose of Italian immigrants, A. P. Giannini founded his bank, originally known as the Bank of Italy, to serve immigrants and people of small means who were shunted aside by less compassionate financial institutions. When the 1906 earthquake struck, Giannini personally rescued his bank's deposits ahead of the flames, hauling them hidden in orange crates to San Mateo. Before other banks' super-heated vaults could cool, Giannini was back in business, investing heavily in San Francisco. It proved a sound bet, as did later investments in California's fledgling farms and small towns. Giannini's most famous gamble was a preposterous bridge across the Golden Gate; and once again, he backed a winner.

Wells Fargo, a name that still calls up images of cracking whips and rattling coaches, keeps the vision alive in its **Wells Fargo History Room**, at 420 Montgomery. An original Wells Fargo stagecoach, route maps, postage stamps, weapons, and displays of Western paraphernalia crowd the two floors. Among the most interesting items are samples of Emperor Norton's currency, a half-completed coach box, which you may try for comfort as you listen to a passenger's recorded diary, and memorabilia of one Charles E. Bolton, alias Charles Boles, alias Black Bart. Bart was a dapper little fellow who, in the 1870s and 1880s, earned his living by highway robbery. His fame rests not only on his 28 stage holdups, but on the leaves of doggerel that he occasionally left behind with the pilfered strong boxes, signed "Black Bart, Po8."

> *I rob the rich to feed the poor,*
> *Which hardly is a sin;*
> *A widow ne'er knocked at my door*
> *But what I let her in.*

> *So blame me not*
> *for what I've done,*
> *I don't deserve your curses,*
> *And if for any cause I'm hung,*
> *Let it be for my verses.*

Unfortunately for Bart and po8try lovers, he carelessly dropped a handkerchief at his final robbery. Special Detective Harry N. Morse traced it to a laundry on Bush Street, San Francisco, and was waiting there when Charles Bolton came to call. Engaging him in conversation about mining ventures, the detective invited Bolton back to his offices at Wells Fargo and Company, where he arrested him for highway robbery. Convicted, Bolton was given a remarkably (in those days) light sentence of seven years at San Quentin State Penitentiary in Marin County. He served four years before being paroled for good behavior, and has never been heard from since. The bighearted, two-fisted Wells Fargo museum is free, and keeps banking hours.

The country's largest stock exchange outside New York is the **Pacific Coast Stock Exchange**, at the nearby corner of Pine and Sansome. Visitors may enter only by special arrangement (telephone 415-393-4133), but you can usually catch a glimpse of the oft-frantic trading action through the open front door.

The original U.S. Subtreasury Building, at 608 Commercial, was erected in 1875 on the site of San Francisco's first U.S. Mint, which operated there from 1854 to 1874. The sturdy walls and basement coin vaults of the old Subtreasury have now been magnanimously incorporated into the modern Bank of Canton tower, and transformed into the elegant **Pacific Heritage Museum**, a skylit venue for changing exhibits of Asian art. (The Chinese Historical Society Museum, treated on page 104, is just up the street.)

The most distinctive landmark of San Francisco's skyline, the **Transamerica Pyramid**, rises at the end of Leidesdorff. At 853 feet (260 m), it is the tallest building in the city. On a warm day, to sit in the shade of the redwood grove growing on its eastern side is a delicious pleasure. When the fog blows in, parting at the needle like a silent, pale river round a monolithic rock, it's an almost zen-like experience.

The Pony Express once stopped across the street, at Montgomery and Merchant, where a plaque marks the end of the 1,966-mile (3,164-km) run from St. Joseph, Missouri. Yet it is the Pyramid's site itself that is most haunted by history, and most mourned by those who love San Francisco. The Montgomery Block, affectionately known as the Monkey Block by many generations of citizens, once stood here. Built in 1853 by the soon-to-be Civil War general, Henry Halleck, it was for decades the largest, sturdiest building west of the Mississippi, accommodating law offices, newspapers, and bars that contributed enormously to the culture and history of the city. Here it was that James Casey gunned down James King of William in 1855, activating the Second Vigilance Committee, which hanged Casey for his crime. It was here also that Mark Twain met the original Tom Sawyer, who owned a Turkish bath in the basement, and where he downed Pisco Punches in the Exchange Saloon while admiring the painting of Samson and Delilah above the bar (as did most male patrons, noted Twain). Twain kept rooms here; so did Ambrose Bierce, George Sterling, Frank Norris, Charlie Stoddard, Joaquin Miller, Gelett Burgess, and other writers. Dr. Sun Yat-sen also settled in for a spell to write the English version of the Chinese constitution while on world tour in quest of funds for the revolution. And at the turn of the century, Pappa Coppa's restaurant on this site was San Francisco's most frequented rendezvous of bohemian writers, poets, and artists, who decorated the walls with their works. Thus, through peace, revolution, rollicking nights, decadence, and stolidity, the Monkey Block nursed in classic San Francisco style as egalitarian an array of characters as ever graced a city. It survived the earthquake and, even more remarkably, the fire of 1906, but it could not survive the wrecker's ball, and fell for a parking lot in 1959.

■ JACKSON SQUARE

On to the Barbary Coast, alias the International Settlement, nowadays more properly called the Jackson Square Historical District, which is found across Washington Street north of the Pyramid. Once infamous as the most perverted hell-hole on Earth, San Francisco's Barbary Coast in its heyday set standards of wickedness and depravity that would have made Shanghai blush. At least that's the legend; whatever it was *really* like—and no doubt was a mean and dirty place—it couldn't *possibly* compare with the legend.

Spawned in the Gold Rush to cater to the lusts of a huge city of males drained of hope and with no passage home, the Barbary Coast coaxed the worst of mankind to do their worst, and the best to do no better. The Coast's main thoroughfare was Pacific Street, known to aficionados as "Terrific Pacific," a string of saloons, gambling dens, raunchy dance halls, and other attractions stretching some half a dozen blocks west from the waterfront. Choice sections of the Coast acquired their own sobriquets: Murderer's Corner, Battle Row, Devil's Acre, Dead Man's Alley. Brutality, prostitution, murder, drunkenness, and bestiality were commonplace. Vicious men lurched through torchlit streets, meeting casual death in grog shops with names like the Morgue, the Goat and Compass, Bull Run, and Devil's Kitchen. Human beings were reduced to the lowest forms in performances of the grossest degradation. Hundreds of prostitutes worked the "cowyards" in narrow cribs stacked up to four stories high, or performed on stages with horses, pigs, and grizzly bears. One pathetic creature known as Oofty Goofty built a reputation by selling the privilege of beating him with a baseball bat across the backside, until the fighter John L. Sullivan crippled him with a pool cue for 50 cents. Another gent by the name of Dirty Tom McAlear made his living (and severely taxed his clients' imaginations) by eating anything that was plopped down before him, for pennies. Here also was sanctuary for the brutal gangs of hoodlums (a word said to have been coined in the Barbary Coast) who terrorized Chinatown. (Another Barbary Coast coinage was the word "Shanghaied," which described what happened to unsuspecting sailors who imbibed spiked drinks, called Mickey Finns. Mr. Mickey Finn himself, incidentally, was the Barbary Coast chemist who supplied the drugs.)

The Barbary Coast raged on for over six decades, eventually feeding on its own notoriety by catering to intrepid tourists and local slumming parties. Outraged preachers and newspaper editors called for divine punishment, or at the very least, government action, to clean up the Coast. Not surprisingly, Heaven made the first move. In April of 1906, the day of reckoning came. The earth shook, buildings crumbled; fire storms swept through the Financial District, the mansions of Nob Hill, the tenements of Chinatown, North Beach, Russian Hill, and South of Market. Five hundred square blocks of San Francisco were incinerated. The streets, parks, Presidio, and transbay ferries swarmed with 250,000 refugees. But curiously, as the smoke and flames cleared, the very heart of the Barbary Coast was seen yet standing amidst the coals, miraculously spared. The party wasn't over! Not until 1917 did a government decree even attempt to bring the Coast to heel, and even then a smaller, tamer version called the International Settlement staggered on until mid-century.

Today, the Barbary Coast is well and truly dead, though fortunately, many of its buildings live on for our edification. It is now a thoroughly gentrified district of old brick structures quaintly renovated to quarter architects, antique sellers, and design studios, some of which cater only to professionals and are not welcoming of casual browsers (unless they be very well-padded, and in any event, possessing of

Old Barbary Coast inmates take a break from the action.

an appointment). Even the old name has been turned out in favor of a peculiarly inappropriate euphemism, Jackson Square. You won't find a square here, but it is very worth your while to wander through the elegant, tree-lined streets, peering through windows and hunting down a few old landmarks. The Belli Building and its neighbors on the **700 block of Montgomery**, for instance, are curious relics of the 1850s, though sadly weakened in the Loma Prieta quake of 1989. At number 728, Bret Harte purportedly wrote "The Luck of Roaring Camp." Around the corner on Jackson, the brick and cast-iron buildings at 451, 445, and 463 once housed **A. P. Hotaling's offices**, including his wholesale whiskey operation. This latter establishment occupies an esteemed position in the lore of the Barbary Coast, for its survival in the fire of 1906 inspired an immortal ode on cosmic justice:

> *If, as they say, God spanked the town for being over-frisky,*
> *Why did He burn the churches down and spare Hotaling's whiskey?*

Other points of interest include the bawdy **Hippodrome Theater**, now a show-room at 555 Pacific, but still preserving a resplendent foyer in carved relief once considered very shocking indeed. **Gold Street**, an alley that predates the Barbary Coast, appears little changed since the 1850s, though most building interiors have been fortified against earthquakes. Its western end is marked by the **Bank of Lucas, Turner & Company**, 1853, better known today as the bank once managed by William Tecumseh Sherman, who later went on to burn Atlanta in the Civil War. Stout's bookstore, required browsing for anyone with the faintest interest in architecture and design, now occupies part of the building.

Broadway and Kearny streets mark the edges of downtown San Francisco. To the north lies North Beach, to the west, Chinatown; both are covered in the next chapter. But downtown San Francisco expands on other fronts, so let us backtrack to Market Street. . . .

■ THE MARKET STREET CORRIDOR

Market Street is San Francisco's main transport corridor, where BART and MUNI rush commuters in and out through tubes and tunnels, while buses, taxis, cars, bikes, and pedestrians vie for space above. When Jasper O'Farrell laid out the street plan in 1847, he envisioned Market as a grand thoroughfare cutting in a wide diagonal from the bay to the foot of Twin Peaks. But O'Farrell failed to

(following pages) A Hyde Street cable car slices through a morning fog.

foresee the havoc his plan would wreak on modern traffic. North of Market, he laid out small, human-scale city blocks in a grid aligned on a north-south axis. South of Market, he planned a much larger grid, better suited for vehicular traffic than pedestrians, and running roughly on a northwest-southeast axis. In consequence, every street intersecting Market hits at an awkward angle, and worse, the streets north of Market never meet the ones from the south, except by luck or some fancy driving. Instead of becoming a focal point for the Financial District, Market Street became the barrier to its southward expansion for the next 140 years. The barrier has been breached on a large scale only since the 1970s, thanks to building-height restrictions and spiraling real-estate prices north of Market.

In **Number One Market Street**, architects Michael Paynor and Associates incorporated the 1917 Southern Pacific Building into their 1978 structure, which features a huge mosaic clock, an indoor plaza, and a cheerful fountain that curtains off a plaza restaurant. Southern Pacific was the successor of the Central Pacific, builder of the first transcontinental railway, linking California to the East. The railroad also opened enormous tracts of California to farming and settlement, while acquiring vast landholdings and influence. By the latter third of the nineteenth century, railroad corporations had become the most powerful private institutions in the state. Frank Norris fiercely attacked their monopolistic rape of a Central Valley farming community in his novel *The Octopus*.

Immediately behind stands **Rincon Center**, incorporating a 1940 post office annex. Murals on the annex walls stirred bitter controversy when painted after World War II by Anton Refregiar, a Russian immigrant, because they showed the dirt under San Francisco's nails. A case in point is his rendition of Vigilante Days, depicting the assassination of James King of William by James Casey, while a menacing Vigilante Committee marches in the background and a man gets lynched. Other panels illustrate the anti-Chinese rabble-rousing, the transcontinental railway, the Mooney case, the 1906 earthquake, and an imaginary convocation of writers associated with San Francisco, including Mark Twain, Bret Harte, Jack London, Robert Louis Stevenson, and Ambrose Bierce. Through the modest annex door, the center bursts into a soaring atrium surrounded by little bistros and soothed by the patter of fountain water falling like rain from the lofty skylight.

The **Jewish Community Museum** at 121 Steuart Street provides a cultured venue for frequently changing exhibits on Jewish art and history. Past exhibitions, for example, have dealt with such diverse themes as Jewish ghetto life in Italy from the fifteenth century, the plight of Ethiopian Jews in Israel, and political art inspired by the trial and 1953 execution of Julius and Ethel Rosenberg.

Anyone uninitiated in the workings of the Financial District will want to stop by for an explanation at the **Federal Reserve Bank** at 100 Market, where they may study an interpretive display and film explaining its role as the "bankers' bank." Much more fun is the **Chevron Oil Museum** in the Standard Oil Building at 557–75 Market, where you can try your hand at discovering oil reserves by computer.

An excellent travel book store, with an enormous selection of maps and books, is Rand McNally, at the corner of Second and Market. A short block west, opposite the strategic intersection where Montgomery spills into Market, William Ralston built the **Palace Hotel** in 1873. With well over 700 rooms, it was the largest and most celebrated hostelry in the world at the time. Ralston had big plans for his little city, and furnished the hotel with little regard for reason or expense. Champagne and oysters were standard fare, and traveling royalty made it their home away from home. From the Crystal Roof Garden on the top floor, resident millionaires gazed down upon the carriages arriving in the Grand Court, seven stories below. Oscar Wilde and Rudyard Kipling lodged at the Palace in the 1880s, and opera sensation Enrico Caruso got the snub of his career here on an April morning in 1906, when he was rudely awakened by a falling ceiling. The Palace burned in the fire that followed, and the heartily offended virtuoso left town swearing never to return.

A new Palace rose on the foundations of the old. Make a point to visit it, if only for a peek at the elegant **Garden Court**, inspired by the earlier Grand Court and one of the grandiose dining rooms in the city. The famous Maxfield Parrish painting of the Pied Piper of Hamelin in Maxfield's Restaurant evokes strong memories of long-forgotten bedtime stories.

American Indian Contemporary Arts, on the second floor of 685 Market Street, exhibits crafts and art of the many native cultures of the United States. Hand-made Navajo blankets and jewelry, books, art, traditional clothing, taped music, and various other cultural treasures are sold in the gallery shop.

The **Crocker Galleria**, across Market Street and a half block west on Post, has an attractive arcade of gardens and shops under a barrel-vaulted roof. Framed at

the northern end is the **Hallidie Building**, at 130 Sutter, reputed to be the world's first glass-curtain-walled building. (If glass-curtain walling fails to induce shivers up and down your spine, try thinking of it as the original glass-walled skyscraper.) When architect Willis Polk completed it in 1918, he was way ahead of his time. Polk, who left his mark throughout San Francisco, was a man devoted to perfection and indifferent to the petty interests of ordinary mortals. Once, when a New York corporate potentate seeking his services tried to praise his designs, the architect replied, "I would feel complimented if I thought you knew anything about art."

■ SOUTH OF MARKET

No area of San Francisco has changed so much and so fast as the South of Market district. Wealthy people began to flock to the up-and-coming residential enclave of Rincon Hill in the 1850s, but they just as rapidly left it when the new cable cars turned Nob Hill into the city's mansion district. As the rich took flight, middle-class, and later working-class, people moved in. The district became known as South o' the Slot, in reference to the cable car lines (which have slots for the cables)

Old San Francisco's dash and opulence were mirrored in the Palace Hotel (left). South Park is a quirky remnant of the district's brief fling as the city's pedigreed residential district (above). Today it's home to artists, as well as innovative high-tech firms (above photo, Kerrick James)

that ran up Market Street. In the 1906 fire, the blocks of cheap wooden houses burned so fast and hot that iron melted. The district was rebuilt with factories, warehouses, train yards, and businesses serving the port at China Basin. For the next 70 years, select streets of South of Market, particularly Howard, were known as Skid Row.

Today, most of the factories, train yards, and warehouses have closed or moved away. The sailors, and many of the hotels that catered to them, have followed the port out of town. Even the drunks and other sad down-and-outers have mostly moved up to Fifth Street and beyond. In deference to New York's SoHo (South of Houston) district, Frisco trendies have rechristened South of Market as "SoMa." Like SoHo, SoMa's gentrifying vanguard were the painters, photographers, dancers, sculptors, and multimedia artists who moved into the low-rent warehouses and abandoned factories, converting them into studios. On their heels came factory retail outlets for designer clothes, with lunch-time cafes in their train, and nightspots catering to a mostly young and city-savvy crowd.

Meanwhile, rising land values north of Market were pushing the Financial District steadily south of Market along an expanding frontier line of offices and restaurants. The opening of the Moscone Convention Center, Yerba Buena Gardens, hotels, restaurants, and suave residential developments are attracting ever larger numbers of middle-class residents and visitors to SoMa. Along the shore as far south as China Basin wharfs, even the old harbor has been gussied up into docks for private pleasure craft. Like the sailors and pensioners before them, the struggling artists and factory outlets are in retreat—though many still hold their own in the nether regions south of Folsom and west of Fifth.

Also holding their own are some of the nightclubs opened here in the '80s, especially those further south along Harrison and Folsom, which have become established dance and music venues. Meanwhile, new (or newly named) hotspots seem to pop up every week. Leave your car parked on Folsom and Seventh on a Saturday night, and you'll come back to a windshield littered with flashy postcard notices for one-night-a-week clubs like "Bondage-a-Go-Go" or "Faster Pussycat."

South Park, on the other hand, is a quirky remnant of the district's brief fling as San Francisco's pedigreed residential district. Built in 1856 on a plan inspired by London's Berkeley Square, the oval park was fenced and surrounded by mansions, whose owners kept the keys to the gate. With the invention of cable cars, the rich departed South Park for Nob Hill, abandoning it to poorer families, factories, warehouses, and sailor hotels. It bottomed out as a skid row when construction of the Bay Bridge leveled Rincon Hill for its western anchorage. South Park remained depressed until quite recently, when artists and designers discovered that its abandoned warehouses made great studios. Now, a wealthier class is once again returning to South Park. The sidewalk tables of the South Park Cafe add a touch of class to the oval. Jack London was born in 1876 around the corner from South Park, at 615 Third Street. The house burned in the fire of 1906, but the approximate site is marked by a plaque.

No section of SoMa has been so completely transformed as the waterfront. Plans are afoot to build a new baseball stadium at China Basin, and already new housing developments have replaced the dockland atmosphere south of the Bay Bridge.

One prominent maritime reminder is the **SS** *Jeremiah O'Brien,* now anchored at Pier 32. The last Liberty Ship still in regular operation, the *Jeremiah O'Brien* carried grain, arms, and cargo in both the Atlantic and Pacific during World War II. It was present at the D-Day invasion, and returned 50 years later for the anniversary in June of 1994. Visitors always have free run of the ship, but by all means do try to see it when the steam's up and crew's aboard, when you can climb to the chart rooms for a chat with the captain, or crank round the gun turrets under orders of the gunnery mate. The descent to the stifling engine room, skirting pounding pistons and scalding pipes, is a spectacle of well-crafted and cared-for machinery. Wander about the engine room, inspecting the gauges and boilers, pumps and pistons; squeeze down the narrow screw shaft passage to the ship's stern. Crew members will demonstrate how it all works, even to the point of reversing the engine upon request—truly the highlight of any mechanic's visit to San Francisco. But you don't have to be a mechanic to appreciate such power and dynamism. Kids love it. The crews fire up the engines on the third weekend of every month, except December, and periodically take her out for a run on the bay or the Sacramento River.

The **Sailing Ship Restaurant** at Pier 42 is another actual sailing vessel, once called the *Ellen.* After service on the southern oceans at the turn of the century, she was drafted for troop and supply transport during World War I, and followed that with a stint of smuggling during Prohibition. Bought by Columbia Studios to star

in *Mutiny on the Bounty*, she was later sold to a San Franciscan restaurateur. Winched ashore, she now sits high and dry, with food and drink for all hands.

The symbolic heart of the new SoMa is **Yerba Buena Gardens,** a committee-designed green where artist and patron, conventioneer and tourist all meet on common turf. Decades passed from its first proposal till its opening in autumn of 1993, and many more years will pass before all the full contingent of promised gardens, playgrounds, hotels, and museums see light of day. The **Esplanade Gardens** and dining terraces are very pleasant oases in the midst of a metropolis. A rushing waterfall partially conceals the **Martin Luther King Jr. Memorial,** comprising of panels translated into several languages, advocating peace and tolerance.

The vanguard of the development was **Moscone Center,** San Francisco's prime convention complex, which occupies the entire block of Howard between Third, Fourth, and Folsom streets. Named for San Francisco's assassinated mayor, George Moscone, the exhibit hall is an engineering curiosity well worth contemplating, if you happen to be there anyway. The arched roof supports are designed like a series of great, taut hunting bows, with the ends strung together by cables running under the floor. By tightening the cables, structural engineer T. Y. Lin was able to spring enough upward thrust to counter the enormous weight of the ground-level gardens on the roof, without employing a single interior column. The result is a vast, open hall, one of the largest underground spaces in the world.

Yerba Buena Gardens is a true crossroads of artists and art patrons. Anchoring one corner of the square is the **Center for the Arts at Yerba Buena,** which comprises galleries for the visual arts, a sculpture court, and a 755-seat theater. Together they serve as prominent showcases for contemporary visual and performing artists, particularly those from the Bay Area and San Francisco neighborhoods.

Across the street from the Center for Performing Arts stands the dazzling new home of the **San Francisco Museum of Modern Art.** With five floors of galleries designed around a spectacular skylight, vast collections of paintings and works on paper, sculpture, architectural drawings, furniture and graphic design, photography, video, film, and other time-based media, this is a world-class showcase of twentieth-century art, and an inspiration to the local art scene. Among the museum's spectacular collection are works by Georgia O'Keeffe, Andy Warhol, Imogen Cunningham, Paul Klee, Willem de Kooning, and others, including Diego

(previous pages) Yerba Buena Gardens comprises the Esplanade Gardens (foreground) and the Center for the Arts (gray building behind gardens). The San Francisco Museum of Modern Art is the cylindrical building at rear. (Kerrick James)

Rivera's *The Flower Carrier,* Jackson Pollock's *Guardians of the Secret,* Picasso's *Women of Algiers,* and *Woman with a Hat,* by Matisse. All the major schools and artists of the twentieth century are represented, with substantial holdings from Fauvists, German Expressionists, and American Abstract Expressionists; numerous pieces by Mexican and California artists round out the exhibits. The biggest star of the museum, however, is the building itself; Swiss architect Mario Botta's classically receding hallways, dramatic spaces and curiously placed picture windows are very much enhanced by the works of art that they are meant to enhance. A 125-foot (38-meter) skylight, gingerly crossed on the top floor by a dramatic footbridge, scoops in most of the light for the museum's five sprawling stories. The bookshop is one of the largest retailers of art books, posters, cards, catalogs, artistic toys, and T-shirts on the Pacific Coast.

On the western side of Yerba Buena Gardens, at 250 Fourth Street, the **Ansel Adams Center** hosts five galleries devoted to the art of photography, a research library, bookstore, photography classes, and other programs. One gallery is permanently set aside for the work of the eminent photographer and San Francisco native, Ansel Adams, whose black-and-white landscapes of Yosemite and the American West are among the world's most widely recognized photographs.

An even quirkier gallery near the northwest corner of Yerba Buena Gardens, the **Cartoon Art Museum** (814 Mission) devotes itself to the preservation and study of a vigorous American art form. In addition to its rotating displays, this small archive maintains a gift shop and permanent library of comic books, editorial cartoons, comic strips, animation, advertising, greeting card art, and more.

Historical paintings and other artifacts are exhibited at the **San Francisco Historical Society Museum** (678 Mission), the guardian of a vast treasure trove of manuscripts, photographs, books, prints and other documents from the city's fascinating past. A more specialized historical collection occupies a side-room off the ornate lobby of the 1925 Pacific Tel and Tel headquarters building, on the corner of Natoma and New Montgomery. The **Telephone Pioneer Communications Museum** displays an old-style telephone booth, model satellite, San Francisco's first phone book, hands-on electronic displays, vintage switchboards, and other assorted telephone equipment dating back to the 1870s illustrate the first century of an ever-more crucial technology. One intriguing exhibit shows how beep baseball is played by the blind.

Natural light floods the atrium and catwalk inside the Museum of Modern Art. (Kerrick James)

■ THE SHOPPING DISTRICT

Powell slams into Market at **Hallidie Plaza**, crossroads of the city. The lion's share of San Francisco's hotels are located nearby, as are many prominent theaters, restaurants, art galleries, shops, and department stores. The cable cars prelude their clanging journeys to Nob Hill, Chinatown, and Fisherman's Wharf with a clumsy, yet charming, pirouette on the Powell Street turntable. Here, the trajectories of callow executives from nearby office buildings collide with the paths of sheepish tourists, Tenderloin panhandlers, suburbanites with shopping bags, and park-bench prophets ruminating on the world's end. Meanwhile, information and maps can be gathered at the main **Convention and Visitors Bureau** office downstairs near the Powell Street BART station.

San Francisco's downtown retail shopping district is the second largest in the country in terms of sales, and it whips number one, New York's Fifth Avenue, for compactness and convenience. Some of the most elegant shingles in the world hang in the side streets. The district is well served by buses and the Powell Street station of BART and MUNI, and has more than 5,500 parking spaces for those shortsighted shoppers who insist on driving. And believe me, you might have to wait to get one of those spaces.

San Francisco Centre, on the corner of Fifth and Market, is a vertical mall whose main tenant is the sumptuous, Seattle-based department store, Nordstrom. It boasts the country's first semi-spiral escalators, which wind mantra-like up the eight-story central well to a dome that opens to the sky on fine days.

Union Square, at the heart of the shopping district, was named for the pro-Union rallies held here during the Civil War, when there was a controversy whether California (and its gold) would throw in its lot with the North or South. Largely by the oratory of San Francisco preacher Thomas Starr King, the city went firmly pro-Union; and as San Francisco went, so went the state. Union Square is now the grassy roof of the world's first underground multi-level parking garage. A column and statue commemorating Dewey's victory at Manila during the Spanish-American War gathers pigeons at center stage. Flower stands at its busy corners splash color through the streets.

On the west side of Union Square, the landmark Saint Francis Hotel was gutted in the 1906 fire. You can stroll through the elegant arcade, or rocket to the top of the new tower annex in spectacular, outside glass elevators. It was

At San Francisco Centre, shoppers ascend to Nordstrom on semi-spiral escalators.

here that President Gerald Ford made his lucky escape from an assassin's bullet in 1975, and here also that Miles Archer, Sam Spade's partner in The Maltese Falcon, commenced the job that would shortly result in his murder on nearby **Burritt Street**, a site now marked by a plaque.

Rambling, many-storied department stores like Macy's and Neiman-Marcus have doors near Union Square. Perhaps their most popular commodity, especially during the Christmas season, is the festive atmosphere of big-city bustle, lights, rich scents, music, color, and a thousand other delights that even window-shoppers can afford. For just a bit more, give your feet a rest and your nostalgia a rush by taking tea under the grand glass dome that for decades surmounted the now-defunct City of Paris. (It now overspreads Neiman-Marcus, at the corner of Stockton and Geary.) And don't miss the festive Yuletide decorations at F.A.O. Schwarz, the dazzling toy store at Stockton and O'Farrell. East of Union Square, framed by the four-block rectangle of Stockton, Geary, Kearny, and Sutter, are among the most unapologetically luxurious shopping streets in the country. Among the names here that bespeak exclusive tastes and wealth one may find Tiffany, Dunhill, Cartier, Gucci, Louis Vuitton, Shreve's, Bullock & Jones, Mark Cross, Wilkes Bashford, and Brooks Brothers, to name but a few. The lavish San Francisco institution at 135 Post Street, Gump's, has an old-world feel that matches the rarity of its wares. Much of what they sell you will not find anywhere else, for Gump's specializes in one-of-a-kind treasures. Their jade collection is renowned the world round. Their furniture and decorations are works of art, and their works of art are, well, exceedingly expensive. Sally Stanford, San Francisco's favorite madame (and a woman of discriminating tastes), once referred to Gump's as "the Metropolitan Museum with cash registers. . . ."

The magical extravagance of their autumn promotion, for which a score of buyers and artisans prepare all year, is legendary. **Maiden Lane,** the petite darling of these blue-blooded streets, has a risqué past. She was once none other than notorious Morton Street, yet another of San Francisco's red-light districts. Frank Lloyd Wright designed the Circle Gallery Building at 140 Maiden Lane, a smaller version, but an obvious prototype, of his famed spiral interior in the Guggenheim Museum in New York.

■ THE THEATER DISTRICT

San Francisco's answer to Times Square, albeit a quiet answer, begins with **Lotta's Fountain** at the intersection of Geary, Kearny, and Market, presented by the actress Lotta Crabtree, who got her start as a child dancer in California during the Gold Rush. Here San Francisco celebrated its most sentimental Christmas Eve, in 1910, when the Italian coloratura soprano, Luisa Tetrazzini, expressed her passionate gratitude to the city that "discovered" her five years earlier, by singing free to a crowd of thousands that filled the streets.

San Franciscans love and have always loved the theater and its troupers. During the Gold Rush, miners used to lob bags of gold dust on stage when young Lotta Crabtree danced, though rotten vegetables and worse were kept on hand for more critical judgment calls. The forty-niners were not really a brutish lot; in fact, Gold Rush San Franciscans were on average better educated than New Yorkers of their day. They enjoyed poetry, sat through Cantonese opera, and were passionately devoted to Shakespeare and grand opera, even in the most far-flung mining camps. San Francisco's first opera house opened to clamoring audiences as early as 1851. Though woolly and remote from European capitals, from the start it was pulling in stage companies from the grand opera and theater circuits, solely by the extraordinary enthusiasm of its audiences (and gate receipts). European superstars Lola Montez and Lillie Langtry forsook their royal lovers for San Francisco's adulation, and settled for a time in small California towns. As the great nineteenth-century actress Helena Modjeska, used to say, "If they like you in San Francisco, you're all right."

Aside from Lotta Crabtree and Tetrazzini, San Francisco launched the careers of Adah Menken, Edwin Booth, and native son David Belasco. Ironically, San Francisco cannot claim discovery of her most influential daughter of the footlights, Isadora Duncan. Duncan's fortune and fame as the progenitor of modern dance were first recognized in New York and the capitals of Europe. Appropriately, Isadora's birthplace is the heart of San Francisco's theater district. The original building, at 501 Taylor Street, is gone, but a plaque marks the site.

The Bay Area supports a tremendous number and range of theaters and drama companies, so it seems a bit confining to pin the name "Theater District" on one small area. After all, several other nationally celebrated theater companies are in other neighborhood districts and around the Bay Area. Still, if blue-haired theater matrons and jaded cabbies alike agree to call the half-dozen scattered blocks west of Union Square "The Theater District," who am I to argue? Scores of other Bay Area theaters present "Broadway" plays, musicals, and classic drama, but the Theater District offers them professionally produced, with larger budgets than are available to smaller neighborhood companies. Adding to the special theatrical atmosphere are the late-night cafes.

Generalizations about most Theater District venues are difficult. For an up-to-date schedule of all performances, check the pink "Datebook" in the Sunday *Chronicle*. By and large, the doyen of the city's troupes is the American Conservatory Theater (ACT), a highly professional repertory company housed in the 1,300-seat Geary Theater (415 Geary Street). The Curran (445 Geary) offers Broadway drama road shows, while the 2,400-seat Golden Gate Theatre (25 Taylor) tends to specialize in musicals. The ornate Romanesque movie palace, the Warfield (982 Market) was built for Twentieth Century Fox in 1921, and renovated to its former glory as a venue for live music, mostly rock. Farther down in the Tenderloin, the Orpheum (1192 Market) struts and frets its hours upon the stage in its sadly benighted neighborhood.

Farther west, the Great American Music Hall (859 O'Farrell) promises a very good time for ears, with music ranging from Grand Ol' Opry to jazz fusion.

Walking north from the Theater District, the steep rise of Nob Hill quickly becomes noticeable. The finer things in life come thick and fast here: hotels, shopping, restaurants, galleries, clubs. The ironically exclusive **Bohemian Club,** on the corner of Taylor and Post, was founded by people who would have laughed uproariously to see it now, a sanctuary for the likes of Henry Kissinger, Gerald Ford, and other powerful Establishment figures. In its early days, George Sterling, Jack London, Ina Coolbrith, Ambrose Bierce, John Muir, and Joaquin Miller were the *original* bohemians.

■ CIVIC CENTER

No spectacle of civic architecture in the country is more grand than San Francisco's Civic Center. City Hall's magnificent dome is a symbol of proportion and reason, a triumph of beauty and benevolent power. The proximity of the Tenderloin and its army of transients is another symbol, an ambiguous one that says little for control and order, ideals, or compassion. Where to house them, of course, is a problem with no easy answers, but until a solution is found, visitors should be prepared to deal with a gauntlet of panhandlers.

Civic Center is a supreme example of the Beaux Arts style in America. Beaux Arts was a movement initiated by young American architects who had studied at the French Ecole des Beaux-Arts. Inspired by classical architecture and infused with the City Beautiful movement, the new school of civic planning called for formality in design, with wide boulevards, colonnades, parks, and plazas. Its ideas swept the country at the turn of the twentieth century. When enthused San Franciscans asked Chicago architect Daniel Burnham to draft new plans for their city, he retreated to the top of Twin Peaks for two years of study and sketching. Published in 1905, his Burnham Plan called for a Paris-style revamp of San Francisco's streets, making use of the hills as great, park-like pedestals for monuments, with

---

HOT ON THE BLACK BIRD'S TAIL

Spade went to the Geary Theatre, failed to see Cairo in the lobby, and posted himself on the curb in front, facing the theatre. The youth loitered with other loiterers before Marquard's restaurant below.

At ten minutes past eight Joel Cairo appeared, walking up Geary Street with his little mincing bobbing steps. Apparently he did not see Spade until the private detective touched his shoulder. He seemed moderately surprised for a moment, and then said: "Oh, yes, of course you saw the ticket."

"Uh-huh. I've got something I want to show you." Spade drew Cairo back towards the curb a little away from the other waiting theatre-goers. "The kid in the cap down by Marquard's."

Cairo murmured, "I'll see," and looked at his watch. He looked up Geary Street. He looked at the theatre-sign in front of him on which George Arliss was shown costumed as Shylock, and then his dark eyes crawled sidewise in their sockets until they were looking at the kid in the cap, at his cool pale face with curling lashes hiding lowered eyes.

"Who is he?" Spade asked.

Cairo smiled up at Spade. "I do not know him."

—Dashiell Hammett, *The Maltese Falcon,* 1929

grand boulevards leading off from a magnificent Civic Center.

The 1906 earthquake wiped the slate clean, and seemed a God-given opportunity to institute the Burnham Plan. But San Franciscans were in a hurry to rebuild, and before the bureaucrats could rouse themselves, the city's commercial and residential sections were already rising on the old street grid. Fortunately, government sloth for once paid off at Civic Center, which was rebuilt more slowly on City Beautiful principles. Old City Hall had crumbled in the quake, a victim of government corruption that siphoned off construction funds and used substandard materials. Outraged San Franciscans mandated a new government, and a new Civic Center. One of the first acts of Mayor "Sunny Jim" Rolph when elected in 1911 was to call for bids for a new city hall. The winning design came from the firm of Bakewell & Brown, two local boys who had submitted it with no serious expectation that San Francisco would choose such an extravagant plan.

Arthur Brown, Jr., a graduate of the Beaux Arts school, was the designer. His old fraternity partner, John Bakewell, Jr., ran the business end of the operation. They went on to build other great buildings, including Civic Center's War Memorial Opera House, Berkeley's city hall, several structures on the Stanford and

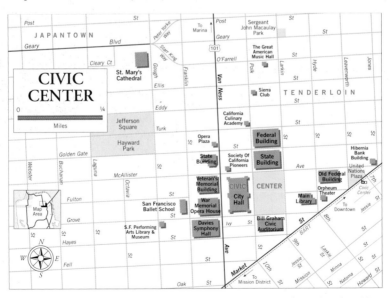

This stately view of City Hall (opposite) can be had from Franklin Street, one block west of Van Ness. (Kerrick James)

Berkeley campuses, and Coit Tower; but **San Francisco City Hall** was both the cornerstone and capstone of Brown's long, distinguished career. The dome, modeled after Saint Peter's at the Vatican, rises three feet higher above its floor than that of the nation's Capitol. To stand below that ornate dome and flowing staircase inspires awe for the powers of Caesar. Henri Crenier's Renaissance-style sculptures over the Polk Street entrance represent the figures of San Francisco, California's Riches, Commerce, and Navigation. Watching over the Van Ness Avenue entrance are Labor, Industry, Truth, Learning, the Arts, and Wisdom. Long may they live!

United Nations Plaza, between Market Street and City Hall, commemorates the charter meeting of that august body, which took place in June 1945 at the War Memorial Opera House. A largely Asian farmers' market sets up on the plaza on Wednesdays and Sundays. Rich in color and vitality, the **Civic Center Market** is a cornucopia of fresh, hard-to-find Southeast Asian vegetables and processed foods.

Kitty-corner to the newly refurbished Bill Graham Civic Auditorium, San Francisco's **Main Library** fronts the plaza. Opened in April 1996, this splendid monolith is the nation's most high-tech storehouse of knowledge, offering hundreds of on-line computer terminals to supplement its miles of bookshelves. So pervasive is the technology, and so high-tech the interior design, that readers accustomed only to shelf-browsing and card catalogs might find the new building somewhat daunting at first; but with a little practice, all but the most determined luddite should be able to navigate their way through. With children's facilities, collections of historical documents, specialty libraries devoted to singular San Francisco neighborhoods and communities, the new Main Library is a resource for researchers and for casual browsers, and all are welcome into its soaring, sunlight spaces. (The old Main Library building, on the north side of the plaza, is scheduled to be converted into the new home of the Asian Art Museum.)

Outside the Van Ness entrance to City Hall, an ornate iron gate joins the twin Veterans Memorial Building and the War Memorial Opera House (presently closed for renovation). The ultimate place to see and be seen in San Francisco is at the opera during its September to December season. Dressed to the nines, San Francisco's glitterati arrive in limousines on opening night, tailed by paparazzi and society editors. Devoted fans of more modest means jam the standing-room-only section when stars come to shake the rafters. The lavish costumes and settings are

awe-inspiring; all in all, the San Francisco opera is among the world's most criti-
cally acclaimed.

Like its opera, San Francisco's ballet and symphony are internationally distinguished. One of the nation's oldest dance companies, the **San Francisco Ballet** performs in the **War Memorial Opera House** when it is not on the road, and presents
contemporary as well as classical repertory works. The San Francisco Symphony
keeps house at **Louise M. Davies Hall,** built in 1981 on the corner of Van Ness
and Grove. The symphony season runs from September through May. Davies Hall
is equipped with the largest concert hall organ in North America, built by the Ruf-
fatti brothers of Padua, Italy. Its 9,235 pipes are played with the help of a sophisticated computer.

A mandatory side-trip for aficionados of local theater, opera, dance, and music
is the **San Francisco Performing Arts Library and Museum,** one block west of
Davies Hall, at the corner of Grove and Gough streets. A wealth of trappings of
the footlit stage—theater posters, playbills, newspaper clippings, and some 4,000
books on the performing arts from the Gold Rush to the present—invest the
archives and gallery walls with the smell of greasepaint, the roar of crowds.

The culinary arts are also well represented in the Civic Center area, thanks in
large part to the city's premier training ground for chefs, the **California Culinary
Academy** (625 Polk). In their 16-month course on classical French, Italian, and
nouvelle cuisines, the students' training runs the gamut of pastries, wines, appetizers, salads, dressings, canapés, decorative meats, entrées, terrines, garnishes, cut
vegetables, soups, and desserts, while learning the economies and etiquette of
kitchen and restaurant. The best part is that you can taste the fruits of their labors.
Besides operating a retail bakery and small cafe, the academy serves lunch and dinner at set times on weekdays in the Carême Room—a glass-enclosed hall, permit-
ting diners to watch the ongoing work in the kitchens—and in the basement
Academy Grill. Service is excellent and prices are extremely reasonable for such
high quality dining.

Headquarters of the Sierra Club, the international environmentalist organization founded by John Muir to preserve and foster appreciation of California's
Sierra Nevada range, stands one block north at 730 Polk Street. Its street-level
store sells books on travel, nature, and conservation.

GOING HOME

Where are they going
all these brave intrepid animals
Fur and flesh
in steel cabinets
on wheels
high-tailing it
Four PM Friday freeway
over the hidden land
San Francisco's burning
with the late sun
in a million windows
The four-wheeled animals
are leaving it to burn
They're escaping
almost flying
home to the nest
home to the warm caves
in the hidden hills & valleys
home to daddy home to mama
home to the little wonders
home to the pot plants behind the garage
The cars the painted cabinets
streak for home home home
THRU TRAFFIC MERGE LEFT
home to the hidden turning
the hidden yearning
home to San Jose
home to Santa Cruz & Monterey
home to Hamilton Avenue
home to the Safeway the safest way
YIELD
LEFT LANE MUST TURN LEFT . . .

—Lawrence Ferlinghetti, from
"Home Home Home,"
Landscapes of Living & Dying, 1979

■ THE TENDERLOIN

The dreariest high-crime district in San Francisco is the Tenderloin. It is easy to stumble into because it lies between the downtown shopping district and the Civic Center, at the edge of the greatest concentration of hotels in the city. Its exact boundaries are fuzzy, but it is generally pinned down between Larkin, Mason, and O'Farrell streets, with a dogleg over Market and down Sixth Street toward Howard.

The Tenderloin, in case you wonder, is a kind of vigorous skid row and red-light district of porn shops, pimps, streetwalkers, and massage parlor fronts. It attracts runaways and their exploiters, as well as drug dealers, drunks, transvestites, and down-and-outers—not to mention stag businessmen and conventioneers. The Tenderloin has the highest rate of rape in the city, and ought to be avoided by unaccompanied females, even by day. Because of cheap rents, the Tenderloin also has the largest concentration of elderly poor people. Many live a life of fear, barricaded behind locked doors.

But all is not a tale of woe. The Tenderloin is in the midst of change. Within the past decade, Southeast Asian families have been quietly colonizing a large swatch of territory here, especially in the blocks along Ellis Street. Most of them are ethnic Chinese from Vietnam, Laos, and Cambodia, many of whom survived 40 years of warfare and unbelievable hardship to get here, and who do not flinch easily at the mere reputation of mean streets. The Southeast Asian influence may yet transform the Tenderloin from a no-man's land to a thriving family community. Already, its markets and restaurants are attracting patrons from other neighborhoods, and even some tourists. Especially inviting are the small neighborhood cafes, mostly of the cheap and hearty Vietnamese type called *phö,* where a huge bowl of spiced beef noodle soup, with a condiment of fresh bean sprouts, lemon, pepper, and mint leaf, is the pièce de resistance.

NABOBS, SOJOURNERS,
B O H E M I A N S

THE LOW HILLS RISING UP BEHIND DOWNTOWN San Francisco are no Rocky Mountains, but they are a formidable barrier nonetheless. The principal civic, financial, and commercial functions of San Francisco cluster on the flat lands around the foot of these hills, where bureaucrats and capitalists (and their esteemed clients) can tread the course of least resistance. But climb any hill out of downtown San Francisco, and you turn your back on the world of big business and big government.

Nob Hill, Telegraph Hill, and Russian Hill, with their attendant communities of North Beach and Chinatown, were among San Francisco's earliest residential areas, nurturing a succession of outcast communities, eccentrics, and escapists, not to mention plenty of just ordinary family folk. Within five minutes' walk of the hard-nosed towers of Montgomery Street, you can buy a Chinese pear or hear Puccini sung on a jukebox. Within 10 minutes, you can watch a game of bocce or pay respects to Kuan Kung, god of war and literature. Within 15, the all-seeing Top of the Mark can be your throne, or if you prefer, a wooden step beneath dangling fuchsias on Telegraph Hill. And all around you, tens of thousands of local residents and passers-by are playing out their lives in neighborhood bistros, schools, markets, churches, temples, restaurants, clubs, newspapers, hospitals, and funeral parlors, while cable cars rattle and clang through the boisterous streets.

Cynics lament that some of these neighborhoods have become mere symbols of what they used to be. Yes, commercialism has made gross inroads at Fisherman's Wharf. Beatniks and nabobs, for the most part, have gone the way of cheap rents and unregulated monopolies, and even the Italians of Little Italy are growing thin on the ground. Yet, as long as red wine, jasmine tea, Napier Lane, dim sum, fettuccine, and City Lights Bookstore survive, these most San Franciscan of San Francisco's old neighborhoods will continue to salve the soul and feed the senses.

■ NOB HILL

San Franciscans like to say that the *Nob* of Nob Hill is a contraction of *nabob*, meaning a Moghul prince. This etymology is dubious, but it has poetic license.

Nob Hill (opposite) is famous for its cable cars and its grand historic hotels. At the Fairmont Hotel (top), classic high tea (bottom) is served every day in the lobby. (Kerrick James)

Some of America's favorite nabobs, who ripped their fabulous fortunes from the silver mines and railroad rights-of-way of the American West, built their mansions on the gilded crown of Nob Hill.

Hemmed in on the south by Union Square, the Theater District, and the Tenderloin, on the west by busy Polk Gulch, and on the east by teeming Chinatown, Nob Hill stands aloof from the tumultuous city. Today, however, it's not as exclusive as when Robert Louis Stevenson called it "the hill of palaces." The dapper doormen at the grand hotels cater to a newer, more transient breed of mini-nabob. But the ghosts of the old Big Four and the Bonanza Kings live on, not only in Nob Hill's place names, but in its rarified air of understated wealth (not that there was anything understated about the hill's colossal Victorian prosperity). Today's fortunes are more restrained, more evenly spread. The palaces have shrunk to town houses, penthouses, and hotel suites. The corps of servants that once bowed to one master and mistress now pamper hordes of splurging tourists.

The invention of the cable car in 1873 sealed Nob Hill's fate as a suitable aerie for Victorian millionaires. It was said that Leland Stanford built the California Street line for his wife's convenience, laying the tracks right past their door at the corner of Powell and California. Today, you can eyeball those tracks clear down the California Street canyon of the Financial District, past Ralston's and Gianinni's and the Wells Fargo banks, to the imposing Southern Pacific Building on Market Street. Southern Pacific, of course, was the reincarnation of the Central Pacific, the company founded by Stanford and the other Big Four (Hopkins, Crocker, and Huntington) to build the first transcontinental railway. The Big Four reaped obscene fortunes and power from the arrangement. In time, their empire straddled much of the American West, rolling over all who got in its way.

The ultimate triumph of Stanford's life, however, eluded him. He and his wife had a son, whom they doted on, Leland Stanford, Jr. Leland was raised in the lap of Nob Hill, a privileged quarter of chiming clocks and scurrying servants, where rare and wondrous toys for the lad arrived from around the world. The best of everything was lavished upon him, and he grew up showing great talents in several disciplines, particularly archaeology. But sadly, in his sixteenth year, while on European tour, the boy died, plunging his parents into sorrow unallayed by all the money in the world. They returned to San Francisco and channeled their grief into building a memorial to perpetuate his name for the benefit of other sons and daughters of California. That monument is Stanford University.

Like all the other wooden palaces on Nob Hill, the great Stanford mansion burned in the 1906 fire. The massive granite wall that once surrounded it still partially encloses the present structure, the Stanford Court Hotel. It is, in the best tradition of nabobbery, one of the finest hotels in the world. Stanford's California Street cable cars still come trundling up from the lowlands, pausing briefly outside his vanished front door. The Powell-Mason and Powell-Hyde street lines, climbing up Powell from Market, cross the California Street line at this same corner.

Mark Hopkins, the Big Four's number two man, built his mansion next door to Stanford's, at the top of California Street. Today, the Mark Hopkins Hotel (1 Nob Hill) rises on the site, capped by the city's most famous view-bar, the **Top of the Mark**. You can see for miles from every window, the celebrated view (though maybe not the venue) that inspired the city's signature song, immortalized by Tony Bennett: "I Left My Heart in San Francisco."

Another elegant landmark of after-hours San Francisco rises across the street. Named for Comstock millionaire James Fair, the Fairmont Hotel was built by his daughter, and is a grand survivor of the quake of 1906, though it was gutted in the fire. The stately marble lobby in its day has greeted many a blue-blood. The **Fairmont Crown**, reached by a heart-grabbing ride in a glass elevator up the outside of the hotel's modern tower, is San Francisco's loftiest watering hole. The Tonga Room offers dancing by a South Sea lagoon, complete with a tropical thunderstorm.

Across the street from the Fairmont stands the solid brownstone **Flood mansion**. The only Nob Hill mansion to survive the fire of 1906, Bonanza King James Flood's one-time residence (1000 California Street) is now the exclusive Pacific-Union Club. It's called the P-U in local parlance. Don't even bother to knock.

Alone among his partners, Charles Crocker lacks the posthumous honor of having his name grace a Nob Hill hotel. Instead, his old mansion made way for San Francisco's supreme Episcopalian house of God, **Grace Cathedral**. Gazing at the towers and spire of that high-minded edifice, it is difficult to envision this as the scene of San Francisco's most grotesque example of filthy-rich rascality. There was a time when Charlie Crocker owned *most* of that block and wanted it *all*. That elusive corner lot, however, was owned by an undertaker named Nicholas Yung, who declined to sell. In retaliation, Crocker built a 40-foot "spite fence" around Yung's property, boxing in the house on three sides. San Franciscans were outraged, but neither Crocker or Yung would budge. Historian Randolph Delehanty

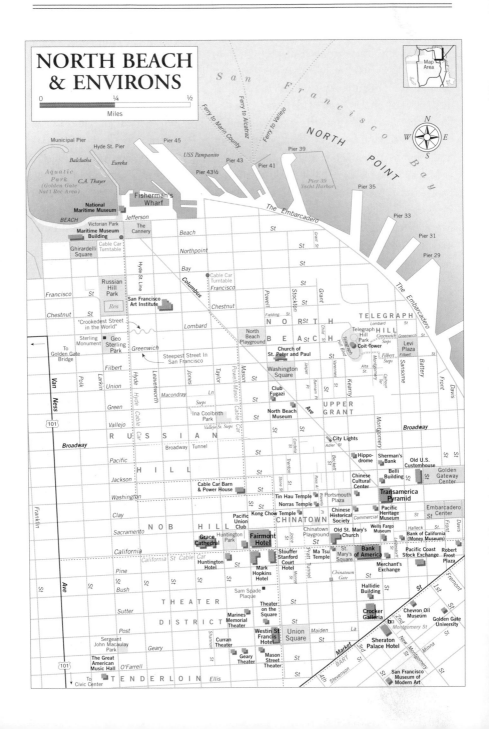

NORTH BEACH & ENVIRONS

0   ¼   ½

Miles

notes that both men died with the stalemate unresolved, leaving their heirs to settle the matter. The Yung estate eventually was sold to the Crocker estate, and all passed quietly to the Episcopal Diocese after the 1906 earthquake rendered the property untenable for worldly use.

No matter how lovely Grace Cathedral looks—and it is a beaut, inspired by Notre Dame in Paris—one can never escape the nagging fact that it is made of reinforced concrete. Why that should detract from the *idea* of religious beauty is not hard to understand. The great cathedrals of Europe, built block by block over decades, sometimes centuries, physically embody their builders' inspired, personal devotion. A cathedral erected in compliance with a building code established to protect worshippers from earthquakes and other acts of God just does not epitomize the same fervor of piety. Still, Grace is a lovely cathedral, from the doors (cast from Lorenzo Ghiberti's *Gates of Paradise,* from the Cathedral Baptistry in Florence) to the great rose window (built in Chartres in 1970). Most beautiful of all is the flood of music that pours out during the choral evensongs, and when the pipe organ or carillon is played, especially in the Christmas season. Also wonderful, if more secular, are the jazz and contemporary classical concerts which Grace hosts from time to time.

Collis P. Huntington, last of the Big Four, once owned the site of Huntington Park, across the street. Huntington bought the land from the widow of Southern Pacific's lawyer, David Colton—which is odd, since the Big Four had accused Colton of embezzlement and sued for a piece of his estate. This lawsuit was the sensation of its age, an unfolding drama of graft and bribery among the rich and famous, which titillated a fascinated public for eight years and scandalized Congress into a flurry of reform laws directed against the robber barons. Today the grand house is gone. Huntington Park is a quiet, sedate place with a charming little fountain, much beloved by elderly Chinese ladies who do their morning *tai chi* above the ashes of the Big Four's mansions. Those who wish to further contemplate this great American saga in an atmosphere evocative of the era may retire across California Street to The Big Four, a splendid restaurant in the posh Huntington Hotel.

The California Street cable car line drops down the west side of Nob Hill five blocks farther to Van Ness Avenue. This valley is known as **Polk Gulch**, after Polk Street, which runs north from City Hall to Aquatic Park, parallel to Van Ness. Polk Street was the setting of McTeague's dentistry office in Frank Norris's

McTeague. It was also one of the earliest established gay neighborhoods of the city, but has since been eclipsed by Castro Street. Polk Street south of California has gone seedy, but the northern stretch remains a vigorous commercial and residential area with an increasing Chinese influence.

■ CABLE CAR BARN

Dynamic powerhouse for the nation's only moving National Historical Monument, this historic brick building is both the "garage" and central powerhouse for the world's last remaining cable car system. Originally built in 1909, the building hums with power, and is one of the city's most spectacular sights, both sensually and intellectually. Between 1982 and 1984 it was gutted and reinforced against earthquakes, and the interior rebuilt within the original exterior walls.

The cable car was invented by Andrew Hallidie, a British-born mining engineer who specialized in building cable systems used for hauling ore. Hallidie's inspiration, the story goes, came after watching a horse-drawn streetcar slip down one of San Francisco's steep streets, dragging the horses behind. After many experiments, he devised a mechanical system that could pull cars up steep hills and around 90-degree turns. Hallidie successfully tested his first cable car on Clay Street in 1873. Though devilishly complex, it was a work of genius. Before long London, Sydney, and several other American cities had adopted the technology, as well as several other companies within San Francisco, providing a field day for Hallidie's patent attorneys. But as bus, streetcar, and automobile rendered them obsolete, cable cars eventually disappeared from every city, except their sentimental birthplace. Despite their expense and questionable safety record, they are arguably the best-loved symbol of San Francisco.

Operating a cable car is a work of art. They carry no engines. The kinetic energy is all in the continuous loop of steel cable, pulled through a slot in the street at a constant speed of 9.5 miles per hour by engines anchored to the floor of the powerhouse. The system's three cables (one for each cable car line) are steered through their circuitous routes—around 90 degree corners and up and down steep hills—by a series of subterranean sheaves (pulleys). To drive the car forward, the cable car gripman yanks the grip lever, forcing the grip into the slot to seize (or *grip*) the cable; to stop he lets go, and applies the brakes. The gripman's finesse shows up best at corners and where two lines cross, when he has to release the grip before it binds or smashes against the sheaves. After coasting free of the impediment, the gripman then reapplies the grip, and the cable car continues its journey. The brakeman receives his workout on the descent of the city's steep hills, a real test of nerve and machine, particularly on the Hyde Street grade of Russian Hill.

From the mezzanine floor of the Cable Car Barn, you can look down on the humming engines, which drive the 14-foot sheaves that wind the cables. Be sure to walk downstairs to the Sheave Room for a peek under the street, where $8\frac{1}{2}$-foot sheaves steer the moving cables (one for each cable car line) in and out of the powerhouse on their subterranean loops through the city. The small museum preserves an early cable car and some well-annotated specimens of the grip and braking mechanisms. You can buy souvenirs and books explaining the operation in much greater detail from the mezzanine shop. The museum is free, and is open daily.

Outside the barn, before turning up Clay Street for Russian Hill, the cable car conductors shout, "Chinatown!" Stockton, the main shopping street for Chinatown residents, is only one block down.

The Cable Car Barn hums as its powerful sheaves steer the cables.

■ CHINATOWN

Chinatown is a clash of five senses, a crush of humanity, a blur of ambrosial steams and flavors, a cacophony of clattering pots and market cries, the grim whir of sewing machines behind windowless walls, an odor of dried fungus.

Rudyard Kipling called it "a ward of the city of Canton," setting a theme for later tour guides, who prefer to compare Chinatown to Hong Kong. Which is nonsense. In fact, it's a little like comparing Grover's Corners to the City of London.

Chinatown is a distinctively American hybrid of a Cantonese market town— *Cantonese* inasmuch as most of its residents are ethnically Cantonese, and *American* inasmuch as fortune cookies, Chinese New Year parades, dragon-wrapped lampposts, Miss Chinatown contests, Chinatown tourist kitsch, chop suey restaurants, and much more, are distinctively American phenomena. And that's just scratching the surface.

Chinatown's founders were mainly from two classes. City merchants, mostly from Guangzhou (Canton City), were few in number, but they rose to prominence in the community by virtue of their wealth, polish, and ability to speak English. The vast majority of early Chinese immigrants, however, were rural males, laborers largely from Toishan County, whose local dialect is unintelligible to people from Guangzhou. Most of these were sojourners, that is, men who intended to return to China after making their fortune—as indeed many did, bringing back new ideas that hastened the downfall of the Qing Dynasty. Few learned English, which contributed to their isolation in America. They banded together in clubs, or *tongs*, based on their surname or county of origin. The word "tong" has a negative connotation in English today, but in Chinese it means only "association." Most "tongs," or associations, in Chinatown were and are perfectly benign social clubs. The tong was the principal political and social force of old Chinatown, most benevolently in the form of a confederation of tongs called the Six Companies; but least so in the form of the fighting tongs of the late nineteenth century.

This peculiarly masculine, working-class society was mummified by the Exclusion Act of 1882. Instead of developing into a family-oriented neighborhood, San Francisco Chinatown remained for years a stunted frontier settlement in the midst of a city, where flourished all the vices comforting to lonely men—drugs, gambling, prostitution, and the corruption and violence associated with the control of same. Ironically, the *real* opium dens, slave girls, and highbinders that inspired sinister Hollywood movies about Chinatown were themselves kept in business largely by the American Exclusion laws. (Chinatown's unique character also inspired stereotypes in the *Chinese* cinema: a stock character of Hong Kong movies and anecdotes up until the 1960s was "Uncle from Gold Mountain"—an aging, rich, spendthrift, good-hearted oaf on the lookout for a young wife.)

Today's Chinatown is a whole different world. Since immigration laws were relaxed in the 1960s, the influx of immigrant families from Hong Kong, China, Taiwan, and Southeast Asia have rejuvenated it. Crusty old Toishan bachelors and Cantonese merchants still hold their own, but they are part of a far richer tapestry of lanky peasants, fry cooks, spoiled-brat starlets, sober-sided professionals and shell-shocked refugees, sophisticates and factory workers, aunties with their daily shopping and, most precious to a once-stagnant community, children.

Most of this new "community" no longer lives in Chinatown. The prosperous, the educated, and the ambitious move on to the suburbs. In fact, most prosperous immigrants from Hong Kong today completely bypass a stay in Chinatown, though they may own a business there. Non-English-speaking poor immigrants from China, and the elderly poor, for the most part, stay behind. Life for them can be hard. Chinatown is the most densely populated neighborhood in the States outside of Harlem. Housing is poor. Sweatshops exploit immigrants ignorant of American labor laws. For those who move away, however, the grimmer realities of Chinatown fade behind a kind of spiritual, or perhaps visceral, symbol. Here, suburbanites can and do regularly repair to eat Chinese food, read Chinese newspapers, shop for Chinese groceries, browse through the Chinese library and bookstores, go to a Chinese movie, and, in short, retouch some aspect of their (or their forebears') heritage.

Not all of Chinatown's "suburbs" are distant. The nucleus of Chinatown remains the 24-block area bounded by Kearny, Bush, Powell, and Broadway, but the contiguous community now incorporates the less hectic streets of North Beach, Telegraph Hill, Russian Hill, and Nob Hill. Stockton Street is the main Chinese thoroughfare, while Grant is the Mecca of tourists. The streets in between— Pacific, Jackson, Washington, Clay, Sacramento, and the alleys that connect them— best retain the atmosphere of old Chinatown.

The only way to tour Chinatown is on foot. The streets are too congested for comfortable driving, and finding a parking space is like winning the lottery. Even the parking garage under Portsmouth Square often has a line of cars *waiting just to get in the door.* You may have better luck parking beneath the Holiday Inn across the street, or under Saint Mary's Square. Visitors might well consider joining one of the walking tours that go "behind the scenes" in Chinatown. (Contact the San Francisco Convention & Visitors Bureau at 415-974-6900.)

Chinatown, for most visitors, begins at the **Chinatown Gate** on Grant at Bush. It is an ornate, touristy version of the ceremonial gate that you might find in Chinese villages. Outside the gate, **Grant Avenue** is one of San Francisco's swankiest shopping streets (described in the previous chapter). Within the gate, the two blocks to California Street are the tidiest of Chinatown, attracting classier shops selling silks, gems, embroidered linens and blouses, antiques, furniture, and art goods. You can find some nice things, but in regard to the prices, bear in mind that Grant Avenue caters especially to tourists.

The corner of California and Grant is one of the city's most photographed scenes, embracing cable cars, pagoda-roofed buildings and **Old Saint Mary's Church.** Looking down through the Financial District, you can see the Bay Bridge above Market Street. The cable car runs up California to the top of Nob Hill, intersecting Grant about mid-slope. Old Saint Mary's was San Francisco's Catholic cathedral from 1853 to 1891. Its famous brick tower bears a clock and inscription, "Son, Observe the time and fly from evil." Though gutted by flames in 1906, its sturdy foundation (imported from China) and walls (imported from the East Coast) survived. Emperor Norton, while waving at a passing cable car, collapsed and died here in 1880.

Old Saint Mary's is not the only religious building on this corner. Two floors up at 562 Grant Avenue you will find the **Ma-Tsu Temple of the United States of America.** This modern temple combines shrines to Buddha and the popular gods Tin Hau (Queen of Heaven), Kuan Kung, Kwun Yum, and an earth god. As in all Chinatown temples, visitors are welcome, though the caretakers seldom speak English. Photography is not permitted in temples.

A half block down from California, **Saint Mary's Square** basks quietly amongst taller buildings. Saint Mary's restful mood is enhanced by Benjiamano Bufano's peaceful statue of Sun Yat-sen, founder of the Republic of China. A native of Guangdong (Canton) Province, but educated in Hawaii and Hong Kong, Sun sought to overthrow the Qing Dynasty. Under sentence of death in his own country, he traveled around the world drumming up money for the revolution. During his stay in San Francisco, he founded a newspaper and wrote the English version of China's constitution in the Montgomery Block, a short stroll down from Saint

The Li Po (top), a Chinatown watering hole for many years, was named for China's most famous poet. Portsmouth Plaza is the living room of many Chinatown elderly (bottom).

Mary's Square, though now demolished. He also made many trips to Chinese communities around the state. Through their generous contributions, Californians were thus instrumental in founding the Republic of China.

Chinatown grows more frenetic in the six-block walk along Grant between California and Broadway. Here you will find many of Chinatown's big restaurants and tourist knickknack shops, but also others that offer more curious browsing, such as the Chinatown Kite Shop (717 Grant), the Wok Shop (718 Grant), and the Ten Ren Tea Company (949 Grant). A uniquely Chinese-American creation, the cave-like Li Po Bar (916 Grant) is named after China's most famous poet, a wildly romantic warrior and wine-loving courtier, who drowned while drunkenly embracing the reflection of the moon in a river. The last block of Grant before it hits Broadway is the business heart of old Chinatown, now eclipsed by Stockton Street.

Be sure to detour down Commercial Street, a narrow, partially cobbled lane that contains the only museum in the country devoted exclusively to Chinese-American history. The **Chinese Historical Society** attempts to trace and preserve a record of the myriad Chinese contributions to the growth of America, and especially California, where Chinese played key roles in agriculture, fishing, mining, industry, and civil engineering, not to mention the arts, science, military, and service industries. Among the historical treasures in the society's collection are a tiger fork from the Weaverville "tong war," a papier-mâché dragon's head, old photographs, gold rush paraphernalia, and the old, handwritten Chinatown telephone book. The museum, at 650 Commercial Street, is open Wednesday through Sunday afternoons. It's free, but donations are appreciated. (The Pacific Heritage Museum at 608 Commercial Street is noted on pages 61–62.)

The block of Grant between Washington and Clay was the original street of Yankee San Francisco. Back when the waves of Yerba Buena Cove still lapped at what is now Montgomery Street, Grant Avenue (then called *Calle de la Fundación,* or Foundation Street) was laid out by an English sea captain and his Mexican wife. Their village plaza, just down the hill, proved very useful for corralling the horses and livestock of visiting *vaqueros,* as well as the occasional goat. After American Marines raised the flag there in 1846, seizing San Francisco for the Union, they christened it after their ship, the USS *Portsmouth.*

Young Portsmouth Square (*Square* changed back to *Plaza* in 1927) was the heart of Gold Rush San Francisco, hosting a motley array of civic assemblages, town meetings, celebrations, duels, and lynchings, as well as the city's first school, bookstore, and newspaper, and the finest hotels of the Gold Rush era. As landfill pushed the waterfront farther east, however, the business district moved with it, and Portsmouth Square lost its luster. Union Square, and later Civic Center, took over its public duties. Today, though rather ill-kempt and sprinkled with panhandlers, **Portsmouth Plaza** serves as a much-needed backyard for densely packed Chinatown.

When Robert Louis Stevenson lived in San Francisco (1879–1880), he liked to sit in Portsmouth Square to watch the tide of humanity roll by. A **monument to Stevenson** stands at the northwest corner of the plaza today—a model of the *Hispaniola* from *Treasure Island*, with some lines from his "Christmas Sermon." Today it shares the square with a replica of the "Goddess of Democracy," the symbol of the Tiananmen Square protests of 1989 in Beijing, when so many students were killed.

The tide of humanity that so fascinated Stevenson still flows through Portsmouth Plaza. At dawn, novices and old hands assemble here for *tai chi*, an ancient Chinese exercise that resembles a slow-motion ballet. In the afternoons, the plaza fills with scores of men playing checkers, cards, *go*, and other games. Many are single, elderly, boarding-house tenants who have no other family. Having come of age during or just after the Exclusion Act, which restricted Chinese immigration between 1882 and 1943, they were unable to find wives from the male-dominated Chinatown community, and fell into lifelong habits of bachelorhood. Portsmouth Plaza is both their living room and social club.

The **Chinese Cultural Center** occupies the third floor of the Chinatown Holiday Inn, across the footbridge from Portsmouth Plaza. The lectures, seminars, and exhibitions of works by Chinese-American artists and writers are geared more for community than tourists, but the center does have a small gift shop.

Backtracking to Grant, head uphill along the steep lateral lanes of Chinatown: Pacific, Jackson, Washington, Clay, and Sacramento. Keep your eyes open for **herbalist shops**, windows cluttered with medicinal and aphrodisiac potions, ginseng roots, fungus, elk horn, and occasional oddities like snake wine. The old-fashioned herbalist shops are most atmospheric, jammed with chests of Chinese roots and herbs. Many herbalists are scattered through Chinatown, but Washington Street seems particularly rich in them.

Ross Alley is the shadiest-looking thoroughfare in Chinatown. Its history lives up to its appearance, but today its most sinister aspect is the whine of hidden sewing machines in the garment factories. Visitors are welcome in the tiny **Golden Gate Fortune Cookie Factory** at 52 Ross to see the cookie machine in action.

Waverly Place, between Washington and Sacramento, is called the "street of painted balconies" for reasons obvious to anyone who looks up. During the tong war era, Waverly was known as the toughest street in Chinatown. Today it's better known for its temples. The **Tin Hau Temple** at 123 Waverly, a long climb to the fourth floor, is the most atmospheric of Chinatown's temples, hung with lanterns and smokey from incense and the fires of burnt offerings. The main altar is dedicated to Tin Hau, Queen of Heaven and protector of seafarers and sojourners, but the temple also accommodates shrines to other gods. The Buddhist Association of America oversees the **Norras Temple** at 109 Waverly. From the street, you can often hear the saffron-robed monks chanting and striking bells, while the drums of kung fu clubs practicing lion dancing resound from elsewhere in the building.

Sacramento Street, once Chinatown's main stem, is still known by the name that signifies "Chinatown" to overseas Chinese—*Tang Yahn Gai*, literally "Tang People's Street." (The Tang Dynasty is considered the most brilliant era of Chinese history, hence the Cantonese fondness for referring to themselves as Tang people.)

Children are the most vital ingredient of Chinatown's future.

A Chinatown apothecary measures herbs for use in a traditional Chinese medicine.
(Kerrick James)

Between Waverly and Hang Ah streets is one of the outstanding children's playgrounds of San Francisco, with a maze of climbing ladders and slides, and plenty of sand. On the block above Stockton, the clinker-brick Donaldina Cameron House (920 Sacramento), named after the Chinatown crusader, replaced the earlier mission that burned in 1906.

Broad Stockton Street is the main market street for Chinatown residents. Its southern end enters Chinatown by way of the Stockton Tunnel, connecting with the Union Square shopping district at its other end. At the Chinatown end of the tunnel, on the corner of Stockton and Clay above the post office, the **Kong Chow Temple** (855 Stockton Street) looks out over Chinatown and the Financial District from the top floor. Though the building itself is entirely modern, some say this is the oldest Chinese temple in the country. Its carved, gilded altars and furnishings are venerable and magnificent. The main shrine honors the god Kuan Kung, a fierce, yet noble, poetry-reading general during the Three Kingdoms era (A.D. 220–280), who was deified after being captured and executed. Kuan Kung is now the patron god of warriors and literature, much beloved by persons in professions requiring courage and fighting skill, including both police and criminals.

Nearby, at 843 Stockton Street, stands the modern headquarters of the Six Companies, the patriarchal government body of old Chinatown. Now called the Chinese Consolidated Benevolent Association, its influence these days is considerably more token than toothy. The Taiwan flags advertise its political orientation.

Unlike the dingy alleys down the hill, Stockton Street's appeal is not historic, but immediate. No more crowded street exists in San Francisco than the stretch of Stockton between Sacramento and Broadway on a Saturday afternoon. Pedestrians throng the sidewalks outside markets crammed with fresh fish, bok choy, cabbages, mangos, bitter melon, apples, oranges, roast ducks, pressed ducks, barbecued pork, dry goods, oils, sweets, and shoppers shouting orders to the quick-fingered meat choppers. Curbside, hawkers haggle over live chickens and ducks from the backs of flatbed trucks, while vats of squirming fish and crabs are hoisted down to aproned butchers.

Beyond Broadway, Chinatown presses along Stockton into traditionally Italian North Beach, clear to Columbus Avenue. Chinatown's largest supplier of books on China is East Wind Books, in the basement of 1435 Stockton Street. Their English-language store is upstairs on the second floor. Tea connoisseurs should drop in for a Chinese tea-tasting session at the Imperial Tea Court, an exquisitely old-fashioned establishment at 1411 Powell.

This neighborhood used to be (and to a lesser degree still is) the city rendezvous of the Basques brought to the United States on contract to tend sheep in the high deserts of the Great Basin. The Obrero Hotel, upstairs near the corner of Stockton and Pacific, is a longtime lodging house for Basques. The Obrero now caters to the general public, but still maintains clean and cheap pension rooms—a real find for the budget traveler who appreciates a simple, homey, friendly setting. Around the corner at 732 Broadway is Des Alpes, a long-time local Basque restaurant.

Speaking of food, no visit to Chinatown should neglect the stomach. Chinese is the emperor of world cuisines, and Cantonese is China's own undisputed king—though American palates seem to prefer the spicier northern styles of cooking, which explains the proliferation of Hunan, Sichuan, and Mandarin restaurants in the city. Chinatown's new immigrants are also opening restaurants serving Vietnamese food, as well as the Hakka and Chaozhou variations of the Cantonese. Still, Chinatown's main culinary focus remains traditional Cantonese food, with its two outstanding offerings of dim sum and seafood.

Dim sum are light snacks—little dumplings of shrimp, pork, and scores of other fillings, little pastries, and minced meats—served traditionally from passing carts or trays, with tea. Aside from a few organs that might make the uninitiated queasy—a bit of tripe, a duck's foot, a piece of pig's intestine—dim sum is invariably a happy revelation. Dim sum is traditionally served for breakfast or lunch. Most popular to Western tastes are the wrapped shrimp (*ha gow*), wrapped pork with shrimp (*siu mai*), rice pasta stuffed with meat or shrimp (*cheung fun*), and roast pork buns (*char siu bao*). Most dim sum restaurants are noisy affairs where the varieties of dishes are belted out in piercing tenors and sopranos by the passing serving ladies. If you can't get into the rumbustious spirit of these clamoring, packed-out restaurants, where the maitre d's patrol with walkie-talkies and you may have to order by hunt-and-point methods, then stick to the more genteel northern-style restaurants. But if you like great food in a truly hang-loose setting, then by all means come prepared for an invigorating experience. Any Hong Kong expatriate will tell you, however, that the best dim sum is found *outside* Chinatown, at huge Hong Kong-style restaurants, such as North Sea Village in Sausalito, the Hong Kong Flower Lounge in Millbrae and the Richmond District, Yank Sing and Harbor Village in the Financial District, and East Ocean in Emeryville.

Tai chi, an ancient Chinese form of exercise, is performed in controlled slow motion, rigidly disciplined, painstakingly methodical. Some have called it "Chinese shadow boxing," an inadequate description, for the movements only vaguely resemble the more crudely martial Western form of boxing. If performed diligently over one's lifetime, tai chi is said to keep the muscles and cardiovascular system toned and healthy. Every morning brings devotees, many of them elderly, to the open spaces around Chinatown, particularly Portsmouth Plaza, Huntington Park, and Washington Square, where teachers lead them through the graceful moves.

Seafood dishes are readily available in most Chinatown restaurants. You can get good seafood at the big, fancy restaurants catering to tourists and special Chinese banquets, or you can pay less for a meal just as good in a modest, casual setting catering to locals. Most of the big, expensive restaurants congregate along Grant Avenue. Washington and Jackson streets are packed with crowded, tiny restaurants, some downstairs, some up. These are not tourist places, and if you don't mind homey cooking and service, they offer some of San Francisco's best dining bargains.

The Chinatown equivalent of the American diner is the noodle and *juk* shop. They keep late hours and serve quick short-order meals like fried or soup noodles, rice plates and *juk* (rice porridge).

Chinatown groceries are usually stocked with fresh bok choy, ginger, and other produce typically used in Chinese cooking. (Kerrick James)

■ NORTH BEACH

The beach has long been buried by landfill, but its potent name still carries meaning beyond mere geographical reference. On a local level, North Beach represents the focus of the ethnic Italians, a place of trattoria, cappuccino, aromatic delicatessens, and music. On a national level, North Beach means *Bohemia*, or more specifically, *beatnik*. Between the Italians and bohemians, North Beach has been christened San Francisco's Latin Quarter. The reputation is increasingly hard to keep up.

North Beach fills the floor of the valley that hangs between Russian and Telegraph hills. Columbus Street cuts a wide diagonal right down the middle, and is the main road between downtown San Francisco and Fisherman's Wharf. The northern edge of North Beach, which once pushed almost to Fisherman's Wharf (itself a long-time Italian stronghold) is now obliterated by the hotels and gift shops that cover the waterfront. The southern boundary, traditionally, is Broadway.

Broadway was long known as the Marco Polo Zone because it marked where Chinatown ended and Little Italy began. This is no longer the case. Chinatown now pushes far into North Beach, and the predominant ethnic group in North Beach today is Chinese. A lot of old-time Italians bitterly grumble about this, and no doubt the weakening Italian influence is disheartening to those who love the fascinating distinction between these two wonderful neighborhoods. Sad it may be, but an ethnic community cannot be preserved as a museum. Neighborhoods change. Before North Beach was Italian, it was Irish. Before the Irish came, it was Chilean. (The old church of Nuestra Señora de Guadalupe at 908 Broadway still recalls its Hispanic parishioners.) And for that matter, before Fisherman's Wharf was Italian, it was *Chinese*.

Though Italians were early immigrants to San Francisco, the Italian community of North Beach took root relatively late in the nineteenth century, filling out after the turn of the century during the heyday of immigration from Italy. By 1940, they were the predominant foreign-born group in the city. Their families prospered, their children grew up as Americans, and they moved to the suburbs, selling the family homes and businesses. The heyday of Chinese immigration, on the other hand, came much later in the century, during the 1970s and 1980s (though, of course, the 1850s and 1860s were also boom decades of Chinese immigration). The old boundaries of Chinatown were rendered inadequate. Paralleling the Italians, the Chinese also prospered, supplanting them as the largest foreign-born

Molinari's deli is a paradise for lovers of Italian salami and salads.

group in the city. And like the Italians, the Americanized generations have moved out of the old neighborhood center. As a community of first-generation immigrants in the late twentieth century, Little Italy simply cannot match the vitality of Chinatown.

But let us not sing a dirge for Little Italy. North Beach is still a colorful focus of the Italian-American community. The annual Columbus Day Parade in October is the biggest celebration of the year here. Italian teams still gather at the bocce grounds at North Beach playground. Best of all, the gustatory pleasures are fully celebrated in North Beach. Its many Italian restaurants, coffeehouses, bakeries, pasta makers, gelato stores, and other establishments make it one of the supremely stimulating neighborhoods of San Francisco.

The Financial District, Chinatown, Telegraph Hill, Jackson Square, and North Beach all chafe against one another at **Broadway**, a strip of clubs and sleazy porno joints, barkers, and more than a few perfectly decent establishments. Starting with the infamous Barbary Coast, one block south on Pacific, this area has been a major center of the city's nightlife since the Gold Rush. In the fifties and sixties, comedy and folk clubs like the Purple Onion and the hungry i (both around the corner from Broadway, under new ownership) booked such upstarts as the Smothers Brothers, Dick Gregory, Mort Sahl, Barbra Streisand, Bill Cosby, Lenny Bruce, and Phyllis Diller. Then, in 1964, Carol Doda danced topless at the Condor, revolutionizing the Strip, as it was and is still known. Two years later, the Strip went bottomless, starting a new craze. Strip joints opened up and down, and one place even raised a platform on a pole outside, where go-go dancers shimmied and wiggled for passing cars. Some old-timers still wax nostalgic when they contemplate the strip's bawdiness of yesteryear; today's efforts have so much less *pizzazz*. Someone's even gone so far as to erect a pretentious bronze plaque on the wall of the Condor, at the corner of Columbus and Broadway, crediting the Strip as the birthplace of the world's first topless and bottomless stage shows. These claims must be viewed with skepticism. Even without accounting for the grosser perversities of the Barbary Coast, one block and a hundred years south, surely the honor of hosting the first topless dance must belong to Babylon or Gomorrah, to name but two possible precedents.

A good spot to watch the passing scene is **Enrico's**, San Francisco's most venerable alfresco hang-out, right on Broadway. Once frequented by Beats, though now under new management, the sidewalk seats are made endurable on chilly nights by space-heaters and hot music.

San Francisco's most famous bookstore is Lawrence Ferlinghetti's **City Lights Bookstore**, at 261 Columbus, on the corner between Broadway and Jack Kerouac Street (which was known in Beat days as Adler Alley). City Lights was the first all-paperback bookstore in the country; but more than that, its odd-shaped, rambling rooms and basement are the literary focus of North Beach. Overflowing with small-press periodicals and literary programs, City Lights is an inspiration to writers and poets and people who get a charge from ideas that run against the grain.

City Lights is forever associated with the watershed event of the Beat Generation. In 1956, Ferlinghetti published *Howl*, Allen Ginsberg's raging eulogy for an alienated generation. Ginsberg had written it in one weekend in San Francisco, and two weeks later read it to a wildly enthusiastic crowd at the Six Gallery in the Marina District. After publication, local police brought charges of obscenity against Ginsberg, Ferlinghetti, and City Lights' manager Shigeyoshi Murao. The long court battle was followed by acquittal, with the judge ruling that an author "should be real in treating his subject and be allowed to express his thoughts and ideas in his own words."

Unfortunately for North Beach, the publicity turned unwanted national attention on the new Bohemia. The alienated generation that congregated in its coffeehouses and clubs were called the Beat Generation, a phrase coined by Jack Kerouac in his romantic portrayal of a manic subculture, *On the Road*. New York may have spawned them, but North Beach became their most identifiable symbol. With handy, cheap Chinese and Italian food and wine, and an urbane indifference to eccentric manner and dress, North Beach nurtured the beats, and they in turn cultivated its cafe society and folksy clubs. The beats (or *beatniks*, as San Francisco columnist Herb Caen called them) rejected established mores as absurd, and sought fulfillment (or extinction of conventional behavior and thought) in spontaneous self-expression—free-style poetry, prose, music, art, endless talk, and obsessive hungering for new sensations.

The public loved the caricature of the beatnik: ragged and dirty, angry but cool, libertine, digging everything, lost in a haze of cheap wine, marijuana, and be-bop music. Before long, tour buses were crawling through the streets of North Beach. To make a long story short, as North Beach became a tourist attraction, the things that *real* bohemians thrive on—cheap rent, cheap eats, and cheap drink—disappeared. The beats, for the most part, went straight or moved on—many of them to the Haight-Ashbury.

Though North Beach today is harder on the pocketbook, fortunately it's still good for the soul. It remains a haunt of cafe society, where locals and visitors still cultivate that fine old European habit of frequenting coffeehouses and bistros, listening to music, chatting, or just sitting and watching the other patrons. The best spots are patronized by neighborhood Italians and a few bohemian-like characters, lovers of conversation, scowlers into morning newspapers, thumbers of noses at establishment values, sketch artists, scribblers of poetry and other hacks, not to mention haughty young wannabes who, for want of talent, cultivate attitude. Plunk down your four bits and join the club.

Vesuvio Café (or "Vesuvio's") is exactly such a place. Across the alley from City Lights, on Jack Kerouac Street, it has been serving bohemians and other folks since 1949. It's a quirky bar, full of curiosities and interesting people. The Welsh poet Dylan Thomas, on his literary tours, relished his visits there. Across Columbus Avenue, Spec's is another atmospheric watering holes, chock-full of curios. Nearby Tosca, with its operatic jukebox and Tuscan murals, is said to be the origin of the North Beach Cappuccino, an Italian-inspired answer to Irish Coffee (which was itself purportedly introduced to the States at the Buena Vista Cafe, on Beach Street at Hyde, at the other end of boozy old North Beach).

Old bohemians still repair to Vesuvio's (above). A street musician (right) plies his trade on Maiden Lane (right photo by Kerrick James).

The heart of Beatnikdom used to be upper Grant, between Broadway and Filbert. The bar in the Saloon, on the corner of Vallejo, has been propping elbows since 1861, while the old beat Coffee Gallery is now a Blues joint called the Lost and Found Saloon. Most of the other old haunts are gone, but Caffè Trieste still battens down the corner of Vallejo at Grant, where it opened in 1956, making it the oldest coffeehouse on the West Coast. It stays open late. The jukebox plays Italian folk music and opera. On Saturdays at 1 P.M., the family owners sing opera for their patrons, always drawing a large crowd. (For a detailed listing of other beatnik sites, read Don Herron's *The Literary World of San Francisco*.)

The four blocks of Columbus between Broadway and Filbert, and their lively side streets, are the busiest of Little Italy. By night, their window-side tables glow with warm light and jovial company. By day, the lunchtime crowds and shoppers fill the sidewalks. Columbus Avenue hosts the city's largest collection of cafes: Caffè Puccini, Caffè Michaelangelo, Café Stella, Caffè Greco, and Café Roma, to name but five, not to mention the venerable Bohemian Cigar Store (Columbus at Union), purveyor of espresso and good cheer—though its signs now warn "No Smoking!" A forest of cheeses and sausages and other Italian treats at Molinari's (373 Columbus) enraptures with the smell alone. For another whiff of heaven, tootle round the corner to Vallejo and Stockton, where Victoria Bakery's basement ovens turn out breads, cakes, and cookies from several regions of Italy, including festival and wedding treats. Cafferata Ravioli Factory (700 Columbus) has a small restaurant in tow for those who can't wait until they get home to try the tortellini, ravioli, and other specialities.

Take a short detour to 1435 Stockton to see the small **North Beach Museum**, on the upstairs level of a bank. Rotating collections of photographs and artifacts illustrate the changing demographics of North Beach, its social movements and immigrant families—Italian, Chinese, Irish, and others. The museum keeps banker's hours, and is free. Nearby, Cavalli & Company (1441 Stockton) sells Italian books, magazines, and recordings. Across the street, the U.S. Restaurant fills out the triangular corner of Stockton and Columbus. It is famous for its hearty portions of good, solid, reasonably priced Italian and American breakfasts, lunches, and dinners.

Club Fugazi (678 Green) has been running Beach Blanket Babylon so long now that it has become a San Francisco institution. The cabaret-style show is famous for its outlandish, gigantic hats, outrageous musical parodies of pop-culture icons, and affectionate lampoons of all things San Franciscan; reservations needed.

Washington Square is the heart of North Beach. Here, mostly Chinese and elderly Italians gather on (usually separate) park benches to talk about the Old Country. Backed by the spectacular **Saints Peter and Paul Catholic Church**, the "Italian Cathedral" of San Francisco, the square really does exude a Mediterranean ambience. As the church was being built in 1922, Cecil B. DeMille showed up to film the construction for a scene in *The Ten Commandments*. A good place to soak it all in is Malvina's, an old North Beach cafe now in newer quarters on Stockton at Union. It opens early for the first cup of the day, with pastries and breads at the ready. Kitty-corner is the city's oldest Italian restaurant, Fior D'Italia, in business since 1886.

The old statue of Ben Franklin in the middle of the park stands above a time capsule. It expired in 1979, giving up a hoard of nineteenth-century temperance tracts. (The statue's patron, a crusading teetotaler named Dr. Cogswell, intended this as a water fountain; note the defunct fountain heads around the base.) The capsule was promptly refilled with a poem by Ferlinghetti, a recording of the Hoodoo Rhythm Devils, a pair of Levi's, and a bottle of wine. Next opening: 2079.

Another statue in Washington Square is a sentimental monument to San Francisco's once-beloved firemen, donated by the eccentric Lillie Hitchcock Coit. The scene shows two fire fighters with a rescued child. One fireman stands with an outstretched hand, which passers-by contrive to keep filled with all manner of objects, usually beverage containers. Once upon a time, fire fighters were the dashing heros to every child of San Francisco, and to none more so than Lillie Coit. As a child trapped in a house afire, she never forgot the thrill of the clanging engines, and the strong, fearless fireman who climbed up to rescue her. Throughout her life, whenever she heard the bells and horses, she would drop any business (even a wedding) and chase after them, cheering them on. She was a wealthy woman, and before her death she donated the money to build Coit Tower on the top of Telegraph Hill, one of San Francisco's most cherished monuments, and easily visible on Telegraph Hill, above. Look closely; legend claims that it was designed to resemble a fire nozzle, but don't believe it.

A quiet statue of a drinking man stands in the small iron-fenced triangle of park at the southwest corner of Washington Square, on the west side of Columbus Avenue. The sculptor was Melvin Cummings, a professor at the precursor of the San

Francisco Art Institute on Russian Hill. The model is said to be the same that Rodin used for *Saint John the Baptist* (which you may see in the Palace of Fine Arts).

■ RUSSIAN HILL

Telegraph and Russian hills both were cultivating reputations as bohemian neighborhoods long before North Beach received the call. Of these, Russian Hill was the earlier. Today, it is a retreat of the elite, but its stairways and vistas are open to all. Russian Hill takes its name not from any large Slavic presence, but from the belief that visiting Russian ship crews down from Sitka to hunt sea otter used to bury their dead here.

Movie producers love Russian Hill. It has what many believe to be the most classic San Franciscan vistas: stunning backgrounds of white hill and blue bay, with foreground settings of old bay-windowed houses and suddenly plunging streets, just perfect for dramatic car chases.

To reach Russian Hill, you can ride the Powell-Hyde cable car; in fact, you *ought* to ride it at least once in your life. But neither should you miss the chance to walk around Russian Hill, one of the rarer pleasures of the city. A spectacular walking route from North Beach climbs steeply up **Vallejo Street**; so steeply, in fact, that the road gives way to stairs beyond Mason Street. The city falls away as you rise, opening up Hollywood backdrops of bridges, bay, Coit Tower, and the downtown highrises. Puffing up to Ina Coolbrith Park, at Taylor, you can well understand why Russian Hill was long neglected by the worthies of the community, but greatly appreciated by poor souls with fine tastes. Naturally, it became something of a writers' colony.

Ina Coolbrith Park is named after one of San Francisco's most undersung poets and literary inspirations. She was the first American child to enter California in a wagon train, crossing over Beckwourth Pass in a saddle shared with the trailblazing mountain man, Jim Beckwourth. After an unhappy marriage to a businessman in the hamlet of Los Angeles, she relocated to San Francisco, where she made her home on Russian Hill, wrote poetry, and helped to edit the *Overland Monthly.* More than one local scribbler was reputed to have fallen in love with her, including Mark Twain, Bret Harte (who reportedly offered to divorce his wife for her), Charlie Stoddard (who threatened suicide if she didn't marry him), and bitter Ambrose

The "Italian Cathedral" rises over the rooftops of North Beach.

Bierce (who ordinarily hated women, at least intellectually). She never did remarry, however, but invited all to join her literary circle at her house on Russian Hill. She corresponded with European and East Coast poets, and became a librarian both for the Bohemian Club and the Oakland Free Library. It was in that latter capacity that she met 12-year-old Jack London, and set him on a course of reading that defined his formal education. In 1919, she became California's first Poet Laureate.

Cross Taylor Street and continue up the Vallejo Street stairs to the southern "summit" of twin-peaked Russian Hill. This small warren of lanes at the top, now quite exclusive, was once home to an eclectic array of creative types, including Bierce, Gelett Burgess, Frank Norris, and Willis Polk, who built his own house at the top of the stairs (1013 Vallejo). Don Herron notes a tradition that Burgess was inspired by the sight of a cow grazing on Russian Hill to pen his best-known rhyme:

> *I never saw a purple cow*
> *I never hope to see one,*
> *But I can tell you anyhow,*
> *I'd rather see than be one.*

Tiny, pretty **Florence Street** leads off to the south, halting at a small staircase where you should stop to admire the downtown view, including a romantic broadside of Grace Cathedral. Step on down to Broadway. This is not the Broadway of big lights and dancing mammaries. *That* Broadway was channeled by tunnel under Russian Hill to Polk Gulch in the early 1950s. *This* Broadway is the *old* route that climbed over the hill. You can see why they built the tunnel: At this point, Broadway slips so suddenly from underfoot that some thoughtful city planner has built a wall across it to stop cars from going over. Ina Coolbrith's last Russian Hill house (her earlier abode burned in 1906) stands at 1067 Broadway.

The second summit of Russian Hill—six blocks farther north on Hyde Street—is the one best known to tourists. If you're walking, you might want to detour by way of romantic **Macondray Lane**, an Arcadian lane that starts at a rickety staircase on Taylor Street. Less quaint, but certainly more fun, is the **Filbert Street hill**, which drops suddenly down from Hyde Street. Actually, to call Filbert a "hill" is like calling Beethoven's Fifth a snappy tune. At 31.5 degrees, it's the steepest driveable grade in San Francisco. Be warned; if you take it Steve McQueen-style, barreling over the brink and screeching into a right turn up Leavenworth, your car's going to need a fresh set of shocks and a new transmission when you get out of the hospital. Take it easy, and you can do it *twice.*

From the corner of Greenwich and Hyde, poetry lovers (if indeed such creatures still exist) should walk up the Greenwich steps past the Alice Marble tennis courts, to the secluded **George Sterling Glade**. This spot was treasured by Sterling, San Francisco's King of Bohemia, Ambrose Bierce's disciple, Jack London's best friend, a founding member of Carmel's artist colony, a poet called the finest of his age by many of his contemporaries, but also an alcoholic, and finally, in 1926, a suicide. A small monument in the park is inscribed with one of his San Francisco poems:

Tho the dark be cold and blind
Yet her sea fog's touch is kind
And her mightier caress
Is joy and the pain thereof;
And great is thy tenderness
O cool, grey City of Love!

QUOTATIONS FROM BITTER BIERCE

Discriminate: v.i. To note the particulars in which one person or thing is, if possible, more objectionable than another.

Happiness: n. An agreeable sensation arising when contemplating another's misery.

History: n. An account, mostly false, of events mostly unimportant, which are brought about by rulers, mostly knaves, and soldiers, mostly fools.

Love: n. A temporary insanity curable by marriage.

November: n. The eleventh twelfth of a weariness.

Piracy: n. Commerce without its folly-swaddles, just as God made it.

Quill: n. An implement of torture yielded by a goose and wielded by . . . an ass.

Rash: adj. Insensible to the value of our advice.

Rear: n. In American military matters, that exposed part of the Army that is closest to Congress.

Riot: n. A popular entertainment given to the military by innocent bystanders.

Saint: n. A dead sinner, revised and edited.

—Ambrose Bierce, "The Devil's Dictionary," 1906

Sterling died in the Bohemian Club, leaving behind some half-burned snatches of poetry that have since become legends in the cult of Sterling, which appeals to literate romantics, occultists, and counterculture figures, as well as to lovers of intensely beautiful language and imagery. In his day, Sterling was known for (among other things) his sense of horror and demonic imagery, a quality no doubt encouraged by the macabre Bierce. Sterling's most famous lines in this vein, inscribed on the wall of the now-demolished Papa Coppa's restaurant on Montgomery Street, read *"The blue-eyed vampire, sated at her feast, Smiles bloodily against the leprous moon."* Strange, sad, and beautiful character, George Sterling; deserves to be better known.

Another literary touchstone stands on the northwest corner of Lombard and Hyde: Mrs. Robert Louis Stevenson's house. The writer died before Willis Polk built it. The crowds of tourists outside are probably not here to admire it, however. They are more interested in flagging down the Hyde Street cable car or snapping pictures in front of San Francisco's two most famous streets: Hyde and Lombard.

"The crookedest street in the world" is the block of Lombard between Hyde and Leavenworth. You can walk down, enjoying its views, gardens, red cobblestones, and the little mid-block terrace called Montclair. But hey, you really ought to enjoy it the way God and Karl Malden intended you to, at the wheel of a sedan, grinding fenders on every turn.

Back at the top of the hill, look straight north, down Hyde Street and over the tall masts on the wharfs, toward Alcatraz and beyond. If you had a nickel for every time a photographer shot a cable car with this backdrop, you could probably retire to Russian Hill. The steep stretch of the Hyde Street grade, between Francisco and Bay streets, registers 21.3 degrees.

Most visitors will want to continue down Hyde to Fisherman's Wharf, but if you wish to explore Russian Hill a little further, you will be rewarded for your efforts. Those who strike west on Francisco, around the terrace to Chestnut, will be within whistling distance of one of Russian Hill's nicest surprises. The **San Francisco Art Institute** (800 Chestnut Street), established in 1871, is the oldest art school in the western U.S. It's an eccentric building, very conducive to artistic temperaments. The entrance brings to mind a medieval Italian monastery, with courtyard, cloisters, tiled fountain, and bell tower; the overgrown vacant lot across the street adds to the effect. It's somewhat of a letdown to know it was built of reinforced concrete (in 1926, by the same outfit that did City Hall and Coit

The "crookedest street in the world" becomes a winding parade of pink hydrangea in spring.
(Kerrick James)

Tower—Bakewell and Brown). The fact that it's concrete doesn't seem to bother the ghost who lives in the tower, however.

The small cafeteria in back is one of the few places in residential Russian Hill where you can enjoy a cup of coffee with a view over Fisherman's Wharf. Saving the best for last, before you leave, visit the **Diego Rivera Gallery**, to the left of the main entrance on Chestnut. One wall is illuminated with a massive fresco painted by Rivera in 1931, entitled *The Making of a Fresco Showing the Building of a City*. Rivera's work, celebrating the power, color, and epic saga of people who toil, had great influence on San Francisco Depression-era artists, as you can see when you visit the more famous (because more public) murals in Coit Tower on Telegraph Hill.

■ TELEGRAPH HILL

Telegraph Hill was named for the semaphore installed at its crest in 1850 to notify downtown merchants of ship arrivals. As anyone who stands on the top today can attest, its sight lines still reach through the harbor and out the Golden Gate.

Telegraph Hill rises from Broadway in the south so abruptly that residents just half a block up Kearny and Montgomery streets look down on Broadway neon and rooftops. The rise on the west side from North Beach is likewise steep, but neither can match the cliffs of the east side, falling sharply away to the old wharf and warehouse district. These cliffs are largely man-made. Quarries blasted away at the hillside, mostly for landfill and sea walls, until 1914. In earlier days, ships' crews quarried the rock for ballast. As they took on goods in other ports, they left the ballast as paving stones. Thus, the east slope of Telegraph Hill today spreads halfway around the world.

The hill has always been a neighborhood of immigrants. During the Gold Rush, Chileans were among the largest groups to settle on there. As San Francisco settled down, the Irish moved up in droves, followed by smaller numbers of Italians, Spanish, Mexicans, Portuguese, Scandinavians, Germans, Chinese, and even some Yankees. After the earthquake of 1906, when the Irish departed for the Mission District, the Italians filled the vacuum, making Telegraph a distinctly Italian hill until recent years. Today, the Chinese have probably surpassed the Italians as the major ethnic group, especially on the North Beach side.

Eastern Telegraph Hill's relative remoteness from the rest of the city in the 1890s made it, like Russian Hill of an earlier era, an attractive district for bohemians, artists, and theatrical people. Even the humblest shacks offered spectacular views. Wine and rent were cheap. The Muses flourished. Charles Stoddard, a writer who spent his youth on Telegraph Hill, described this wonderful bohemia in his book, *In the Footprints of the Padres:*

> The cottages were indeed nestlike: they were so small, so compact, so cozy, so overrun with vines and flowering foliage. Usually of one story, or of a story-and-a-half at most, they clung to the hillside facing the water, and looked out upon its noble expanse from tiny balconies as delicate and dainty as toys. . . . They loomed above their front yards while their backyards lorded it over their roofs. . . . They were usually approached by ascending or descending stairways, or by airy bridges that spanned little gullies where ran rivulets in the winter season. There were parrots on perches at the doorways of those cottages, and songbirds in cages that were hidden away in the vines. There were pet poodles there. I think that there were more lap dogs than watch dogs in that early California.

By the 1940s, the artists were gone. The crest and eastern side of Telegraph had become chic—and so it remains today. It was, in many ways, San Francisco's first gentrified neighborhood, and the artists have been on the run ever since.

To drive on Telegraph Hill requires patience. Between Broadway and Bay Street, nine wide blocks to the north, there are no through roads. Parking is horrendous. If you drive to **Coit Tower** (up Lombard from North Beach), expect to wait. And wait and wait. It's better to walk, though the steep climb from Washington Square is not for sissies. Filbert and Greenwich streets, densely packed with houses, give way to stairs and greenery at Telegraph Hill Boulevard, which hooks around from Lombard to Pioneer Park and Coit Tower, on the summit. A statue of Columbus, erected in 1957, stands in the middle of the parking circle, gazing off toward the ex-federal penitentiary on Alcatraz.

Coit Tower was built with money left by Lillie Hitchcock Coit as a monument to San Francisco's pluck in the face of frequent blazes. The firm of Arthur Brown drew up plans for a cylindrical observation tower on the top of Telegraph Hill. Work started early in 1933; by October of the same year, the tower was finished. Though only 180 feet tall, Coit Tower gets a 284-foot boost from Telegraph Hill. From the top, the Bay Area spreads out gloriously in every direction. There are coin-operated telescopes for closer looks. You can pick out landmark after landmark: Mount Diablo on the eastern horizon, the Claremont Resort and Spa in the

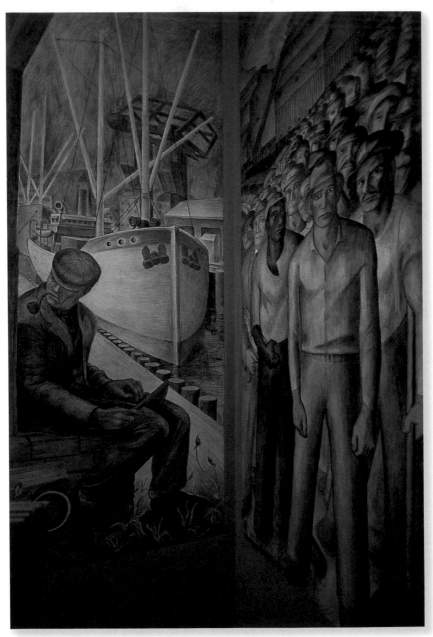

A mural at Coit Tower recalls the drama and vitality of the old waterfront. The nobility of work is the overriding theme of the murals.

Oakland hills, the Campanile at Berkeley, the Richmond Bridge, Alcatraz, Sausalito and Mount Tamalpais in Marin County, the Golden Gate Bridge, the Presidio, Fisherman's Wharf, wiggly Lombard Street, the rooftops of Nob Hill and Chinatown, Grace Cathedral, Twin Peaks, the downtown towers, the Bay Bridge . . . .

Back in the tower lobby, take a closer look at the murals on the walls. Commissioned during the Great Depression by the Civil Works Administration, the **frescoes** were painted by a team of 25 local artists. The murals present an incredibly vigorous picture of California life during the 1930s, a gallery of characters and scenes embracing crowded city streets, rich agricultural valleys, the mineral-rich mountains, libraries, ranch and farm hands, engineers, machinery, working animals, and a lunch counter, bank, department store, and press room. For subjects, the artists painted their friends and supervisors, and even Coit Tower's watchman. Their themes celebrate the richness of California's resources and people, the dignity and brotherhood of honest labor (as well as its exploitation), economic injustice, and political anger. The paintings are spiked with signs of militancy—a clenched fist, ominous newspaper headlines, the idle rich gazing at the tattered poor, a robbery in progress in the crowd at the corner of Market and Montgomery—portents of a revolution that many expected and even yearned for in 1934. The controversy over these powerful images delayed their unveiling, and smoldered for years afterward.

From its perch on Telegraph Hill, Coit Tower overlooks "the Rock"—Alcatraz. (Kerrick James)

If you have time for but one walk in San Francisco, turn your dogs loose on the eastern flank of Telegraph Hill. The steep **Greenwich and Filbert steps** nurture some of the most sylvan cityscapes in the country, most of it unapproachable by automobile. Both stairs start on the east side of Coit Tower: Greenwich Street stairs descend from the parking circle, while the Filbert Street stairs descend just a little farther down the road, where Telegraph Hill Boulevard swerves right. Whether Greenwich or Filbert makes the nicer walk is a moot point. Walk down one and up the other, and you will know the best of both.

Brick-paved Greenwich meanders down through thick foliage to emerge near a cliff on the dead-end of Montgomery Street, where perches a crenelated old wooden restaurant, Julius' Castle. Until they "widened" the street, there used to be a turntable here for automobiles. Glance over the edge before bearing right to the second stretch of Greenwich stairs, marked by a street sign, but otherwise looking like private steps to the side yard of the building. Dropping past old houses and small urban pastures of dog fennel, nasturtium, and fenced garden flowers, the Greenwich stairway lands on Sansome Street, at the eastern foot of Telegraph Hill. Turn south to meet the Filbert steps.

Filbert is the more formally landscaped stairway, a charming companion of roses, fuchsias, lilies, ivy, and other garden flowers and trees. Like Greenwich, the public steps are continuously met by private paths and stairs and picket gates that lead off to houses, coddled in flower pots and foliage, some old, some not. Just above Montgomery, near a romantic, rambling restaurant called The Shadows, there are some small terraces with benches. From here, you can study the handsome art deco apartment house at 1360 Montgomery, on the corner of Filbert.

Take some time to explore **Montgomery Street** before descending to Sansome. This was the street where heroic Italians made a last stand to rescue their little homes from the great fire of 1906. In desperation, according to the story, they broke out casks of red wine and doused their houses with vino, cooling and saving them from the flames. It's a pity the tactic didn't work with developers. Still, a handful of these wine-baptized houses *reportedly* survives. A likely candidate is 9 Upper Calhoun Terrace, which dates from 1854. Other nineteenth-century survivors can be spotted by walkers. If you like heights, take a look at the views from **Upper Calhoun Terrace** and the end of **Alta Street**. People with vertigo can't live on Telegraph Hill.

Below Montgomery, the Filbert steps turn to wood—rickety wood, with the nails sticking out. Unpainted and enchantingly cushioned in baby tears and ferns, it leads down to the rarest of San Francisco's country lanes, Napier. Last of the city's wood plank streets, **Napier Lane** seems to be heavily populated by beautiful cats. By all means, clomp to the end of the lane and back for a look at the old houses, which survived the fire of 1906, but for the sake of the residents and their precious atmosphere, let us strangers keep our grosser presence fleeting. Below Napier Lane, the Filbert steps drop down to Sansome Street on a new concrete stairway.

The stretch of flat ground between Telegraph Hill and the Embarcadero wharves is covered landfill once given over to brick warehouses and train tracks. The industries have long since moved. Today many of the warehouses have been beautifully remodeled into designer studios, condos, restaurants, and offices, at least one with rooftop tennis courts. Even the old roundhouse engine shed for the San Francisco North Belt Railway, at the corner of Sansome and Lombard, has been converted to an attractive office called (somewhat contradictorily) Roundhouse Square. The area is known as Media Gulch for its abundance of graphic design, advertising, and broadcast TV and radio stations.

Levi's Plaza, between Sansome and Battery streets at Filbert, is the corporate headquarters of Levi Strauss, manufacturer of blue jeans. During the Gold Rush, Levi Strauss came to San Francisco, where he no doubt met a good number of men with holes in their britches. He set about to invent some sturdier pants using rivet-studded tent canvas. Levi's blue jeans not only tickled forty-niners' fancies, but were destined to become perhaps the greatest fashion statement of the latter half of the twentieth century. Like fortune cookies, steam beer, and cable cars, blue jeans rank as a San Francisco original.

Even without its historical context, the Levi Strauss headquarters should be seen for its admirable design. The staggered lines of the building, set against the staggered housing on Telegraph Hill, enhances the view, while its brick facade echoes the surrounding warehouse walls. Bookstores, bakeries, restaurants, and a cafe on the plaza have turned an erstwhile industrial zone into a stimulating and pleasant place to relax. But best of all is the splashing fountain in Levi Plaza, built of Sierra granite, inviting you to climb through it, as you might with a real mountain stream. Across Battery Street, this mountain "creek" flows through a grassy, boulder-studded "meadow" designed by landscape architect Lawrence Halprin. How much more civilized a corporate statement than a mammoth steel tower!

■ FISHERMAN'S WHARF

Before the Virgin Mary's name was ever invoked to bless San Francisco's fishing fleet, Tin Hau looked after her fishermen. The Chinese pioneered the business at Fisherman's Wharf. The Genoese came soon after, pushing out the Chinese, and in turn were edged aside by the Sicilians. The harbor of Fisherman's Wharf was known as an Italian lake for much of its life, and the daily sailings out and back of the fleet were a colorful sight in old San Francisco.

With over-fishing and pollution, San Francisco Bay fisheries grew slack after World War II. Though you can still find boats and fishermen at the wharf, the big money-earner today is tourism. Broad swaths of the neighborhood have been given over to the tawdriest kinds of schlock shops and amusements. But don't be scared away. There is a lot to see and do at Fisherman's Wharf, even if the hucksterism turns you off.

In a poll of San Francisco children, a majority once voted **Pier 39** as their favorite place in the city—a high endorsement. But judging by the crowds that gather here on weekends, adults seem to like it well enough, too. Refurbished as an ersatz New England wooden fishing wharf in 1978, this erstwhile cargo pier

Lunchtime at the Cannery, along Fisherman's Wharf (above). (Kerrick James)

Full of fun in the water, sea lions can become real pests on the wharfs (opposite).

now sports two decks of shops and amusements, including a carousel with a mezzanine, a calliope, street performers, and a resident colony of sea lions. Visitors to Underwater World visitors can also meet the submarine residents of the bay on an amazing conveyor-belt ride through a transparent underwater tube, surrounded by sharks, rays, rockfish, and a host of other specimens usually served on platters in this neighborhood. With bucking seats and a giddy motion picture, the Turbo Ride simulates the thrill of a roller-coaster, while a multi-media extravaganza called The San Francisco Experience treats visitors to an earthquake, Chinese New Year celebrations, fog, and other tokens of local history and culture. One lone reminder of the past, a longshoreman's diner called The Eagle, yet remains, though now raised intact from its original ground-level site to a second floor perch.

Between Pier 39 and Pier 45, you can hire three-wheeled pedicabs for local tours, take a dinner cruise on the bay, or catch a ferry to Vallejo, Angel Island, or **Alcatraz**. Once the most notorious federal penitentiary in the country, Alcatraz is now administered as part of the Golden Gate National Recreation Area. Known as "The Rock," Alcatraz was a prisoner's prison, whose inmates were men unable to live by the rules of other penitentiaries. Famous guests included such superstars of crime as Machine Gun Kelly, Al Capone, Alvin "Creepy" Carpis, and Robert

The dismal prison on Alcatraz now hosts only tourists.

Stroud, the Birdman of Alcatraz who, in fact, did all his bird research at Leaven-worth before being sent to Alcatraz for a prison murder. What did The Rock have that Sing Sing didn't? Aside from its terrible reputation, a tough and mostly silent regimen, and a tantalizing view of civilization at its most hedonistic, probably not much. True, Alcatraz was surrounded by a frigid bay, raked by powerful currents. On the other hand, it had good food and warm showers—the better, it was said, to keep prisoners too soft to escape.

After a scenic ferry ride from the wharf, contemporary visitors are loosed on The Rock to explore on their own. Climbing up the grim hill through the sally port, most people head straight for the large cell block on the top of the island. There they wander quietly through the hospital ward (where the crazed Birdman spent much of his time), cafeteria, recreation yard, and solitary confinement in "D" block, where bullet holes in the wall testify to the bloody prison uprising in 1946. Most sobering of all is to stand among the tiers of empty cell blocks and imagine what life was like here. The rangers (whose ranks are sometimes bolstered by ex-prisoners and guards who served time here) have many stories to tell of life on The Rock.

One of the most mysterious stories involves Frank Morris (portrayed by Clint Eastwood in *Escape from Alcatraz*) and the Anglin brothers. After digging through the ventilation shafts in their cells, they prepared for their escapes by fashioning lifelike decoy masks from plaster and hair gathered from the barbershop. On the appointed night, they tucked the dummies into their beds and escaped to the roof. Having manufactured a raft from raincoats, they inflated it with an accordion bellows, and shoved off the island in the dark. They were never seen again. Officially, they are presumed dead—drowned and swept by currents through the Golden Gate—but intriguing reports of sightings still crop up from time to time. Their extraordinary getaway hastened the prison's closure a year later, in 1963. You can see a dummy setup in the main cell block (jocularly called Broadway), but the real masks are in the Maritime Museum archives at Aquatic Park (see below).

Back on the mainland, stop by Pier 45 to see the USS *Pampanito*. This fighting submarine sank six Japanese ships and damaged four others during the Second World War, narrowly escaping destruction on two occasions. She participated in the tragic raid that sank the *Kachidoki Maru* and *Rakuyo Maru*, which were carrying British and Australian POWs, though she managed to rescue 73. Keep in mind,

A SUPERMARKET IN CALIFORNIA

*W*hat thoughts I have of you tonight, Walt Whitman, for I walked down the sidestreets under the trees with a headache self-conscious looking at the full moon.

In my hungry fatigue, and shopping for images, I went into the neon fruit super-market, dreaming of your enumerations!

What peaches and what penumbras! Whole families shopping at night! Aisles full of husbands! Wives in the avocados, babies in the tomatoes!—and you, Garcia Lorca, what were you doing down by the watermelons?

I saw you, Walt Whitman, childless, lonely old grubber, poking among the meats in the refrigerator and eyeing the grocery boys.

I heard you asking questions of each: Who killed the pork chops? What price bananas? Are you my Angel?

I wandered in and out of the brilliant stacks of cans following you, and followed in my imagination by the store detective.

We strode down the open corridors together in our solitary fancy tasting arti-chokes, possessing every frozen delicacy, and never passing the cashier.

Where are we going, Walt Whitman? The doors close in an hour. Which way does your beard point tonight?

(I touch your book and dream of our odyssey in the supermarket and feel absurd.)

Will we walk all night through solitary streets? The trees add shade to shade, lights out in the houses, we'll both be lonely.

Will we stroll dreaming of the lost America of love past blue automobiles in driveways, home to our silent cottage?

Ah, dear father, graybeard, lonely old courage-teacher, what America did you have when Charon quit poling his ferry and you got out on a smoking bank and stood watching the boat disappear on the black waters of Lethe?

—Allen Ginsberg, "A Supermarket in California," 1955

as you squeeze through the tight passages, that this ship carried a complement of 10 officers and 70 enlisted men. The *Pampanito* gives new meaning to the word *claustrophobia.* It's open daily for self-guided tours.

The success of the famous Italian seafood restaurants of Fisherman's Wharf— Scoma's, Castagnola's, Alioto's, A. Sabella's, and others—demonstrates the relative profitability of *cooking* fish over *catching* them. In the hubbub of tourists and smelly crab pots cluttering the walks in front you can still find live and cooked shrimp and crabs for sale. Unfortunately, the shell-fish have to share the stalls with

trinkets, postcards, and such unseaworthy snacks as chicken. To try the local specialty, Dungeness crab, come between mid-November and June; the peak of the season is around December.

If you want to see, hear, and smell the *real* **Fisherman's Wharf**, go behind the restaurants to the boat harbor, where wheeling gulls and barking sea lions try to bum free meals from the fish handlers. Walk out along the shore-facing side of Pier 45 to see the working boats.

Crab vendor Tony Cresci is a Fisherman's Wharf fixture. (Kerrick James)

Many today are owned by Vietnamese and Korean fishermen. The fish-processing plant, one of the largest on the West Coast, hits its stride in the wee hours of the morning, finishing up most of its work long before the tourists begin their morning crawl.

If you came to San Francisco to buy a T-shirt, you're also in luck. Among the busy crowd-pleasers along Jefferson Street are the **Wax Museum at Fisherman's Wharf** and the Haunted Goldmine. In the breathless spirit of the old cartoon series, the **Ripley's Believe It or Not Museum** regales visitors with its two-headed calf, a wax figure of the man with two pupils in each eyeball, humorous tombstone inscriptions, and many other such curiosities. The **Guinness Museum of World Records** enshrines such marvels as the world's smallest printed book; an energetic statue of "Wheelie King" Doug Domokos riding 145 miles (242 km) on the back wheel of his motorcycle; a model of the 62 pancakes that a certain gent devoured in six minutes 58 seconds for a world record; and an admittedly *astounding* video of the "fastest draw in the world," in action.

The **Cannery**, at 2801 Leavenworth, was one of the country's first brick factory buildings to be converted into a shopping mall. This old fruit-canning factory now entices browsers with dozens of restaurants, clothing boutiques, galleries, and specialty shops selling such eclectic items as collector dolls, candles, designer fishing gear, and Native American arts and crafts. With so rich a subject under its dominion, the **Museum of the History of San Francisco** sadly remains a modest collection of pictures and artifacts intriguing to aficionados, but unlikely to fire up much enthusiasm among the uninitiated. One hopes that funding may some day change that situation; till then, it quietly bides time on the third floor of the Cannery.

The most sophisticated and attractive of the Fisherman's Wharf shopping centers is **Ghirardelli Square**. Most of its red-brick factory buildings, erected between 1900 and 1916, were part of the Ghirardelli chocolate factory. The Ghirardelli sign on the roof is a local landmark. The maze of passages, warm buildings, and sunny plazas are delightful for walking or sitting. The highly browsable shops display an array of crafts, foods, clothing, jewelry, books, and toys, though some of the specialties are hard to classify. The Nature Company sells wonderful things like crystals and birdcalls, not to mention nature books and prints, telescopes, dinosaur-bone excavation kits, plant presses, time-zone clocks, natural science experiments, and recordings of evening storms passing over Big Sur. The Sharper

Image is harder to pin down, with rare toys for grown-ups, like globes that hover on a column of air, and crystal balls that flash with darting lightning bolts. The Ghirardelli Chocolate Manufactory, on the plaza below the Clock Tower, sells the famous chocolate, although it is now manufactured in San Leandro. You can mull over the old chocolate-making machines while waiting for a sundae.

Across Beach Street from Ghirardelli Square, at the foot of Polk Street, the **San Francisco National Maritime Museum** building sits like an ocean liner run aground in **Aquatic Park.** Its halls are filled with ship models, nautical instruments, and old photographs and paintings that recount the spirited maritime history of San Francisco Bay. Maps, charts, books, and archives are stored in the J. Porter Shaw nautical library at Fort Mason, a short walk to the west. Nautical books and cards are also sold at the Maritime Store on Hyde Street Pier.

The pride and joy of the Maritime Museum is its collection of vintage ships from the Pacific and San Francisco trade, most of which are docked at **Hyde Street Pier.** The *Balclutha* is the flagship of the museum, a magnificent, three-masted Cape Horn veteran launched in 1887. The *Balclutha* used to make two round trips yearly between the British Isles and San Francisco, trading coal and whiskey for California wheat. Later she worked in the Alaskan fish-packing trade, spending winters in San Francisco Bay. Walk the decks and explore the cabins and hold, where displays from the packing business and other seagoing paraphernalia lie about in colorful clutter.

The handsome paddle-wheeler *Eureka* was originally launched as a train ferry in the 1890s, and then ferried autos and people between her present berth and the North Bay from 1922 to 1941. The magazine store (for display purposes only) on the upper deck has some interesting period magazines.

The *C.A. Thayer*, another three-masted sailing ship, used to sail in the lumber trade along the Pacific coast. She retired in 1950. The tiny *Alma*, a lumber scow from the North Bay, is too small to allow landlubbers. The *Eppleton Hall*, a British paddle-wheel harbor tug, is closed while awaiting restoration. Other vessels under care of the Maritime Museum are scattered at other berths. The *Wampama*, a steam schooner from the Pacific coast trade, is at dock in Sausalito undergoing refurbishment. The submarine *Pampanito* (already mentioned) is at Pier 45 on the other side of Fisherman's Wharf.

Aquatic Park is popular among a certain kind of swimmer who is immune to cold water. The rest of us can enjoy the stirring maritime scenery on the usually brisk walk along curving Municipal Pier. The steeples, towers, masts, and crowded hillsides, the white sails on the bay, and the Golden Gate Bridge fill the eyes, as the robust sea air fills the lungs. If you're in a mood for more of the same, turn west toward Fort Mason.

The real Fisherman's Wharf still harbors many fishing boats (above). Once a fruit-canning plant, the Cannery is now a fancy mall (left).

THE CULTIVATED
Q U A R T E R

THE NORTHWESTERN CORNER OF SAN FRANCISCO encompasses some of the city's most opulent, poised, and cultivated neighborhoods. Sure, there are decrepit sections, too, but over all, the hard realities of urban life are less apparent there than in any other quarter. San Franciscans treat this section rather like their own backyard—jamming favored shopping and supping precincts, like Union, Clement, and Fillmore streets; puttering around the museums; retreating to the cultivated solitudes of Golden Gate and Lincoln parks. This is San Francisco's most romantic quarter, a bright collage of noisy markets and thundering seacoasts, Old Masters in silent rooms, spiked cannons, and overgrown gardens, haunted by cypresses and foghorn music.

■ GOLDEN GATE NATIONAL RECREATION AREA

What other major American city comes boxed in a national park? Embracing San Francisco's northern and western shores, Golden Gate National Recreation Area (GGNRA) links a number of abandoned military properties in San Francisco with extensive tracts of the Marin Headlands, a semi-wilderness across the Golden Gate Bridge. With nearly 80,000 acres, the GGNRA is more than twice as big as the city itself, and receives 20 million visitors per year.

Park headquarters for the GGNRA is Fort Mason, command post for the U.S. Army in the West from the 1860s through the 1880s, and a major military depot during America's Pacific wars. Fort Mason still retains its warlike mien, but the old quarters, warehouses, and docks are now given over to the fruits of peace. One of San Francisco's most important cultural centers, Fort Mason today shelters a host of museums, theaters, galleries, and nonprofit institutions promoting culture and conservation. A free monthly newspaper, *Fort Mason Center,* keeps track of events. A quarterly publication, *Park Events,* promotes the GGNRA's activities. For up-to-the-minute news, maps, and information, go to the headquarters building one block in from the Franklin Street Gate.

Then make your way across the Great Meadow and down the steps toward the bayside wharfs. From these piers, where fishermen now try their luck, one and a half million U.S. soldiers embarked for the Pacific theater during World War II. The converted warehouses are a smorgasbord of curious sights, lively arts, and noble causes. The tiny **San Francisco Craft and Folk Art Museum** (Building A) exhibits and sells handmade crafts from around the world. A phenomenally popular vegetarian restaurant next door, Greens offers splendid views of bobbing yachts and the Golden Gate Bridge. If you don't have reservations, you can still buy something from their bakery. The **J. Porter Shaw Library** (Building E) preserves an extensive collection of maritime charts and books.

The **Mexican Museum** (Building D) displays the arts and culture of Mexico and Mexican Americans. Their adjacent shop sells a variety of Mexican handicrafts and has a free map of Mission District walking tours. Contemporary Italian and Italian-American artists display their works at the **Museo Italo Americano** in Building C, while across the hall, the **African-American Historical & Cultural Society** maintains a library, gallery space, and exhibits of African arts. Its museum of African-American history and culture honors some of San Francisco's early pioneers, among them William Alexander Leidesdorff. A Virgin Island sea captain, Leidesdorff sailed his ship, the *Julia Ann*, into San Francisco Bay in 1841. He liked the place, and stayed. Before his death at 38, he built a fortune in the shipping business, opened San Francisco's first hotel, and served as city treasurer, American vice consul of Yerba Buena, and administrator of the first American public school in California. His warehouses stood on the present site of Leidesdorff Street, in the Financial District. Leidesdorff is buried under the floor of Mission Dolores.

Some of San Francisco's premier experimental theaters are at Fort Mason. The intimate, avant-garde Magic Theater (Building D) has premiered the works of Pulitzer Prize-winning playwright Sam Shepard. Young Performers Theater (Building C) is both an acting school and playhouse for children, the perfect place to introduce your kids to the magical world of live theater. (Its counterpart in the art world, the Children's Art Center, is on the ground floor.) The Cowell Theater (Pier 2) and Life on the Water Theater (Building B) also host dramatic productions.

The **Golden Gate Promenade**, a scenic 3.5-mile pathway along San Francisco's north shore from Aquatic Park to the Golden Gate Bridge, crosses Fort Mason. Linking San Francisco's urban core with its wilder hinterlands, the Promenade traverses rocky coast, driftwood beach, historic army land, and exclusive city

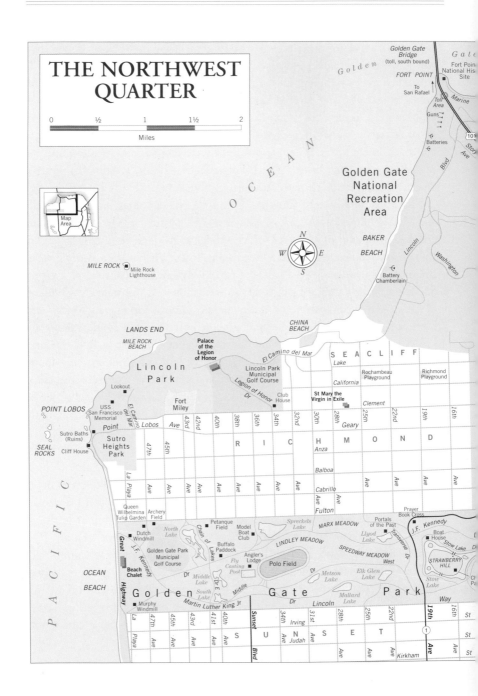

THE NORTHWEST QUARTER

0   ½   1   1½   2

Miles

Map Area

Golden Gate Bridge
(toll, south bound)

Golden

FORT POINT

Gate

Fort Point National His Site

To San Rafael

Toll Area

Guns

Marine

Batteries

Story Ave

101

Golden Gate National Recreation Area

BAKER BEACH

Lincoln

Washington

N
W   E
S

MILE ROCK   Mile Rock Lighthouse

Battery Chamberlain

LANDS END

CHINA BEACH

MILE ROCK BEACH

Palace of the Legion of Honor

El Camino del Mar

S E A C L I F F

Lake

Lincoln Park

Lincoln Park Municipal Golf Course

Rochambeau Playground

Richmond Playground

Legion of Honor Dr

California

Lookout

Fort Miley

Club House

St Mary the Virgin in Exile

Clement

POINT LOBOS   USS San Francisco Memorial

El Camino del Mar

Point   Lobos   Ave

43rd   42nd   40th   38th   36th   34th   32nd   30th   28th   Geary   25th   22nd   19th   16th

Sutro Baths (Ruins)

Sutro Heights Park

R   I   C   H   M   O   N   D

SEAL ROCKS   Cliff House

47th   45th   Anza

Balboa

P A C I F I C

La Playa   Ave   Ave   Ave   Ave   Ave   Ave   Ave   Ave   Cabrillo   Ave   Ave   Ave   Ave

Ave   Ave

Queen Wilhelmina Tulip Garden   Archery Field

Fulton

Prayer Book Cross

Portals of the Past

J.F. Kennedy

North Windmill

Great

Chain of Lakes

Petanque Field   Model Boat Club

Spreckels Lake

MARX MEADOW

Lloyd Lake   Boat House   Stow Lake Dr

Dutch Windmill

J.F. Kennedy

Buffalo Paddock

LINDLEY MEADOW

SPEEDWAY MEADOW

Transverse Dr

West

STRAWBERRY HILL

Golden Gate Park Municipal Golf Course

Angler's Lodge

Fly Casting Pool

Polo Field

Dr   Metson Lake   Elk Glen Lake

Stow Lake

OCEAN   Beach Chalet

Dr   Middle Lake   Dr E   Middle   Golden   G a t e   P a r k

Highway

BEACH   South Lake

Mallard Lake   Way

Murphy Windmill   Martin Luther King Jr   Dr   Lincoln

19th   16th   St

La   47th   45th   43rd   41st   40th   Sunset   34th   31st   28th   25th   22nd   Irving   St

Playa   Ave   Ave   Ave   Ave   Ave   S U N S E T   Ave   Judah   Ave   Ave   Ave   Ave   Kirkham   St

Blvd

O   C   E   A   N

1

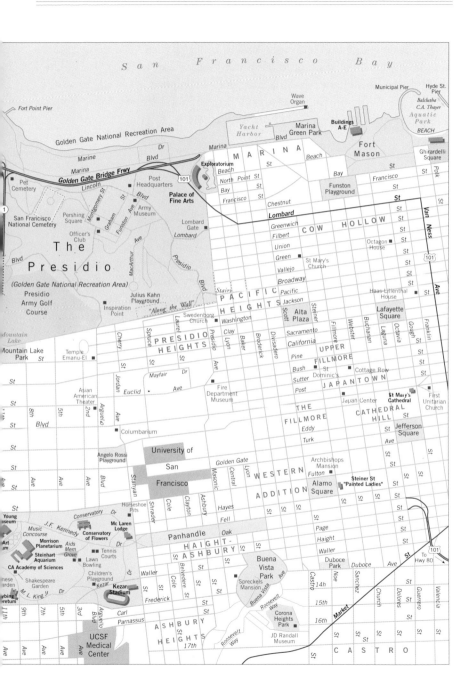

enclaves, ending at Fort Point, in the shadow of the Golden Gate Bridge. From there, hikers can strike south on the 9.1-mile Coastal Trail to Baker Beach, Lincoln Park, the Cliff House, Ocean Beach, and Fort Funston, or north across the Golden Gate Bridge on backpack trips to the Marin Headlands, Muir Woods, Mount Tamalpais, and Point Reyes National Seashore.

■ THE MARINA

The Marina District is a flat, tidy, pastel neighborhood of wide, swept sidewalks, smacking of respectability. Because it was built on landfill, notoriously unstable in a tremor, the Marina was one of the two city districts hardest hit in the 1989 earthquake (the other being South of Market). Only minutes after the quake, pictures of collapsed Marina District housing and a fire were flashing across the country, and indeed the world, inadvertently leading many to believe that flames were engulfing the entire city. In fact, most of the scenes of greatest residential damage in San Francisco were shot in the Marina. Though the district's particular vulnerability in the next quake no doubt worries most residents, life has returned to normal here.

Chestnut, the Marina's main shopping street, was long considered exactly that—a chestnut—until the trendy commercialization of nearby Union Street taught Marina residents to cherish its neighborly virtues. Chestnut's quiet mix of delis, restaurants, cafes, and boutiques, with a homey bookstore and magic shop thrown in, still caters to a mostly local clientele.

In contrast, Marina Green is the promenade *par excellence* for the young moneyed set, who come from miles around to walk their dogs or tend their boats moored at the adjacent St. Francis and Golden Gate yacht clubs. The Green also rates high among kite fliers for the unobstructed winds that blow fine and fresh from the Golden Gate. Views are superb.

At the west end of Marina Green, walkers can continue west on the Golden Gate Promenade to Fort Point, or they can turn east to the end of the West Harbor jetty to see the world's most peculiar musical instrument. Frankly, the **wave organ** resembles no Wurlitzer you've ever seen. What it looks like most, in fact, is a jumbled rostrum of broken tombstones strangulated by pipes crawling up from the sea bed. Waves striking the submerged ends of the pipes force air out through the other ends, moaning and gurgling, a true sea ditty if ever there was one. Stonemason George Gonzalez and the assistant director of the Exploratorium, Peter Richards, designed the wave organ to play loudest at high tides.

If you turn south at Marina Green, walking one block on Baker Street, you will come to the **Palace of Fine Arts**, San Francisco's last vestige of its most glorious fair. The Panama-Pacific International Exposition of 1915 officially marked the opening of the Panama Canal, but most San Franciscans knew it was really a monumental coming-out party for a city risen from the ashes of 1906. Its splendor was, by most accounts, unmatched by any world's fair before or since. Local poet Edwin Markham, admittedly fond of rhetorical hyperbole, deemed it "the greatest revelation of beauty that has ever been seen on earth," but even the sobersided *New York World* swore it was so "indescribably beautiful" that "it gives you a choky feeling in your throat as you look at it." Visitors delighted in the fairyland of brilliant electrical lighting, the Tower of Jewels, a five-acre working model of the Panama Canal, the "palaces" of Education, Horticulture, and Industry, and the fair's lovely centerpiece, the Palace of Fine Arts, designed by Bernard Maybeck as a colonnaded mock-Roman ruin built beside a reflecting pool. (A complete model of the Panama-Pacific fair, incidentally, is displayed at the Presidio Army Museum.)

When the fair closed and the buildings were dismantled, San Franciscans could not bear to raze the Palace of Fine Arts, sparing it for a half century's slow decay until a Marina resident generously donated the funds to rebuild it in 1962. A monumental salute to art for art's sake, the Palace of Fine Arts still rises enchantingly from its sylvan duck pond, a fantastic rotunda transported from a romanticized classic age. Sculptured maidens atop the colonnades weep piteously, filling the palace with a melancholy air of mystery.

Immediately behind the rotunda, at 3601 Lyon Street, stands the **Exploratorium**, dubbed the finest science museum in the country by *Scientific American*. Even people who find science a bore are engrossed by the Exploratorium, and no one has more fun than kids—older kids, that is. The Exploratorium was founded by Frank Oppenheimer (brother of A-bomb inventor J. Robert Oppenheimer) to encourage people to explore the wonders of physics and the human senses. Visitors do not merely learn how things work; they actually take hold of the more than 400 hands-on displays and experiments and *make* them work. You can custom design a bubble, engineer a water spout, create fog or St. Elmo's fire in a vacuum, step into an optical illusion, or crawl through the sound- and light-proof

The Palace of Fine Arts (right) was originally constructed for the Panama-Pacific International Exposition in 1915, as depicted in the diorama at top. Immediately behind the Palace stands the kid-oriented Exploratorium (above), where hands-on exhibits illustrate scientific laws and phenomena. (above photos, Kerrick James)

Tactile Dome to test your reaction to an environment free from most sensation. Other experiments explain the behavior of light, color, motion, sound, plant and animal behavior, and electricity. There are also classes, a film program, and a marvelous store stocking scientific toys, maps, books, and experiments.

■ THE PRESIDIO

The main gate of the Presidio stands ajar on Lyon Street at Lombard, three blocks south of the Exploratorium. The Presidio was founded by the Spanish in 1776 to guard the entrance of San Francisco Bay. The Americans inherited the Presidio from Mexico when they annexed California, and turned it over to the U.S. Sixth Army. After more than two centuries as a military reservation, it closed in 1995 and was turned over to the National Park Service for operation. Although the most important features of the historic site are already open as part of the GGNRA, a wide swatch of the 1,480-acre Presidio cannot be maintained under the present budget, and remains in limbo while Congress debates its fate.

The Presidio contains the largest tract of forest in the city and more than 800 buildings. Among the most interesting attractions are the Presidio Army Museum, a National Cemetery, beautiful walking paths, rows of nineteenth-century officers' houses and barracks, El Polin Spring (revered by the Ohlone and the Spanish for its fertility-inducing properties), Fort Point and gun batteries above Baker Beach. A car is handy here. Get your bearings at the Visitor Center, housed in one of the brick Montgomery Barracks houses along the northwestern edge of the old Main Post parade ground.

Pershing Square, at the southern end of the Parade Ground, was named for General John Pershing, the first commander of American troops in Europe during World War I. The general served at the Presidio for several years prior to departing for Mexico in pursuit of Pancho Villa, in 1916. General Pershing suffered a personal calamity here in 1915, when fire destroyed his house, killing his wife and three daughters.

The tragic heroine of San Francisco's most famous love story was born and raised on the Presidio. In 1806, when Concepcion Arguello was 15 years old, a seasoned Russian diplomat, Nikolai Rezanof, arrived in San Francisco Bay seeking aid for the starving Russian colony at Sitka, Alaska. As *comandante* of the Presidio, Concepcion's father entertained him with the best Hispanic hospitality, despite well-justified suspicions of Russian intentions. Completely green in the ways of the politic world, Concepcion fell in love with the Russian, who in turn proposed marriage. Before sailing through the Golden Gate with his hard-won supplies, he reminded her that since he was Russian Orthodox and she a Roman Catholic, he would have to get permission from both the czar and the pope. The journey, he noted, would take years, but Concepcion said she would wait.

Rezanof never returned. In time, Concepcion retired to a Dominican convent, disavowing all connection with the world, and burying her sorrow beneath decades of silence and daily ritual. Then one day came bittersweet news: her fiancé had not abandoned her. He had frozen to death in the snows of Siberia some 40 years before, en route to petition the czar. Concepcion died in the convent, and is buried in Benicia, where strangers still strew her grave with flowers.

The Officers' Club on Moraga Avenue, at the southern end of Pershing Square, incorporates some of the adobe walls of the Spanish-era fort where Concepcion's father served (and indeed, where the young lady lived). The oldest complete building on the Presidio, however, is the handsome Old Station Hospital, now the **Presidio Army Museum.** Built in 1863 on the corner of what is now Funston and Lincoln, it is surrounded by spiked artillery and mothballed missiles. The Army carried away most of its property when it departed—including exhibits dealing with the American military era. The National Park Service will be working for years to reshape the focus and acquire new displays. In the meantime, the museum still recounts the Presidio's role as a refuge after the 1906 earthquake, displays a model of the 1915 Panama-Pacific International Exposition, and houses other exhibits of local military interest.

The **National Military Cemetery**, where American war veterans are buried, lies farther west on Lincoln Boulevard. Less dramatic than the cemeteries of Normandy or Gettysburg, where every stone marks a life cut down on the field, the National Military Cemetery is nonetheless a compelling spot to reflect on the generations and individuals that bore the brunt of sacrifice in America's wars. The flag here is never lowered. Among the more famous gravestones you may find the names of the Indian scout, Two Bits, and Union Civil War spy Pauline Cushman Fryer, an actress by profession.

Judging by the burgeoning number of new markers at the **pet cemetery** on Crissy Field Avenue, civilians have apparently usurped this graveyard once reserved for four-legged military personnel. Behind the white picket fence lies many a

Military animals and pets are laid to rest in the Presidio pet cemetery.

beastly hero, including General Pershing's horse.

Other military pets lie at rest here, with such epitaphs as "Trouble 1956–1965/ He was no trouble" and "Here lie our beloved rats/Chocolate/Candy" and "Skipper/ Best damn dog we ever had."

As guardian of the sea approaches to San Francisco Bay, the Presidio hosts several abandoned artillery emplacements, some dating back to the nineteenth century. Its Pacific-facing ridge once bristled with the guns of batteries Marcus Miller, Godfrey, Dynamite, Crosby, and Chamberlain. This formidable pack, now defanged, are linked along the Coastal Trail, which runs south from the Golden Gate Bridge. The 1906-vintage **Battery Chamberlain** still contains a 95,000-pound disappearing gun carriage, designed to avoid incoming shells by ducking behind reinforced concrete walls. The mechanism still works. Rangers offer weekend tours.

Baker Beach, below, like most north coast beaches, is dangerous for swimming. It does offer fishing and panoramic views, while the planted forests of Monterey pine and cypress provide shelter from the wind for picnickers. Drivers can park on Bowley Street.

Army officers once inhabited the brick homes which line the Presidio's shady cul-de-sacs.

■ FORT POINT

The most spectacular fortress on the California coast is Fort Point, crouching with spine-tingling drama beneath the southern arch of the Golden Gate Bridge. You do not find too many Civil War-era forts west of Vicksburg, but Fort Point is the genuine article, built between 1853 and 1861 to guard the entrance of San Francisco Bay from marauders. Planted a mere 10 feet above the water, and exposed to rough winds that sometimes whip the sea over the approach road, Fort Point is one of San Francisco's most exhilarating surprises.

Fort Winfield Scott, as it is officially known, once bristled with 126 cannons, but never fired a shot in anger; just as well, too, because it was obsolete almost before it was completed. Of similar design to historic Fort Sumter, Fort Point's brick walls were likewise rendered vulnerable to the new rifled-bore artillery barrels (which put a spin on fired shells) and heavier munitions developed in the Civil War.

Visitors enter through great, studded doors to a sally port, where defenders firing through gun embrasures could pick off storming parties before they breached the next door. The massive walls are built around a courtyard, where three tiers rise up on vaulting arches to a barbette roof. On the ground floor, southeast corner, the powder room is arranged much as it used to be, encased behind 15-foot thick walls. The extraordinary vaulting brickwork is a rarity in San Francisco, where the abundance of good timber encouraged wood-frame housing. Amazingly, Fort Point survived the 1906 quake with flying colors.

Living quarters occupied the east side, with officers on the second floor and enlisted men on the third, 70 to each barracks. Among their regular duties, the men were under orders to wash their feet twice a week, and to take a bath once a month. Their quarters now contain a small but interesting museum, with pictures, uniforms, and weapons. All in all, Fort Point must have been a cold, bleak, and very boring assignment.

Casemates overlooking the Golden Gate mark the business end of operations, presenting four tiers of formidable firepower to any enemy ship that got within a three-mile range. Climbing to the rooftop barbette, where rotating guns could fire over the parapets at moving ships, visitors are usually blasted with cold Pacific winds. It's worth every goose bump for the spectacular views of bridge, bay, rocks, and the craziest clique of wind surfers you've ever seen. Watching them skirt and dart about the hulking, frigid, green Pacific waves in the shadow of the gargantuan bridge piers makes for one of the most riveting and dramatic cityscapes in the world.

Entrance to the fort is free to the public daily. Regular tours are given by docents dressed in Civil War garb, but you can wander about at will. Check the bookstore for schedules, information, and a terrific array of historical publications.

■ THE GOLDEN GATE

The skylines of New York, Paris, and Hong Kong are potent symbols of earthly power and order, but San Francisco at the Golden Gate is radiant beyond compare. The Golden Gate Bridge is arguably the Earth's most harmonious mastery of nature by mankind. What other structure radiates such majesty, such complexity of character? Viewed from any angle, or comprehended statistically, the bridge is marvelous both to rational minds and romantic ones, a symbol of serene grace in the midst of roiling clouds and open sea, a beacon of vaulting triumph, reason, beauty, and mathematical truth, and yet, a brooding mystery, a haunting presence, a siren song of suicides.

The view from Fort Point is awesome, from Lincoln Park, majestic, and from the Marin Headlands, almost unbelievably sublime. From the Berkeley Hills it is seen tenuously stretched, as if faintly threading a continental rift; looking up from below, it is overpoweringly vast. To motor across on a sunny day is to consort with elegance; to walk it on a windy one is pure exhilaration—or terror, if you fear heights. From the deck of a ship approaching from a long Pacific crossing, it can move a wandering native soul to tears, or cheers.

Like most complex personalities, the Golden Gate Bridge is easier to appreciate when you know its history. Three miles long and one mile wide, the Golden Gate is the largest gap in the Coast Ranges for many miles, and yet it was completely missed by Cabrilho, Drake, and other European explorers over the centuries. How could anything so big and important have been overlooked for so long? Perhaps it was foggy; but it's also true that from a distance at sea, the narrow gate appears solidly plugged by the Berkeley Hills behind it. Once discovered by Europeans, however, the excellent bay attracted envious scouts from many nations. When Washington finally sprang for it in 1846, some congressmen were calling it the greatest natural asset of the Far West.

An asset, yes; but no candy-asset. The tidal surge through the gate sucks out a volume of water equal to 14 times the flow of the Mississippi at speeds up to 60 miles per hour. The currents have carved a deep canyon beneath the Gate. Wracked by storms and fogs, the rocky shores outside the Gate have claimed their share of shipwrecks. Against such extraordinary odds, bridging it was unthinkable to all but madmen and poets.

Appropriately enough, Emperor Norton was one of the first to propose it. He was followed up by a poet named Joseph Strauss, who also happened to be an engineer. Strauss and his associates drew up plans and built models that showed it could be done. Yet even as the physical problems were solved, an unsympathetic public still scorned the idea of defacing such a magnificent work of nature. Over 2,000 lawsuits were filed to stop the bridge. In the first half of the twentieth century, it was still possible to win such a number of suits in a lifetime. Bonds were passed in 1930 by Bay Area voters who were willing to give it a try. (Construction fees of $35 million were paid off by bridge tolls in 1971.)

Actual work started in 1933 under supervision of engineer Clifford Paine. Eleven workmen were killed during construction, and storms once wrecked access

(following pages) The Golden Gate Bridge is the perfect collaboration of man and nature.
(Kerrick James)

piers, but the bridge was completed and opened in May 1937. When financier A. P. Giannini of the Bank of America asked how long it would last, Strauss replied "forever" if cared for properly. More levelheaded engineers say it's good for 200 years—which portends a bonanza year for scrap dealers in 2137.

The sheer size of the bridge is astonishing, especially if you walk out on it, as everyone should. Its art-deco towers rise 746 feet above the water, about as high as a 48-story building. If you include the underwater portion, the tallest tower is almost as high as the Transamerica Pyramid. When it was built, its towers were the highest west of Manhattan, and the 4,200-foot main span was the longest in the world; it has now been surpassed on both accounts. The bridge can sway 27.5 feet from east to west in a wind (or earthquake). It takes four years to paint the bridge, an ongoing job to prevent it from rusting.

You can park on either side of the bridge and walk across. On the San Francisco side, be sure to see the section of cut bridge cable displayed in the gardens near the parking lot. The cables contain enough wire to encircle the earth three times at the equator. The statue of Joseph Strauss, nearby, honors the tiny man who proved it could be built. Though Strauss was the force behind the bridge, he has too long received sole credit as *the* bridge builder. In fact, his assistants (like Clifford Paine) deserve much of the credit for the engineering feat.

Climb the steps to the Roundhouse store, where you can stamp a penny with an image of the bridge for 50 cents, or choose from a wide assortment of other mementos; no other American structure, save perhaps the Statue of Liberty, has inspired more schlock. Those who fancy flirting with their own immortality can have a brick inscribed with their name and a message, which then is used to pave the concourse.

The walk across the bridge is about two miles, one way. At 246 feet above the sea, it is like walking a catwalk around the top of a 16-story building. Looking down on Fort Point and on ships passing under the bridge, or looking up the precarious cable walkways, spotting dangling painters at work, a person with respect for heights can feel giddy. The Bay gives scant cushion for anyone falling from such heights, but amazingly, a handful of attempted suicides has survived the jump. The number of those who have not surpasses 1000.

■ COW HOLLOW

The Marina District is walled in on the south by the rather abrupt rise of Pacific Heights. The trough at the foot of Pacific Heights, now engraved by Union Street, was once known as Cow Hollow for the score or so of dairy farms that operated here in the nineteenth century. Alas, the pastures, richly watered by springs, disappeared with the advance of progress. In 1891, the last of Cow Hollow's namesakes was sent, kicking and mooing, into exile.

After six decades as a stodgy residential neighborhood, **Union Street** in the fifties underwent a second rejuvenation. With a paint job to the gingerbread and wrought ironwork, old Victorian houses were transformed into boutiques, coffee houses, restaurants, and fine shops. Soon, Union Street was enjoying a reputation among cognoscenti as a chic shopping district. Word spread, and by the seventies, outlanders and tourists were arriving in droves to hobnob on Union Street, driving much of the chic set over the hill to Upper Fillmore.

Though sometimes verging on preciousness, one of San Francisco's hallmark pleasures is the eight-block stroll down Union between Van Ness and Steiner, poking through the courtyards, shops, and bookstores, idling in the cafes, chatting in the bars, expounding in the galleries, supping in the nosheries, and, in general, completely indulging one's lounger instincts. There's something for everyone: purveyors of crystals, pies, herbs, futons, masks, African jewelry, paper products, Afghan rugs, lingerie, bath potions, tribal art, down comforters, French pastry, ceramic cows, and metaphysical books. The fernier Union Street watering holes cater to a singles crowd.

The **Octagon House**, at the corner of Union and Gough, is an architectural curiosity, built in 1861 with the idea that an octagonal shape allows maximum sunlight into a house. You won't have a chance to test that theory because the original interior has been altered. The house is now the only colonial museum west of Texas, and displays the decorative furnishings of the Colonial and Federal periods. A small donation permits you to wander among the antique tables and chairs, and to inspect the prize collection of autographs by the signers of the Declaration of Independence.

Redwood-sheltered **Allyne Park**, next door behind the white picket fence, is San Francisco's most charming city park. Let yourself in at one of the gates. It has the feel of somebody's backyard.

Another local oasis is the churchyard of **St. Mary's Episcopal** (2301 Union), where one of Cow Hollow's springs still flows up to water long-vanished pastures. The spring, hidden from the street by a hedge and lych-gate, endows the rustic scene with the peace and solitude of an English country churchyard.

Accommodations are available on Union Street in bed-and-breakfast houses, where the comfy flowers-and-sherry ambience matches the neighborhood character. For those who want to soak up one of San Francisco's most charming neighborhoods, if you have the budget, consider lodging in Cow Hollow.

■ PACIFIC HEIGHTS

The western end of Union Street halts at the Presidio wall, where **Lyon Street** bounds southward and upward to Pacific Heights. Here dwell San Francisco's bluest-bloods. It is by no means a small neighborhood. Pacific Heights commandeers the crest of a long, high ridge rising in the east from Van Ness Avenue and rolling 14 blocks west to the Presidio's eastern wall. On the north side, overlooking the Bay, the mansions and apartments march down terraces as far as Green

Pacific Heights is one of the city's wealthiest neighborhoods.

Street. On the south side, overlooking Hayes Valley and Twin Peaks, the streets drop more gradually to California Street. Presidio Heights, an even more exclusive enclave, takes up the torch at the Presidio wall, and runs several blocks farther.

The best way to get a feel for the Heights is to walk, enjoying the splendid architectural wealth of Gothic door-knockers, mansard roofs, fairy-tale turrets, gables, statuary, Tudor facing, wrought iron fences, topiary, burnished lamps, carved doors, and clinging ivy. Bay vistas are the best that money can buy. By night, some half-opened curtain might treat you to a fleeting glimpse of a fine old library or a roaring fire, which you may, if you wish, enjoy vicariously. The Christmas holidays herald a special profusion of lights and decorations.

Where to walk? If not quite aimlessly, let it at least be wherever fancy takes you. Certainly Lyon Street above Union is a good place to start. As you climb its landscaped steps, magnificent views open up over the Marina District to the Bay, the Palace of Fine Arts floating like a magic castle in the foreground. At intersecting streets, like Broadway and Vallejo, avenues of mansions march solidly east. Finally, cresting the top, look west down Pacific at one of the city's most romantic views: the partially red-brick street plunges steeply down into a secluded kingdom known as Presidio Heights, whose rich hinterland embraces the parallel blocks of Jackson, Washington, and Clay. This particular stretch of Pacific between Lyon and Spruce is known as "along the wall," in deference to the low stone Presidio wall that separates civilians from warriors. "Along the wall" means old money and cultivated tastes. Governesses gather with their little charges at Julius Kahn Playground, beyond the wall at Spruce Street. Surrounding cypress woods, rolling across the Presidio hills, absorb the fog and hush the footfalls of passers-by.

A few blocks west along the Presidio wall, Presidio Terrace nurses a clutch of palatial mansions on a circular drive, in the shadow of **Temple Emanu-El.** Inspired by the grandiose dome of Santa Sophia in old Constantinople, this landmark synagogue was built by Arthur Brown, whose other works include City Hall and Coit Tower. The temple is open to the public during the afternoon from Monday to Friday. Enter at the corner of Arguello and Lake.

A humbler, but still genteel, architectural statement is made by the **Church of New Jerusalem**, better known as the Swedenborg Church, at 2107 Lyon, between Jackson and Washington. Designed and assembled with loving care by architects and artists of the American Craftsman Movement in 1894, the church and its garden show the careful attention to detail and beauty that characterized much of

Renaissance or classical Japanese workmanship. Yet, the tiny church is distinctively Californian. Its carved wooden beams, wood-burning fireplace, stained glass windows, and even its chairs handcrafted of hardwood and woven tule bulrush exude the cozy, yet reverent, atmosphere of a California forest. No wonder it's San Francisco's most popular wedding chapel.

The farther east you go in Pacific Heights, the more the old mansions have given way to apartment houses. Clusters of fine old Victorians still stand between the monoliths, hidden like Russian Easter eggs in the nooks of a garden wall. Many of these remaining mansions have become too expensive to maintain as dwellings, and have been transformed into schools, nonprofit foundations, and even hotels. Lodging in a Victorian is an ideal way to get to the heart of San Francisco.

The **Haas-Lilienthal House** at 2007 Franklin Street is one of the eccentric wooden Victorians that typifies old San Francisco. Owned and operated as a museum by the Foundation for San Francisco's Architectural Heritage, the house was built in 1886 with the jaunty bay windows, luxuriant ornamentation, fanciful gables, and Queen Anne-style circular tower so characteristic of the exuberant Victorian era. The rooms are still furnished with many of the Haas and Lilienthal family heirlooms. Foundation guides lead tours on Wednesdays and Sundays.

Detail of a circular tower on a Queen Anne–style Victorian.

Two of San Francisco's prettiest hilltop parks are in Pacific Heights, surrounded by handsome architecture and elegant views. **Lafayette Park** is a delightful garden, flowery and well-wooded, smelling of pine and eucalyptus. **Alta Plaza**, on the other hand, rises in vigorously symmetrical terraces like a great, green Mayan pyramid—an oddly forceful monument in an otherwise well-groomed, genteel neighborhood.

The lights of nearby **Upper Fillmore**, the main shopping street of Pacific Heights, sparkle long into the night. Catering to a stable, well-to-do, and largely youthful clientele, urbane Upper Fillmore is the epitome of contemporary American trendiness, the domain of sushi and designer foods, luxury services, nail salons, import groceries, hot tubs, dessert boutiques, cafes, and rich young things with mannequin faces. The popular Clay Cinema, on Fillmore near Clay Street, shows art and international films. If Proust were alive and living in San Francisco, no doubt his Swann would have felt at home on Upper Fillmore.

■ WESTERN ADDITION

Ironically, until recently Fillmore was known as one of San Francisco's poorer streets. The Lower Fillmore (between Geary and Haight) still retains this intimi-

The Victorian Archbishops' Mansion stands on Alamo Square in the Western Addition.

dating cachet, though it is also known as an exciting neighborhood for music, especially with the re-opening of the Fillmore nightclub. The rising and falling fortunes of Fillmore Street are typical of the Western Addition in general.

The district acquired its name in the 1870s, when a spate of building to the east of Van Ness Avenue affixed a *western addition* to the old city core. Surviving the 1906 earthquake and fire virtually unscathed, it became the city's largest Victorian neighborhood.

Probably its most famous resident was a woman named Mary Ellen Pleasant, once better known as Mammy Pleasant, who lived in a house owned by Thomas Bell near the corner of Bush and Octavia. (The house is gone, but six venerable eucalyptus trees that she planted still grow in front, where a memorial plaque has been placed by the African-American Cultural Society.) Few figures in San Francisco history have inspired more mystery. Her notoriety followed hard on the death of her employer, Thomas Bell, who was killed in a fall from his third-floor balcony. Some claimed that he was pushed by Mary Pleasant, but no one ever claimed it in court or to her face. Nonetheless, rumors circulated until her death, and after, that she was a procuress, a murderess, and a witch. Modern accounts don't dispel the mystery, but are more likely to credit her as a consummate businesswoman, an ardent abolitionist, and a commanding, fearless person who demanded and received respect. The daughter of a black mother and Cherokee father, Mary Pleasant arrived in San Francisco during the Gold Rush. She opened a successful boarding house (which some say was a discreet bordello), and used her personal fortune to help finance the western terminus of the Underground Railway. Her San Francisco home was a sanctuary for runaway slaves. When John Brown was seized at Harper's Ferry, Maryland, a conspiratorial note signed with her initials was found on his person, but she escaped before any investigation could be mounted. Her interest in the plight of African Americans did not end with the Civil War. In 1865, she sued a San Francisco streetcar company over rude treatment to black riders, and won.

Of the many ethnic groups that have settled the Western Addition, among the most prominent were the Jewish community, which congregated here during the first third of the twentieth century, the Japanese, who built "Little Osaka" around Post Street, and African Americans, whose community centered along Fillmore. Little Osaka was uprooted during World War II by Japanese-American internment, though many returned after the war. Conversely, the African-American community grew rapidly during the war as workers arrived from the South to build ships. When war jobs died out and unemployed black workers were passed over by private-sector companies, the neighborhood fell on hard times. The old Victorians deteriorated into slummy firetraps, and were replaced with ugly urban renewal projects.

Today, the Western Addition is undergoing rampant gentrification of its remaining Victorian enclaves. Modern city planners, wiser from their earlier mistakes, are designing with much more attention to aesthetics and social use. Still, many of the government housing projects of the Western Addition are plagued by high crime rates, especially in the blocks south of Geary.

One of San Francisco's most charming Victorian streets is **Cottage Row**, between Sutter and Bush, a half block east from Fillmore. Like Macondray Lane on Russian Hill, Cottage Row is another of those little country lanes so improbably spirited to the midst of the metropolis. While there, walk the extra block to Marcus Books (1712 Fillmore, between Sutter and Post) for a large selection of works by black authors and about African-American history and culture.

One block west of Fillmore, on the corner of Bush and Steiner, stands one of San Francisco's most popular religious shrines. Catholic pilgrims, many from Latin America, search out **St. Dominic's Church** to pay their respects to the statue of St. Jude, patron saint of lost causes.

Fillmore marks the western edge of Nihonmachi, or **Japantown**, a compact neighborhood loosely rounded by Geary, Octavia, and Pine. For persons completely unfamiliar with Asian cultures, the comparison between Japantown and Chinatown could serve to show that China and Japan are as different as, say, Italy and Denmark. Of course, Japantown does not attempt to be a faithful recreation of "the old country." Like Little Italy, it is a distinctively American hybrid, but harboring a treasury of details that can evoke a sense of Japan, much as a bonsai may evoke a whole forest, or a bite of *sfrappole* can bring back memories of old Bologna. Keep your senses primed as you walk through the district, and you may find such cultural touchstones in the hardware stores, the family-owned markets and bakeries, the Zen and Konko missions, and the comfortable, human scale of the streets and architecture. The one-block, open-air **Buchanan Mall**, between Post and Sutter, is the most self-consciously old-style Japanese street. Paved with riverine cobbles and lined by Japanese restaurants and shops, it is a comfortable, pleasant place to stroll or sit.

A more ambitious vision of modern Japan stands beyond Post Street. **Japan Center** is a three-block concrete mall, hemmed in by Fillmore, Geary, and Laguna, which many find ugly and impersonal. The interior, however, can be inviting, and certainly provides some fascinating cultural insights. Among the Japanese goods and provisions available are futons, cooking utensils, arts and crafts, clothing, furniture (including items specially designed for small-apartment living), antiques, fine paper products, pearls, tourist knickknacks, and a wide selection of Japanese books, videos, cassettes, and compact discs. The center also contains about 30 restaurants, from coffee shops to sushi bars, noodle houses to formal Japanese restaurants, some with tatami rooms. Visitors are fascinated by Isobune, where the sushi boats float by on a miniature river, and by the table-side chefs at Benihana, who put on skilled knife demonstrations while preparing meals. Casual Sapporo-ya, which makes its own noodles on an antique ramen machine, is popular for snacks. The adjacent Miyako Hotel, while blending Japanese trappings (like kimono-clad waitresses) with Western comforts (such as chairs), also offers some genuine Japanese-style rooms with tatami floors and Japanese baths.

Traditional costume, dancing, and a barrel of sake *spice up a Japantown festival.*

Japantown's sometimes sleepy facade belies its cultural vigor. Language and cultural classes, including such arts as cooking and flower arrangement, are advertised on the Japan Center community bulletin board. Seasonal festivals bring dancers, drummers, artists, and craftspeople from around the Bay Area. The Kokusai Theater (1746 Post) devotes itself to Japanese-language films. The AMC Kabuki 8 Theaters, anchoring the Fillmore end of Japan Center, offer first-run features and independent films, and also host major San Francisco film festivals.

Downstairs, the Kabuki Hot Spring bathhouse at 1750 Geary mollifies the soul as it cleanses the body—or rather, *after* cleansing the body. The idea in a Japanese bath is to lather, scrub, and rinse yourself *thoroughly* before getting into the hot bath to soak. The Kabuki has a traditional communal bath, as well as sauna and steam rooms, and is open to men and women on different days. As gentle New Age music soothes away stress, you can relax under an after-bath *shiatsu* (finger-pressure) massage. (And yes, sir, I mean a *real* massage.) The works aren't cheap, but you will come out feeling like a new person.

From Japantown, you can walk two blocks up Geary (east) to the top of Cathedral Hill, named for **St. Mary's Cathedral**, an unabashedly modern edifice rising at the corner of Geary and Gough. However peculiar the exterior (its likeness to a washing maching agitator has earned it the nickname St. Maytag's) the vast interior is astounding, even in this atrium-jaded city. Built in 1971, it speaks boldly of an age of faith bolstered by the worldly powers of science and engineering. Enormous compound arches lift the cross-shaped dome 190 feet above the floor, opening the walls to expansive views out over the city. The majestic Ruffati organ explodes from the depths on an enormous concrete pedestal like a throne rising up to glory. If you like your cathedrals exuberant, you'll love St. Mary's.

The **First Unitarian Church** across the street is a much more staid, though handsome, stone structure dating from 1889. First Unitarian was the church of Thomas Starr King, the preacher credited with swaying California to the Union side in the Civil War. So enamored was California of this service that Thomas Starr King is one of the two statues that represent the state in the Hall of Fame in Washington. (The other is Father Junipero Serra.) King died before the war ended, in 1864. His tomb is outside the southeastern corner of the church.

Nearer the western edge of the Western Addition, the **Museum of Russian Culture**, at 2450 Sutter Street, keeps a large collection of icons, artifacts, and memorabilia of the Bay Area's scattered Russian community. This small, quiet repository of art and books welcomes researchers, and is open Saturdays or by appointment. Firehouse buffs will want to visit the nearby **Fire Department Museum**, at 655 Presidio Avenue, which captures the real veneration San Franciscans have for their fire companies—not a strange phenomenon for a city of wood. The paraphernalia here reflects the glory days when fire companies used to compete for the honor of extinquishing blazes.

South of Geary, **Alamo Square** anchors down another gentrifying section of the Western Addition. Many old Victorians line the park, including the famous row along Steiner Street so often pictured in books of the city. The old Imperial Russian Consulate still stands at 1198 Fulton; and the Archbishops' Mansion on the corner of Fulton and Steiner, once the official home of local Catholic prelates, has now been converted into one of the most palatial bed-and-breakfast inns in the country. Guests may sip sherry in the lap of Edwardian luxury, or play a few bars on Noel Coward's piano.

From the southwestern corner of Alamo Square, you can see the enchanting towers of St. Ignatius church and the forested slopes of Buena Vista Park and Mount Sutro. Though still a bit frayed in places, the neighborhood surrounding Alamo Square is one of San Francisco's most breathtaking. Look north across the valley for another view of Alta Plaza's Mayan symmetry. Some say it's a landing platform for spacecraft.

■ THE RICHMOND DISTRICT

The name of Lone Mountain has struck a chord of terror in more than one generation of San Francisco children. That's because it stood for years at dead center of the city's necropolis, surrounded in all directions by acres of bone yards.

Where have all the graveyards gone? Gone to Colma, every one; at least the ones that they could find. Richmond District gardeners have been surprised more than once while planting their petunias.

In a city as small as San Francisco, the enormous cemetery plots were needed for the living, and so in 1914, Mayor Sunny Jim Rolph ordered all persons owning or claiming lots in the cemeteries to move their occupants to Colma, a city just south of San Francisco devoted to caring for the dead. Unclaimed bodies were buried in mass graves in Colma, and the stones were used, in part, to pave the city's sea walls. You can still see some on the jetty at the wave organ.

Today, Lone Mountain is crowned by a tower that is part of University of San Francisco. Founded by the Jesuits in 1855, USF is the oldest university in San Francisco, though it moved three times before settling on its present spectacular hilltop. The campus contains the most majestic church in the city, **St. Ignatius.** Its handsome dome and campanile, and its 210-foot twin spires, spectacularly lit at night, ennoble more than one city vista.

Only one remnant of Lone Mountain's cemeteries remains today—the **Columbarium.** Once surrounded by the Odd Fellows cemetery, it is now engulfed by buildings, and approached from the appropriately dead-end Loraine Street. The Columbarium is a splendid neoclassical rotunda filled with urns and memorial niches. Capped with a copper roof and decorated with precious vases and a Tiffany window, the four-story building keeps the cremated remains of some 6,000 people, many of them pioneer families. If you bring a companion, you can test the building's marvelous acoustics on any of the upper floors. Standing on one side, you should be able to hold a quiet conversation with someone hidden around the opposite side. The Columbarium is open to the public on mornings from Tuesday through Saturday.

Clearing the cemeteries made way for San Francisco's Richmond District, by far a worthy trade-off. This western third of San Francisco, combined with the Sunset District south of Golden Gate Park, is known collectively as "the Avenues," because most of the streets running north and south are numbered avenues. At one time the Richmond was called the Outer Lands, and even the Great Sand Waste, for the obvious reason that it *was* a wasteland of shifting sand dunes and a few scraggly knolls. The land was opened for settlement largely through the efforts of a Prussian named Adolf Sutro, sometimes called the Father of the Richmond, who owned a good stretch of the Outer Lands. Sutro had made his fortune in the Comstock, and retired to a mansion across from the Cliff House, which he also owned. Next door he erected the largest bathhouse in the world, Sutro Baths, and connected it to the city with a steam railway. Thus, he built both the inducement and the means for people to go to the Richmond.

Today, the Richmond is a solidly middle-class neighborhood of great ethnic diversity happily sandwiched between the Presidio and Lincoln Park on the north, and Golden Gate Park on the south. The Russians were among the first major ethnic groups in the outer Richmond, when some 10,000 White Russians arrived in the years after the 1917 Revolution. Their passage to America was eased by the

(right) St. Ignatius is thought by many to be the city's most beautiful church.

tireless lobbying of an extraordinary priest, known as John the Barefoot, who was to become San Francisco's first Russian Orthodox bishop. His bishopric was **Saint Mary the Virgin in Exile**, the golden, onion-domed church on Geary between 26th and 27th avenues. The church opens for Mass in the morning, when visitors (long pants for men, modest skirts or dresses for women) *may* be allowed to view its enormous chandeliers, icons, and relics, including the *body* of St. John the Barefoot. Another notable landmark is Russian Renaissance, a restaurant at 5241 Geary. The icon-like murals that cover the walls and ceiling with scenes from Russian folklore and history took the late artist Serge Smernoff 14 years to complete. If you stop by in the evening and can stand a stiff drink, try an icy *zebrovka*, the house's buffalo grass–infused vodka. You can still find Russian newspapers in the stores, and a scattering of onion-domed buildings in the side streets. The 1990s are witnessing a resurgence of Russian immigration to San Francisco.

Many elderly Russians still congregate on the playground benches of **Mountain Lake Park**, a pretty spot on the Presidio's border near Park Presidio Boulevard. Anza camped here when he came to found the Presidio, in 1776. Thousands of refugees followed suit on the nearby golf course in 1906. Kids and adults alike will love the playground's large swings and rolling-pin slides.

The most prominent ethnic group in the Richmond nowadays is Chinese. The stretch of the Avenues between Arguello Boulevard and Park Presidio, especially along Clement Street, is known as **New Chinatown**, which lacks both the tourist glitz and squalor of Grant Avenue's Chinatown, while its markets and restaurants can beat it for quality and convenience.

Attracted by the strong Asian American presence in the Richmond, the Asian American Theater has settled into a new home on Arguello at the corner of Clement. One of the premier small theaters in the country, it has produced works by Tony Award-winning playwright David Henry Hwang and other local artists.

The Richmond's restaurants attract more locals than tourists. The long stretch of Clement and Geary in the Richmond has long been known as San Francisco's premier restaurant row, celebrated for its great culinary diversity and quality. Nowadays the restaurants are more plentiful than ever, but the Richmond's once exceptional diversity now decidedly emphasizes East Asian cuisines. Chinese offerings are the most prolific, with *dim sum* and seafood (Cantonese), Mandarin, Shanghai, Hunan, Sichuan, Chaozhou, Hakka, and vegetarian. Vietnamese, Italian, French, Mexican, Japanese, Thai, American, and Korean are amply represented, but you can also find such rarer cuisines as Cambodian, Russian, Moroccan, Peruvian, Spanish, Danish, Laotian, Armenian, Indonesian, Singaporian, and Burmese—not to mention all the ubiquitous cafes, delis, dessert and ice cream parlors, and Irish pubs. You can idle away the hours between meals and late into the evenings at bookstores like Green Apple and Albatross II, or at night spots like the Plough & Stars or Ireland's 32.

All in all, the Richmond is nothing spectacular in the Disneyland sense of the word; but with good food, good drink, good books, and entertaining company, it is one of the most comfortable and stimulating neighborhoods in the city. And as if that weren't enough, it is well placed for escaping to the parks.

■ LINCOLN PARK AND LAND'S END

Seacliff, an exclusive neighborhood of stirring sea views, is incomparably coddled between the Presidio and Lincoln Park. The Coastal Trail from the Presidio passes through the streets of the neighborhood. You can hook into it on the east side at Baker Beach, at the end of 25th Avenue north, and on the west side near where El Camino del Mar meets Lincoln Park.

In Seacliff, devotees of Ansel Adams can take a small detour to the house at 129 24th Avenue, where he grew up. In those days, this was out in the sticks. The house is not open to the public.

Another detour takes you to **China Beach**, named for the Chinese fishermen who used to camp here in earlier days. China Beach is an exception to the no-swimming rule of thumb at San Francisco beaches. The water is safe enough here, though never warm. The beach has changing rooms, showers, restrooms, and a lifeguard station.

San Francisco's most rugged stretch of seacoast is **Land's End**, west of Seacliff. Until closed by landslides, El Camino del Mar once ran through here to the Cliff House. Sutro's railway also passed through. Nowadays, both road and rail rights-of-way are footpaths administered by the GGNRA and Lincoln Park. Between the two parks, San Francisco enjoys both its wildest landscapes and its most rarefied vision of civilization, the Legion of Honor.

Few museums in all the world have a setting as magnificent as the **California Palace of the Legion of Honor.** Approached by car through Lincoln Park Golf Course from 34th Avenue and Clement, the Legion rises handsomely from its Lincoln Park hilltop like a classical French palace, fronted with colonnades, a tri-

umphal arch, and heroic equestrian bronzes of El Cid and Joan of Arc. One of five original castings of Auguste Rodin's famous statue, *The Thinker*, cogitates in the formal courtyard at the front of a pyramidal skylight. A shockingly incongruous sculpture, George Segal's *The Holocaust*, clings half-hidden behind a corner of the balustrade. Its emaciated corpses and barbed wire shriek out with shameless effrontery amidst the Legion's perfect setting—which, of course, is precisely the point.

Founded by Alma de Bretteville Spreckels, the French-born wife of a local sugar baron, the Legion was dedicated to American soldiers fallen in France during World War I. Marshals Joffre and Foch both attended the opening in 1924, each marking the occasion by planting a cypress on the Legion's southern side. For years devoted exclusively to the display of French Art, the Legion of Honor absorbed the European collection from the M. H. de Young Museum in the 1990s, giving it a much broader scope. Francophiles may grumble, as indeed they do, but the Legion still exudes a staunchly Gallic air.

Surveying eight centuries of European art, the permanent collection contains works by El Greco, Rembrandt, Rubens, Van Dyke, Van Cleve, Renoir, Seurat, Cézanne, Degas, Boucher, Monet, Manet, Courbet, Cellini, and Rodin, who

The Thinker *is one of several works by Rodin at the Legion of Honor (above, Kerrick James).*
St. Mary the Virgin in Exile *(left) is the religious center of Russian life in the Richmond.*

alone accounts for more than 70 sculptures. One of the most impressive pieces is an 11-foot high bronze wine vase by Gustave Doré, depicting cherubs and vermin in drunken revel. Of special note are the period rooms, particularly the somber Medieval Mudejar ceiling from Spain, and the paneled French period room. The **Achenbach Foundation for Graphic Arts**, downstairs, cares for the largest collection of graphic prints in the western United States, including a splendid selection of Japanese woodblock prints.

Aside from the collections and exhibitions, the Legion of Honor organizes regular docent tours and hundreds of film, lecture, painting, and music programs, including weekly pipe organ concerts in the Rodin Gallery. Its Florence Gould Theater, one of the most intimate venues in town, hosts regular programs of chamber music, jazz, and dance, as well as demonstrations of historical musical styles and instruments. A small shop at the entrance offers a nice array of cards and books. On the lower floor, Café Chanticleer is a cheery setting for a light lunch.

Outside again, if you like the Legion's facade, stroll around back for another perspective. En route, take note of the black engraved stone on the north side of El Camino del Mar. It is a monument to the *Kanrin Maru*, the first Japanese ship to arrive in San Francisco Bay bearing emissaries to America. Its American counterpart sailed simultaneously in the other direction. The year was 1860.

Behind that monument, a hard-to-find path cuts down the edge of the golf course to the **Coastal Trail**, which leads between the Golden Gate Bridge and the Cliff House via Land's End. (You'll find a second path to the west, at the end of the parking lot.) There are no roads here. Stay on the paths; the cliffs crumble easily, and someone falls or is swept away by freak waves nearly every year. The seas off Land's End are shipwreck waters. On foggy days, the sound of the horns and the smell of fog and the sea produce the kind of atmosphere that make Byronic hearts swoon with sweet melancholy. On clear days, the vistas sweep from Seacliff past the Presidio and the Golden Gate Bridge to rugged Point Bonita Lighthouse, in Marin County, the north channel's outside gatepost. In the foreground, Mile Rock Lighthouse blinks its lonely vigil through rough seas and calm. A spur off the Coastal Trail winds down to tiny Mile Rock Beach, a favorite of stalwart sunbathers.

As the Coastal Trail rounds **Point Lobos**, skirting thick, matted tunnels of cypress, it feeds into Merrie Way, near the Cliff House. Stairs lead uphill at this point to the bridge of the USS *San Francisco*, overlooking the sea at El Camino del Mar. Torn by shells, the piece of ship now stands as a memorial to 107 crew and officers killed in the 1942 Battle of Guadalcanal. The wooden observation house on the hill behind is the old Marine Exchange Lookout. Built to watch for ships entering the Golden Gate, it would announce the news to the more centrally located Telegraph Hill by semaphore. On the hill above the lookout, military buffs can explore Fort Miley's abandoned gun emplacements, built to greet less friendly ships.

A FOGGY EXCURSION

*F*rom the moment we left the stable, almost, the fog was so thick that we could scarcely see fifty yards behind or before, or overhead; and for a while, as we approached the Cliff House, we could not see the horse at all, and were obliged to steer by his ears, which stood up dimly out of the dense white mist that enveloped him. But for those friendly beacons, we must have been cast away and lost.

—Mark Twain's description of an early morning jaunt to the Cliff House, *The Golden Era,* 1864.

This most spectacular version of the Cliff House burned in 1907.

■ THE PACIFIC SHORE

The **Cliff House** was one of the city's first tourist attractions. Mark Twain described a visit here in the 1860s, when it was already garnering a reputation as a fast place for fast people. When Sutro bought it in the 1880s, he stopped the hanky-panky and started to run it as a family resort. After the old Cliff House burned in 1894, Sutro erected a wondrous wooden castle on the site, bolstering business with a huge bathhouse next door. Unfortunately for lovers of the Gothic, the building burned in 1907. Be sure to see its picture in the lobby of the contemporary Cliff House, which dates from 1908.

Still a tourist shrine, Cliff House bars and restaurants mix warm repast with stirring views of sea stacks and rugged breakers. The GGNRA runs a visitor center downstairs, with a view over Sutro Baths. On the patio outside, visitors can step inside a large camera, the Camera Obscura, for views of landscape, seascape, and fellow tourists. Barking sea lions play just off shore on **Seal Rocks**. Their ghostly roars take on added drama in fog or murk of darkness. On clear days, Point Reyes stands out clearly in the north, protected as far as you can see by state and national

Now a hole in the ground, Sutro Baths was once the world's largest bathhouse.
Ocean Beach is pretty to look at, but a menace to swimmers.

parklands. By night, the towns of Muir Beach, Stinson Beach, and Bolinas glow small and bright amidst the black hills and sea. Thirty-two miles to the west, you can sometimes pick out San Francisco's farthest outpost, the Farallon Islands, a rugged sanctuary for birds and sea lions. During the Gold Rush, enterprising businessmen used to collect murre eggs from there to sell for breakfast in the city.

The gulf between the Farallon Islands and the Golden Gate is part of the Red Triangle, a somewhat lurid name for a patch of ocean that the Great White Shark calls home. Recorded attacks on humans here are not overly common; but then, neither are swimmers.

The Cliff House also shelters the **Musée Méchanique**, a collection of coin-operated mechanical games and devices, the kind that used to be found in penny arcades around the civilized world. Plunk your quarters down to play the vintage pinball machines, mechanical fortune teller, miniature carnival, automated band instruments, and more. Admission is free, but bring plenty of pocket change for the machines.

The ruins in the rocks north of the Cliff House are **Sutro Baths**, a Victorian pleasure palace opened in 1896. Its six salt baths and hundreds of dressing rooms had room for 24,000 swimmers under a soaring glass dome. An aerial cable car, the Sky Tram, once ran from the Cliff House to the rocks beyond, where visitors could view the crashing seas from a tunnel cut clear through the rocks. The baths burned in 1966, and the tram was dismantled soon after. You can still walk to the tunnel, and clear through the now-exposed opening above the rocks. Watch out for holes in the floor of the cave, where the surf pounds and gurgles through subterranean passages at high tide.

Sutro lived on an estate high on the hill across the road from the Cliff House. The house was torn down after his death, and his estate turned into **Sutro Heights Park**. Old walls and feral gardens lend a romantic air of ruin to the grounds. Views from high ground here reach to Ocean Beach, the Richmond and Sunset districts, Golden Gate Park, Fort Funston, and beyond, a tremendous study in perspective— all the streets, the park boundaries, and the beach itself intersect at 90-degree angles.

The waters off **Ocean Beach**, running four miles to San Francisco's border and beyond, are not very hospitable. Chill winds usually render sunbathing uncomfortable, while severe undertow makes swimming perilous, not to mention illegal. Ocean Beach still pulls the crowds in on the hottest days, however, and almost always provides a magnificent backdrop for seashore strolls or horseback rides.

■ GOLDEN GATE PARK

Like the Golden Gate Bridge, Golden Gate Park was built despite a litany of nay-sayers who insisted that it couldn't be done. With 1,017 acres, it is probably the largest cultivated park in the United States, if not the world.

In a league with the Hanging Gardens of Babylon, Golden Gate Park is a work of art on a heroic scale, where lakes, forests, glades, waterfalls, streams, hills, and even the earth itself have been designed by human hands. Yet, what mankind nurtured, Mother Nature has now good-naturedly adopted as her own. A more botanically vibrant piece of ground would be difficult to find in any temperate clime.

When plans for a park first started tickling the fancy of boosters like William Ralston, the likeliest pieces of real estate near the center of town were already taken. Instead, the city acquired an oblong piece of the Great Sand Wastes, three miles long and a half-mile wide, at its closest point about three miles from down-town. It was the largest stretch of sand dune on the California coast. Such folly no doubt caused many a guffaw in the saloons and press-rooms of Montgomery Street. Even Frederick Law Olmsted, the landscape designer who built New York's 840-acre Central Park, threw up his hands in disgust at the site, which he thought incapable of supporting trees. He graciously admitted his mistake later.

In 1871, the contract for designing Golden Gate Park went to an engineer named William Hammand Hall, who had already surveyed the Outside Lands for the federal government. Hall went straight to work. First, he had to secure the blowing sand. He did this by sowing barley, then lupine on top of that, and grass on top of the lupine. With a mat of grass established, he planted trees. At the same time, he started constructing a wall on Ocean Beach to stop the dunes from blow-ing inland. He proceeded to grade, build roads, lay water pipe, and plant thou-sands of trees in the eastern section of the park, which had more promising soil than the coastal side. He also built the Panhandle, a long strip of park designed as an elegant carriage entry.

Hall's work was soon appreciated by San Franciscans, who started flocking to the young park for picnics and carriage races. But though San Franciscans loved the new park, government corruption and political shenanigans were eating at the park bud-get. After repeated attacks and trumped-up charges of extravagance and corruption, Hall resigned in disgust, in 1876. Funds were slashed, and Golden Gate Park drifted into a decade of decline. Plants and roads were neglected, crime and corruption flourished. Finally, in desperate straits, the government called Hall back again.

The great outdoors for many San Franciscans is Golden Gate Park.

Hall took the job on the condition that he could appoint his own successor, a man capable of pressing on with the park's construction while fending off the rascally politicians. His appointment, a Scotsman named John McLaren, took over as Superintendent in 1890 and served for the next 53 years. Fondly known as "Uncle John" by his staff and generations of grateful San Franciscans, McLaren was not only a master gardener who personally planted thousands of trees, but a canny handler of people.

McLaren believed that parks should be natural, beautiful settings where people can retreat from such urban trappings as buildings, statues, and roads. Under McLaren's trusteeship, Golden Gate Park blossomed into the masterpiece of landscape gardening that it is today. He brought in exotic plants from around the world and earned international fame for his extraordinary abilities to make them flourish. Against the pressures of developers he fought like a terrier, outplaying politicians at their own games. Once, for instance, when plans were hatched to bisect the park with another road, McLaren deftly nominated a plot in the planners' path for a police academy. The Police Department rushed to McLaren's support, and the road stopped dead in its tracks. The academy, of course, had to be built, but in due course it was reabsorbed back into the park as the Senior Center, as it stands today, at 37th Avenue.

McLaren eventually outlived all opponents, escorting his park beyond their reach into the middle of the twentieth century. Until he expired, still Superintendent, at the age of 93, his staunch loyalty to the Vegetable Kingdom never wavered. When asked what he wanted for his 90th birthday, the Superintendent demanded without hesitation a load of manure to spread around his park. He was joking, of course; McLaren had been commandeering the city's manure supply for years.

The genius of Hall's plan and McLaren's implementation was that it was so well hidden. The land and woods appear so naturally lovely that it seems impossible to be by human design. Yet, nothing is by chance. Strategic pockets of fuchsias, camelias, roses, tulips, dahlias, cherry, magnolia, and other bright-blooming shrubs were placed to lend spectacular color to every season. The roads and walkways were laid out meanderingly, not only to discourage speeding, but to preserve the sense of exquisite seclusion. Even the prevailing winds have been checked and deflected by careful grading and planting. Golden Gate Park is a treasure; and yet more like a treasure hunt, for exploring it is quite as good as finding what you seek. The park never overwhelms. Rather it rewards quietly, with layer on layer of unlimited discovery for the visitor who can spend a lifetime or two getting at the heart of its mystery.

Golden Gate Park accommodates an amazing number of special activities without any one encroaching on another. Of course, all major sports—tennis, baseball, soccer, football, golf, bicycle racing, handball, jogging, basketball, horseback riding lessons, hiking, skating, archery, rowing, and lounging in the shade—are amply represented, but more obscure special interests are also royally cared for. Lawn bowlers have their lawns, fly fishermen their special casting pool, horseshoe pitchers their own elaborate grounds, card-players their designated shelter. There is a field for playing *petanque,* a French species of lawn bowling. Children have three special playgrounds. Model yacht sailors have their own lake. Even dogs have four grounds set aside for their training and other personal needs.

Cultural activities are also well looked after: there are art museums, an aquarium, planetarium, museum of natural history and science, band shell, botanical garden, merry-go-round, and clubhouses for anglers, golfers, beach-goers, model boat sailors, and senior citizens.

All this is put together in a setting of unrivaled botanical wealth. The richness and complexity of the park's special gardens are mind-boggling. Surely, the only way to do Golden Gate Park justice is to get a good map and follow your own interests. A tour of the park can begin at **McLaren Lodge**, on the western edge of the park near the corner of Stanyan and Fell. In the days when park-keepers resided in the parks, Uncle John lived here. At the beach end of the park, a more ambitious visitor center now occupies the historic **Beach Chalet,** designed by Polk. Drop in just to see Lucien Labaudt's Depression-era frescoes, which depict various tableaux of local scenes and personalities, such as John McLaren. The upstairs micro-brewery pays homage to another locally popular form of recreation.

There are many good ways to tour the park. A car is not the best of them, save perhaps on a rainy day. With 27 miles of footpaths and 7.5 miles of equestrian trails, walking and horseback riding are pure joy. Many roads in Golden Gate Park are closed to motor traffic on Sundays from 8 A.M. to dusk, providing a perfect place for bicyclists and skaters. (With up to 20,000 skaters on the roads on a sunny Sunday, walkers may prefer to deal with the cars.) You can rent bikes and skates from outlets on the edge of the park.

The most magical spot in the park for youngsters is **Children's Playground**, the oldest public playground in the United States. Generations of San Franciscans have filled their imaginations in this enchanted sand-garden of swings and slides and make-believe fortresses. Younger kids especially love the carousel, a nineteenth-century Greek temple where storybook horses, cats, pigs, and other beasts prance to the music of a stirring band organ. Fittingly, adults are not allowed on the playground unless accompanied by children.

The oldest and most stately building in the park is the **Conservatory of Flowers**, imported from Europe and assembled in 1878. A jungle of orchids, ferns, water lilies, tropical flowers, and even some sporadic birds thrive in the humid atmosphere. A small entrance fee is charged. The gardens around the Conservatory are particularly lush. Paths lead through thickets of oak, blooming flowers, and a primeval glade of giant ferns. The nearby John McLaren Rhododendron Dell is enchanting in bloom. A small statue of Uncle John himself—a man who hated statues—poses in front, as if picking a pine cone from a tree.

Most visitors to Golden Gate Park congregate in the area around the **Music Concourse**, at the heart of the park's busy eastern half. The Concourse was site of the California Midwinter Fair of 1894, a grand affair despite McLaren's teethgrinding. Bands play free on summer Sundays in the ornate band shell known as the Spreckels Music Temple.

Fronting the Concourse on the south is San Francisco's oldest science museum, the **California Academy of Sciences**. With natural displays of African and North American animals, an aquarium and planetarium, and tens of thousands of reptiles, mounted plants, insects, minerals, and fossils all under one roof, the Academy has long been the Bay Area's most popular science museum. A wonderful store stocks science and natural history books, art, and thoughtful games that attract parents and children alike.

Leopards, lions, monkeys, antelope, a large gorilla, and other animals stare from landscaped dioramas in the **African Hall**. Sit near the zebras and giraffes at an African watering hole through a simulated cycle of day and night, surrounded by the sounds of unseen insects, birds, and roaring lions.

The spectacular **Wild California Hall** centers on a huge diorama of Farallon Island cliffs, complete with churning surf, screeching gulls and enormous sea elephants. Other displays of California flora and fauna feature grizzly bears, condors, oak woodlands, salt marshes, and dioramas of kelp and seawater magnified 50 times to show plankton, shrimp, beetles, and flies the size of your Uncle Herman's hunting dog.

In **Steinhart Aquarium**, 14,000 fish, crabs, turtles, dolphins, penguins, sea horses, eels, an octopus, and other specimens swim in lushly appointed tanks.

To best sense the Japanese Tea Garden's subtle spell, avoid the crowds. (Kerrick James)

Docents at the tide pool tank invite you to touch the starfish, sea urchins, anemones, and other animals. Walking up the spiral ramp to the **Fish Roundabout**, you will be completely surrounded by a doughnut-shaped tank filled with shoals of sharks, bass, snapper, rays, and yellowtail. **The Swamp**, an alligator pit bordered by the snake and lizard terrariums, always attracts a lot of attention. **Life Through Time** traces the history of evolution with models of prehistoric animals roaming through ancient habitats.

The galleries of earth and space sciences display model dinosaur skeletons, a piece of moon rock, a large revolving globe, a scale for measuring comparative weights on the earth and its moon, and the hypnotic **Foucault Pendulum**, which slowly marks the earth's rotation. The most dynamic display is the **earthquake platform**, which demonstrates how earthquakes of differing magnitudes feel, working up to the big one of 1906.

The star projector of **Morrison Planetarium**, which was built in Germany before the Second World War, ranks as one of the most well-crafted instruments of its kind. If you have never been to a planetarium, you will be impressed by the realism of the Morrison's night skies, glowing with stars of differing magnitudes and hues. Even if you are already familiar with planetarium shows, the high technical quality of the Morrison, with its regular program changes, makes repeat visits always interesting. Sometimes the Planetarium is commandeered by the **Laserium**, a computerized krypton-gas laser synchronized to music, and played across the planetarium's ceiling. Music and patterns are always different, but the organizers preserve a choice between classical and modern. (Planetarium and Laserium tickets are purchased separately from the tickets at the main entrance.)

The **M. H. de Young Memorial Museum** and the Asian Art Museum share a building across the concourse from the Academy of Sciences. The museums' forecourt contains the sculptor Earl Cummings' *Pool of Enchantment*—a young Indian boy piping to a pair of mountain lions.

The de Young offers a broad survey of American and British art, with a smattering of Mediterranean, Oceanic, African, and pre-Columbian American artifacts. Special galleries highlight Western landscapes, American furniture of the Federal Period, still life, sculpture, and British decorative arts. Among the American artists featured are George Caitland, Frederic Remington, Albert Bierstadt, Thomas Moran, Charles Russell, Thomas Eakins, Grant Wood, John Singleton Copley, Benjamin West, James Whistler, Rembrandt Peale, John Singer Sargent, and silversmith Paul Revere.

The **Asian Art Museum** houses the largest gathering of Asian art outside of Asia, a collection so vast (and a display area so small) that only 10 per cent of it can be shown at one time. (Plans are afoot to move the museum to a larger new location, at the old Main Library building in Civic Center.)

The arts of China and Korea occupy the ground floor, dazzling the eye against the lush, emerald backdrop of the Japanese Tea Garden. The collection draws from over 5,000 ceramic and lacquer articles, scrolls, sculptures, and other objects dating from as far back as the Zhou and Shang dynasties (1400–1000 B.C.). Among the rarer items are scores of exquisitely translucent white ceramics, and other pieces of fluorescent blues and greens; the oldest known Chinese sculpture of Buddha inscribed with a date (equivalent to A.D. 338); Tang Dynasty (A.D. 618–907) earthenware animals; and a seventeenth-century bowl and pedestal decorated with dangling rings that was carved for a Qing Emperor from a single piece of white jade. The rest of the jade collection, ranging over 30 centuries, is no less astounding.

Upstairs, collections from Japan, India, Nepal, Burma, Kampuchea, and other countries include Khmer stone carvings, Indian gods and goddesses, a sixteenth-century suit of samurai armor, *netsuke* (small, carved pieces of wood and ivory), and an amazingly petite nineteenth-century wooden palanquin from Japan, decorated with red and black lacquer and gold leaf.

A single fee provides entry to both the Asian Art and de Young museums. Docent tours of special galleries run regularly through the day. A small but bursting shop sells art books, cards, and prints. Cafe de Young offers light refreshments, sandwiches, and hot meals either indoors or in the Oakes Garden, surrounded by camellias and classical statuary.

The **Japanese Tea Garden** has been one of San Francisco's most enduring attractions since the 1894 Midwinter Fair. When the fair ended, the park commission hired a full-time gardener, Makota Hagiwara, to tend the gardens and operate the tea concession. The Japanese Tea Garden flourished under the Hagiwara family's care until politicians, goaded by anti-Japanese sentiments, forced their removal at the turn of the century. McLaren, who valued good gardening more than bad politics, asked them back, and the family kept the garden until they were interned during World War II. A plaque honoring the Hagiwara family stands by the main gate.

The garden's carefully tended paths and shrubbery, ornamental gates and lanterns, and pools swarming with gold and black carp are delightful, provided you can visit early on a weekday morning, or on a rainy day. During weekends, the garden can be almost too crowded to appreciate, with tourists clamoring to be photographed on the famous steep-arched bridge, or in front of *Amazarashi-no-hotoke-Buddha*, alias the *Buddha who Sits through Sun and Rain without Shelter*. Cast in Japan in 1790, he is probably the largest bronze ever exported from Asia. The cherry trees bloom in April, a special sight.

A small souvenir shop and a pavilion serving green tea and cookies stand in the garden. San Francisco's most famous culinary invention originated here in 1909—the fortune cookie. Although Makota Hagiwara was the first to make them, the fortune cookie was popularized by Chinatown restaurants as a *Chinese* "tradition." In fact, you do not find fortune cookies at all in China.

A very special English garden grows across the Concourse, beside the Academy of Sciences. The **Shakespeare Garden** contains only flowers and plants mentioned in Shakespeare's works. In case you forget your lines, the relevant ones are cast in bronze on the garden wall. A rare bust of the Bard himself is kept in a box under lock and key, a copy of a cast made in 1814 from a stone bust in Stratford-Upon-Avon, which was itself hewn by Gerard Johnson upon Shakespeare's death. Being only thrice removed from the actual face of Shakespeare, it is thus reputed to be one of the most realistic likenesses. If you want to see it, ask first at McLaren Lodge.

Golden Gate Park's most concentrated collection of rare and exotic plants grows in **Strybing Arboretum and Botanical Gardens.** In addition to representative species and gardens from Australia, New Zealand, Africa, Asia, and the Americas, several gardens maintain special themes, including the New World Cloud Forest, and the succulent, dwarf, Biblical, and California gardens. Medical and culinary herbs grow in the Garden of Fragrance, designed for the blind to appreciate through touch and smell. Plants are labeled in Braille. The Asian Garden, built around the simple Moon-Viewing Pavilion, is lovely and quiet even when the Japanese Tea Garden is overrun with tourists. Nearby, a small stream winds through a grove of stately California redwood trees. Look for the rare Dawn Redwood from China, the only species of redwood that grows outside of California and southern Oregon. You can buy wildflower seeds, cards, and books on nature and horticulture at a small store near the main entrance, or peruse some of the 12,000 volumes on plants at the Helen Crocker Russell Library, housed in the adjacent County Fair Building. (The San Francisco County Fair is really a flower show.) Encircling 428-foot-high Strawberry Hill, **Stow Lake** is the park's largest lake, and a favorite for rowers, who rent their boats at the northwest corner of the lake. A circumnavigation of Strawberry Hill Island takes in its two bridges, Huntington Falls, and the Chinese pavilion. A gift from the city of Taipei, the pavilion was shipped in 6,000 pieces and assembled on the island. **Prayer Book Cross**, a copy of a Celtic cross from the British isle of Iona, stands on a hill above Rainbow Falls, a McLaren-made creek inspired by a California mountain stream. The creek flows into **Lloyd Lake**, in which is reflected San Francisco's sentimental monument to the 1906 earthquake—**Portals of the Past**. The portals were all that was left standing of a Nob Hill mansion after the fires were quelled.

The western half of Golden Gate Park is far quieter than the busy eastern half. Here, during the week, a stroller on Speedway, Marx, or Lindley meadows, or along the Chain of Lakes, meets few passers-by. Holding down the westernmost corners of the park are two windmills from Holland, installed at the turn of the century to irrigate the park. It has been said that the southern one, the Murphy Windmill, is the largest of its kind in the world, though it is in want of renovation. The northern **Dutch Windmill** has been restored. The Queen Wilhelmina Tulip Garden blooms in spring at its foot.

■ THE INNER SUNSET

Something about Golden Gate Park makes a person hungry. Of course, you can eat in the museums or pack a picnic, but two commercial districts are also handy to the park's eastern end. Everyone has heard of Haight Street, of course, but the other little neighborhood just beyond the **Ninth Avenue gate** is a local secret.

Most people think of the Sunset District as boring—a nice place to live, but you wouldn't want to visit there. Some of Golden Gate Park's magic seems to have rubbed off on its northeastern corner, however, where Irving and Judah cross Ninth Avenue. Just a 10-minute walk from the Music Concourse, this homey little neighborhood offers several excellent restaurants, cafes, and shops. Come for a hearty breakfast, pop in for lunch, or browse through the bookstores till late at night. If you're heading back downtown, the N-Judah MUNI streetcar runs right through the neighborhood. But what's the rush? Just outside the Ninth Avenue entrance stands the Little Shamrock Pub, established in 1893, when the Sunset was a giant sandflat. Have a pint of Guinness and check out the historic photographs.

On the thickly wooded slopes of Mt. Sutro, the gargantuan University of California (UCSF) Medical Center sets the serious mood of Parnassus Avenue. One of the last cobbled streets in the city, **Edgewood Avenue** climbs up UCSF's eastern boundary, ending in a eucalyptus forest. Walkers can reach it via **Farnsworth steps**, enjoying a grand view over the Richmond District and the red, steep roofs of Haight Street. Walking east on Parnassus, you'll soon hit Stanyan Street and, two blocks later, Cole Street, both fair and friendly prospects of thriving restaurants and little shops which serve the charming neighborhood of **Cole Valley.** Turning left onto either will guide you into the district known to San Franciscans as **the Haight,** and to everyone else as Haight-Ashbury.

■ HAIGHT-ASHBURY

Like North Beach, Nob Hill, and the Barbary Coast, Haight-Ashbury is a name that transcends mere geographical designation. A mishmash of images comes to mind when one hears it: pop Zen, black-light posters, incense, flowers, purple velvet, buckskin, proffered joints, tambourines, Victoriana, long hair, psychedelia, acid rock, free love, peace signs, cosmic harmony, and bongos in the park. No one can ever forget Haight-Ashbury in the '60s, even those who never saw it. The 1967 Summer of Love lasted a scant three months, but it defined the city for the generation who came of age at that time, and it still generates its own pervasive mythology. Some 200,000 young people came to San Francisco that year, drawn by an enchanting vision of freedom and social harmony.

Haight-Ashbury started life as a solid family neighborhood along Haight Street, a commercial center for the new Golden Gate Park. Large, rambling, wooden houses sprouted on its cross streets, named for city supervisors Stanyan, Cole, Clayton, Shrader, and Ashbury. The wide, green **Panhandle**, designed as a carriage entry to Golden Gate Park, was lined by Victorian rows of Queen Anne towers and gables that lent a kind of Parisian grandeur to a city otherwise choked by dense housing. After the streetcar tunnel under Buena Vista Park was completed in 1928, however, middle-class citizenry started departing for the suburbs in the Sunset, and the bypassed Haight-Ashbury began its long, slow decline in fortune. By the early 1960s, it was a run-down district of cheap rents in subdivided Victorians. Still, the almost exotic beauty of its architecture and grand planning remained.

Bohemian heir to North Beach of the fifties was Haight Street of the 1960s and '70s.

Almost completely surrounded by parks, and haunted throughout by decaying stateliness, Haight-Ashbury seemed a lyrical, almost magical setting to the generations raised in insulated suburbs and small towns. Seeking to shed the restraints of Establishment, they came to indulge their senses through communal living, drugs, music, free love, and outright fantasy, to *live* their protest against materialism, the war in Vietnam, racial strife, social inequality, and parental control. The *San Francisco Examiner* called them "hippies." Decked out in scruffy clothes and long hair, they were not, of course, an exclusively San Franciscan phenomenon, but "Hashbury" (as it was called in the press) became their most celebrated mecca. The music industry spread the gospel. Local rock groups like Jefferson Airplane and the Grateful Dead played free around the Haight and Golden Gate Park, and scores of other stars were made in the nearby Fillmore West and Winterland auditoriums by rock impresario Bill Graham. Psychedelic concert posters from the Haight appeared on bedroom walls across the country, and across the Atlantic. Songs like Eric Burdon's "San Francisco Nights" inspired many to come and experience the "street called Love" for themselves. (And taking a cue from the Scott MacKenzie ode, many really *did* wear flowers in their hair.)

By autumn, the Summer of Love was already changing. Tourist buses and media exposure soured the novelty. Thousands of curious wannabe flower children swelled the Haight population, straining the resources, easy prey for streetwise manipulators. Drugs and pushers took their toll. The war in Vietnam blazed on, intruding on the celebration of life. Many true believers left the district for communes and small towns. The Haight lurched toward decrepitude and violence.

Like much of Victorian San Francisco, the Haight today has once again gentrified. It's hardly surprising. Few neighborhoods harbor such beautiful houses, and none can match its bosky parkland "backyard." Many of the pre-'60s businesses—like the bike rental outlets—are prospering. New bars and restaurants along Haight cater to a politically aware *and* financially secure clientele—a contradiction of terms in the old Hashbury. The head shops have closed, but you can still have your mind expanded at places like Pipe Dreams, where water pipes and Grateful Dead paraphernalia are sold. The scores of street people who congregate on the edge of Golden Gate Park, at the head of Haight, are not a community of quaint, aging hippies.

Six blocks down Haight from Golden Gate Park, a forest of twisting, matted trees rises abruptly, like some fantastically overgrown Tuscan hillside. When seen from below, or from a distance, **Buena Vista Park** presents one of the wildest, most enchanting aspects of San Francisco. Climbing up the steep paths into the park is less exalting, except for the views, if you can find the holes through the trees. From the middle of the hill, where the pitched roofs of Ashbury Heights tumble down toward the Panhandle, look north across the marble-white city and the parks' green rectangles, beyond the church towers of St. Ignatius to the bridge-spiked headlands of the Golden Gate, as exotic as Istanbul, more beautiful than Paris. You can almost understand how such an enchanting place might inspire tangerine dreams of a New Jerusalem.

■ ASHBURY HEIGHTS

Now you are climbing into real hill country, where winding streets finally start to shake the standard San Francisco grid. Submerged under an aging but respectable neighborhood, the little peak of **Mt. Olympus** still nurtures a curious pedestal, where Sutro once erected a statue of the goddess of liberty, the *Triumph of Light*. Sadly, the lady was vandalized and carted off years ago, and even the views are blocked by buildings.

Like Mt. Olympus, **Corona Heights** is a purely local curiosity, an ugly red hill gouged out by brick-making operations in the last century. Excellent views from the Heights bore straight down Market Street, and south to Eureka Valley. Avoid the cliffs on the eastern edge. Below the peak on Museum Way is a nifty little museum for city kids to learn how Mother Nature runs her show. The **Josephine Randall Junior Museum** keeps a menagerie of snakes, owls, raccoons, lambs, goats, and other animals for youngsters to touch and care for. Summer classes and simple displays make science fun for kids.

Leaving Ashbury Heights by the back door, you can descend toward Market Street and the Mission District via **Vulcan Stairs**, one of the more exotic city walks. Departing from Levant Street, Vulcan enters another country, where quiet, almost *rural* houses peer out from behind small gardens of dangling fuchsias, stalks, pines, roses, daisies, succulents, and fennel. In summer, plump blackberries and plums hang ripe for the picking—I mean by the residents, of course. The views fall dramatically from craggy Corona Heights down to Eureka Valley, where rainbow-striped "Freedom" flags festoon the Victorians with an air of fantasy; and indeed, it is something of a brave new world.

THE UNDISCOVERED HALF

SAN FRANCISCO'S SOUTHERN HALF is left pretty much to those who live there. Every day, to be sure, a few tourist buses can be found parked in front of Mission Dolores or inching around the heights of Twin Peaks. But of these, how many of their passengers stop to smell the *flores* along thriving 24th Street, or sidle down the secluded stairways that hang from the city's highest slopes? Almost none.

The tourist industry's neglect of the southern neighborhoods is, for better or worse, a situation that will probably reverse itself in time. It just so happens that the gentrification of San Francisco's "quaint" neighborhoods started at Telegraph Hill, working its way across the city by slow degrees. The Upper Fillmore, South of Market, Western Addition, and Haight-Ashbury, each in their turn, have braced against the tide of higher rents and wealthier tenants that followed their "discovery," washing up a flotsam of boutiques and restaurants, and a reputation among the trendy as a fashionable "new" neighborhood.

For now, fortunately, most of San Francisco's southern half simply does not

Sunbathing at Mission Dolores Park: a beach towel with a view. (Kerrick James)

The Mission District's 16th Street is a hotspot of cafes, restaurants, and nightclubs. (Kerrick James)

appeal to the sight- and action-oriented tourist. The southern half contains the city's most desolate post-industrial zones, its largest stretches of residential poverty, and its greatest concentration of neighborhoods just bland enough to discourage exploration. But it's also true that you will find a lot of what has already been celebrated in the northern half, mercifully unprettified by three decades of rampant tourism. For the traveler who appreciates vibrant cultures and cuisines, enchanting cityscapes, neighborly folks, and a good cup of coffee in a cultivated setting, the southern half deserves to be discovered.

■ THE MISSION DISTRICT

The most *naturally* hospitable spot in San Francisco is the Mission District. Like the Spanish clerics who followed them, the local Ohlone tribe (they called themselves the Ramaytush) chose this broad, sheltered valley to build their largest settlement. The mercantile Americans shifted the focus of settlement to the harbor at Yerba Buena Cove, now the Financial District, leaving the Mission Valley largely undeveloped until the 1860s. The district became one of San Francisco's first suburbs. By the early part of this century, a preponderance of Irish immigrants in this neighborhood even gave it a distinctive accent, called "Mish," which was said to sound something like Brooklynese. The greater portion of the Mission District was spared destruction in the 1906 fire, and today retains some of San Francisco's finest examples of Victorian architecture.

Ironically, the predominant ethnic flavor of the Mission today is once again Hispanic. Since the 1960s, increased immigration from Mexico, Central America, and South America has made this San Francisco's largest Latin American neighborhood. Spanish alternates freely with English in the shops and on the streets. About half the residents are Hispanic; of these, roughly half trace their roots to Mexico and the rest to other Latin countries, including El Salvador, Panama, Nicaragua, Colombia, Peru, and Guatemala.

The Mission District is San Francisco's most visually colorful district—culturally vibrant, yet down at the heel. Twin Peaks blocks the Pacific fogs, making it the brightest and warmest neighborhood in the city. Its low rooflines and wide streets seem to catch the sun. Crowds of people fill the streets in a way that never happens in the Sunset or Marina: shy country folk, fast-talking businessmen, panhandlers, dancers, artists, mothers with babies, muscle-bound teenagers, aging revolutionaries, the walking wounded. Market fruits and vegetables, pounding music, and deep, rich aromas of cooking food spill out onto sidewalks. Higher up, brilliant murals ignite the walls in monumental tribute to families, community, work, the harvest, political strife, and dreamier, fanciful themes. You can tour these colorful murals, a major Mexican art form, by picking up a free walker's map from the Mexican Museum at Fort Mason.

The largest public festival of the Mission District is Cinco de Mayo—the Fifth of May, which celebrates the victory of Mexican troops under command of General Zaragoza over the French invasion forces of Napoleon III, in 1862. Highlight of the festivities is a parade through the Mission. It is followed in late May by Carnaval, a good excuse to dress up in exotic costumes and parade through the streets. Another colorful festival, the Day of the Dead, culminates on November 2 with a nighttime candlelight parade of skeletal celebrants. It might be called a Latino version of Halloween, but more macabre, though with a streak of graveyard humor, and religious roots intact. Local bakeries and crafts shops prepare for the festival days beforehand with eerie (or gaudily devotional) altars, skull candies, and bone-shaped breads called *calaveras*.

The Pan-American character of the Mission is enshrined in its restaurants. Mexican sets the tone, but you can also find authentic Argentine, Nicaraguan,

Brazilian, Cuban, Puerto Rican, Salvadoran, Peruvian, and other Latin American kitchens, many of them intimate, hearty, and cheap neighborhood establishments where expatriates gather to eat and socialize.

The Mission around 16th and Valencia is the likeliest candidate for San Francisco's reigning bohemian district, a perfect example of how alternative intellectual strains prosper best amidst cheap eats and rents, *not* quaintness. Bohemia isn't tidy; but that doesn't mean it can't comfortably entertain its guests with good coffee and company, and evening poetry readings. On any given evening, patrons of neighborhood bars, bookstores, and coffeehouses will likely enjoy (or revile, as the case may be) the company of off-duty dancers, writers, and artists, as well as on-duty pool hustlers, chess players, and poets. If you like the scene, then eat and drink today, for tomorrow the yuppies will drive it down beyond 24th Street.

Mission Dolores stands at the corner of 16th and Dolores streets, as it has since before the streets existed. Built in 1791, it's the oldest standing building in San Francisco. It was the sixth mission to be founded in California, on orders from Father Serra, whom California honors with a statue in Washington's Hall of Fame (the other statue being Thomas Starr King). Father Serra was beatified by the Catholic Church in September 1988, and may yet become California's first Roman Catholic saint—though he remains controversial as the symbol of Native California's demise.

Visitors are charged a small fee to enter the walled mission compound to see the church, a small museum, gift shop, and the beautiful graveyard. The walls were built of brick made from sun-dried mud and manure, called adobe. Though not the strongest material, Mission Dolores survived the 1906 earthquake, while the American-era basilica next door crumbled. On rare hot days, Mission Dolores exudes a musty coolness. Its beautiful painted ceilings are based on original Ohlone designs done with vegetable dyes. The bells, altars, and statues were carried from Mexico by mule.

The peaceful, overgrown cemetery, watched over by a brooding statue of Father Serra, has many a tale to tell. (One of them is not, as fans of Hitchcock's *Vertigo* might wish, the whereabouts of Kim Novak's double.) A number of mostly Hispanic, Italian, and Irish pioneers are buried here and in the church, including William Leidesdorff, the Noé Family, Don Luis Antonio Arguello, first Mexican governor of California, and San Francisco's first mayor, Don Francisco de Haro. It was said that de Haro died of lingering heartbreak after Kit Carson, while in the

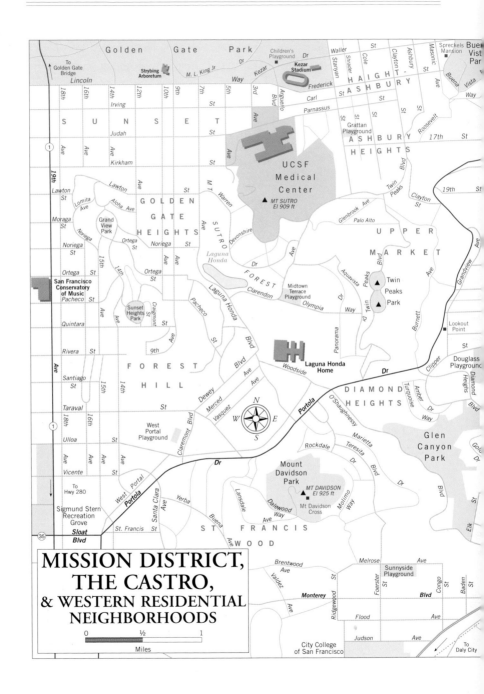

MISSION DISTRICT,
THE CASTRO,
& WESTERN RESIDENTIAL
NEIGHBORHOODS

0   ½   1

Miles

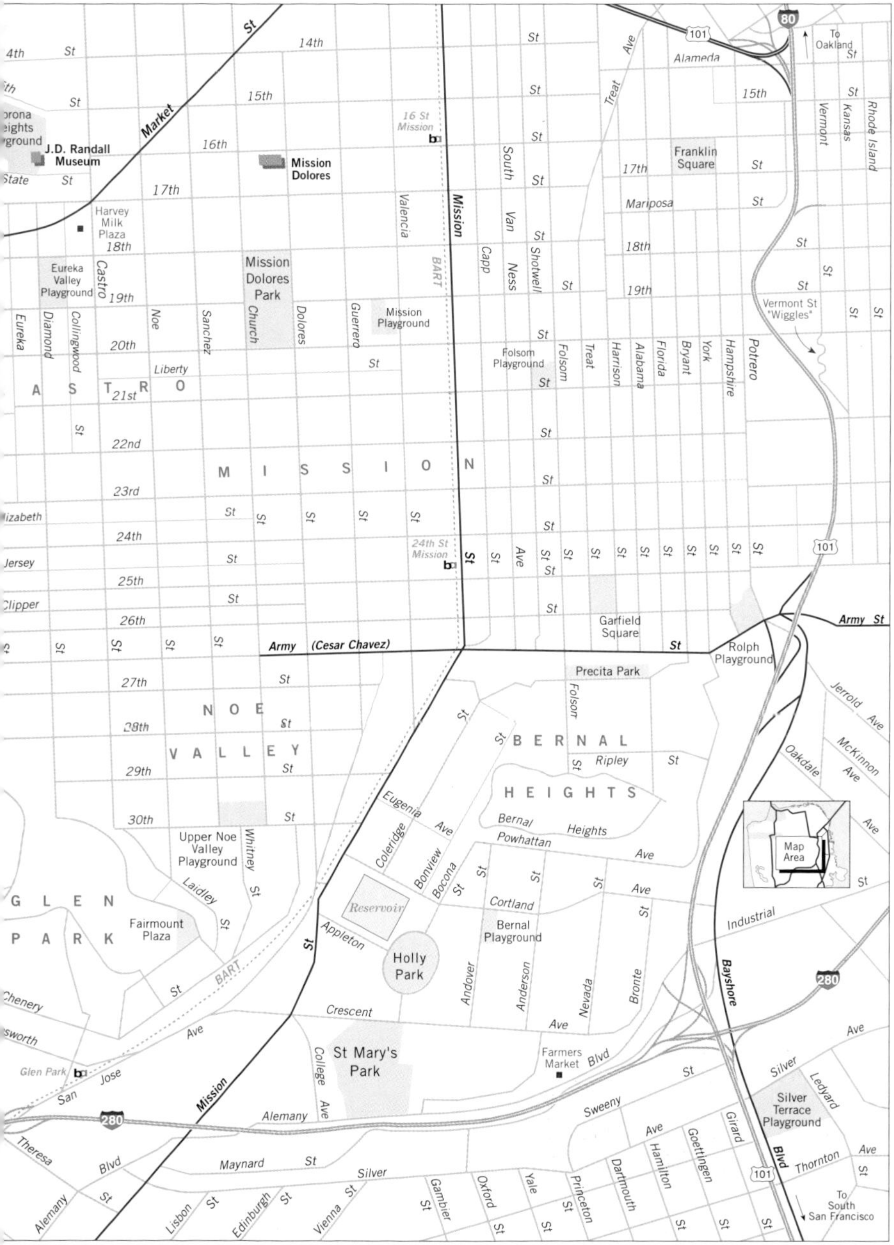
Market St
14th
15th
16th
17th
18th
19th
20th
21st
22nd
23rd
24th
25th
26th
27th
28th
29th
30th
J.D. Randall Museum
Mission Dolores
Harvey Milk Plaza
Eureka Valley Playground
Castro
Mission Dolores Park
Church
Dolores
Guerrero
Valencia
Mission
BART
16 St Mission
24th St Mission
Mission Playground
South Van Ness
Capp
Shotwell
Folsom
Folsom Playground
Treat
Harrison
Alabama
Florida
Bryant
York
Hampshire
Potrero
Treat Ave
Alameda
Franklin Square
17th
Mariposa
Vermont
Kansas
Rhode Island
Vermont St "Wiggles"
To Oakland
80
101
Eureka
Diamond
Collingwood
Noe
Sanchez
Liberty
CASTRO
MISSION
NOE VALLEY
Army (Cesar Chavez) St
Army St
Garfield Square
Rolph Playground
Precita Park
BERNAL HEIGHTS
Ripley
Bernal Heights
Powhattan Ave
Jerrold Ave
McKinnon Ave
Oakdale Ave
Map Area
Industrial
Eugenia Ave
Coleridge
Bonview
Bocona
Cortland
Bernal Playground
Reservoir
Appleton
Holly Park
Andover
Anderson
Nevada
Bronte
Bayshore
280
Upper Noe Valley Playground
Whitney
Laidley
GLEN PARK
Fairmount Plaza
Chenery
Crescent
St Mary's Park
College Ave
Farmers Market
Glen Park
San Jose Ave
Alemany
Sweeny
Silver Ave
Ledyard
Silver Terrace Playground
Girard
Goettingen
Hamilton
Dartmouth
Princeton
Yale
Oxford
Gambier
Thornton Ave
Theresa
Alemany Blvd
Maynard St
Lisbon
Edinburgh
Vienna
To South San Francisco
Elizabeth
Jersey
Clipper
State

service of Captain John C. Frémont, shot his twin sons during a poor excuse for a revolutionary skirmish.

Another poignant story is buried with Charles Cora, who was hanged by vigilantes in 1856. His wife of one day, Arabella, lies at his side. The couple were married at the prompting of the priest who had come to deliver last rites before Cora's execution. Arabella had played an unintentional part in Cora's downfall. As Cora's mistress, she was snubbed one evening at the opera by U.S. Marshal William Richardson. Cora and the lawman exchanged words over the incident, which escalated to a fight, during which the gambler shot the marshal dead. By all accounts, including the one accepted by the jury, Marshal Richardson was the aggressor and the homicide justified. The vigilantes did not accept the jury's verdict, however, and the fruits of their justice lie here for all to see. Aside from Cora, two other victims of vigilante justice, James Casey and James "Yankee" Sullivan, are also buried here.

The most tragic tale of Our Lady of Sorrows is also the one least known. In this quiet churchyard, about 5,000 Ohlone men, women, and children are buried in unmarked graves; the large rock grotto in the middle of the cemetery is their memorial. Most died of measles in the early 1800s. In 1850, when California's first U.S. Indian agent came here to take a census, he found only one Native American left, a man named Pedro Alcantara, who spoke of his love for a missing son, and said that he was the last of his tribe.

Lively, low-rent Mission Street is the district's main thoroughfare, but the stretch of **24th Street** between Mission and Potrero has a more neighborly Latin ambiance. Restaurants and piñata-hung family grocery stores cater to the local community. This is the place to go for such Latino specialties as *nopales* (cactus leaves), fresh and dried chilies, *paletas* (frozen fruit-juice bars), Mexican cheeses, tropical American fruits (including a wide variety of bananas and plantains), and ready-made burritos, tamales, tacos, and pies. If your nose leads you to the corner of Alabama and 24th, stop in for cake, cookies, *churros* (twisted, fried-dough snacks), or pastries at La Victoria, a wonderful Mexican bakery. The **Galeria de la Raza**, on the corner of Bryant, exhibits the works of Hispanic artists, and is a good place to find the often bizarre altars for the Day of the Dead.

The southern edge of Mission Valley is marked by the rise of **Bernal Heights**. It is, in fact, one of the homelier hills of the city—but homely doesn't mean we don't love it, for its character is endearingly San Franciscan. One story says that Bernal Heights was settled by a clever ruse in 1876, when developers triggered a miniature gold rush (and raised land prices) by lacing the summit with gold. Bernal Heights has an almost rural feel in places. Take Franconia Street, for instance, as it rambles around the side of the hill, angling in and out in ways that genteel city streets are taught not to do, and even going so far as to turn to gravel around the middle. Plunked down on the heights are big, fiercely independent, hillbilly houses that sit askew, with land around them. Some were built after the earthquake of 1906 with timbers salvaged from wreckage. Long considered a bit of a bumpkin, Bernal Heights has been able to preserve its comfortable and affordable lifestyle up to now. But alas, in the San Francisco scheme of things, yesterday's rustic neighborhood is today's quaint victim of gentrification—and tomorrow's exclusive district. Residents of Bernal Heights are worrying that the secret may be out.

■ THE CASTRO

The slope of Twin Peaks rises abruptly to the west of Mission Valley. In the best San Franciscan tradition, its hillside streets below Market were built on a right-angle grid, so that they appear on a map to be as flat as Mission Street. Don't be fooled—Noe Valley and the Castro are two of the hilliest neighborhoods in the city. This natural barrier to easy public access has kept them remote from major transport arteries, and therefore quiet, stable, middle class, and Victorian in appearance, though not in character. Still, Noe Valley and the Castro District are very different from one another.

The Castro, known better to old-timers as Eureka Valley, is the city's largest gay neighborhood. Its standing in the Gay Rights Movement is of international scope, for in no other major city do gay men openly comprise such a large percentage of the population, enjoying such social freedom and political clout. The exact population of gay men and women in San Francisco is wildly disputed (and impossible to count), but 100,000 is a commonly quoted figure that *seems* reasonable.

The neighborhood's main commercial crossroads is the corner of **Castro and Market streets**. Harvey Milk Plaza, the southwest corner, is named for San Francisco's first openly gay supervisor, who was assassinated with Mayor George Moscone by a disgruntled ex-supervisor, Dan White, on November 28, 1978. When White was convicted the following May of an incredibly lesser offense (voluntary manslaughter by reason of "diminished capacity"), thousands of protesters besieged Civic Center in riotous anger. Every June, the annual Gay Freedom Day

Halloween in the Castro is an all-day costume party. (Kerrick James)

parade marches from City Hall, scene of the murders, to Main Street, downtown.

The Castro has a strong sense of community. All goods and services necessary for a happy and fulfilling urban life are locally available, so that it can be a world unto itself for those who wish it. Bars, greeting-card shops, restaurants, cafes, furniture stores, hair salons, delis, bookstores, and scores of other shops cater to a predominantly gay clientele. The **Castro Theater**, a vintage movie palace with an Arabian nights interior and a Wurlitzer on a hydraulic lift, shows classic films. The neighborhood hosts a "Pink Saturday" party the day before the Freedom Parade, as well as a street fair in August. While the Castro no longer officially hosts its legendary Halloween party, shopkeepers and customers alike dress in costume on October 31.

The Castro is a beautifully maintained neighborhood, stylish in that a good deal of money and effort go toward cultivating a distinctive ambiance. Along Castro, Victorian parody vies with avant-garde, and fine taste clashes with the outrageous. Shop signs pun cleverly. Patrons stroll in and out of hip boutiques and crowded cafes. Beyond the commercial district, pitched-roof Victorians leapfrog up the hillsides, brilliantly decorated and wrapped in well-tended gardens. Even the cats lounging in the sunny windows seem placed there by design.

■ NOE VALLEY

If you climb up Castro Street to the ridge above, a long, steep haul, you will crest the hill near 22nd Street before dropping into Noe Valley. This dividing ridge between Noe and Eureka valleys—where 21st, Hill, and Liberty cross Collingwood,

Castro, Noe, and Sanchez—is one of the prettiest residential enclaves in the City. Quiet, attractive streets and stairs lead to views that tourists seldom see.

Noe Valley is the Switzerland of San Francisco, Hilly, clean, prosperous, and stable, it cherishes its lofty seclusion high above the teeming flatlands. Overhead, the barren summits of Twin Peaks, with their bone-chilling winds, will put you in mind of the Alps—on a foggy day, of course, and better yet, with a nip or two of brandy. Even the steep-pitched Victorian rooftops seem to be eternally awaiting snow, which never comes. Its residents are loyal to their community. They do not maintain a standing army, but they do have a neighborhood library on Jersey Street, where lectures, films, seminars, local art shows, and publications keep everyone abreast of community affairs. A free neighborhood newspaper, the *Noe Valley Voice*, is published in a wooden church built in 1888 at 1021 Sanchez. At night the church becomes Noe Valley Ministry, an intimate venue for offbeat but consistently high-quality folk, world, and jazz concerts.

Noe Valley's stretch of **24th Street** contains all the conveniences of big city life with the scale and character of a small town's Main Street. The heavy concentration of cafes and breakfast spots along here rate high from people with time on their hands and change in their pockets. A very fine mystery bookstore stands on the

Cafe Flore (known locally as Cafe Hairdo) is a Castro institution. (Kerrick James)

corner of Diamond and 24th. The neighborhood boasts several good restaurants, clothing boutiques, toy stores, and even an old-fashioned grocery or two, where you may find the proprietor sitting at the counter watching the ball game on TV.

■ TWIN PEAKS

As you climb toward Upper Market and Diamond Heights, the City spreads out like a child's counterpane, with toy houses stacked in the tucks and ridges, their roofs of black, gray, red, blue, and green. Romantics say that San Francisco has seven hills. Nit-pickers, in fact, have counted a total of 43. The most famous ones—Russian, Nob, and Telegraph—are midgets compared to the range of hills that rise in the geographic center of the city. Of these, Twin Peaks, Mount Sutro, and Mount Davidson all top 900 feet.

When Daniel Burnham required a View of Views from which to make his master plan for San Francisco, he retreated for two years to the top of **Twin Peaks**. Burnham and his plan have long blown town, but Twin Peaks and its view are still there, more magnificent than ever—the night expanse of lights was never so magnificent in Burnham's day. Twin Peaks Boulevard encircles both peaks near their summits, with parking.

Wooded Mount Sutro is the platform for San Francisco's tallest structure, a much-hated (because very obtrusive) radio antenna called Sutro Tower. Red-striped and gigantic, it's visible from all over the Bay Area.

Mount Davidson is the highest hill in the city. Thick woods obstruct the views afforded from naked Twin Peaks. Paths from the surrounding neighborhood wind to the top, where a huge cross stands, visible from miles around. At 103 feet (31 m) tall, it just might be the largest cross in the New World. Every Easter, thousands of people gather here for sunrise services. The cross also attracts its share of detractors, who demand that it be dismantled because it stands on public land in violation of the constitutional separation of church and state. Legalistically, they may have a case; let's just hope nobody tells them where the City and County of San Francisco gets its name.

Between Mount Davidson and Twin Peaks, a wilder aspect of pre-Yankee San Francisco still survives in **Glen Canyon Park**. Once part of a Spanish cattle ranch, the rugged canyon is now a day camp and playground for local kids.

The neighborhoods on the slopes of these peaks are newer than most in the flatlands, and their streets were built to follow the contours of the hill, not a surveyor's grids. Were it not for their spectacular views, many of these neighborhoods would be rather plain. Some of the terraces are linked by stairways. Partly overgrown Pemberton stairway is the best in the Upper Market area. Wooded Mount Sutro supports Oakhurst Lane, the longest, highest stairway in the city, as well as the Ashwood, Blairwood, and Glenhaven stairs. One of the least-known stairway walks is Harry Street, a ramshackle affair that clambers between Beacon and Laidley streets, on Glen Park's eastern edge, with a bird's-eye view of Noe Valley. San Francisco's most elegant stairway sweeps up from near Dewey Boulevard into sheltered Forest Hills, an affluent enclave on the western slopes of Twin Peaks. Adah Bakalinsky's *Stairway Walks in San Francisco* is an excellent guide for searching out these and other hidden steps.

In a city of outstanding views, some shock even natives, mainly because they have not been snapped to death by photographers. **Sunset Heights** is one example. Fantastically situated on high, steep, exposed hills west of Mount Sutro, the area offers surprise views around almost every corner, with steep stairways connecting different levels. Looking west, the cross-hatched Richmond and Sunset districts resemble an unfolded map, on which you can pick out Seal Rocks, the Farallon Islands, Golden Gate Park, Point Reyes, and other landmarks. Climb the stairway to the lofty knob of **Grand View Park** for the best views.

■ WEST PORTAL

Saint Francis Wood is yet another of San Francisco's moneyed neighborhoods. Frederick Law Olmsted, who designed New York's Central Park, helped John Galen Howard lay out these urbane streets, with their fountains and gateways, in 1912.

West Portal, next door, is its main shopping street. West Portal refers to the western entrance of the 2.25-mile streetcar tunnel under Twin Peaks. The tunnel opened in 1917. Until the Market Street section was put underground in the 1970s, the tunnel's eastern portal was on Market Street at Castro. Nowadays, when you ride the K-Ingleside, L-Taraval, or M-Ocean View streetcars from downtown, your first glimpse of sunlight is at West Portal.

There is something vaguely romantic about West Portal. Imagine sitting in a restaurant overlooking the street at dusk, perhaps with streaks of rain on the window, watching the streetcars come and go. Commuters returning from downtown rush off to do their grocery shopping, while others scurry aboard for the ride back—perhaps for an evening at the theater. All the hallmarks of San Francisco chic are here, the tidy shops and ethnic restaurants. Despite its cosmopolitan airs, West Portal most resembles some nondescript Central European streetcar suburb. It's a great place for a romantic rendezvous, not least because it provides an expedient getaway should that prove necessary.

■ THE SUNSET DISTRICT AND POINTS SOUTH

As mentioned earlier, the Inner Sunset where Ninth Avenue crosses Judah and Irving is by far the most interesting section of the district for outsiders. Otherwise, the Sunset is an overwhelmingly orderly, middle-class residential area sandwiched between the peaks and Ocean Beach. The summer fog here is relentless. San Franciscans from other neighborhoods occasionally find their way out to a Sunday concert in Stern Grove, a recital at the San Francisco Conservatory of Music (1201 Ortega), or a Chinese dinner on Taraval (which has been christened by some as *new* New Chinatown!). But on the whole, the Sunset keeps pretty much to itself.

Once upon a time in what is now **Stern Grove**, there was a roadhouse of ill repute called the Trocadero Inn. It achieved its greatest notoriety as the place where Abe Ruef, the corrupt political boss of Mayor Schmitz's regime, was captured after a gunfight with police. For better or for worse, the Troc has long since been rehabilitated.

The main gate of the **San Francisco Zoo** is on Sloat Boulevard, a stone's throw or two from Ocean Beach. Though not ranked as one of the best American zoos, some of the individual animal habitats themselves do rank quite highly. The gorillas' new home gives them room to roam, rocks and trees to climb, and a thick window through which they may safely observe the *homo sapiens* at close range. Silkworms, tarantulas, black widows, termites, beetles, crickets, scorpions, and other vermin dwell in the Insect Zoo, where you can also observe bees at work in a living hive, without getting stung. The Children's Zoo lets kids feed and touch barnyard animals. In the Kresge Nocturnal Gallery, visitors can study a bush baby, slow loris, and other nocturnal animals in their natural settings. The Phoebe Hearst Discovery Hall uses computers to stimulate questions and answers about primates. Other zoo attractions are Wolf Woods, Koala Crossing, the Lion House, the Gorilla Habitat, Musk Ox Meadow, and a host of rhinos, elephants, hippos, tigers, giraffes, zebras, bears, penguins, and other birds and beasts. A roaring good show is feeding time in the Lion House, daily at 2 P.M., except Monday. The zoo operates guided tours, snack bars, a gift shop, a popular playground, and a magnificent carousel, built in 1921 by William Dentzel.

The last of the exposed sand wastes that once overspread the Richmond and Sunset districts survives at **Fort Funston**. Now part of the GGNRA, this old military property on San Francisco's southernmost coast was once used for trial beachhead landings by the army. The barren, windy cliffs are popular for hang gliding.

Lake Merced is another natural area that has miraculously survived the city's expansion. Now protected as a park, San Francisco's largest lake provides a natural habitat for wildlife, as well as recreation for fishermen, boaters, joggers, golfers, and birdwatchers. Bring your own (non-motorized) boat, or rent one from the Boat House on Harding Road.

San Francisco State University's modern campus stands on the eastern shore of Lake Merced. One of the most academically acclaimed schools in the state university system, the school is home to the Sutro Library (480 Winston Drive), inherited from the Sutro estate, and one of the West's earliest and largest collections of books. Another intellectual property of note on campus is the American Poetry Archives, the world's largest videotaped collection of poets reading their works or being interviewed. The archive is open to the public in room 117 of the Humanities Building.

Beyond the University is the suburban neighborhood of **Ingleside**. Ingleside's greatest claim to fame is that it has the world's second-largest sundial—or is it the third? Sundial worshippers can make the pilgrimage to Entrada Court to genuflect before the 26-foot-high device.

■ THE BORDER NEIGHBORHOODS

The residential districts along San Francisco's southern border—Hunters Point, Visitacion Valley, Bayview, Ocean View and the Outer Mission—are *terra incognita* to most San Franciscans who do not live there. That's not to say that they aren't interesting, so long as you realize that they are working class or poor residential neighborhoods that do not cater to tourism.

The Excelsior and Crocker-Amazon neighborhoods, lumped together with the **Outer Mission**, are down-home cosmopolitan places. The residents trace their roots in roughly equal numbers to Asia, Africa, Europe, and the Americas. Unlike the prosperous, international Richmond District, the Excelsior is the poor-man's

Until the new stadium in China Basin is completed, the Giants and the 49ers play at the "Stick"—Candlestick Park in Hunters Point. (Kerrick James)

polyglot, vibrant in a colloquial, unflamboyant way. Sure, it needs a little "softening up" before it's ready to entertain visitors. In the meantime, local residents take it for granted and enjoy the lower rents.

Sandwiched between the Excelsior and Visitacion Valley, **McLaren Park** preserves a large hill from development. Most of the park has been left alone as natural, uncultivated grassland. The views are unique. Look south across Visitacion Valley to Mount San Bruno; the hulking Cow Palace, an all-purpose auditorium, dominates the valley from the Daly City side of the city line. Look north, and the towers of San Francisco rise like an Emerald City behind the grid of the Bayview District, tossed over its hills like a checkered quilt.

Bayview-Hunters Point has strong name recognition among San Franciscans, almost none of it favorable. Outsiders don't come here much, except en route to Candlestick Park to see the Giants or 49ers play, or to the Cow Palace for rodeos and stock shows. During World War II, Hunters Point was the largest shipyard on the West Coast, attracting large numbers of out-of-state workers, who settled in makeshift housing beyond the docks. Hunters Point became, and remains, the largest predominantly African-American district in the city. Since the war, the largest predominantly African-American district in the city. Since the war, the speed and quality of urban renewal has not been universally inspiring, though many of Bayview's hills and old houses, punctuated by wooden church steeples, retain distinctively San Franciscan qualities admired by visitors to other districts. Unfortunately, Bayview-Hunters Point is ravaged by high unemployment, drugs, and violence. Parts are heavily industrialized, and many residential neighborhoods are extremely depressed. Many artists have retreated to studios at the old navy base on Hunters Point. Once a year, the Open Studio program offers a peek to the general public.

■ POTRERO HILL

Long a quiet backwater in the midst of the city, Potrero Hill is one of the latest districts to feel the winds of gentrification. So far, the southern half of the hill, closest to Hunters Point, remains in the lee, but the northern half is very much a community like Noe Valley, with a quiet, pleasant shopping street along 20th.

Colorful murals adorn many a wall in the Mission District.

Views to the west over the Mission, and north toward downtown, are inspiring. Vermont Street from McKinley Square squiggles down the hill like a miniature Lombard, but without the tourists. Potrero Hill even has its own library (on 20th), newspaper, (*The Potrero View*), playhouse (Theater Artaud), and brewery (Anchor Steam).

Anchor Steam Brewery, at 1705 Mariposa Street, ranks as a San Francisco original. Unlike all other lagers, steam beer is made without ice—a rare commodity in San Francisco at the brewery's founding in 1851, when Gold Rush thirsts could not be quenched by imported stock. The founding family had to devise a cooling method that used air instead of ice. As the idea caught on, other steam-beer breweries started up, but all disappeared with the advent of refrigeration, except for Anchor Steam (which actually adopted its present name a half-century after its founding—in 1896). The modern plant now brews three ales, two lagers, and a delicious wheat beer by their special methods. They also partake of the old brewers' custom of making a special Christmas vintage ale (it's actually a barley wine). Beloved by San Franciscans, Anchor Steam has a devoted following. Beer fanciers who want a taste of the Gold Rush should seek it out, and tours are a special treat.

Eastern Potrero Hill drops down to the docks, a working mixture of old brick warehouses and modern cranes. If you like the smell of the docks, the sight of ocean-going vessels, and the sounds of a solid Miles Davis tune, go to the Ramp, an outdoor jazz bar on the southern end of China Basin Road. On sunny weekend afternoons, patrons crowd the deck's tables to imbibe huge margaritas and take in the view across Central Basin to huge ships draining their bilge at the docks.

■ THE BAY BRIDGE

Bay Area residents love their bridges. The span across the Golden Gate inspires a virtual cult following, who garland it with all manner of glorious praise. Fans of the **San Francisco-Oakland Bay Bridge** don't have much truck for that kind of hogwash. And why should they?

The Bay Bridge is a big old hairy-chested roustabout span that does the work of two Golden Gate bridges. Five lanes wide, two decks deep, it joins causeway, truss, cantilever, tunnel, and double suspension spans to make the largest high-level steel bridge on Earth. About 2.25 billion vehicles crossed it during its first half-century of work. Today, the rate is about 250,000 *daily*. When it was completed in 1936, there was none bigger. How big? In length, about 8.25 miles, of which 4.25 miles are over water. The tunnel bored through Yerba Buena Island was the world's widest when built. The massive center anchorage, which anchors the ends of the two suspension spans in the middle of the bay, alone is bigger than the Great Pyramid at Giza and deeper than any other pier in the world. The bridge was designed by Charles Purcell, who called it a tribute to the intelligence of the American workingman. When you consider that the Bay Bridge and the Golden Gate Bridge were built *simultaneously*, who can fail to marvel at the vigor and confidence of the San Franciscans of yore!

The earthquake of 1989 severed the bridge where the cantilever section and the Oakland approach ramp join, knocking out 50-foot sections of both decks. Fortunately, neither section dropped into the water, but the crossing was closed for one month of repairs. While engineers rejoined the sections, road crews completely resurfaced the decks, a job that normally takes two years to do.

The Bay Bridge is not open to pedestrians. Drivers can exit the bridge midway at **Yerba Buena Island** to hunt for the classic view of the suspension span marching into San Francisco. Another stupendous view is from adjacent **Treasure Island**. When completed in 1937, it was the largest man-made island in the world. It was originally intended as the site of San Francisco's first airport, but only Pan Am's *China Clipper* flights to Asia and the Pacific ever flew from here. Instead, the city gave Treasure Island to the U.S. Navy in exchange for the site of the present airport. And now the Navy is giving it back, and the city is wondering what to do with it.

In the meantime, visit the **Treasure Island Museum** on the Navy Base after signing in at the front gate. Dedicated to the Navy, Marine Corps, Coast Guard, the museum occupies the *China Clipper* terminal building. On permanent exhibit are mementos of the Golden Gate International Exposition, a world's fair held here in 1939 and 1940 to celebrate completion of the bridges. Uniforms, weapons, nautical instruments, paintings, murals, a lighthouse lens, and other treasures help illustrate the history of the maritime services. You can buy pictures of naval ships from a large selection at the counter. The museum is open daily, and it won't cost you one red cent.

THE EAST BAY

WHEN SLIPPING OFF FOR A DAY IN THE COUNTRY, San Franciscans prefer to head north to glamorous Marin, or south to the coastline of San Mateo. The East Bay hills are considered little more than a backdrop for dazzling city views. But to the original San Franciscans, the Ohlone Indians, the ranges to the east were far more than just another pretty vista; they were the origins of life itself. In bygone ages when the rest of the world was drowned in sea water, so they believed, the highest peak, Mount Diablo, was an island, home of Coyote, creator of mankind. For thousands of years, the Ohlones drew life from the ranges, an existence beautifully described by Malcolm Margolin in *The Ohlone Way*. In annual journeys to the interior valleys and slopes, they gathered acorns, seeds, and wild game from the bursting, natural storehouses of native oak and riparian woodlands. Hailed as the year's happiest season, these cyclical migrations moved from the bay to favorite camps, past rocks and glens and woods revered by the Ohlone, perhaps as we might cherish a Taj Mahal or Westminster Abbey.

The eighteenth century, however, abruptly ended this way of life. The Spanish arrived at San Francisco Bay, overawing the Ohlone with European technology and confining them on harsh mission farms, where they died by the thousands of European diseases. Those who escaped were hunted down and punished. Within one generation, their villages, their ancient traditions, and most of their people had been extinguished. The hills, oaks, and sacred places may live on, but no one can ever know them as intimately as the Ohlone once did.

The East Bay comprises Alameda and Contra Costa counties. Oakland and Berkeley are the most obvious destinations for travelers, but scores of other less well-known towns and suburbs have some very exciting things to see, depending on the traveler's special interests. Among these are John Muir's house in Martinez, playwright Eugene O'Neill's house, and the wilder reaches of the East Bay parklands.

■ DOWNTOWN OAKLAND

The eastern end of the Bay Bridge drops down to Oakland, passing docks and train yards, and merges into one of the biggest, busiest freeway interchanges in the country.

The Bay Bridge is the region's busiest bridge, carrying over 250,00 commuters between the East Bay and San Francisco every day. (Kerrick James)

For old-time San Franciscans, Oakland was the perfect butt of many a joke. Herb Caen once pointed out that when you cross the Bay Bridge into San Francisco, you have to pay a dollar toll; but to go to Oakland doesn't cost a plugged nickel. And of course, there is that famous, oft-quoted line by Gertrude Stein about Oakland, where she lived as a child: "There is no there there."

It's a pity that Oakland must be forever stigmatized by a noted writer's second most quoted line (the first being, of course, her immortal "A rose is a rose is a rose"). As Don Herron points out in his *Literary World of San Francisco*, however, if you put the quote in context, it doesn't seem so barbed. What Stein actually wrote was "what was the use of my having come from Oakland it was not natural to have come from there yes write about it if I like or anything if I like but not there, there is no there there." Heavy stuff, but down-to-earth Oaklanders prefer one of Hemingway's least famous quotes: "A stone is a stone is a *stein.*"

Oakland has many problems—drug problems, high crime rates, ghettos, and poverty. But it's also true that very few of Oakland's finer qualities ever find their way into print. Oakland's museum is one of the best in the West. The regional parks in the Oakland Hills are splendid. Oakland's skyline, from the shores of Lake Merritt, is postcard pretty. The downtown district is busy, friendly, and readily accessible from BART. Cafe society and the arts are flourishing. Oakland's port, manufacturing base, railways, BART service, professional sports facilities, *and* weather are superior to San Francisco's. Potential for tourism is growing apace, and most of the sights that appeal to tourists are close to BART stations.

Visitors can easily make a full day of exploring downtown Oakland. You can walk around Lake Merritt, taking in Chinatown, the public markets, Victorian Row, the Oakland Museum, a few good bookstores, coffee, and shopping, and still have time for dinner at Jack London Square.

The focus of Oakland's Civic Center ought to be City Hall, at the three-street intersection of Broadway, 14th Street, and San Pablo Avenue. It is upstaged, however, by the **John B. Williams Plaza**, a lively forum of fountains and Victorian inspired modern architecture, leading straight to the striking new Federal Building. Across Broadway, bustling DeLauer Newsstand (1310 Broadway), an institution reeking of cigars and imported newspapers, keeps its finger on the pulse of the world, 24 hours a day.

Four blocks up Broadway, the 1931-vintage **Paramount Theater** (2025 Broadway) was built in the best tradition of the great movie palaces of Hollywood's heyday. Restored to its original beauty, the Paramount is one of the supreme examples of art-deco design in the country. It is now hosts live theater as well as classic films, but you can tour the building only for a look at the historic interior on the first and third Saturdays of every month.

Down Broadway in the other direction, at 10th Street, you will find the most splendid and evocative of Oakland's old-time districts. **Victorian Row**, also known as Old Oakland, comprises two square blocks of solid wood and brick buildings built between the 1860s and 1880s to serve passengers at the western terminus of the transcontinental railway. Among the tenants of the neighborhood are the Pacific Coast Brewing Company pub—a friendly night spot—and the historic Washington Hotel. Every Friday from 8:30 A.M. to 1:30 P.M., the **Outdoor Market** spills over the cross streets of Ninth and Washington, marshalling a bazaar of fresh produce and other delicacies. Meanwhile, the **Housewives Market** is thriving one kitty-corner block farther, on the corner of Clay and Ninth. The Housewives is a United Nations of markets, where butchers, bakers, and cooks with traditions hailing from around the world meet to mingle and sell their foods, cooked, preserved, and fresh: Portuguese sausages, Filipino fish heads, Korean pickled cabbage, Asian pig snouts, Mexican tamales, Middle Eastern breads, dried goods from Asia, French and English cheeses, down-home barbecued ribs, and ever so much more. You can eat here, or shop for a different ethnic feast every meal for a week.

Another marvelous international grocer in the neighborhood is **Ratto's**, at 821 Washington. A new century has dawned since Ratto's was founded, bringing with it several wars, new waves of immigrants, and countless changes brought by new technology; but despite heavy damage in the 1989 earthquake, it's *still* 1897 in Ratto's. The old wooden floors and shelves stacked with sacks and bottles and racks of foods from around the globe exude an aroma that's one third salami and two-thirds indescribable. The list of stock is mind-boggling: Irish porridge, sundried tomatoes, Russian mustard, Brazilian soda pop, sushi rice, horehound candy, olive oils from six different countries, escargot, Hungarian peppers, Ethiopian *berbere*, hickory mist, Haitian vanilla, bonbons, curries, Chilean mushrooms, raspberry vinegar, hummus, Thai chiles, juniper berries, Indian chutneys, cooking chocolate, Australian ginger, Kenyan coffees, truffles, coconut, Turkish dried apricots, European garlic, Indonesian satay, Cajun sauces, goose fat from France, and scores of cheeses and pastas from Italy. To the side of the grocery section, Ratto's runs a cafeteria. Friday and Saturday nights bring Pasta Opera, when visiting virtuosos serenade guests with arias as they dine on pasta and vino.

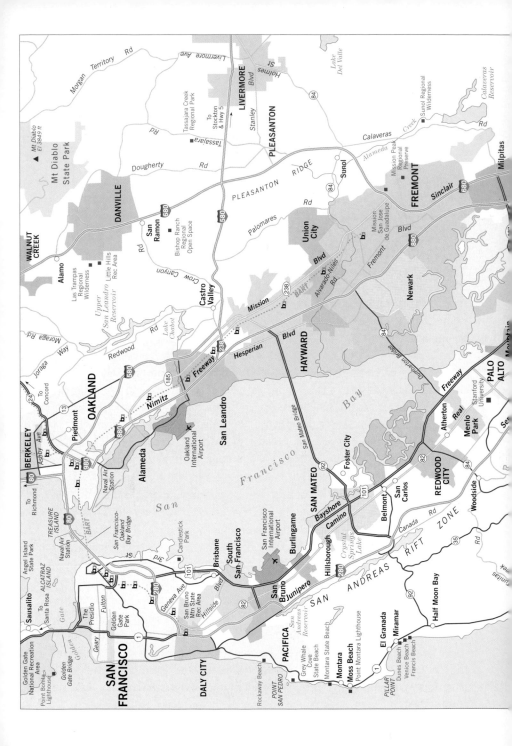

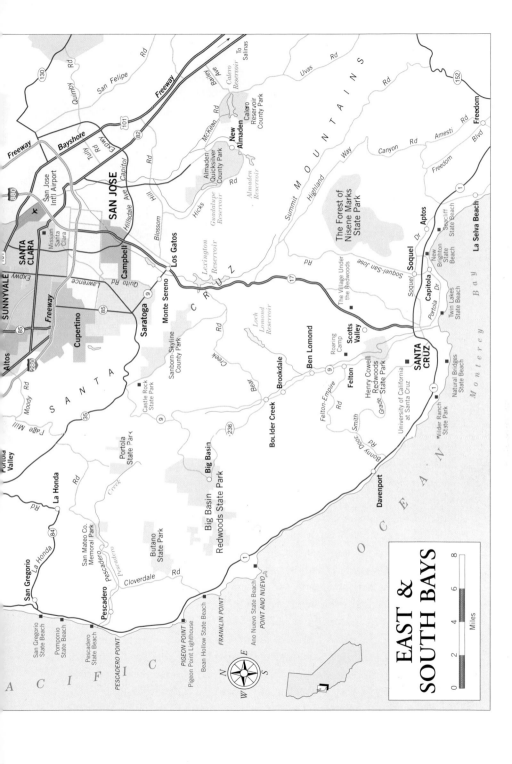

EAST & SOUTH BAYS

Miles

0   2   4   6   8

Even more restaurants and markets await across Broadway from Victorian Row in **Oakland Chinatown**. Founded in the 1870s, this neighborhood is today enjoying a renaissance sparked by immigration, investment, and new construction. Compared to San Francisco's Chinatown, Oakland's is more homey; it does not cater to tourists. Because so many residents are Koreans, Filipinos, Vietnamese, Cambodians, Laotians, Burmese, and Thais, many call the neighborhood Asiatown; still, most of these residents are *ethnic* Chinese.

The heart of Chinatown is the blocks bounded by Broadway, 8th, 11th, and Harrison, but a large concentration of Chinese Americans have settled all the way to Lake Merritt, and beyond. The Oakland Chinatown Chamber of Commerce publishes a handy brochure map listing the names and addresses of Chinatown businesses, which you can pick up at the Hyatt Regency on Broadway. But it's just as interesting to wander through the district without a map, skirting the crates of vegetables that spill onto the sidewalk, eyeing the produce and fish, dodging the deliverymen's dollies, sampling the dim sum or Vietnamese noodles.

■ THE OAKLAND ESTUARY

From Victorian Row and Chinatown, Broadway continues south under the Nimitz Freeway (Interstate 880) seven blocks more to Jack London Square, on the Oakland Estuary. A short detour one block east at Third Street runs into the **Oakland wholesale produce market**, at its most bustling in the morning hours, when the streets are jammed with trucks, loading and unloading. Though by no means a tourist "sight," there is something undeniably engrossing in the old wooden buildings, broad sidewalks roofed in corrugated metal, stacks of crated fruits and vegetables, and the commotion of people at work. Those who need an eye-opener, or just breakfast, should repair to the Oakland Grill.

The San Francisco ferry and Amtrak trains meet at **Jack London Square**, named for Oakland's most famous writer, who spent much of his stalwart youth on these docks. The splendid plaza, with stores, hotels, harborside restaurants, and late-closing bookstore, is a delightful place to spend an evening. The passing ships on the estuary and the yachts tied up at the waterfront make a pretty enough picture from window-side seats at the seafood restaurants. Looking up the channel, past Oakland's hard-working container harbor, you can glimpse the distant towers of San Francisco. The Port of Oakland offers personal tours of President Roosevelt's (FDR's) yacht, the *Potomac,* docked at the western end of the public waterfront.

Although born in San Francisco, Jack London was raised in Oakland, where he was coached in his reading at the Oakland Free Library by the librarian, Ina Coolbrith. Several of the houses where London lived still stand in Oakland (which you can find with the help of Don Herron's aforementioned guide), but it is the waterfront that he is most powerfully associated with. It was along here that he docked his boat, the *Razzle Dazzle*, which carried him on night raids of rivals' oyster beds. So adept was he at this dangerous game that he earned the title "Prince of the Oyster Pirates." It was here, also, that he drank in the bars and met many of the characters who would later appear in his novels.

One authentic London hangout still stands by the wharf, a saloon called **Heinold's First and Last Chance** (so called because the ferry to the "dry" city of Alameda docked nearby). London supposedly bought the *Razzle Dazzle* here when he was 16 years old. Still open for business, Heinold's is a curious shack half sunken below present street level. Nearby stands part of the cabin where London lived during the Klondike Gold Rush of 1897–98. Rediscovered in Yukon Territory in 1960, it was spirited back to its present site overlooking the Oakland Estuary.

The small Jack London Museum at **Jack London Village**, to the south of Heinold's, preserves the author's books and photographs, and sells his works. The rambling wooden walks and shops and restaurants of Jack London Village resemble San Francisco's Pier 39 without the crowds. Views from the restaurants over the estuary to Alameda's thickly sparred and masted waterfront are enchanting at night. The tiny Ebony Museum, on the floor above, displays a collection of African arts, including masks and carvings; it is a good place to buy African handicrafts.

■ LAKE MERRITT

Only a short stroll east from the heart of Chinatown, the Lake Merritt BART Station hides underneath Madison Park, between Eighth and Ninth streets. The **Oakland Museum of California**, devoted to California's art and history, both natural and human, is only one block north of the station. One of the West's most exciting museums, it rises in three meandering, landscaped terraces around a central garden court, handsome and intriguing.

In the Hall of California Ecology on Level One, you'll get a sense of the state's complex geography and biology by taking an imaginary cross-country walk from the Pacific eastwards across the state, visiting complex dioramas showing the life and terrain of the Coast Ranges, Central Valley, the Sierra Nevada and, finally, the high deserts of the Great Basin. The displays are packed with plants and animals illustrating the interdependency of species; so carefully displayed are many of the beasties that their natural camouflage continues to hide them, and visitors who study any given diorama on many different occasions will find something new every time. The aquatic dioramas are works of art, possibly the best examples of their kind to be seen anywhere.

The Cowell Hall of California History on Level Two maintains one of the largest and most eclectic collections of Californiana. Not only do you get a wonderful sense of the California myth—the images of Hollywood, Hell's Angels, oranges, and Mel's Drive-in—but you also glean a sense of how *real* people *really* lived, from prehistoric times to the present. It does this through an ingenious grouping of everyday objects, evoking a distinctive sense of our ancestors' times, and of our own.

The Art Gallery on Level Three focuses on painters and photographers with California connections, including Albert Bierstadt, Eadweard Muybridge, Dorothea Lange, and Imogen Cunningham. The museum is renowned for its early California paintings, especially its romantic oils of Yosemite and the Sierra, and the rivetingly detailed paintings of old San Francisco.

The Oakland Museum, the state's best for history, is strong on Californiana.

Galleries for temporary exhibits and the cafeteria round out the top floor. The museum store, a good place for books on California, is on Level One.

The chief architect of downtown Oakland's exquisite setting is **Lake Merritt**, a saltwater rendezvous of migrating birds, which became the first state game refuge in America in 1870. A few years ago, newspapers were reporting that the lake, connected by channel to the Oakland Estuary, had become a living refuge for thousands of foreign sea creatures, which had arrived here as unwitting passengers aboard oceangoing ships docking in Oakland's inner harbor. Whether any truth rests therein is debatable, but it's nice to speculate that some strange species of octopus dwells beneath those beautiful blue waters. Surrounded by a paved three-mile path for pedestrians and cyclists, Lake Merritt is a brilliant foil for the offices and apartments that ring its shore.

Lovely **Lakeside Park**, with its small aviary and science center, shades the northern shore under green woods and gardens. Youngsters love to visit **Children's Fairyland**, where they can play among scenes from nursery rhymes and stories. You can rent a boat from one of two boat houses (north and west sides), or take a ride on toy miniature paddle-wheel boats.

An Oakland version of "Rocky" works out on the shore of Lake Merritt.

Grand Avenue, sweeping across the edge of Lakeside Park and up toward the hills, is a pretty commercial district designed, in a more leisurely era, for strolling. Elegant lampposts, tidy lawns, warm-windowed restaurants, drugstores, soda fountains, and the Egypto-Art Deco **Grand Lake Theater** give the street the urbane, slightly formal feel of a Hollywood back lot set.

■ OTHER OAKLAND SIGHTS

The East Bay ranges, of which the Oakland and Berkeley hills form the vanguard, mark the eastern rampart of one of the most spectacular, diverse, and extensive urban greenbelts in the country. The East Bay Regional Park system preserves more than 63,000 acres spread through 46 parks, crossed and linked by a thousand miles of trails. The range of things to do here confounds the inveterate city dweller. You can hike, fish, watch birds, climb rocks, or practice archery. You can go sailing, picnicking, swimming, golfing, shooting, camping, biking, canoeing, or backpacking. You can tour a mine, ride a miniature steam train, study fossils, or watch a blacksmith pound a red-hot horseshoe into shape. And no matter what you do, you can still be back in San Francisco, refreshed in body and soul, in time for dinner.

The best thing about the parks is that they provide an escape from the harried pace of civilization. Their pungent, creaking forests of gum invite wanderers to leave the city far behind, to experience the simple insect hum of summer in the hills, the drone of bees, a blue jay's raucous cry, the rustle of a fox creeping through fat tule bulrushes, the splash of spring water pumped cold from the earth, the clang of a hiker's gate closing on empty fields. Such soothing airs and fancy scents, tranquility, and sensual rejuvenation would cost a pretty penny in the city; out in the East Bay parklands, it goes for nothing.

The stretches of trail through the forests of Oakland's **Redwood Regional Park** are perhaps the East Bay's most enchanting. Standing among these noble second-growth redwoods, it is hard to imagine the awesome monsters that lived here until only last century. They were logged for timber to build the cities below. At least one rotted stump, now marked by a ring of its second-growth offspring, hints of a vanished behemoth that may have been larger than any tree now known to mankind. Another famous giant of the last century, the Blossom Rock Tree, was so huge that ships entering the Golden Gate some 18 miles west used it as a navigation marker.

Green in winter, yellow in summer, the East Bay hills offer year-round hiking.

Joaquin Miller poses with Japanese poet Yone Noguchi at his home in the Oakland Hills
sometime in the late 1880s. (Oakland History Center, Oakland Public Library)

The **Skyline National Trail** passes through the heart of Redwood Regional Park en route between Wildcat Canyon north of Berkeley, and **Lake Chabot Regional Park**, at Oakland's southern border. Placidly set amongst steep hills studded with oak, gum, and bay trees, Lake Chabot is one of the Bay Area's best-stocked fishing reservoirs. Every pleasant morning brings out scores of anglers to its piers and rowboats in quest of elusive bass and trout, as well as less-elusive bluegill, catfish, and crappie. Chabot Park attracts crowds of campers, target shooters, and picnickers on weekends, but there's still plenty of space to lose yourself in.

> ## SUNSET OVER OAKLAND
>
> *The* brave young city by the Balboa seas
> Lies compassed about by the hosts of night—
> Lies humming, low, like a hive of bees;
> And the day lies dead. And its spirit's flight
> Is far to the west; while the golden bars
> That bound it are broken to a dust of stars.
> Come under my oaks, oh, drowsy dusk!
> The world and the dog; dear incense hour
> When Mother earth hath a smell of musk,
> And things of the spirit assert their power—
> When candles are set to burn in the west—
> Set head and foot to the day at rest.
>
> —Joaquin Miller, "Twilight at the Hights."

Closer to civilization is a site above Oakland's Montclair district first settled by the poet and outlandish character, Cincinnatus Hiner Miller, better known as Joaquin Miller. The poet's modest home and much more ambitiously planted property are now preserved by the city of Oakland as **Joaquin Miller Park**. In his day, Miller claimed to have been a farmer, miner, Indian fighter, and Pony Express rider, but in truth, it's hard to separate his real accomplishments from his own embellishments. What is known is that Miller fancied himself a great poet, and he was by every account a charmingly colorful character.

Miller showed up in San Francisco in the 1850s, presenting his poetry to Bret Harte, then editor of the *Overland Monthly*, who rejected it as doggerel. On Ina Coolbrith's advice, Miller then departed for England, where his eccentric manners, sombrero, and red shirt won him a following in fashionable society. His galloping verses were praised as primitive but genuinely spirited Americana; in short, they sold, and Miller became a celebrity.

When he returned to the Bay Area in the 1880s, he found the as-yet uncivilized San Franciscan magazines still disinclined to idolize humbuggery. Miller retired to

(following pages) Heading home on BART, East Bay commuters enjoy a sunset over San Francisco.

the more receptive wilds of the Oakland Hills, which he called **The Hights** [*sic*]. There, he built a house called The Abbey and started receiving his curious admirers. One of these was a Japanese poet, Yone Noguchi, who also took up residence. Miller was particularly fond of lady visitors, whom he would impress with a rain dance that he had learned from the Indians. (Noguchi worked the sprinkler atop the Abbey.) The Abbey still stands amidst the forests that Miller planted.

Three sites in eastern Oakland have very strong appeal to children, as well as adults. **Knowland State Park** contains a small but well-designed zoo with tigers, lions, elephants, monkeys, and other mammals and birds, as well as a children's petting zoo. An old-time favorite of old-time Oaklanders is the **Chabot Observatory**, where the Friday and Saturday night science shows attract a very small contingent of local astronomy fans for a first-rate planetarium show, a peek through the 20-inch telescope, and a chance to hobnob with the friendly astronomers. The **Western Aerospace Museum**, located in an old hanger at the North Field of the Oakland Airport, displays a fully functioning World War II Link instrument trainer, special exhibits sponsored by the Black Pilots Association, and several vintage planes, including a 1946 four-engine Flying Boat. Designed to take off and land in the water, the plane measures 90 feet from nose to tail, and was used for passenger flights to Australia, England, and South Africa. It was later owned by Howard Hughes, and had a starring role in *Raiders of the Lost Ark*.

For those who can't get enough espresso in San Francisco, Oakland has cultivated yet another marathon coffeehouse gauntlet along **College Avenue** in the **Rockridge** area. Actually, given Oakland's superior weather and the sidewalk tables along the street, many hedonists would argue that it is an improvement over anything San Francisco has to offer. Strung for some two miles between the California College of Arts and Crafts, on the corner of Broadway in Oakland, and the University of California in Berkeley, College Avenue attracts a slightly offbeat, mellow crowd, including many college students and yuppies. Besides coffee, College Avenue also nurtures bookstores, ethnic restaurants, a host of children's clothing stores and curious specialty shops, and more designer pizzas than you can eat in a lifetime. Parking is increasingly tough, so come by BART; College passes right under BART's Rockridge Station. If you do, you can't miss the Rockridge Market Hall on College and Keith: it houses an excellent bakery, a coffee and tea counter, a delicatessen stocked with fine cheeses and interesting salads, a butcher and fishmonger, a wine purveyor, and a spotless and colorful produce market.

Just before the Berkeley city line, Claremont Avenue angles off College toward the hills and the palatial **Claremont Resort and Spa**. Completed in 1915, it remains the most picturesque hotel in the Bay Area. An enchanting vision of wooden towers, chimneys and gables, the Claremont is so vast that you can easily see it with the naked eye from San Francisco. With a cavalier ambiance reminiscent of the carefree Roaring Twenties (the exterior more so than the remodeled interior), the Claremont seems happily lost in a world where tea is served on the tennis courts, and people still dress for dinner—not because of tradition, but for the fun of pretending that they are part of the tradition. Even the casually dressed drop by the Terrace Lounge for smashing views out over the lowlands and the Bay.

The **Judah L. Magnes Memorial Museum** occupies a four-story brick mansion at 2911 Russell Street, just over the Berkeley line. Lectures, film shows, the Blumenthal Library, a museum shop, and special exhibitions supplement a collection of historical artifacts pertaining to Jewish history, from classical times to contemporary. Among the items kept in this third-largest Jewish museum of the Western Hemisphere are paintings by Marc Chagall and Max Liebermann, antiquities from Jewish communities in India and Turkey, and ceremonial art treasures from Europe.

■ BERKELEY

Berkeley—you either love it or hate it. There is no middle ground, save perhaps a love-hate relationship.

Intellectually, Berkeley is the most exciting city in the West, jammed with scholars from around the world, new ideas and discoveries, Nobel laureates, books, classic cinemas, and seekers of revolution, social freedom, or just a soapbox. There's also a wealthy, liberal Berkeley, crusaders in quest of a gastronomic Holy Grail, a new breed of Medici whose generous patronage has fueled a renaissance of bakers, paper-makers, organic farmers, espresso-pourers, micro-brewers, and other inspired artisans.

But ask anyone from outside the Bay Area what Berkeley is famous for, and they will say crackpots, revolutions, and protests. That's hardly a fair assessment, especially nowadays, when Berkeley's student population is going through a decidedly conservative stage. But the colorful history of Berkeley in the 1960s and '70s, when it was a socialist town with its own foreign policy and a spectacular lunatic fringe, still lives on in the minds of Middle America—and in more than a few yet-lively characters and corners of the city.

When the **University of California at Berkeley** was founded in 1868, it was called the Athens of the Pacific. The campus grew to be one of the largest and most beautiful anywhere, with a faculty and alumni who have, quite literally, changed the way the world thinks. To list all its contributions to science and the humanities is a task too daunting for these pages, but probably the two most momentous events in the popular imagination were the development of nuclear science, and the protest movements of the 1960s.

You can reach the campus easily from the Berkeley BART station, on Shattuck Avenue, the city's main business district. Though downtown Berkeley has a life of its own, it is overshadowed by the nearby campus, which starts at University Gate, a two-block walk up toward the hills. Free campus maps are available at the visitor center in University Hall, at the corner of University Avenue and Oxford Street.

The Berkeley campus was planned along twin branches of Strawberry Creek by Frederick Law Olmsted. Although the hallmark Beaux-Arts buildings of John Galen Howard set the tone, a montage of architectural styles graces the campus,

Between students and street life, Berkeley is never dull.

from log cabin to high-tech. Glens and garden-like settings abound between the buildings. The eucalyptus trees to the right of the West Entrance at the end of University Avenue are reputed to be the tallest in the world. The forks of Strawberry Creek meet in the grove before being swallowed up under the pavements of downtown Berkeley.

The gargantuan **Valley Life Sciences Building,** a Hollywood Egyptian monstrosity distinguished by bas-reliefs of bison skulls, saber-tooth tiger heads, and Babylonian scientists, houses the university's enormous collections of plant and animal specimens. Foremost among them is the **Paleontology Museum,** which contains an enormous Tyrannosaurus skeleton, a Triceratops skull, a frozen mammoth carcass (not on public display) and other prehistoric specimens.

Doe Library is the central depository of books on campus, supplemented by several department libraries and the large Moffitt Undergraduate Library. The collected papers of Mark Twain are kept in the adjacent **Bancroft Library,** which maintains the university's rare book collection and a small museum of Californiana, including Gold Rush paintings and the brass plate supposedly left by Sir Francis Drake during his sixteenth-century visit to California. The consensus nowadays is that it's a fake.

Sather Tower, better known as **the Campanile** because of its likeness to the *campanile* (bell-tower) of Saint Mark's Cathedral in Venice, is Berkeley's most famous landmark. Visitors can ride the elevator 200 feet to the top for a superlative view of downtown Oakland, San Francisco, Marin County, and straight out the Golden Gate to the Farallon Islands. Though the tower strikes the hours automatically, a bell-ringer ascends to play the carillon three times a weekday during semester. You can hear it all over campus, and though it is interesting to watch the carillonneur at work, you'll have to cover your ears or suffer being (one hopes only temporarily) deafened. There is a small charge to ascend.

Though modest in size and aspect, Le Conte Hall has burned a trajectory across the history of science for its role as Berkeley's venerable physics department. Berkeley's reputation as a leader in physics was already established before Ernest Lawrence won the Nobel Prize in 1939 for inventing the cyclotron, which he built on the hill above campus. Experiments in the cyclotron by Glenn Seaborg and other scientists resulted in the discovery of plutonium in 1941. Berkeley scientists went on to explore new frontiers of nuclear physics, building the bevatron, and discovering 13 synthetic elements (including berkelium and californium), the antiproton and antineutron, and carbon 14 (one of the keys to understanding radiocarbon dating and photosynthesis). The most notorious offspring of this brave new world, however, came in 1941 when, realizing that war was imminent, the U.S. government approached Lawrence with a secret project. A team of scientists, including Edward Teller (who later helped develop the hydrogen bomb), met under the direction of J. Robert Oppenheimer in Le Conte Hall, where they roughed out the first plans for a new type of bomb. The project soon moved to New Mexico for development and testing, and the results fell on Hiroshima and Nagasaki in 1945.

One of the most handsome buildings on campus is Hearst Mining Building, built in 1907 and entered through an impressive rotunda. Its mineral displays and pictures of western mining operations give the place an atmosphere of old-time California before it was flooded with quiche-eaters. A nice touch is the mine tunnel in the hill beside the building, no doubt used for engineering demonstrations.

The **Phoebe Apperson Hearst Museum of Anthropology** occupies a ground-floor corner of Kroeber Hall. Exhibits change regularly, but the permanent collection features thousands of artifacts of Native American, European, Asian, African, and Pacific cultures, including the weapons and tools made by Ishi, the last California Indian to come into contact with whites. Ishi walked into Oroville, California, from his mountain home in 1911. Anthropologist A. L. Kroeber invited Ishi to live at the Museum of Anthropology in San Francisco, now the site of the U.C. Medical Center, where Ishi taught him firsthand about the Yana language, handicrafts, music, and customs.

Wurster Hall, the College of Environmental Design across the courtyard, is a splendid example of where the Brutalist movement in architecture gets its name.

The 8,500-seat Greek Theater above the main campus on Gayley Road was designed after the theater at Epidaurus, Greece. California Memorial Stadium is the Berkeley venue of the fiercely contested annual Big Game between the Berkeley and Stanford football teams. On the knoll beyond, the building that resembles a Scottish castle is Bowles Hall, a fraternity.

Foreign and American students share the residence hall called International House, or I-House, on Piedmont at the top of Bancroft Way. Its friendly little cafe is open to the public. Frat Row extends south on Piedmont.

The **University Art Museum** at 2626 Bancroft Way is a concrete sculpture of open galleries dovetailing into a central hall. The museum has works from Asian and Western artists, a sculpture gallery, and cafeteria. The **Pacific Film Archive**, with a door around the corner on Durant, screens celluloid obscurities and classics nightly, and provides screening rooms for film researchers. The museum charges a small admission fee.

The liveliest part of the university is **Sproul Plaza**, just outside **Sather Gate**. Activists and leafleteers are thick on the ground here, a Berkeley tradition since 1964. That was the year that students challenged university regulations controlling public speech on campus. The Free Speech Movement gained momentum, culminating in a sit-in at Sproul Hall and the largest mass arrest in California's history. The movement spread throughout the country and to campuses around the world. Throughout the Vietnam War, Sproul Plaza was a forum for anti-war protests, some of which were met with tear gas and the National Guard. Ludwick's Fountain, near the Student Union, honors Ludwick Von Schwaranburg, a dog whose passion for cleanliness led to a life-long habit of bathing here daily, which clearly impressed both students and regents.

Sproul Plaza feeds into **Telegraph Avenue** on the south side of campus, where the streams of humanity flow with almost Gangetic fecundity. Here, undergraduates rub karmas with anarchists, musicians, crafts-sellers, prophets, lunatics, booksellers, revolutionaries, artists, missionaries, runaways, pushers, professors, and assorted riffraff. For big-city people accustomed to running a gauntlet of street people, Telegraph Avenue holds no terrors. For more timid souls, it is a chance to turn one's thoughts to the woof and warp of the human condition. Nirvana of book lovers, the south side packs in more booksellers per acre than any other corner of the Bay Area—and probably the country, west of the Appalachians. Among the book emporia on Bancroft, University Press Books stocks publications of university presses from around the world, while the tiny Map Center sells travel and wilderness handbooks from the back of an alley. Three blocks up Telegraph, beyond Haste Street, Berkeley opens up its big guns. Cody's not only sells books; it fosters literacy with coffee and regular readings by local and visiting authors. Moe's is reputed to be the largest used book store in the Bay Area. Shambhala deals in metaphysics, Eastern religions, and Asian medicine. Shakespeare and Company anchors down the corner across the street. At least five more major booksellers and buyers flesh out the neighborhood, and business is always booming during term. And if book-hunting makes you a bit peckish, or if you want a cozy place to read

Sather Gate (top) and an Egyptian motif from Berkeley's Life Sciences Building.

your latest purchases, you'll be happy to know that coffeehouses thrive in this neighborhood.

Berkeley's most infamous symbol of radicalism is **People's Park**, which sits a half block up from Telegraph, on a rectangle of land bounded by Haste, Bowditch, and Dwight. Although owned by the university, the land was seized for a park in 1969 by a coalition of hippies, activists, and radical students. Attempts by the university to retake the land sparked rioting, in which one man was killed, another blinded, and scores injured by county sheriff buckshot. The property has sat in limbo ever since, and though it is a vibrant symbol to radicals and conservatives, in reality today it is almost anti-climactically park-like.

The **Botanical Gardens** are both reached by ascending Centennial Road, above the stadium. You *can* walk, but it's so long and steep that you're better off driving or riding the shuttle from Mining Circle, in front of Hearst Mining Building. The gardens shelter more than 7,500 species from around the world, arranged in thematic gardens linked by paths. Californian, Asian, African, European, South American, and other sections are used for scientific research, but are also beautiful just for walking. A small botanical bookstore and information center stands at the gate.

Further up Centennial Road, the **Lawrence Hall of Science**, like the Exploratorium in San Francisco, inspires people, especially children, with the wonder and excitement of science. Using holograms, computers, lasers, telescopes, a planetarium, laboratories, and other resources, visitors can reach an understanding of such difficult concepts as evolution, prehistoric human migration, atomic theory, random selection, biological engineering, and the history of science, while having fun. Traveling exhibits and science fairs are set up regularly, including the ever-popular displays of enormous (though not quite life-size) mechanical dinosaurs, called Dynomation. A magnificent array of books, experiments, and scientific toys is sold in the lobby store. The Hall of Science charges a moderate admission fee, and is open daily. By night, incidentally, the view of the city lights from the parking lot is astounding.

At the top of Centennial sprawls **Tilden Regional Park**. It has something for everyone. The local model railroad club has set up a miniature steam train yard there, where weekend engineers are happy to take small passengers on a chug around the park. Everyone is always welcome on the granddaddy of the tiny locomotives, The Little Train. For youngsters, there are pony rides, a children's farm, and a vintage merry-go-round with a jaunty honky-tonk music box. Tilden also has an enchanting botanical garden, specializing in California landscapes. Swimmers can escape the summer's heat at Lake Anza. Best of all, Tilden is a great place to hook into the huge trail system of the East Bay hills.

North Berkeley is famous for its food. Upper Shattuck Avenue, between Virginia and Rose, has been christened in the press as **Gourmet Ghetto**, a reputation initiated by Alice Waters at Chez Panisse, celebrated as an innovator of what is now known as California cuisine. Scores of other kitchens dedicated to creative French-inspired cookery—or to unreconstructed ethnic cuisines—have sprung up along Solano and University avenues, upper Shattuck, the up-and-coming Fourth Street (at the foot of University), and the aforementioned College Avenue, turning them into the reigning restaurant rows of the East Bay. Many of the retail shops on these streets, likewise, deal in the unusual and the exquisite.

The neighboring town of Emeryville has also made its mark on the East Bay culinary scene. Amble over to one of the upstart eateries on Hollis and Doyle streets near Powell for Watersesque cooking. Many of the chic cafes here are done up in steel and concrete to match the neighboring warehouses. At the **Emeryville Public Market,** prepared foods from a patchwork of cultures make this lively, easygoing venue perfect for a casual lunch or dinner.

■ SOUTHERN ALAMEDA COUNTY

Most San Franciscans think it nothing but a sprawling bedroom community, but southern Alameda County's link with Bay Area history is fascinating and tangible. A car will be handy to reach these far-flung sites.

The Ohlones lived for centuries in what is now **Coyote Hills Regional Park,** west of Fremont. The hills themselves are peculiar, rising abruptly from the surrounding marshes and mud flats of San Francisco Bay. Mounds of these Indian's castoff shells and debris are now being excavated by archaeologists, who have resurrected some of the village ways in park seminars open to the public. Kids of all ages enjoy learning how to make acorn mush, chip obsidian arrowheads, weave cord and netting, build tule boats, and kindle fires by the ancient Ohlone methods.

Yankee-era history is preserved at nearby **Ardenwood Historical Farm.** The fields and barnyards are still worked as they were between the 1870s and 1920s. The land is plowed by horse-power and the crop harvested in the neighborly fashion of the threshing bee, where all comers can lend a hand. Kids can get a feel for bygone country life by learning how to milk a cow or crank-wring the laundry, and by watching the blacksmith, farrier, and quilters at work. On special occasions, you can even taste Victorian recipes, or play Victorian games on the mansion house lawn.

After founding Mission Dolores in San Francisco, the Spanish set out to develop the more fertile and heavily populated regions of what is now Fremont. Established in June 1797, **Mission San Jose de Guadeloupe** grew famous for its music. Examples of Ohlone instruments and handicrafts are displayed in the old living quarters of the mission, one of the most absorbing small museums of the Bay Area. The graveyard, olive groves, and detached church, painstakingly reconstructed in the 1980s, exude a strong feeling for the vanished era. Perhaps that is because the hills behind the mission are preserved by Mission Peak Regional Preserve, in much the same state that the Ohlones would have known.

For those who wish to experience it for themselves, the **Ohlone Trail** starts at the end of Stanford Avenue, about two miles south on Mission Boulevard from Mission San Jose. Traversing canyon and mountain, forest and glen, opening wide on the ridge tops to grand vistas of earth and sky, yet thoroughly secluded from

Mission San Jose was rebuilt in the 1980s to its original design.

the noisy distractions of civilization, the trail straggles some 30 miles through three regional parks—**Sunol, Ohlone,** and **Del Valle.** Designated campgrounds have hand-pumped water, a superlatively cool refreshment in the hot days of summer, when the Ohlone Trail is a real test of stamina. In spring and on clear winter days, the hills glow a bright shade of winter-green, a treat for the eyes.

■ THE DIABLO VALLEY

Mount Diablo, the 3,849-foot summit of the East Bay hills, dominates the back end of the East Bay, and is usually seen above the horizon from San Francisco. *Monte de Diablo*—the devil's mountain—was named after a frightening encounter on its slopes with an Ohlone shaman, whom the Spaniards mistook for Satan himself. At least that's one story. Bret Harte told another—of a Spanish cleric who was treated by the devil to a mountaintop vision of Yankee hordes storming into California, seizing the land from Spain. Today, the mountain is protected as part of **Mount Diablo State Park,** which you can reach in a car by way either of Danville or Walnut Creek. A two-lane road winds clear to the top for a view that sweeps east on clear days from the Farallones to the lofty Sierra Nevada range—the widest view that can be seen from any point in the United States. Kids love to climb on the sandstone formations at Rock City, on the mountain.

The suburban town of Danville has a claim to fame unbeknownst even to most local residents. Arguably the greatest dramas of the American stage were written here by its foremost playwright, Eugene O'Neill. On a visit in 1936 (the same year that he won the Nobel Prize for literature), O'Neill fell in love with the beautiful views of Mount Diablo. He and his wife, Carlotta, bought 157 acres on the slopes of Las Trampas Ridge, west of Danville, and built **Tao House.** Between 1937 and 1944, he wrote his last five plays there, including *The Iceman Cometh, A Moon for the Misbegotten,* and *Long Day's Journey into Night.* Now protected as a national historic site, Tao House is still relatively remote, and can be visited only on scheduled free tours that meet in downtown Danville. Make an appointment with the National Park Service by calling (510) 838-0249. The house is being refurnished as O'Neill knew it, right down to the books on his writing room shelves.

Blackhawk is one of the Bay Area's most exclusive communities. Sightseers will be turned away at the gate, but they can come for a turn around **Blackhawk Plaza,**

(following pages) The peerless view toward San Francisco from the Lawrence Hall of Science.

the dazzling neighborhood shopping mall. It's something like Rodeo Drive with a concerted theme of pink Mediterranean, built around luxuriant fountains and a spectacular, ever-flowing artificial stream. Everything is done to a tasteful excess. At one end of the plaza, the **Behring Auto Museum** offers an absolutely scintillating collection of vintage roadsters, polished to a splendid sheen and enchantingly arranged about a darkened hall. The Jazz Age models put to shame anything on the road today for style and pure snob appeal, not to mention comfort. These are the most beautiful machines in the world, and the Behring Museum is an ideal setting. Next door, the **University of California at Berkeley Museum** presents a somewhat curtailed glimpse of its vast paleontology and other collections in an otherwise splendid setting.

A more earthy experience can be had at the **Lindsay Museum** in Walnut Creek, where handling snakes and petting rabbits are part of the guidelines. This small wildlife museum is designed with kids in mind. Note the stuffed California Grizzly, an extinct species.

■ CARQUINEZ STRAITS

Martinez is an old town by California standards, built on the Carquinez Straits where San Francisco Bay squeezes down to its narrowest point between San Pablo and Suisun bays. Legend says that the martini was named after this town when a San Francisco Bartender invented it as fortification against the chilly transbay ferry crossing to Martinez. (If this story be true, however, why wasn't the drink called a *martinez?*)

John Muir, known around the world as the prime mover of the conservation movement, lived for 25 years, and is buried, in Martinez. His farm is now a national historic site. You can wander at will through the 1882 white frame house. Notice especially the cluttered study where he wrote while managing his fruit orchards. Photographs from his life hang on the walls, and some of the period furnishings are originals. On the grounds, you can also see the two-story Martinez adobe, built by the town's namesake, Don Vicente Martínez, in 1849. Muir's books are on sale in the park office at the gate, where you can also see a short film on his life. Muir was buried nearby on what is still private property; ask directions from the park office.

The hamlet of **Port Costa**, about five miles west of Martinez on the Carquinez Scenic Road, hangs on to a history much larger than itself. When the first transcontinental railway train chugged down from Sacramento, no bridge crossed the

Carquinez Straits, as two do today at Martinez and Vallejo. The tracks ended at Benicia, on the north side of the Straits, where the cars were loaded on waiting ferries and floated across to Port Costa. The largest train ferries in the world, the *Solano* and *Contra Costa*, operated on these waters until the completion of the rail bridge at Martinez in 1930. Port Costa today has changed little from the beginning of this century.

The historic Solano County town of **Benicia**, seen across the straits from Port Costa, can be reached from Martinez by the Benicia-Martinez bridge. Looking east from the high span, you can see the remnants of Liberty Ships from World War II for which the Navy no longer has any use. Anchored in the straits, they are known as the Mothball Fleet. Arriving on the north shore of the Carquinez Straits, you are now in Solano County.

Benicia, a small, quiet town, has had a fascinating role in California history. Its low-key appearance does not exactly dazzle the eye, but for those who make an effort to learn the stories behind it, Benicia is an unspoiled beauty. It was founded on land owned by General Mariano Vallejo, who was egged on in the venture by two Yankee leaders of the Bear Flag revolt, Robert Semple and Thomas Larkin. They named it after Mrs. Vallejo. Benicia was an early rival to Yerba Buena, and was almost certainly the better situated of the two for trade, sitting midway between the Central Valley hinterland and San Francisco Bay. Competition between the two villages prompted the citizens of Yerba Buena to rename their burg after the famous bay of San Francisco, a shrewd move that brought recognition from strangers around the world. As noted already, the first transcontinental railroad passed through here, reinforcing Benicia's *natural* superiority over peninsular San Francisco; but by then, the city by the Golden Gate was already fixed as the economic capital of California.

When Concepcion Arguello joined a Dominican monastery to forget the unhappy promises of Nikolai Rezanof, she retired to Benicia. She died in 1857, and was buried in Saint Dominic's Cemetery, on Hillcrest Avenue between East Fifth and Sixth streets. Her gravestone, carved with the name of Sister Mary Dominica, is at the end of the second row, on the left. A larger monument stands beside it.

Benicia's main stem, First Street, hosts a few antique shops, cafes, restaurants, and historical houses. For a self-guided tour of the town, pick up a map and brochure from the **old State Capitol** on the corner of First and G streets. This handsome Greek Revival building dates from 1852, and served as California's capital house in 1853 and 1854. For a small admission fee, you may visit the Assembly and Senate chambers, set up as they were during the 1853 session. Note the interior pillars: they were masts from ships abandoned off Benicia during the Gold Rush.

The U.S. Army established a barracks in Benicia in 1849, adding an arsenal in 1852. Remnants of the base, which closed in 1964, still stand around the east side of town, including the formidable sandstone powder magazine built in 1857, the Clock Tower Fortress, the post hospital and cemetery, the 1860 Commandant's house, and the old guardhouse. Actually, this is the third guardhouse on the site.

A little-known story is connected with the first one, built in 1852. A young soldier named Hiram Grant, passing through San Francisco en route from the Mexican War to Humboldt County, California, was tried and briefly imprisoned here in 1852 for getting roaring drunk in public, during which time he allegedly fired the post cannon off in front of the commander's house in the middle of the night, waking him with a start. This hardly gives Benicia a pivotal role in American history, but it does have an interesting twist in that Grant went on to become supreme commander of the Union army in the Civil War, and eventually, President of the United States. How many other towns can boast of having locked a future president in their cooler for being drunk and disorderly? (Quite in character with his unpretentious manner, Hiram Ulysses Grant never bothered to change the name that West Point erringly recorded in his files as Ulysses S. Grant.)

Another military site worth visiting is the **Camel Barns**, on Camel Road north of Highway 780. The camels came to Benicia after a failed experiment by then-Secretary of War Jefferson Davis, who imported them for use in the American deserts. Actually, the camels performed well under arid conditions, but weren't to the liking of American handlers, who failed to understand their impertinent manners. The camels were stabled in the Benicia Camel Barns in 1863, and auctioned off in 1864. Today, the barns are part of the Benicia Historical Museum.

West of Benicia, and just across the Carquinez Bridge from western Contra Costa County, is the city of Vallejo. Its greatest tourist draw is **Marine World Africa** USA, a combination of aquarium, zoo, marine circus, and water-ski show. For a single entrance fee, you have the run of the park, choosing from among several daily shows by trained dolphins, sea lions, killer whales, birds, elephants, chimps, tigers, lions, and folks on water skis. A playground for kids is built with ropes, nets, bridges, and tunnels. At the aquarium, visitors handle sea animals under supervision of park biologists.

THE PENINSULA
AND SOUTH BAY

ONCE HELD FIRMLY IN THE HANDS OF SAN FRANCISCANS, the economic reins of power that drove the city through its first brilliant century have slipped, and been taken up by other cities around the Bay. A center of finance and cultural hub of the Bay Area San Francisco yet remains; but the South Bay, and specifically Silicon Valley, now controls the manufacturing base which, more than any other single element, drives the regional economy of the San Francisco Bay Area.

Less than one generation ago, the South Bay was a fertile land of walnut, apricot, and prune orchards. Now San Jose is the most populous city in the Bay Area—yes, larger than San Francisco. Santa Clara, Sunnyvale, Cupertino, and other towns have joined in a massive and complex grid of freeways, sprawling city blocks, parking lots, and malls that remind San Franciscans somewhat disconcertingly of Los Angeles. The metropolis is loosely linked under the name of Silicon Valley, in reference to the semiconductor and computer-chip industries that were largely pioneered here in the 1960s. Those were the days when the likes of Steve

Steve Jobs and Steve Wozniak founded Apple Computers in a garage. (Kerrick James)

Jobs and Steve Wozniak (the duo behind Apple Computers), Bill Hewlett, and Dave Packard were working in garages, while John Warnock and Chuck Geschke created the first program for what was to become Adobe Systems in a home bedroom. Hewlett-Packard, Apple Computers, Lockheed, and many other high-tech corporations are headquartered in Silicon Valley.

But the South Bay is not all work and no play! Travelers will find a huge variety of things to do and see in Silicon Valley, and throughout the mountains, beaches, and towns of the Peninsula.

■ THE PENINSULA

With a population of about 1.5 million, **Colma** is easily the largest city of the Bay Area. The only reason you never hear of much stirring in Colma is that only about 500 of its residents actually *live* there.

Colma is San Francisco's necropolis, its City of the Dead. It comprises several cemeteries lining both sides of El Camino Real, just south of Daly City. Some of the cemeteries cater to specific religious or ethnic groups—Italians, Chinese, Japanese, Jews, Serbs, and Greeks. Though each cemetery has its particular character, the most spectacular is Cypress Lawn, which contains hundreds of family crypts scattered like tiny Greek, Roman, and Egyptian temples over the rolling landscape. Other residents of Cypress Lawn rest in an enormous, rambling columbarium, lit during daylight by acres of stained glass. Woodlawn Memorial Park, entered through a massive sandstone chateau-gate, is the cemetery of choice for numerous notable San Franciscans, including Emperor Norton, Ishi, Lillie Hitchcock Coit, James King of William, and Beniamino Bufano. Perhaps the most famous resident of Colma is none other than the celebrated sheriff of Tombstone, Arizona, who fought the shoot-out at the O.K. Corral. Wyatt Earp is buried beside his wife in the Hills of Eternity cemetery.

A few minutes south of San Francisco, Skyline Boulevard and Highway 280 both skirt a long, north-south valley partially submerged under Upper and Lower **Crystal Springs reservoirs.** The San Andreas fault, responsible for the San Francisco earthquake of 1906, runs right up the valley floor, certainly the most visible section of fault line south of San Francisco. Part of the extensive San Francisco State Fish and Game Refuge, the lakes store water, piped from Hetch Hetchy Reservoir in the Sierra Nevada range, for San Francisco's use.

The supposed resemblance of Crystal Springs reservoirs to Ireland's Lakes of Killarney inspired one William Bourn II, in 1915, to build a fabulous 654-acre estate on its southernmost shore. (The fact that he was president of the water company no doubt provided further inspiration.) Bourn, who earned a big hunk of his fortune from his Empire gold mine in Grass Valley, California, named his mansion **Filoli**, an acronym of his motto: **Fight, Love, Life**. Television viewers familiar with the Carrington estate on "Dynasty" already know some of its exquisite gardens and buildings.

Designed by Willis Polk, the mansion is a great pseudo-Georgian manor house set amidst ancient California oaks and unobstructed views of the distant hills. Tours visit the ground-floor kitchen, library, office, and dining rooms, dawdling longest in the gardens. These are a virtual Eden of blooms, trees, lawns, formal alleys, fountains, arbors, courts, and special gardens, such as the English knot garden, the Dutch garden, the Chartres garden (planted to resemble the cathedral window pattern), a sunken garden, and an extensive rose garden. Among the special trees are dawn redwoods, pomegranate, and avenues of Irish yew. Every season brings new blooms, though the peak season for color is probably March.

Filoli feels more like a living house than a museum. The busy gardeners in their slouch hats, the helpers in the kitchen, the small tea shop on the patio, and the gift shop in the carriage house fill the estate with life and purpose. Tours of Filoli run on Tuesday through Saturday, February through November; the house is festively decorated for the special Christmas tour in December.

The city of Menlo Park has three low-key stops of specialized interest. Map collectors will want to visit the **United States Geological Survey**, the government's map-making division at 345 Middlefield Road, where they can buy beautifully detailed maps and satellite photos of the Far Western States. Nearby is the headquarters for *Sunset*, an innovative publisher of books and magazines specializing in travel, cooking, gardening, and home remodeling for residents of the western states. Their experimental gardens, workshops, and kitchens are open for tours on weekdays at the adobe showroom, on the corner of Middlefield and Willow roads. The **Allied Arts Guild** (75 Arbor Road), an enchanting Spanish-style complex of attractive gardens and crafts shops where artists sell their weaving, candles, pottery, painting, needlepoint, and carpentry work.

One of the prettiest and most intellectually stimulating cities of the Bay Area, **Palo Alto** is best known as the home of **Stanford University**. In marked contrast to the manic streets of Stanford's nemesis, Berkeley, the main commercial district of Palo Alto gathers handsomely along a clean, prosperous, charming, and eminently walkable thoroughfare, **University Avenue**. At its head, beyond the Caltrain railroad station, sprawls the Stanford campus—likewise a markedly different scene from Berkeley's, though each is consistently one of the highest-ranked universities in the nation.

The entrance to the campus always surprises first-time visitors with its natural vegetation of sparse native oak and wild weeds. Within these dry Elysian fields stands a lonely white **mausoleum**, guarded by sphinxes, encompassed by trees. Leland Stanford Jr., the namesake of the university, lies entombed therein with his parents. After you pass through this strangely deserted landscape, the Main Quadrangle and Hoover Tower jump up with sudden, refreshing vigor. You can obtain a map of the grounds from the information desks to the left of the entrance to the Main Quad (as it's called) and at Tressider Union.

The **Main Quad** is the focus of the university, surrounded by symmetrical cloisters and buildings made of peach-colored sandstone, heavy, almost monastic, in feel. In the seat of honor basks **Stanford Memorial Church**, a Romanesque affair with brilliant murals and mosaics.

Filoli's gardens are among the most ornate and sophisticated in the West.
Stanford Memorial Church reflects both Californian and Byzantine influences.

The grounds are dominated by the 285-foot square **Hoover Tower**, named after Herbert Hoover, Stanford's most famous graduate. Visitors ride to the top for an overview of the South Bay area. The Stanford University Art Gallery, exhibiting contemporary work, stands in front. Not far behind is White Plaza, home of the Stanford Bookstore, a huge and lively emporium.

While in Palo Alto, you might want to take in the **Barbie Hall of Fame**, a world-renowned collection of the best-selling Mattel doll. According to the museum proprietress, the museum is 99.8 percent complete. Here you can witness not only the evolution of Barbie, but the evolution of American style and social consciousness since the late 1950s: from the original, girl-next-door, hand-painted, 1959 model, through rising and falling hemlines and hairdos, through the hippie and Mod Squad eras and the Jackie Kennedy look, to the present []. Here also you can contemplate the transfigurations of Barbie and her friends, including Ken, in all their professional, multi-racial, international, chrono-progressive, and socio-economic identities. Even if you've never played with Barbie, there's plenty here for an intriguing sociology thesis or two. This small, surprisingly captivating museum is just off University Avenue, at 433 Waverley.

Immediately south of Palo Alto, **Mountain View** nurtures one of the most strollable downtowns of any Bay Area city. Its new City Hall and Center for the Performing Arts, at Castro and Mercy streets, sets the elegant tone, which it carries down Castro Street by means of classy street-lamps and broad, clean, well-manicured sidewalks. Castro Street is noted for its score or more of excellent Mandarin (Beijing, Shanghai, and other northern cuisines) restaurants, making it a sure-fire winner for a cheap bowl of noodles or a banquet. A handful of bookstores, including the glorious Printer's Ink (301 Castro), where coffee, music and, of course, books attract crowds till late at night.

The hottest tour in Mountain View is the NASA (National Aeronautics and Space Administration) **Ames Research Center** at Moffett Field, where scientists test new aircraft design with a score of wind tunnels (including the world's largest) and computers. Visitors are welcome on free, escorted tours, but reservations are mandatory and should be made two to three weeks in advance.

■ SILICON VALLEY & SAN JOSE

Where Silicon Valley actually starts and ends is anybody's guess, but you can recognize it by its general modernity, the monolithic high-tech electronics plants, wide highways, and new business hotels and restaurants. Many long-time residents of Silicon Valley don't actually call it that—they much prefer the old, proper and much more beautiful name of Santa Clara Valley, which they feel preserves a sense of the region's fascinating history.

Reconstructed **Mission Santa Clara de Asis**, established by a Spanish Padre in 1777, was noted for having the largest native population of any in old California. It now stands in the middle of the lovely campus of the University of Santa Clara. Founded in 1851, the Jesuit university is the oldest in the state. Its flower gardens, trees, and the old adobe wall behind the church retain a charming, old mission flavor, though no doubt its bucolic days were hardly so immaculate. See for yourself at the campus **de Saisset Museum**, principally an art gallery with a history section downstairs.

Linked to the mission by a tree-lined Alameda, the Spanish village of **San Jose** was founded in 1777, and is today the oldest city in the state. In 1849, San Jose was declared as California's first state capital under American dominion.

Downtown San Jose is a gracious blend of old-time and high-tech styles. The opera, museums, theater, restaurants, main library, hotels, offices, parks, and convention center all congregate within the few downtown blocks between Almaden and Second streets, and from San Carlos to Santa Clara. The campus of the California State University at San Jose starts two blocks east, on Fourth Street. The clean, handsome streets and plazas invite walkers; pick up a map and directions at the San Jose Metropolitan Chamber of Commerce, at 180 South Market Street. If you don't feel like walking, ride one of the airy cars on the new light-rail system.

Among the congenial surprises in the Spanish mode is the brick-paved El Paseo Court, with its fountain and tiles and colorful South American handicrafts hanging from the balcony of the Machu Picchu Gallery. The shiny, new, open-air mall called **The Pavilion**, on Park between First and Second, provides alfresco tables for enjoying typically balmy South Bay days.

Two landmarks of old San Jose stand on opposite corners of San Fernando and Market streets. The graceful copper domes and stately pillars of **St. Joseph's Cathedral** were raised in 1877 and renovated in 1991. The handsome, sandstone

Post Office Building, a historical landmark from 1892, now houses the old wing of the **San Jose Museum of Art**, a beautiful venue for world-class exhibits and a well-stocked gallery store.

The **Children's Discovery Museum**, a mere stroll from downtown San Jose at the corner of West San Carlos and Woz Way, is a walloping adventure for kids, who can explore the structure of a city by sliding down a sewer pipe, commandeering the stoplights, sending messages by pneumatic tube, and taking over the dentist's office, theater dressing room, fire engine, and waterworks. As wonderful as it is for kids, however, adult interests generally start flagging here faster than they do at the Exploratorium or the Tech Museum of Innovation, both of which are geared for older attention spans.

Fortunately, the **Tech Museum of Innovation** is only just up the street at 145 West San Carlos. You know you've arrived at an enthralling spot even before walking in the door. One glance at the kinetic sculpture *Imaginative Chip* and you're caught for at least 30 minutes watching billiard balls bounce and coil and fly through a maze of track, chiming gongs as they pass.

It's even better inside. Maneuver a spacecraft through a simulated exploration of Mars. Command a robot to pour coffee or clean up a kitchen mess. Design an aerodynamically improved bicycle. See how a silicon chip is made, or run some experiments on new materials. The museum, which is being temporarily housed here while a larger building can be built, is both showcase and shrine of Silicon Valley technology.

The city's older history is preserved at the **San Jose Historical Museum**, on the south side of Kelly Park. Many historic buildings from old San Jose have been removed to this site (or built from original plans) to give a feeling of the earlier days. You can poke through Gianinni's first Bank of Italy (Gianinni was born in San Jose), sip a soda at O'Brien's Soda Fountain, or inspect the equipment at the livery stable and old firehouse. The post office houses the first radio station in the United States—KQW—which was licensed in San Jose in 1912. A number of furnished farmhouses capture the rare scent of Victorian times. The park also preserves a vintage gas station, smithy, dentist parlor, and a reconstructed temple from San Jose's Chinatown. An excellent bookstore, specializing in history and regional travel, mellows out behind the soda fountain.

Of spookier interest is the **Winchester Mystery House**, a legacy of the superstitious heiress of the Winchester Repeating Rifle fortune. Sarah Winchester commenced building the house in response to a fortuneteller's prophecy that she would live only while the house remained unfinished. The clincher was that this revenge would be meted out by the spirits of people gunned down by the Winchester rifle, who would . . . well, we're not quite sure *what*, but something *terrible*. The bottom line is that Mrs. Winchester made sure her carpenters kept busy 24 hours a day for 38 years, until she died. The result is something really weird: a 160-room monstrosity with some 2,000 doors and 10,000 windows, stairs that lead nowhere, secret passages, and sealed doorways. The tour guides milk the story for all it's worth—and who can blame them? The house is intriguing and, naturally, is said to be haunted.

Far fewer tourists ever find their way to the **Rosicrucian Egyptian Museum**, the largest collection of Egyptian antiquities in the western United States. Aside from a large collection of mummies (including a cat, bird, snake, fish, and, of course, people), dioramas of pyramids and ancient cities, and displays of Egyptian, Sumerian, Babylonian, Assyrian, and Persian artifacts, the museum houses the only full-sized reproduction of an Egyptian rock tomb in the Western Hemisphere. Winding your way down the dark, narrow passages to a ransacked burial chamber is exciting and a little eerie.

An exciting destination for older children and amateur astronomers is **Lick Observatory**, atop 4,209-foot (1,283-m) Mount Hamilton. At the time of its founding by San Francisco millionaire James Lick (who is buried beneath the largest telescope), it was the world's first permanently staffed observatory, and its 36-inch refracting telescope had no peer. It still works fine, but the smog and bright lights of the city below interfere with viewing. The visitors' gallery is open daily, but it is more interesting to come for the Friday evening summer programs, between mid-July and mid-September, when some telescopes are open for public viewing.

After all these museums, are the kids are getting restless? The perfect antidote is northern California's answer to Disneyland: **Great America**. People come here for many reasons, and none more compelling than to challenge some of the country's most stomach-wrenching roller coasters, like the double-corkscrew Demon, the Tidal Wave (which does a full loop forwards and backwards), the Vortex (where you ride *standing up*), and the guaranteed-to-get-you-wet Rip Roaring Rapids. Now, if that ain't your style, you may prefer to watch a movie on the country's largest theater screen, or to chat with the likes of Bugs Bunny and Fred Flintstone.

South Bay summers, far removed from Frisco's fogs, are hot enough to make a hit of another theme park called **Raging Waters**, at 2333 South White Road in San Jose. Bring your swim suit to try the water slides.

Nestled against the Santa Cruz Mountains, **Saratoga** is a wealthy, genteel town. Its main street, Big Basin Way, is a delightful place to dine or shop for sweet nothings. San Francisco's ex-Mayor James Phelan, a devoted patron of the arts, chose the hills behind town to build his estate, which he called **Villa Montalvo**. When he died, his will directed that Villa Montalvo be used henceforth to promote the arts and artists. He would be happy today to see what his trustees have done with the beautiful Italian country house. It's now a retreat for artists, musicians, and writers with work in progress. The Mediterranean gardens and pavilions are used to stage plays, poetry readings, and concerts. The gardens are open daily.

Another variation on the sylvan mood is **Hakone Japanese Garden**, one of the most authentic ever created outside Japan. Built on a steep hill where a small artificial creek cascades into the pond, the garden draws visitors in quietly, soothing their senses with gentle sound and beauty. Secluded pavilions invite guests to sit and relax, or to have tea. The garden was designed in 1917 by a master Japanese gardener, Mr. Shintani, on principles of design popular in seventeenth-century Japan.

■ THE SAN MATEO COAST

The western side of the Peninsula is one of the Bay Area's richest treasures. Though developers keep pecking away at Half Moon Bay, the fact that so much of these coastal ranges remain rural and wild is truly a wonderful benefit of their ruggedness.

Sweeney Ridge, which climbs out of Pacifica on the coast south of San Francisco, is the southernmost outpost of the Golden Gate National Recreation Area. A trail leads up to the site where Portola's men first saw San Francisco Bay, a sight today much changed but no less spectacular.

Montara Mountain falls abruptly into the sea at **Devil's Slide**, a very unstable and narrow bit of Highway 1 south of Pacifica. From there, Highway 1 pushes south above the crawling Pacific, past a continuous string of beaches and coves under state park protection. Swimming at any of these is never warm, and almost always dangerous, until you get to Santa Cruz. Aside from a few daring surfers in wet suits, most locals come here for the scenery, sunbathing, and picnicking.

Gray Whale Cove State Beach, reached by a stairway from Highway 1, is popular among nude sunbathers. Next door, long Montara State Beach is crowded on hot weekends. Beyond the 1875 **Montara Lighthouse** (site of a 35-bed youth hostel), the tide pools of Moss Beach stretch down the coast to Pillar Point. The pools are great places to study crabs, starfish, anemones, and other sea creatures at low tide—but remind your explorers not to remove anything. Nature walks are arranged for those who care to join.

Half Moon Bay curves gracefully beyond Pillar Point, providing several popular beaches for picnickers and a working fishing harbor on the north end at **Princeton-by-the-Sea**. The town of **Half Moon Bay**, settled mostly by Portuguese and Italian farmers and fishermen, still has the salty flavor of a seacoast village along its main street. The saltiness has been somewhat sweetened in recent years with bed-and-breakfasts, restaurants, and galleries. The town is famed for its pumpkins, celebrated in the October Pumpkin Festival, when visitors carve jack-o'-lanterns, inspect the heftiest monsters, and eat whatever it is that one makes out of pumpkin, including pie.

The country grows leaner south of town, giving way to windswept hamlets, farm roads, empty beaches (on the typically foggy days of summer), and the ever-present crash of breakers. The many state beaches along here are always beautiful to look at, but usually too brisk for anything less than long pants and sweaters. Winding roads crawl up the canyons and through fog-nurtured woods and county parklands to the ridge at Skyline Boulevard. The rustic village of **La Honda**, a favorite hangout of Ken Kesey and the Merry Pranksters during the sixties, still breathes an alternative air. Another redwood preserve with camping, **Butano State Park**, is hidden on the Cloverdale Road, near Pescadero.

Pigeon Point lighthouse, 15 miles south of Half Moon Bay, is one of the tallest in the country, and a sight to soothe sore New England eyes. Its 115-foot tower is open to visitors on Sundays, and the buildings at its foot serve as a youth hostel. The lighthouse took its name from the nearby wreck of the *Carrier Pigeon* in 1853.

Easily the most astounding sight along the San Mateo coast are the elephant seals of **Año Nuevo State Reserve**. Lest you think these creatures are the sleek black mammals you see tossing beach balls with their noses on TV, dispel the notion. The adult males, with their bulbous noses that give them their name, can grow as long as 20 feet and weigh as much as 6,000 pounds. But just because they're big, don't think they can't move with amazing speed and agility if they don't take a liking to you. To see the elephant seals, visitors have to walk a mile and a half, much of it over shifting sand dunes; reservations are required long in advance. The sea elephants are not present all year round. Females start arriving in December, and stay till May; males are found here between June and September.

The road south from Año Nuevo soon crosses into Santa Cruz County. The county seat and namesake, **Santa Cruz**, about 35 miles south of the park, was once the summer resort capital of northern California. It still preserves its classic Boardwalk on the beach, where day-trippers come to chew on saltwater taffy, play the penny arcades, and ride the bumper cars, carousel, and the The Giant Dipper, a wooden behemoth of a roller coaster built in 1923.

■ THE SANTA CRUZ MOUNTAINS

Arching between Silicon Valley and Santa Cruz, the Santa Cruz Mountains give shady respite from the summery lowlands. One of the oldest and most beloved of all Bay Area state parks is **Big Basin**. Its huge, cool redwood forests invite strollers and more serious hikers through the mountains to waterfalls and ferny valleys. You

The rugged San Mateo coast contains many wild beaches and coves.

can also bicycle the 14-mile dirt road through the park to the sea; bikes and guides are available for rent. The giant redwood groves near the entrance shade picnic tables and campgrounds. Deer like to graze in the nearby meadows in the evening.

Another wonderful redwood forest is preserved in **Henry Cowell Redwoods State Park**. Broad sections of it reach through the mountains clear to the University of California at Santa Cruz, but the main grove is just south of Felton on Highway 9. Lacking the crowds of Muir Woods, it is one of the best places in the Bay Area to sense the majesty of the coastal redwood forests. As in most redwood parks, visitors tend to be most impressed by the oddities of nature, like the walk-through Clothespin Tree and the Grizzly Giant. The most amazing tree of all is the John C. Frémont Tree, named after the ambitious soldier who camped here in 1846, and whose presence forced the American seizure of California from Mexico. The tree is hollow. After crouching through the low entrance, allow a couple of minutes to adjust your eyes to the dark. You will see then that the room inside this living tree is large enough to shelter several people standing up.

In 1875, a freight railroad line was built up the San Lorenzo River from Santa Cruz to Felton. The tracks still pass through Henry Cowell's redwood forests, but today the **Roaring Camp Railway** hauls passengers, who have a choice between chugging up the steepest railroad grade in North America to the top of Bear Mountain, or down through the forested San Lorenzo River canyon to the Boardwalk in Santa Cruz. The trains make the spectacular round-trip journey to Santa Cruz twice a day during summer, and several trips daily up the shorter, steeper line to Bear Mountain.

THE NORTH BAY
& WINE COUNTRY

AMONG SAN FRANCISCO'S MANY RARE ENDOWMENTS, there's none more wonderful than the ease with which you can leave the town. The perfect escape is north, across the Golden Gate or on the splendid little ferries. Whether your tastes run to seascape or mountain scenery, backpack trails or tea in a cultivated setting, sensational shopping or oyster shucking, gargantuan feasting or wine and cheese sampling, you can start your vacation within minutes of leaving San Francisco. The Wine Country of Sonoma and Napa counties, among the richest viticulture areas of the world, is one of the premier attractions of the North Bay.

■ THE URBANE HALF OF MARIN COUNTY

O Exalted Guru, how many Marinites does it take to screw in a lightbulb? The answer, my children, is *three:* one to do the job, two to share the experience. Tsk, tsk, tsk. Everyone picks on Marin—the Bay Area's richest, most famous and beautiful, and therefore most maligned county. The jokes are fueled by jealousy—and who wouldn't be jealous of this beautiful, cultivated county, where mountain and sea, parklands and rolling dairy farms preserve more than half the land from urban sprawl, and where so many of the existing towns and cities retain a charm expunged from so many other Bay Area suburbs? Fortunately, even if we can't all live in Marin, at least we can all come for a visit!

Tourist promoters like to compare **Sausalito** to the Riviera. A certain visual similarity exists, but don't expect warm beaches and bikinis. Built on a steep, wooded hillside tumbling straight into the deep, blue bay, Sausalito is a pretty sight. Yachts and houseboats crowd its harbors, and a carefree air of leisure plays about its shops and restaurants.

Sausalito has not always been thought a pretty face. During World War II, it was a major shipyard. At the turn of the century, it was full of rough-and-ready waterfront bars and gambling parlors. In the Depression, the town was a haven for bootleggers. Today, Sausalito has become a little precious. The colorful old buildings remain, but too many of them are in the T-shirt and knickknack business. Still, Sausalito has managed to keep its charm.

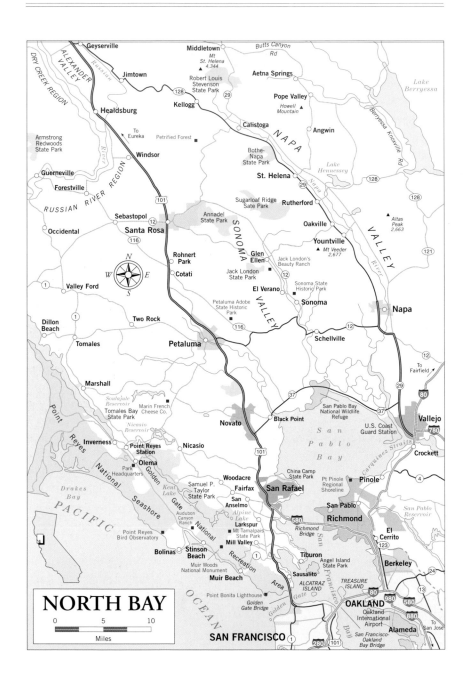

NORTH BAY

0   5   10

Miles

Avoid parking problems by coming from San Francisco by ferry. Near the pier, the old town center of Plaza Viña del Mar is dedicated to Sausalito's Chilean sister city; the twin elephants holding up the lampposts were salvaged from San Francisco's 1915 Panama-Pacific International Exposition. Sausalito's main street is **Bridgeway**, a charming gauntlet of shops, galleries, restaurants, and watering holes, intersected by stairs and steep residential streets from on high, and opening to spectacular views of San Francisco's spires and towers on the shore side, where scuttling crabs and a bronze seal rule the rocks. The boutiques, toy stores, and other shops of the central Village Fair mall, converted from an old garage, climb interior stairs to pretty little patios and overlooks.

Sausalito's most absorbing sight is the **Bay Model**, at 2100 Bridgeway, at the northern end of town. Built by the Army Corps of Engineers to study the effects of engineering projects in the bay and local river systems, the model is a gigantic working map of the Bay Area. You won't see all the familiar *land*marks, but the shape and dynamics of the bay and its tributaries are produced accurately, right down to the tides, currents, salinity, and sedimentation. (The only compromise in accuracy is that the Delta and the Sacramento and San Joaquin rivers had to be

Houseboats at Sausalito.

bent above the Carquinez Straits to fit into the building.)

The Bay Model is a fascinating piece of engineering. Its scale and complexity are downright amazing. As the rivers and streams flow at one-tenth their actual velocity, the tide rolls through an entire cycle in 15 minutes, a month of tides in 7.2 hours. You can watch the salt collecting on the mud flats of the South Bay, or inspect the prevailing flow of water through the bay's shipping channels and submarine canyons. A look at the sunken islands of the delta will show in an instant the disastrous effects of a broken dike. The Army Corps of Engineers has done a magnificent job of presenting the model to the public, with interpretive displays, elevated walkways, and recorded explanations.

Mill Valley started life as a lumber camp on the slopes of Mount Tamalpais. When the first-growth redwoods had been felled, the loggers moved on, while city people built summer homes among the new growth trees. Today, the trees have grown tall again, and summer people now live here all year round. And who can blame them? Mill Valley is one of the nicest little towns in the state, as pretty for walkers as Sausalito, but catering more to community than tourists.

The center of town, where Miller and Throckmorton streets meet, is a redwood-shaded widening in the road called Lytton Square. Homey shops and restaurants stand comfortably about, like small-town gents genially swapping stories at the general store. The streets wander with the contours, hardly ever keeping a straight line, ambling over a creek here, a wooded gulch there, disappearing up a stairway into the forest. Mill Valley has a woodsy yet bustling atmosphere—a prosperous mountain town. Local artists and backpackers pass on the sidewalks. Coffeehouses like the Book Depot, which doubles as a bookstore, do a thriving business.

The 6.8-mile **Dipsea Trail**, darting over the shoulder of Mount Tamalpais to Stinson Beach, starts at Lytton Square. Its famous climb of almost 700 steps out of Mill Valley, between Cascade Way and Edgewood Avenue, has knocked the wind, if not the will, out of generations of hikers. The Chamber of Commerce next to the Book Depot on Lytton Square can point you in the right direction.

Tiburon is an attractive harbor town with much of the quaint feel of Sausalito. Ferries run from Fisherman's Wharf, though not very frequently, so check the schedule before going. Browsers wandering Main Street's refurbished old shops and galleries, or along the new waterfront parade, can make a day of it without spending a dime.

From Tiburon, you can catch a ferry across Raccoon Straits to **Angel Island**

State Park. Far removed from the commotion of the bay around it, Angel Island is a peaceful natural preserve. Hiking trails ring the island and ascend the low peak, linking several nineteenth-century military garrisons (abandoned) and the immigration station, in use between 1910 and 1940.

Larkspur is not a tourist town, but riding the commuter ferry offers a lovely ride right up the middle of the bay past Angel Island, the swaybacked Richmond-San Rafael Bridge, and the huge, forbidding bulk of San Quentin Prison. If you can drive to the village of San Quentin, at the west end of the bridge, and the east gate of the prison, you can briefly enter the prison gate to see the San Quentin Museum—after approaching the guard, presenting your identification, and shedding all cameras, pocket knives, and assorted weaponry, he'll direct you. Exhibits illustrate the lives of guards and inmates, history of the prison and its infamous gas chamber, and a fascinating case of home-made devices used in past prison escapes.

If you've never been shocked by a work of art, you've never seen the Marin County Civic Center. Marching through the hills just east of Highway 101 in San Rafael, it was Frank Lloyd Wright's last commission before he died in 1959. How to describe it? Well . . . it's huge, pink, and blue, with a dome and a spire, and will probably be called futuristic until well into the next century. By all means, enter to see the indoor gardens thriving along the space-age corridor.

China Camp State Park, five miles east of Civic Center, is the last of some 30 Chinese fishing villages that once ringed San Francisco Bay. The Chinese, pioneers of the California fishing industry, were in time legislated out of business by discriminatory laws that stacked the deck against them. China Camp once supported hundreds of people. Today it is just a dock, a handful of buildings, and a vintage diner that serves fresh crab and other seafood on weekends. The visitor center illustrates the history of the town with old photographs and interpretive displays.

The small Marin Museum of the American Indian stands in Miwok Park, at 2200 Novato Boulevard, in Novato. Though contemporary exhibitions include arrowheads, tools, beads, and artwork from different tribes, the main displays concentrate on the culture of the native Miwoks. Of great interest is the garden of native California plants that the Miwok used in their daily lives. A small shop sells Native American books and crafts.

Cheese lovers will not begrudge the extra effort required to visit the remote Marin French Cheese company. Drive nine miles west of Novato on Novato Boulevard to Petaluma-Point Reyes Road, then south (left) for a quarter mile. The factory produces four excellent cheeses under the Rouge et Noir label: Camembert, Schloss, Brie, and Breakfast, a mild white cheese that goes well with jams and fruits. After the tour, you can buy all the fixings for a picnic lunch, and enjoy it right on the grounds. Tours and tastings are offered daily, except on holidays.

■ MARIN COUNTY'S WILDER WESTERN HALF

The dramatic cliffs of Marin County, rising above the northern shore of the Golden Gate, are known as the **Marin Headlands**. The military early on commandeered these strategic heights, closing them to the public, and thus preserving them from development. When modern technology rendered their gun batteries obsolete, the army retreated gracefully, leaving the land most fortunately in the hands of the Golden Gate National Recreation Area. Hikers here can hook into an extensive trail system that leads from Fisherman's Wharf clear to Point Reyes.

The Marin County coastline is often shrouded in fog (above). In summer the fog rolls past the Marin Headlands and under the Golden Gate Bridge, creating surreal scenes, such as the one shown here (opposite photo, Kerrick James).

Stark, windy, and rugged, the Marin Headlands offer ravishing views, solitude, seasonal wildflowers, and a handful of interesting military sites to explore. There are hike-in campgrounds, wildlife tours, and guided walks through the bunkers and garrisons. For information about park events, inquire at the visitor center in Fort Cronkhite's converted chapel on Field Road, or at park headquarters in Fort Mason, San Francisco.

Gazing upon **Fort Baker**'s old, white-frame officers' housing built around the parade ground, now grown weedy, military buffs might well imagine the thrumming chords of the infantry march. Some of the old buildings have been converted to the **Bay Area Discovery Museum**, an educational romp for children. They can, for instance, climb over a make-shift fishing boat, crawl through an "undersea tunnel," investigate glassed-in, working models of plumbing fixtures, and sketch on a drafting table. There's a science store and cafeteria.

The only way into the western headlands is by **Conzelman Road**, reached by following the signs from the Alexander Avenue exit off Highway 101. The road provides, quite simply, the most sublime cityscape this side of Jupiter: the great Golden Gate Bridge looming offshore, beneath the cliffs, with San Francisco framed between its towers.

These hills beyond Conzelman are peppered with gun emplacements. The largest is **Construction 129**, which was built in World War II to accommodate two massive million-pound, 16-inch guns. Park on the turnout and walk through the tunnel, admiring the work of modern Neanderthals, to the empty carriage well, overlooking the Pacific. The guns intended to fit this battery were designed to lob 2,100-pound shells 27 miles out to sea. For better or worse, the rapid advance of aircraft technology during the war rendered them obsolete, and they were abandoned before they were finished.

Rodeo Beach is washed by seas too rough for all but expert swimmers. Trails lead out from here over the hills to the north and south, and around Rodeo Lagoon, a favorite of bird-watchers. Guano-covered Bird Island glowers offshore like a great white whale. On the rise above the lagoon, the California Marine Mammal Center operates a hospital for sick and orphaned seals and sea lions.

The most exhilarating short walk in the Marin Headlands leads to **Point Bonita Lighthouse**, the last lighthouse in California that was tended by a human keeper. This half-mile trail starts at the marked parking area on Field Road, a short drive from the visitor center. Descending a good path on the rocky cape, stupendous views of the sea and the Gate fall away on either side. Passing through a tunnel chiseled by hand in 1877, you emerge on the ocean side of the rocks, then cross to Point Bonita on a shaky wooden suspension bridge built over crashing waves in 1954, after waves washed away the original path. (A Coast Guard officer reported 130-foot waves breaking over the stubby lighthouse in 1967.) The present light-house was built in 1877 on a rocky ledge above rough seas at the mouth of the Golden Gate. It is now controlled automatically. The lens, built in France by Frensel in 1855, weighs 300 tons, and was considered a technological marvel in its day. The light, visible from 18.5 miles out to sea, is now bolstered by an automatic foghorn. When it was first built, the lighthouse keeper had to fire a cannon every 30 minutes in foggy weather.

Muir Woods is a mossy treasure, a grove of ancient redwoods untouched by lumberjacks. Being the closest grove to San Francisco, Muir Woods receives a huge number of visitors throughout the year, though if you come early on a weekday, or on any rainy day, it is an enchanting place. In some ways prettier than the Santa Cruz mountain groves at Henry Cowell and Big Basin state parks, Muir Woods lacks the spectacular specimens and grotesque shapes that titillate the minds of statisticians and exercise the trigger-fingers of amateur photographers. Redwoods can live beyond a thousand years, but few of the trees in Muir Woods are a day over 800. Likewise, coast redwoods are the tallest living things, but the loftiest tree in Muir Woods—a paltry 252 feet—is a good hundred feet shorter than the no-blest specimens growing in Redwood National Park, up the California coast. Still, it's impressive to keep in mind that if this same 252-foot tree were growing on the surface of San Francisco Bay, it would poke about 32 feet higher than the roadway of the Golden Gate Bridge.

Muir Woods National Monument has a small visitors' center, gift shop, and cafeteria. The short, gentle walks through the groves along the valley floor are easy for just about everyone. More strenuous hikes connect the park with Mount Tamalpais State Park and the GGNRA.

Mount Tamalpais is San Francisco's Mount Olympus—a sylvan backdrop to countless cityscapes, an inspiration to writers and artists, an almost pagan symbol of nature worship for generations of city hikers. A road winds up to a point near the 2,571-foot (784-m) summit of East Peak, with extraordinary views down

The Muir Woods contain the area's most impressive virgin redwood stands.

western canyons to Point Reyes and the Pacific, and south to San Francisco and beyond. The best of the park are the meadows, mountain creeks, and redwood canyons reached only by trail. In the best old-world mountaineering traditions, **West Point Inn** offers tea (and lemonade) to hikers on its wooden porch. Floating far off to the southeast, the inconsequential towers of San Francisco fade before the more demanding flurry of a blue jay, begging for your sandwich. The park also offers camping and picnicking, and is popular with mountain-bike riders.

Muir Beach, the first coastal settlement north of San Francisco, is more a village than a town. Pocketed at the mouth of Redwood Canyon, where the creek from Muir Woods makes its entry into the sea, Muir Beach is a nice place for a picnic. The most remarkable thing about the village itself is the **Pelican Inn**, a replica of a sixteenth-century English public house. Though it is of recent vintage, the Pelican is nothing like the thousands of other "olde English pubs" with mock-Tudor beams and bottle glass; there is something extremely convincing about it. Built largely of old timbers and bricks, and hosted by an English publican, the Pelican has the look, feel, and even the *smell* of an old English roadhouse. A garlic wreath hanging near the front door keeps witches at bay, though to be sure, courage is bolstered by the inscription carved above the fireplace: "Fear Knocked at the Door; Faith Answered; No One Was There." Wooden tables, an inglenook with priest's hole, an English lawn, and even bricked-up windows (to avoid the window tax) add to the atmosphere. Rooms are available for the night, and hearty English fare is offered at breakfast, lunch, and dinner. The pub serves London's Pride, Watney's, Harp, Bass, and Guinness for those long Marin winter nights. Local stables rent horses for exploring the nearby trails. If thou desireth, thine host can arrange an evening gallop along the beach, perhaps by the light of a smuggler's moon.

Stinson Beach is the most popular swimming spot in the Bay Area north of Santa Cruz, and one of the few where the water is reasonably protected from riptide currents. The beach, which stretches for about three miles, fizzles out in a beautiful sandy spit across the mouth of Bolinas Lagoon. The quiet town of Stinson Beach has a great bookshop, Stinson Beach Books, as well as stores where you can buy picnic provisions.

The rich, protected waters of **Bolinas Lagoon** attract great flocks of feeding and roosting birds. **Audubon Canyon Ranch**, north of Stinson Beach on Highway 1,

A local dog makes himself at home in Bolinas.

preserves some of the favorite nesting canyons of egrets and great blue herons, which return from their migrations to breed in spring and early summer. A half-mile trail to Henderson Overlook permits nosy birdwatchers to spy on nests without disturbing domestic affairs. The ranch is open on weekends and holidays from mid-March through mid-July.

You probably won't find signs directing you to the town of **Bolinas**. However often the county puts one up, Bolinas residents take it down. It's not that they dislike tourists per se; they simply don't want to encourage tourist development. Should a friendly visitor happen to stumble upon Bolinas (by following the road west, and then south, around Bolinas Lagoon), he or she would undoubtedly find an amenable reception.

Once a booming fishing and lumber town, Bolinas today is a quiet enclave of creative people who derive their happiness from the joys of nature, homemade bread, and small community pleasures. It's an easy-going, shabby-looking sort of place, comfortable like an old pair of shoes. If you seek to know where San Francisco's Bohemians have gone, you could do worse than look in Bolinas. But don't tell them I sent you.

Off the southwest shore of Bolinas is **Duxbury Reef**, one of the richest reefs in temperate American waters. Stretching some 1,000 yards into the sea at low tide, the reef is protected as a marine preserve for starfish, mussels, seaweed, sea urchins, clams, anemones, and other creatures. You can look all you like, but don't disturb or collect them.

Sitting at the bottom of the Point Reyes peninsula, Bolinas is a good base of operations for exploring the wild southern sector of Point Reyes National Seashore. Accommodation is available in Bolinas inns. Mesa Road, leading to the Palomarin trailhead, first passes the **Point Reyes Bird Observatory**, where visitors can get some background on the 361 species that make their home here at least part of the year. Trails from Palomarin lead into the Phillip Burton Wilderness Area. A short, steep path drops down the cliffs to tide pools.

Olema, Point Reyes Station, and Inverness are three more "gateway" towns to Point Reyes National Seashore. All are good places to buy groceries, eat in a restaurant, or find lodging, most fortuitously in one of the many bed-and-breakfast houses. Like Bolinas, they provide civilized, peaceful, and attractive bases for exploring the surrounding parklands. Hikers can also stay at the Point Reyes Youth Hostel, on Limantour Road, in the park itself.

So much for the gateways . . . To get at the heart of Point Reyes is another matter. Point Reyes is an enchanting mystery, a world quite removed from the rest of the Bay Area. It moves to a different rhythm; the natural cycles of bird migrations, rising and falling tides, the crash of waves, the passing of storms, and quiet stretches of utter solitude. The human side also lives in conscious respect of nature—the ranchers tending dairy herds, the fishermen following the shoals, the tourists who migrate in summer and on weekends, and who disappear back down the coast when the big Pacific storms blow in. Point Reyes has an air of big things that happened long ago, mysterious things—of vanished tribes and Elizabethan privateers, sunken Spanish galleons, an English ghost-fort, Russian pelt-hunters, traces of Ming China washed up on the beach. It is the most thoughtful and thought-provoking of landscapes, hauntingly beautiful, often stark, humbling to city people used to bullying around seasons to fit their busy schedules.

Part of Point Reyes' feeling of separateness from the rest of the world is that it *is*, literally, from someplace else. The peninsula is separated from the "mainland" by the San Andreas Fault, which runs up the rift of Bolinas Lagoon, the Olema Valley (under Highway 1), and Tomales Bay, making it the most clearly visible section of the fault in the Bay Area. The peninsula, on the western plate, is moving north at a good clip. Its origins have been traced to some 300 miles south of its present location. During the 1906 earthquake, the Point Reyes peninsula lurched north by some 20 feet in one movement, displacing roads and fences, and destroying buildings. The Earthquake Trail near the park visitor center at Bear Valley makes a short loop past one of these displaced fences, while interpretive displays point out other signs of the earthquake's impact.

The barn-like **Bear Valley Visitor Center** displays dioramas of Point Reyes animals, plants, and birds. This is the place to collect maps, books, postcards, and park information, including tide tables. (The last is extremely important if you intend to hike the beaches, because most of Point Reyes' beaches are backed by cliffs and can be covered at high tide.) The center provides a good introduction to the natural world of Point Reyes' forest, heath, lagoon, and maritime provinces. Outside the visitor center, the Earthquake Trail leads walkers to a fence displaced by the 1906 quake. Another short path leads to **Kule Loklo**, a replica of a native Miwok village.

Other, much-longer trails lead through pristine forest and marsh land, to long, seldom-visited beaches and remote campgrounds. Horseback riders can rent horses at Five Brooks and Bear Valley stables. Swimmers, however, should know that Point Reyes has some of the most punishing surf on the coast.

A good cross section of the park is visible along **Limantour Road**, which runs from the Bear Valley Road through Douglas fir forests and rolling coastal meadow to Limantour Beach. From there, you can see the white cliffs fronting Drake's Bay where, according to historians, the English privateer Sir Francis Drake probably anchored for repairs in the sixteenth century. Drake stayed a month and claimed the land for England. He christened it Nova Albion. (Albion was a poetical name for England derived from the Latin word for "white," probably in reference to the white cliffs of Dover—which the Point Reyes coast resembles.)

Another two-lane country highway, **Sir Francis Drake Boulevard**, goes from Inverness through the partly wooded, moor-like ranch lands of the northern Point Reyes peninsula, to the tip of the point itself.

Farther on, spur roads lead off Sir Francis Drake Boulevard to north and south sections of long Point Reyes Beach, where wild breakers roll in the Pacific, mile after mile. Sir Francis Drake Boulevard ends at the mountainous headland of Point Reyes itself. Many ships have run aground here. **Point Reyes lighthouse,**

The moor-like landscape of Point Reyes.

some 20 miles from the Bear Valley Visitor Center, was built in 1870 to warn ships off this most treacherous headland on the Pacific coast. The lighthouse sits 160 feet above the sea, and some 300 steps down an exposed spine of rock from the parking area. Waves crash and sea lions roar on the rocks below. From mid-December through March, you can watch migrating whales swim past Point Reyes. On clear days, you can see San Francisco, but when the fogs come in, they are thick enough to chew.

■ SONOMA COUNTY

The Petaluma River divides Marin County from Sonoma County. It was once the third busiest river in California, linking San Francisco with the Sonoma County breadbasket of **Petaluma**. Known as "the egg capital of the world," Petaluma also raised hay, grain, and produce, and shipped them from the crowded Petaluma River turning basin at the center of town. Today, the old paddle-wheel steamers and scows are museum pieces, like the river itself.

Petaluma's Old Town, where Petaluma Boulevard and Kentucky Street intersect

A fine country home in Marin County.

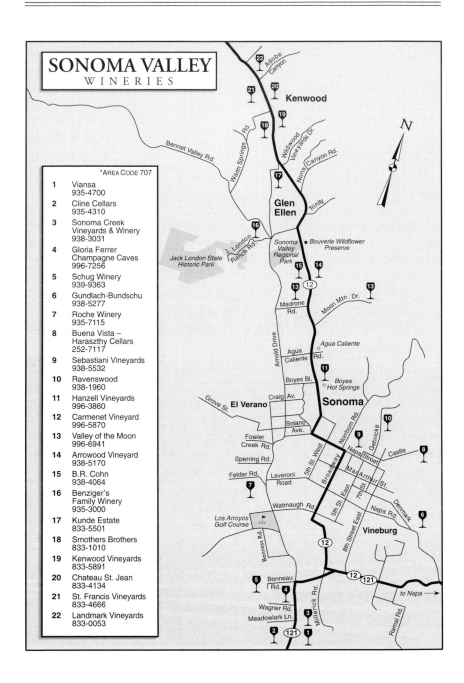

SONOMA VALLEY
W I N E R I E S

Kenwood

N

Glen Ellen

Bennet Valley Rd.

Warm Springs Rd.

Wildwood Vineyards Dr.

Nuns Canyon Rd.

Trinity

Adobe Canyon

*AREA CODE 707

1	Viansa 935-4700
2	Cline Cellars 935-4310
3	Sonoma Creek Vineyards & Winery 938-3031
4	Gloria Ferrer Champagne Caves 996-7256
5	Schug Winery 939-9363
6	Gundlach-Bundschu 938-5277
7	Roche Winery 935-7115
8	Buena Vista – Haraszthy Cellars 252-7117
9	Sebastiani Vineyards 938-5532
10	Ravenswood 938-1960
11	Hanzell Vineyards 996-3860
12	Carmenet Vineyard 996-5870
13	Valley of the Moon 996-6941
14	Arrowood Vineyard 938-5170
15	B.R. Cohn 938-4064
16	Benziger's Family Winery 935-3000
17	Kunde Estate 833-5501
18	Smothers Brothers 833-1010
19	Kenwood Vineyards 833-5891
20	Chateau St. Jean 833-4134
21	St. Francis Vineyards 833-4666
22	Landmark Vineyards 833-0053

Jack London State Historic Park

J. London Ranch Rd.

Sonoma Valley Regional Park

Bouverie Wildflower Preserve

Madrone Rd.

Moon Mtn. Dr.

Arnold Drive

Agua Caliente

Agua Caliente Rd.

Boyes Bl.

Boyes Hot Springs

Grove St.

El Verano

Craig Av.

Sonoma

Solano Ave.

Fowler Creek Rd.

Sperring Rd.

Felder Rd.

Leveroni Road

Watmaugh Rd.

Los Arroyos Golf Course

Bonness Rd.

5th St. West

Broadway

Napa Street

5th St. East

7th St.

MacArthur St.

Castle

Norbom Rd.

Gehricke

8th Street East

Denmark

Napa Rd.

Vineburg

Bonneau Rd.

Wagner Rd.

Meadowlark Ln.

Millerick Rd.

to Napa →

Ramal Rd.

121

Washington Street and Western Avenue, is a pleasant place for strolling. You can pick up free maps and walking guides from the excellent visitor center on the corner of Baywood Drive and Lakeville. Old Town has the atmosphere of an American country town of brick, wood, and iron facades; some buildings date as far back as the 1870s and 1880s. Among the buildings still standing, though given over to other purposes, are old hotels, the blacksmith, feed, and flour mills, the Odd Fellows Hall, and the library at Fourth and B streets, now converted to the city museum. The greatest gathering of shops is at the Great Petaluma Mill at 6 North Petaluma Boulevard, overlooking the turning basin of the Petaluma River.

Petaluma was built on one of the largest ranchos in California, established by General Mariano Vallejo. His two-story **adobe hacienda** stands on a rise southeast of town. Surrounded by fields and built around a courtyard, it is still an impressive sight. Wander around the rooms and verandas to get an idea of the rustic prosperity enjoyed by feudal landholders of the Mexican era.

Sonoma County's largest city, **Santa Rosa**, was built on some of the finest agricultural land in the country. Such was the opinion of America's most famous horticulturist, Luther Burbank, who selected the spot for his home and experimental farm. Here, he scientifically bred and developed over 800 new varieties of fruits, flowers, vegetables, and other plants now common through the United States, including the Santa Rosa plum, the Shasta daisy, rainbow corn, the plumcot, the Royal walnut, the spineless cactus, the Black Giant cherry, and new strains of prunes, nectarines, berries, tomatoes, and apples. His old gardens and house stand in downtown Santa Rosa, at the corner of Santa Rosa and Sonoma avenues. The Luther Burbank Gardens and modest house, now a museum of Burbank's life, are open daily. Burbank himself is buried near his dog under the large cedar of Lebanon on the grounds.

Across Sonoma Avenue and down half a block is a curiosity that's hard to believe—though maybe not. It's the **church built from one tree**, a Russian River redwood that stood 275 feet tall and 18 feet in diameter. Appropriately, the church now preserves the memorabilia of Santa Rosa's most famous native son, Robert L. Ripley, creator of *Ripley's Believe It or Not*. Aside from being a curiosity itself, the building houses a collection of Ripley's cartoons and personal effects, some rotating county history displays, and a handful of Ripleyesque oddities.

Downtown Santa Rosa, centered north of Sonoma Avenue around Santa Rosa Avenue and Fourth Street, is a handsome, sparkling, unabashedly modern district

of plazas, malls, and spruced-up historical buildings. To see the latter, start at the **Sonoma County Museum**, on Seventh Street, and finish at Railroad Square Historic District.

Sonoma County's two main vineyard regions are the Sonoma Valley and the Russian River Valley, including the smaller independent appellations of the Alexander and Dry Creek valleys near Healdsburg. Russian River wineries, of which more than 50 welcome tours, are listed in a free brochure called "The Russian River Wine Road" from the Healdsburg Chamber of Commerce, at 217 Healdsburg Avenue (call 707-433-6935). Many of the wineries have picnic grounds, encouraging you to buy a bottle and enjoy the lovely setting.

The Sonoma Valley has the distinction of being the cradle of the California fine wine industry. Though the mission fathers were first to plant the grape, the Buena Vista Winery was founded in 1857 by a Hungarian count, Agoston Haraszthy. Haraszthy is often credited with being the first to plant imported European vine stock in the region, although it's now known that George Belden Crane, Sam Brannan, and other Napa vintners actually preceded Haraszthy in their European vinifera plantings. Nonetheless, Haraszthy gave the Wine Country its first commercial push. We must also thank the count for two important breakthroughs. First, rather than follow the mission tradition in planting vines close to irrigation sources, Haraszthy planted his vines on dry hillsides, proving that Sonoma's climate was moist enough to sustain viticulture without irrigation. He also was the first to use redwood barrels rather than oak ones to age his wines, a far less expensive storage method which vintners would use for the next 100 years. **Buena Vista Winery** is still in operation northeast of the town of Sonoma, on Old Winery Road, and it offers one of Sonoma's most delightful winery tours. Visitors can picnic on the tree-shaded grounds, and guide themselves on a walk through the foliage-covered stone buildings that front rough-hewn, cask-filled wine caves.

Closer to town, the vast **Sebastiani Vineyards**, on Fourth Street, offers more comprehensive tours. Beyond the handsome tasting rooms, dark and richly decorated with wood carving, rows of enormous redwood tanks and oak barrels march with pungent gusto through the aging cellars.

The town of **Sonoma** was founded in 1823, over the hills east of Santa Rosa. General Mariano Vallejo, the richest and most powerful man in Mexican California,

The mustard blooms between dormant vines in Napa. (left)

moved here to manage his huge rancho, and to lead occasional raids against hostile Indian tribes to the north. In **Sonoma Plaza**, Robert Semple and his American compatriots raised the Bear Flag and declared California a republic, after first seizing General Vallejo at his house across the street (where he calmly treated them to a glass of brandy). A heroic statue stands in the square, but historians disagree on the heroism of the rebels. Imprisoning the statesmanlike Vallejo as a prisoner of war was theatrical, but unjust. When Vallejo was set free, he found that his ranch had been ransacked by the state's "founding fathers," his livestock and tools carried off. Vallejo accepted the Yankee conquest philosophically, and even joined in the new government as one of California's first state senators.

The rich collection of vintage shops, cafes, hotels and historic buildings surrounding the plaza make for a delightful stroll through history. **Mission San Francisco Solano de Sonoma**, last to be founded in California, occupies the corner northeast of the plaza. Especially impressive is the enormous cactus growing in the back. Across Spain Street, Vallejo built a hotel called The Blue Wing. Among his guests were the likes of Kit Carson, Ulysses S. Grant, William Tecumseh Sherman, and, by tradition, the bandits Joaquin Murietta and Three-Fingered Jack.

The barracks, the servants' wing of Vallejo's home, and the 1850-era Toscano Hotel, originally known as The Eureka, are on the north side of the plaza. The two-story barracks is now a museum of early California history, with emphasis on the Bear Flag Revolt. Like the mission, all are administered as part of the **Sonoma State Historic Park**, covered by a single entrance fee also good for visiting General Vallejo's nearby home, Lachryma Montis.

Other points of interest on the plaza are the Sonoma Cheese Factory, and The Sonoma Hotel, on the corner of First West and Spain. The hotel has a venerable western saloon, still in perfect working order.

After retiring from state politics, General Vallejo built a new house on the grounds west of Sonoma, where it stands today. **Lachryma Montis** is an elaborate gingerbread structure, furnished as it was when the general and his family (there were 16 children) knew it.

The town of **Glen Ellen** lies a few miles north of Sonoma. This section of the Sonoma Valley is also called Valley of the Moon, a name made famous by Jack London, who spent the last years of his life at the Beauty Ranch, in the hills above town. The ranch is preserved as **Jack London State Park**. In his day, London sold more books than any other writer in the world, and he remains today probably the best-known American writer outside the country. He used his income to buy the Beauty Ranch, which he developed without heed to cost. His last big project was Wolf House, an immense mansion, which mysteriously burned on the eve of completion. You can see the magnificent ruins after a half-mile walk through the woods from the parking lot. London's ashes, placed in an urn and covered with a boulder, can be visited nearby.

The ranch house where London lived and died (of an apparently suicidal drug overdose in 1916) is also on the property, surrounded by barns and a distillery. Most interesting of all, however, is the House of Happy Walls, built by London's widow after the writer's death, and now a museum of London artifacts, photos, and books.

■ NAPA COUNTY

The Napa Valley, America's most famous wine-producing region, draws so many tourists these days that local wine makers have taken measures to thwart them. Two and a half million visitors annually come to Napa not only to tour wineries, but to dine in gourmet restaurants, shop in smart boutiques, and tootle through and over the valley by wine train, balloon, or glider. In response, Napa vintners have voted for zoning laws to restrict tourist-oriented "boutique wineries." Some wineries have even adopted the drastic measure of charging for tours and glasses of wine.

The glamor of the Napa grape is rooted firmly in the rare beauty of the Napa Valley, especially the section north from Yountville. Here the valley closes in between high, forested ridges, sometimes sharpening to cliffs. The rolling vineyards are dotted with oak trees and old stone buildings, some the scale and shape of French chateaux, others of Rhineland estates. The wine mystique thrives in the old, musty cellars and wine caves in the hills, and the music and food that accompany it. And no doubt, too, it is bolstered by the romantic aura of exclusive quality that surrounds the mysterious art of making, and drinking, wine. Certainly, nobody makes much of a fuss over San Joaquin Valley vintages, which by far outweigh the Napa Valley's in volume. The beauty, the quality, the *mystique* of a Fresno wine grape just can't compete with one from Napa.

Visitors can savor the Napa Valley better if they go on a weekday to beat traffic jams and extra charges. They will enjoy tours and tastings more, too, if they read up on wineries and viticulture before they go. Many famous wineries are found on both Highway 29, on the west side of the valley, and the Silverado Trail, on the

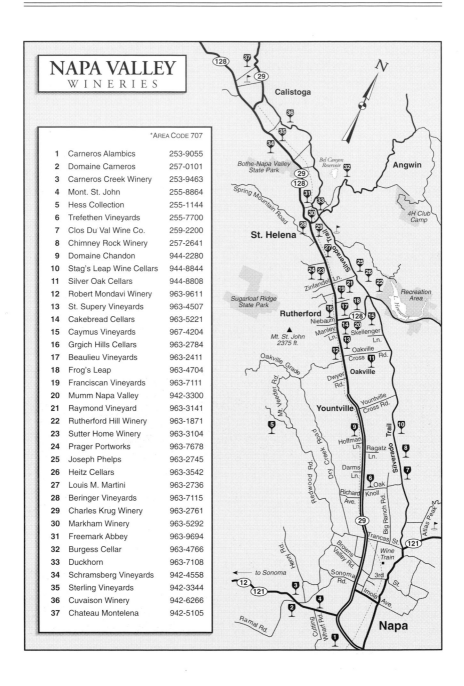

NAPA VALLEY
W I N E R I E S

*AREA CODE 707

#		
1	Carneros Alambics	253-9055
2	Domaine Carneros	257-0101
3	Carneros Creek Winery	253-9463
4	Mont. St. John	255-8864
5	Hess Collection	255-1144
6	Trefethen Vineyards	255-7700
7	Clos Du Val Wine Co.	259-2200
8	Chimney Rock Winery	257-2641
9	Domaine Chandon	944-2280
10	Stag's Leap Wine Cellars	944-8844
11	Silver Oak Cellars	944-8808
12	Robert Mondavi Winery	963-9611
13	St. Supery Vineyards	963-4507
14	Cakebread Cellars	963-5221
15	Caymus Vineyards	967-4204
16	Grgich Hills Cellars	963-2784
17	Beaulieu Vineyards	963-2411
18	Frog's Leap	963-4704
19	Franciscan Vineyards	963-7111
20	Mumm Napa Valley	942-3300
21	Raymond Vineyard	963-3141
22	Rutherford Hill Winery	963-1871
23	Sutter Home Winery	963-3104
24	Prager Portworks	963-7678
25	Joseph Phelps	963-2745
26	Heitz Cellars	963-3542
27	Louis M. Martini	963-2736
28	Beringer Vineyards	963-7115
29	Charles Krug Winery	963-2761
30	Markham Winery	963-5292
31	Freemark Abbey	963-9694
32	Burgess Cellar	963-4766
33	Duckhorn	963-7108
34	Schramsberg Vineyards	942-4558
35	Sterling Vineyards	942-3344
36	Cuvaison Winery	942-6266
37	Chateau Montelena	942-5105

east side. The latter is the more bucolic, and usually less crowded, route.

As with Sonoma, choosing which to visit from the 200 or so wineries in Napa Valley is a task beyond the scope of this guidebook. Detailed discussions of the wineries can be found in Compass American Guides' *Wine Country: California's Napa & Sonoma Valleys;* Sunset's *Wine Country California,* and the *Wine Spectator's Wine Country Guide to California.*

Napa, the town at the south end of the valley, has reestablished its wine country identity in recent years. The old town center has some interesting buildings, nineteenth-century homes, as well as interesting shops and restaurants—some overlooking the Napa River—which are well worth searching out.

Yountville is smaller, with more polish and less urban sprawl. The net result is a tourist attraction. Vintage 1870, an old brick winery building fashioned into a collection of boutiques, is certainly picturesque. If you're in a celebratory mood, visit **Domaine Chandon** for a glass of bubbly. Just north of Yountville and west of the freeway underpass, the sprawling sparkling-wine house manages to blend beautifully into its oak-dotted landscape by being partly underground. As you continue up Highway 29, you'll spy the tower of **Robert Mondavi,** north of the Oakville Grade.

Niebaum-Coppola Estate near Yountville in Napa Valley. (Kerrick James)

Perhaps Napa's best-known winery, it was the first to be built in Napa after the repeal of Prohibition. Try a reserve cabernet sauvignon.

Saint Helena is a beautiful small town with a traditional Main Street. Two of the most famous winery buildings in the Napa Valley stand on the north side of town. **Beringer Brothers**, with its half-timbered mansion, is famous for its wine caves, dug by Chinese laborers in the 1870s. A half-mile north, **Charles Krug** is the valley's oldest winery, built in 1861. The Mondavi family bought the long-bankrupt winery in 1943, and today Peter Mondavi oversees the winemaking. On the Silverado side of the valley, and midway to Rutherford, the modern **Rutherford Hill Winery** shows how even a new vintner can be a classic. Their extensive caverns, bored in 1985, are the highlight of a tour.

Robert Louis Stevenson visited the Napa Valley on his honeymoon in 1880, camping on Mount Saint Helena (now part of the undeveloped Robert Louis Stevenson State Park) and visiting many of the other sights. He described his stay in a short book called *The Silverado Squatters*. In Saint Helena, next to the library on the eastern side of town, a small museum is dedicated to the beloved Scot. The **Silverado Museum** houses some 8,000 pieces of memorabilia, including several first editions by the author, a lock of hair, pictures, and the actual toy soldiers described in his poem "Land of Counterpane" from *A Child's Garden of Verses*.

Ambrose Bierce used to live in a house around the corner from the Evans Studio, at 1515 Main Street. One of the most intriguing and disturbing figures of American literature, Bierce was infamous for his cynical commentary on the state of mankind. His most famous work is the brilliantly misanthropic *Devil's Dictionary*, but he was better known in his own day for his supernatural short stories. Bierce worked as a columnist for the *San Francisco Examiner*, and made it his business to improve the literature of California by attacking what he deemed was bad, and praising what he deemed was good. His fame today stems partly from his mysterious disappearance in Mexico in 1913.

When Bierce stayed in Saint Helena, he would entertain friends like the eccentric Lillie Coit and the photographer Eadweard Muybridge. The house is now a bed-and-breakfast. Bierce's wife and two sons—both of whom died under tragic circumstances—are buried in the verdant, old-world burial grounds west of town on Spring Street.

When the Napa Valley was first cultivated, wheat, not grapes, was the main cash crop. The farmers gathered to have their grain ground at a mill owned by an

English brother-in-law of General Vallejo, Edwin Bale. The old **Bale Grist Mill** still stands in a park north of Saint Helena. It has recently been refurbished to give visitors an idea of how the job was done using a 36-foot waterwheel and two one-ton millstones. The mill is open daily, and there is an admission fee. It is surrounded by the Bothe-Napa Valley State Park, which offers camping and hiking.

Two wineries between Saint Helena and Calistoga exemplify the long and distinguished career of wine-making in this region: Schramsberg and Sterling.

Schramsberg Vineyards still retains the isolated feel that it had when Robert Louis Stevenson described his visit in *The Silverado Squatters*. "Mr. Schram's . . . is the oldest vineyard in the valley," he wrote. (The German had founded it in 1862.) "Now, his place is the picture of prosperity: stuffed birds in the veranda, cellars far dug into the hillside, and resting on pillars like a bandit's cave: all trimness, varnish, flowers and sunshine, among the tangled wildwood." Stevenson tasted every variety on the premises, and expressed his approval of the setting, which "made a pleasant music for the mind." Those who would like to know that music today require an appointment, for the Schramsberg champagnes are of far too limited vintage to allow the large-scale tours and tastings common at some Napa wineries; reservations are required—call (707) 942-4558. Schramsberg is in the hills at 1400 Schramsberg Lane, which is off Petersen Lane. Petersen is about two miles north of the Old Bale Mill, on the west side of Highway 128.

Sterling Vineyards resembles a great white Greek monastery on a high knoll overlooking the vineyards. Accessible to the public only by cable car, self-guided tours take visitors step by step on elevated platforms through the wine-making process, ending in an airy tasting room—a fascinating and elegant experience. Sterling is in the middle of Dunaweal Lane, which runs east (right) off Highway 128 about two and a half miles north of Saint Helena. You pay an entrance fee when you board the cable car.

Calistoga is the town at the northern end of the Napa Valley, 27 miles from Napa. Sam Brannan founded it as a hot-spring resort, with hopes that it would become the California version of Saratoga; hence the name. The venture did not work out for Brannan, and indeed, Californians' enthusiasm for Calistoga has bounced up and down over the decades. Today, however, Calistoga is back in favor. The surging interest in health-oriented resorts, as well as the concomitant success of Napa wineries, has made Calistoga and its spas very fashionable indeed.

Calistoga retains its comfortable, Old West feel in the false-front buildings and

the bracing air of the surrounding mountains. Most businesses, restaurants, and spas are concentrated around Lincoln Avenue, including the old Calistoga Inn at 1250 Lincoln, which brews its own beer above a leafy beer garden. Some of the beautiful old houses in Calistoga's tree-shaded residential neighborhoods have been converted to bed-and-breakfast inns that really strive to impart the slower pace and grace of another century. In fact, you can even stay in one of Brannan's original cabins, the Brannan Cottage Inn.

Calistoga's **hot baths** are today enjoying the business that Brannan hoped to reap. The little industry offers a whole gamut of treatments—saunas, mud baths, facials, herbal wraps, hot-spring soaks, Swedish and shiatsu massage, steam baths, mineral jacuzzi, body wraps, foot reflexology—with, and even more blissfully without, the twentieth-century version of a snake-oil seller's claims. The volcanic mud feels great, but it sure looks ugly.

For timid souls who balk at climbing into mud, there are two other ways to appreciate Calistoga's thermal blessings. First, you can drink a Calistoga Mineral Water. Second, you can visit the **Old Faithful Geyser**, at 1299 Tubbs Lane, about three miles (five km) north of Lincoln Avenue. Not to be confused with the Old Faithful of Yellowstone fame, the Calistoga version is privately owned. Sixty-foot blastoffs occur roughly every 40 minutes.

There's more to Calistoga than what comes from the ground. The town is also famed as a center of gliding and ballooning adventures. The scenery from the air is superb, and the amenities for enjoying it surprisingly plentiful.

History buffs will enjoy browsing through the **Sharpsteen Museum**, at 1311 Washington Street, in the center of town. Aside from a lively diorama of the Calistoga of Brannan's dreams, you can see odds and ends of Brannan memorabilia, pioneer guns, and a good deal of displays on animation. The latter was the special interest of museum founder Ben Sharpsteen, an Oscar-winning animator with Walt Disney Studios. Among his movie credits are *Pinocchio*, *Fantasia*, and *Dumbo*.

Robert Louis Stevenson was disappointed by the **petrified forest** in the hills west of Calistoga, but a lot more of the fossil trees have been uncovered since those early days. The largest of the stone giants is 60 feet long and six feet thick. A store on the premises sells pieces of petrified wood and other fossils.

Lunch on the terrace at Auberge du Soleil affords diners a view of the Napa Valley. (Kerrick James)

Restaurants

RESTAURANTS

DINING OUT IS SAN FRANCISCO'S MOST CONSUMING PASSION. Finicky critics may quibble about the city's place in the culinary firmament, but people who simply *enjoy* eating know that San Francisco is tops. In a recent Condé Nast *Traveler* poll, readers rated the city first in the *world* for restaurants. Certainly those of us who live here appreciate what we've got: we eat out more often than any other citizenry in the nation.

San Francisco Bay Area residents know food and have little patience for a place that's all style and no substance, or one that's mediocre value for the money. As a result, the Bay Area is full of restaurants in every price range that uphold high standards of freshness, innovation, and presentation. While you can expect to be served exquisite food at a pricy spot like Masa's, you might not anticipate relishing the smoky, full flavor of a three-dollar grilled chicken burrito; the baby artichokes on foccacia available at a corner deli; brilliant green water spinach from a Chinese take-out; or red pepper and sweet potatoes sauteed into the hash browns at a sidewalk cafe. Such thoughtful preparations of the region's excellent produce and meats exemplify the operating principle of "California cuisine:" creative yet unpretentious presentation of the finest and freshest ingredients. California cuisine is not just a trend, but an invitation to explore new cuisines, techniques, and ingredients.

California is a hodgepodge of immigrant and transplant cultures, and in San Francisco we enjoy countless traditional cuisines, especially from Italy, various American regions, Latin America, and a whole panoply of Asian nations and provinces. A little borrowing back and forth was inevitable. Granted, chefs at many ethnic and traditional American eateries preserve their specific cuisines (the Tadich Grill is not likely to start serving pad thai anytime soon, and most folks probably prefer it that way), but today many Bay Area chefs, especially those in the vanguard, mix and match ingredients and techniques to create their own eclectic styles. We've seen the impact of French and, more recently, Latin cuisine on local restaurants; currently, the influence of Asian cooking continues to grow. A few restaurants even offer "Asian" or "Pacific Rim fusion" menus, on which dishes from Japan, Thailand, India, and China, are mixed wholesale. More common are restaurants which serve East-West hybrids like polenta with shiitake mushrooms, or tuna carpaccio—sashimi in Italian clothing. Chefs draw upon Far Eastern spices and techniques to accent Mediterranean, say, or classic American dishes. Lemongrass, cumin, and ginger are used to accent Maine lobster, risotto, roast duck, even ice cream. ("Continental cuisine"? What's that?)

Another current culinary style is "regional" cooking (inspired by "country-style" cuisines in rural regions, usually of America, France, and Italy). This means you'll find homey comfort foods like polenta, white beans, potatoes, risotto, braised lamb, and roast chicken even in very formal establishments. Concomitant with this casual style is the trend away from "tall" or "vertical food"—those look-at-me plates on which an overwrought structure of meat and vegetables resembles nothing so much as the Transamerica Pyramid.

The most practical (and perhaps most sociable) trend is giving diners a chance to taste more dishes. Taking their cue from Chinese and European country-style restaurants, places like LuLu and Mecca encourage family-style service, where patrons share a few platters and serve themselves as they please. At a growing number of tapas and antipasti bars, as well as at restaurants like China Moon, customers order from a list of small plates. This way, even a party of two can try the asparagus *and* the mussels *and* the grilled portobello.

Any room for dessert? Currently, polished versions of American sweets—sundaes and parfaits, brownies and devil's food, blackberry and apple crumbles—seem to be preferred at eateries of every stripe. Usually a silky crème brulée (Meyer lemon, perhaps, or vanilla bean) and a refreshing granita, sorbet, or cold fruit soup are thrown in for good measure.

Food fashion aside, every taqueria and trattoria, every bistro and sushi bar is aiming to distinguish itself from the pack and to please its patrons. Ultimately, experimentation with cuisines and ingredients can be considered successful only if it tastes good.

Following are restaurants to know about, listed alphabetically in each region as follows: San Francisco, East Bay, South Bay, and North Bay & Wine Country. At the end of the chapter, on pages 321-325 are cross-referenced lists of restaurants by cuisine; note that many restaurants appear in more than one category. The term *Eclectic* is used to describe restaurants which draw upon a wide variety of cuisines. The term *California*, meanwhile, indicates a style of cooking which emphasizes local ingredients in a simply presented, yet sophisticated manner.

—Julia Dillon

Prices
Per person, excluding tax, tip, and drinks
$ = under $10; $$ = $10 - 20; $$$; $20 - 30; $$$$ = over $40

San Francisco

Acquerello *Italian* $$$$
Polk Gulch 1722 Sacramento St. (Polk);
(415) 567-5432
At this highly regarded restaurant, the talented chef and knowledgeable maitre d' present exceptional dishes covering a range of regional Italian cuisines. You might start with tortiglioni with foie gras and black truffles, or wild boar sausage with greens.

Act IV *California/Mediterranean* $$$$
Civic Center 333 Fulton St. (Franklin);
(415) 863-8400
Hidden away in the Inn at the Opera is this romantic restaurant, where an inventive (if occasionally unreliable) kitchen staff showcases local ingredients in rich dishes such as smoked sturgeon served on a bed of baby greens with onion rings and garlic aioli.

San Francisco Restaurants

Alain Rondelli *French/California* $$$ - $$$$
Richmond 126 Clement St. (2nd Ave.);
(415) 387-0408
This small restaurant in a somewhat un-
likely Inner Richmond location has won
raves from critics and locals alike since day
one. Young Rondelli specializes in hearty
Gallic entrées such as a rustic lamb *pot au
feu,* and bacon-wrapped lobster tournedos
with brussel sprouts.

ALAIN RONDELLI

Alejandro's *Spanish/Peruvian* $$
Mission 2937 Mission (25th St.);
(415) 826-8260
You can come here to nibble on over 40
different tapas, but if you're really hungry,
order the paella for two (or three)—a veritable cauldron brimming with fresh
seafood, chicken, chorizo, vegetables, and
savory saffron rice.

Amelio's *French* $$$ - $$$$
North Beach 1630 Powell St. (Green);
(415) 397-4339
The cherry wood lacquer and chandeliers
of this restaurant—originally established as
a speakeasy in 1926—resonate with old-
world elegance, but cuisine here takes on

Asian overtones, in dishes such as woven
pasta, served with a caviar-topped scallop
and one succulent prawn.

Angkor Wat *Cambodian* $
Richmond 4217 Geary (Sixth Ave.);
(415) 221-7887 $$
The French-trained chef at this serene
restaurant impresses diners with specialties
like lemongrass-charbroiled rabbit and ba-
nana blossoms in lime.

Aqua *Seafood/Eclectic* $$$ - $$$$
Financial District 252 California St.
(Front); (415) 956-9662
With its airy, mirrored dining room and
sophisticated menu, this stylish restaurant
has earned many kudos for highly original
seafood dishes made from the freshest
fish—some local and some flown in spe-
cially. Your starter might be black mussel
soufflé, and your entrée an Idaho trout
with foie gras and chanterelles. Maine lob-
ster is usually available, too; at Aqua it
might come with smoked sturgeon ravioli.
Heavenly desserts are arranged with a
Bauhaus touch.

Baker Street Bistro *French* $$
Marina 2953 Baker St. (Greenwich);
(415) 931-1475
Chef-owner Jacques may draw you in on
personality alone, but his wonderful, classic
French preparations of rabbit and duck (as
well as satisfying but lighter California-style
salads and poached fruit desserts) will pull
you back the second and third times. As
will the prices—almost absurdly low for
food like this.

Betelnut Peiji Wu *Pan-Asian* $$
Marina 2030 Union St. (Buchanan);
(415) 929-8855
Lines of "Melrose Place" types stretch out the door of this boisterous eatery. The small plates of various Asian specialties can be wonderful (such as the spicy house-curied anchovies) but the kitchen is inconsistent and the decor verges on fast-foodish. Nonetheless, the prices are good, and the house-made ale and rice lager are better. Go late at night for a nosh and brew.

The Big Four *American/California* $$$$
Nob Hill 1075 California St. (Taylor);
(415) 771-1140
Historical memorabilia decorates the walls of this clubby restaurant located in the Huntington Hotel. Try grilled whole artichoke with goat cheese and hazelnuts, then move on to smoked pork loin with corn fritters. Popular for power lunches.

Big Nate's Bar-B-Q *American/Barbecue* $$
South of Market 1665 Folsom (12th St.);
(415) 861-4242
"Big Nate" is basketball Hall-of-Famer Nate Thurmond, and in the canary yellow building he owns, a wood-burning brick oven cooks tender chicken, lean ribs, and Memphis pork. The tangy barbecue sauce (in three degrees of spiciness) is perfect, and the homemade corn muffins and sweet potato pie are just as good. Cash only.

Bistro M *California/Eclectic* $$$
South of Market 55 Fifth St. (Market)
(415) 543-5554
It's tough to go wrong here: everything from a cold pepper soup to a roast chicken wrapped in portobello mushrooms to pan-seared scallops over a mountain of beets and burdock is flawless. Don't miss the crème brulée, either. Reasonable wine list.

Bistro Rôti *French/California* $$$
South of Market 155 Steuart St. (Mission); (415) 495-6500
Count on the chicken and rabbit roasting on the huge rotisserie to be a carnivore's dream; seafood and salads are tasty also. Rely on a great cocktail at the lively bar, or sit at the back for stellar views of the Bay.

Bix *American* $$$
Financial District 56 Gold St. (Montgomery); (415) 433-6300
Housed in a historic building on a side street sandwiched by Jackson and Pacific, this 1940s-style supper club offers classic American dishes like steak tartare and grilled pork chops with greens. Owner Doug ("Bix") Biederbeck's martinis are locally famous.

Bizou *French* $$
South of Market 598 Fourth St. (Brannan); (415) 543-2222
This warm (if often noisy) bistro features the robust food of Provence, and sometimes beyond. The varied menu is always appealing and reasonably priced. Batter-fried green beans with fig sauce are the way to kick off a meal here; follow with the signature braised beef cheek.

Boulevard *California/Eclectic* $$ - $$$
Embarcadero South 1 Mission St. (Steuart); (415) 543-6084
With a stylish Art Nouveau interior (by

San Francisco Restaurants

San Francisco restaurant designer Pat Kuleto) and sweeping views. this lively restaurant features Nancy Oakes's impressive brand of California cuisine, which ranges from rare ahi with wasabi and cucumber noodles to roast chicken with mashed potatoes or duck breast with parmesan-champagne risotto.

BOULEVARD

Bruno's *California/Mediterranean* $$ - $$$
   Mission 2389 Mission St. (21st St.);
   (415) 550-7455
After cooking at restaurants from Aqua to Flying Saucer to Lark Creek, James Ormsby helped start this supper club, located just past the edge of the fast-gentrifying Valencia Street strip. Ormsby serves a richly flavored menu: roasted sea bass comes with fennel risotto and spring artichokes, braised oxtails with parsnip mashed potatoes. Once a 1950s family-style Italian restaurant, Bruno's was left largely unchanged: red naugahyde banquettes, glass brick, dark panelling, and a huge sign outdoors.

Around 10, the live music starts two rooms over, and the hipsters show up.

Buca Giovanni *Italian* $$$
   North Beach 800 Greenwich St ()
   (415) 776-7766
In this dimly lit restaurant just below street level (*buca* means cave, and it is a bit cavelike here), chef-owner Giovanni Leoni serves superb, authentic Tuscan dishes to San Franciscans who really know food. Before launching into rabbit in grappa or lamb with black olives, order an unusual house-made pasta or risotto. Don't skip salad, either: Leoni himself grows many of the vegetables he prepares.

Cadillac Bar & Grill *Mexican* $$ - $$$
   South of Market 1 Holland Ct. (4th St.);
   (415) 543-8226
It's loud and noisy, thanks to the crowds and the "poppers"—shots of tequila with ginger ale that bubble over when they're banged on the bar.

Café Bastille *French* $
   Financial District 22 Belden Pl. (Pine)
   (415) 986-5673
Situated on a quiet street in the middle of downtown is this French bistro, which offers delicious niçoise salads and pizzas. Office workers enjoy the outside tables at lunch. Live jazz some nights.

Café Claude *French* $ - $$
   Union Square 7 Claude Ln. (Bush);
   (415) 392-3505
Like Café Bastille, this Parisian sidewalk cafe is tucked away on a narrow street in the Financial District, and attracts the office crowd for lunch. A younger set shows up on

nights when jazz musicians perform. The owner brought the zinc-topped bar (along with the rest of the interior) from Paris.

Cafe Majestic *American/California* $$$
Cathedral Hill 1500 Sutter St. (Octavia); (415) 776-6400
Situated in the Edwardian-era Majestic Hotel (see "Accommodations") and decorated in period style, Cafe Majestic is often voted San Francisco's Most Romantic Restaurant. Some of the best meals include hearty foods like rack of lamb or venison.

Caffe Delle Stelle *Italian* $ - $$
Civic Center 395 Hayes St. (Gough); (415) 252-1110
Almost always crowded, this Italian corner bistro in Hayes Valley features inventive pasta dishes with a Tuscan accent. And although chefs use deluxe ingredients such as truffle oil and chanterelles, a meal here is surprisingly affordable.

Caffe Macaroni *Italian* $$
North Beach 59 Columbus (Jackson); (415) 956-9737
The lively atmosphere and enthusiastic service here guarantee a delightful lunch or dinner. The jovial brothers who own this tiny Southern Italian spot serve up fabulous antipasti and tasty homemade pastas in record time. You won't leave hungry.

California Culinary Academy
American/French/California
Civic Center 625 Polk St. (Ellis); (415) 771-3500
In the main dining room of this eminent cooking school—the **Carême Room** ($$$) —an open kitchen allows diners to watch students preparing the classic French dishes that comprise the prix-fixe dinners. An incredible bargain when you consider that your salmon may be prepared by the Alice Waters of tomorrow. Delicious food is served at the more informal **Academy Grill** ($$), which is below ground level. Make reservations.

CAMPTON PLACE

Campton Place *American/California* $$$$
Union Square 340 Stockton St. (Post); (415) 781-5555
At this intimate, elegant hotel restaurant, chef Todd Humphries conjures savory, flawless entrées such as grilled rouget and turbot with celery root puree in artichoke broth. Try the sumptuous Sunday brunch.

Carta *Eclectic/California* $$
Civic Center 1772 Market St. (Octavia); (415) 863-3516
The name means "map" in Latin, and this storefront cafe features tapas-sized dishes inspired by an atlas of cuisines. Each month the kitchen showcases the cooking of a different region or country.

San Francisco Restaurants

CHA CHA CHA

Cha Cha Cha *Central American* $ - $$
Upper Haight 1801 Haight St. (Shrader).;
(415) 386-5758
The music's always going and the crowd is always hopping at this colorful tropical restaurant, where plates of tapas please the palate. Try the Cajun shrimp, plantains, or spicy calamari. And sangria. Cash only.

Chevy's *Mexican* $$
South of Market 150 Fourth St.
(Howard); (415) 543-8060
A favorite with the downtown and convention-goer crowd. Have a plain margarita (avoid exotic versions like guava) and chips with the house salsa. The air of franchise is unmistakeable, but kids are more than welcome, and the seem to love the place.

China Moon Cafe *Asian/California* $$$
Union Square 639 Post St. (Jones)
(415) 775-4789
At this revamped Art Deco coffeeshop, owner-chef Barbara Tropp deftly weaves Asian and California cuisines in dishes such as Chinese eggplant and chard in French onion sauce. Don't miss the salmon "tiles".

Crustacean *Vietnamese* $$ - $$$
Polk Gulch 1475 Polk St. (California);
(415) 776-CRAB
Dungeness crab, San Francisco's favorite seafood, is the pièce de résistance at this snazzy, colorful restaurant. The Vietnamese proprietors, the An family, serve crab several ways, but they're most proud of the butter-roasted version, which is garlicky and tender. Many other interesting Euro-Asian dishes also appear on the menu.

CYPRESS CLUB

Cypress Club *California/Eclectic* $$$
Financial District 500 Jackson St.
(Montgomery); (415) 296-8555
In this spacious and festive Jackson Square bar/brasserie, the stylized murals and unusual furnishings form a kind of Cubist hallucination of women and, well, chickens. Plates look eccentric too, but the food itself relies on perfect ingredients, prepared simply. "San Francisco brasserie" entrées like venison chop with winter potatoes, black trumpet mushrooms, and huckleberries keep diners coming back for more. Others come to drink a glass of wine with gossipy friends.

Delancey Street *Eclectic* $$ - $$$
Embarcadero South 600 Embarcadero
(Brannan); (415) 512-5179
This waterfront restaurant, one of the city's
best restaurants, is also part of a highly successful halfway house rehabilitation program and a source of pride and strength for
the Delancey Street residents who staff the
kitchen. The varied ethnic and regional
backgrounds of the cooks are revealed in
the wide range of specialties on offer
here— from barbecued ribs to grilled ahi to
Thai stir-fry to salmon mousse.

Des Alpes *Basque* $
North Beach 732 Broadway (Stockton)
(415) 391-4249
Family-style dinners, prix fixe—salad,
soup, and two entrées—are covered by an
extremely reasonable price.

Ebisu *Japanese* $$
Inner Sunset 1283 Ninth Ave. (Irving)
(415) 566-1770 $$
Sushi-lovers in the know come here, order
a sake, and wait outside for fresh and reasonably priced house maki specialties like
the "Tootsie Roll." A huge draw here is the
sushi chef team: by evening's end, they've
downed several glasses of Kirin each, and
joked, toasted, or flirted with everyone at
the sushi bar.

El Nuevo Frutilandia *Cuban* $ - $$
Mission 3077 24th St. (Folsom;)
(415) 648-2958
Beef, pork, and seafood are central to the
dishes served at this casual spot. The house
specialty is *ropa vieja,* flank steak cooked in
a Creole sauce with tomatoes and peppers.

Eleven *California/Italian* $$
South of Market 374 11th St. (Harrison);
(415) 431-3337 $$
In the nexus of SOMA nightspots is this
popular jazz supper club, where the kitchen
pulls off flawless plates such as seared ahi
with field greens or gorgonzola pizza. Sit in
one of the comfy banquettes in the loft if
you want to watch the singles jostling elbows at the bar—or if you want to hear
yourself think.

Enrico's *California/Italian* $$
North Beach 504 Broadway (Kearny);
(415) 982-6223
Although this open air cafe (kept warm
with floor and space heaters) is better
known for its history and jazz, the flavorful
salads, pizzas, and cockles and mussels are
great, too. Don't miss the Aviation cocktail,
born in Havana in the 1930s.

Eos *International/Eclectic* $$$
Cole Valley 901 Cole St. (Carl);
(415) 566-3063
With a spare, airy interior and lots of windows, this corner bistro offers small plates
that usually succeed. Try skirt steak marinated in Chimay ale or polenta with Danish bleu and caramelized onions.

Eric's *Chinese* $
Noe Valley 1500 Church St. (27th St.);
(415) 282-0919
Fresh, healthful, and flavorful, dishes from
varied regional cuisines are served at this
appealing neighborhood spot. Try dry-fried
green beans, any moo shu, and noodles to
round out a meal.

San Francisco Restaurants

Esperpento *Spanish* $
Mission 3295 22nd St. (Valencia);
(415) 282-8867 $
Offering more tapas than you can shake a stick at as well as cheap combination plates, this popular Mission hotspot is worth the unavoidable wait (you might get free sangria anyway). Tortilla de patatas, calamari, and garlicky vegetable sautes.

Firefly *Eclectic /California* $$$
Noe Valley 4288 24th St. (Douglass);
(415) 821-7652 $$$
An instant hit among locals, this neighborhood prize strikes a perfect balance: intriguing, well-executed dishes like Thai- spiced salmon cakes, and gumbo with duck breast. The country-style decor makes patrons feel welcome and relaxed.

Fleur de Lys *French* $$$$
Union Square 777 Sutter St. (Jones);
(415) 673-7779
Long regarded one of the city's best French restaurants, Fleur de Lys's reputation remains solid. Underneath a ceiling dramatically draped in richly colored, hand-painted fabric, diners relish starters like cold cucumber soup with caviar and vodka sorbet. Tasting plates (vegetarian option, too) offer bite-sized treasures. Servers are eager to please, but can be disorganized.

Flying Saucer *French/Eclectic* $$$ - $$$$
Mission 1000 Guerrero St. (22nd St.);
(415) 641-9955
Inventive combinations of feisty flavors come whimsically arranged on every plate. This groovy cafe, with its quirky decor (imagine if Ed Wood redecorated a Victorian

bordello) is extremely popular, so call ahead.

Flytrap *American* $$ - $$$
South of Market 606 Folsom (2nd St.);
(415) 243-0580
Looking for San Francisco's olden golden days? Hankering for hangtown fry, celery Victor, calf's brains? This spot's hopping at lunch; your grandfather would have loved it. Should you prefer something a little more current, the fresh fish and pastas are good, too.

Fog City Diner *American/California* $$$
Embarcadero North 1300 Battery St.;
(415) 982-2000
At Cindy Pawlcyn's always crowded (and noisy!) restaurant at the foot of Telegraph Hill, the chrome and paneling recall a 1940s train diner car, not a highway burger joint—but you *can* order a chili dog. The kitchen puts a spin on a range of American regional fare: try the Maryland crabcakes with sherry-cayenne mayonnaise, along with Southwest-inspired cornsticks with red pepper.

42 Degrees *California/Eclectic* $$$
South of Market 235 16th St. (Third St.); (415) 777-5558
Chef-owner James Moffat's restaurant near China Basin feels industrial but cozy—concrete floors, yes, but giant, curvy banquettes too. Moffat draws from European cuisines at 42° latitude (Provençal, Southern Italian, et al.) for hearty dishes like grilled salmon with white beans and chanterelles, roasted potatoes with aioli, and frisée salad with gorgonzola.

42 DEGREES

Fournou's Ovens *American* $$$$
Nob Hill 905 California St. (Powell);
(415) 989-1910
One of the city's famous classic restaurants,
the Stouffer Stanford Court's flagship dining room is the spot to dine on tender rack
of lamb in an elegant setting.

Fringale *French/California* $$$
South of Market 570 Fourth St. (Bryant)
(415) 543-0573
At this comfortable, cheerful eatery, Basque
chef Gerald Hirigoyen showcases the savory
dishes of southwestern France, emphasizing
their warming Gallic appeal: duck confit
comes with toasted walnuts and mashed
potatoes, and Roquefort ravioli is spiked
with basil and pine nuts.

Ganges *Indian* $
Inner Sunset 775 Frederick St. (Arguel-
lo); (415) 661-7290
Between the UCSF Medical Center and
Kezar Stadium, this cozy, informal restau-
rant serves only vegetarian Surti cuisine.
You choose one or two of the day's often
spicy special dishes, then decide on raita,
papadum, and chutneys.

Geva's *Caribbean* $$
Civic Center 482-A Hayes St. (Octavia);
(415) 863-1220
Caribbean food, extra spicy, is the specialty
at this Hayes Valley restaurant. Best are the
Jamaican jerked chicken legs, marinated in
Scotch bonnet peppers. The coconut
jumbo prawns are a mellower alternative.

Golden Turtle *Vietnamese* $$
Russian Hill 2211 Van Ness (Broadway);
(415) 441-4419
The highly touted dishes at this attractively
decorated, popular restaurant include lotus
blossom salad, five-spice chicken, and cat-
fish clay pot. More formal and a little prici-
er than most Vietnamese eateries.

Gourmet Carousel *Chinese* $
Pacific Heights 1559 Franklin St. (Pine);
(415) 771-2044
In an unlikely spot, this eatery draws Chi-
nese food lovers who flock here for cheap
salt-and-pepper prawns and great veggies.

Greens *Vegetarian/California* $$ - $$$
Marina Fort Mason, Building A;
(415) 771-6222
Affiliated with the Green Gulch Zen Cen-
ter, this converted warehouse right on the
water is the city's most established vegetari-
an restaurant. (Vegans note: dairy and eggs
are used liberally.) Have a brunch of aspara-
gus omelette with roasted potatoes and
enjoy the lovely room with its view. Prix-
fixe dinners on weekends.

San Francisco Restaurants

Happy Immortal *Chinese* $
Richmond 4401 Cabrillo St. (45th Ave.)
(415) 386-7538
This tidy restaurant serves high-quality banquet dishes to the neighborhood's families. Best dishes include clam soup and the Hunan crab clay pot.

Harbor Village *Chinese* $$ - $$$
Financial District 4 Embarcadero Ctr.
(Clay); (415) 781-8833
Where local power-lunchers go for dim sum. In the evening, the chefs serve both creative and traditional Cantonese dishes, all assembled with great care.

Harris's Steak House *American* $$$
Russian Hill 2100 Van Ness (Pacific);
(415) 673-1888
The leather upholstery and wood paneling in this steakhouse resonate with masculine vibes, even though it's run by a woman—Texan Ann Harris, the widow of Harris Ranch's Jack Harris. The aged beef, available in 26-ounce size, is incomparable.

HAWTHORNE LANE

Hawthorne Lane *Eclectic/California* $$$$
South of Market 22 Hawthorne St.
(Howard); (415) 777-9779

David and Anne Gingrass (formerly of Postrio) turned the ground floor of the Crown Point building into a highly acclaimed eatery. Elaborate dishes like seared yellowfin with hummus, maque choux, and frisée salad are perfect cross-pollenations, but occasionally the kitchen gets a little too ambitious. The smaller room features a central oval bar of satiny cherry in the center; the larger one, views of the line chefs. In addition to warm lighting and inviting furniture, both dining rooms boast gorgeous Crown Point prints by Sol LeWitt and Richard Diebenkorn, among others.

Hayes St. Grill *American/Seafood* $$ - $$$
Civic Center 320 Hayes St. (Gough)
(415) 863-5545
This Hayes Valley standby has been a local favorite for years. The concept is simple: your choice of fish (of the dozen or so listed on the blackboard) grilled and served with your choice of sauce (from tomatillo salsa to Szechuan peanut sauce).

The Heights *French/Eclectic* $$$$
Presidio Heights 3235 Sacramento St.
(Lyon); (415) 474-8890
Located in a beautifully converted home and decorated with exquisite flowers, this extremely elegant restaurant offers contemporary French cuisine which features lobster, truffles, and the like.

Hong Kong Flower Lounge *Chinese* $$
Richmond 5322 Geary (18th Ave.);
(415) 668-8998
This highly acclaimed San Francisco outpost of Alice Wong's Hong Kong restaurant features excellent Cantonese soups and

seafood—ask the waiter if there's any fresh rock cod. Two Millbrae locations (see "South Bay Restaurants").

House of Nanking *Chinese* $
North Beach 919 Kearny St. (Columbus); (415) 421-1429
Excellent Shanghai cooking with American and Southeast Asian touches. There's always a line (mostly of Westerners) at this inexpensive hole-in-the-wall. Ask the waiter for recommendations; the menu is almost irrelevant here. Try the onion cakes, then move on to the chicken braised in Tsing Tao beer. Cash only.

Hyde Street Bistro *Austrian/Italian* $$
Russian Hill 1521 Hyde St. (Pacific); (415) 441-7778
This small neighborhood restaurant is just the spot to enjoy an informal but romantic dinner for two. The Austrian chef/owner serves pastas as well as spaetzle, in keeping with the Austro-Italian cuisine of northern Italy's Frioli region.

Il Fornaio *Italian* $$
Embarcadero North 1265 Battery St.(Filbert) (415) 986-0100
With murals and marble inside as well as patio tables outside, this Tuscan eatery on Levi's Plaza offers robust pastas and thin-crust pizzas. The pastries and fresh fruit sorbets are exceptional, so be sure to save room for dessert.

Ivy's *California* $$ - $$$
Civic Center 398 Hayes St. (Gough) (415) 626-3930
A real jewel in Hayes Valley, this corner eatery offers skillfully prepared small plates

and well-conceived entrées—from Asian smoked prawns to venison—for less than you'd expect. Go after 8, when the crowds have gone to the opera, and salad or soup is served gratis with your entrée.

JT's Bistro *French/Eclectic* $$$$
Civic Center 555 Golden Gate (Polk); (415) 861-7827
Adjoining Stars and sharing its front door is Jeremiah Tower's latest venture: a small, plush room where he serves an exquisite prix-fixe menu. Deluxe ingredients such as truffles, foie gras, and caviar figure prominently. A glass-enclosed cigar room on the mezzanine allows you to indulge.

Julie's Supper Club *California/Eclectic* $$
South of Market 1123 Folsom St. (7th St.); (415) 861-0707
This whimsically decorated joint is almost always crowded, usually with banker- or lawyer-looking folk. Order an over-sized martini (and, if you're hungry, a tasty duck confit and red bean tostada) then watch the suits loosen up. Live music some nights.

Kabuto Sushi *Japanese* $$ - $$$
Richmond 5116 Geary (15th Ave.); (415) 752-5652
Considered by many to be the city's best sushi bar, Kabuto serves only the freshest and most expertly prepared maki, nigiri, and sashimi. Chef Sachio Kojima is the knife-brandishing star here.

Kate's Kitchen *American* $
Lower Haight 471 Haight St. (Webster); (415) 626-3984
This homey storefront breakfast spot is a breath of fresh air in a sketchy if fun

nightlife neighborhood. Come early for lemon-cornmeal pancakes with fruit or for the chunky "red-flannel hash." Otherwise you'll have to wait while the pierced and tattooed club-crawlers finish up their java.

Khan Toke Thai House *Thai* $$
Richmond 5937 Geary (23rd Ave.);
(415) 668-6654

At this well-known Thai restaurant (reputed to be the city's first) you might start with a pungent salad built around green papayas or squid, then move on to an impressive pad thai. Plushly carpeted rooms, furnished with low tables (placed over foot wells) and comfortable cushions.

Klein's Delicatessen *American/Deli* $
Potrero Hill 501 Connecticut (20th St.)
(415) 821-9149

This woman-run deli serves high-quality, inexpensive sandwiches, and names its specialties after famous women known for their chutzpah: the "Kahlo" is chicken salad with mango chutney and almonds on wheat, and the "Hepburn" is salmon pâté with sweet-and-hot mustard on sourdough.

Kowloon Vegetarian *Chinese* $
Chinatown 909 Grant Ave.
(Washington); (415) 362-9888

Buddhists and secular vegetarians alike are drawn to this restaurant for items like mushroom cake, as well as mock "chicken" or "pork" dishes made from wheat gluten and soy beans.

Kuleto's *Italian* $$ - $$$
Union Square 221 Powell St. (Geary);
(415) 397-7720

Chef Bob Helstrom cures the prosciutto and makes the mozzarella, vinegar, and bread served in this lively restaurant, beautifully designed by Pat Kuleto and housed in the Villa Florence Hotel. You might enjoy snacking on an antipasta of grilled radicchio and pancetta while sitting at the inviting mahogany bar, which graced the old Palace Hotel before the 1906 quake.

La Cumbre *Mexican* $
Mission 515 Valencia St. (16th St.);
(415) 863-8205

Locals swear by this taqueria, especially for the carne asada (steak) burritos. Cash only.

La Folie *French* $$$$
Russian Hill 2316 Polk St. (Union);
(415) 776-5577

Beneath the clouds painted on the ceiling at this chic yet light-hearted restaurant, Roland Passot and his wife present plates arranged fancifully into swirls and towers. But if the food looks eccentric, Passot's contemporary cooking makes perfect sense on the tongue: a recent starter was roast quail with foie gras and wild fall mushrooms; a refreshing dessert was Meyer lemon and cranberry terrine in raspberry coulis.

LA FOLIE

Laghi *Italian* $$$
Richmond 1801 Clement St. (19th Ave.);
(415) 386-6266
Comfy despite its upscale and ambitious menu, this acclaimed trattoria offers updated regional Italian dishes like cornmeal rigatoni with roasted lamb and a flavorful seafood risotto. Menu changes daily.

Le Trou *French* $$ - $$$
Mission 1007 Guerrero St. (22nd St.);
(415) 550-8169
This relaxed, charming restaurant offers regional French food in a prix-fixe menu that might let you order a warm seafood terrine to start, then an entrée of roast lamb with couscous.

Liberty Cafe *American/California* $$
Bernal Heights 410 Cortland (Bennington);
(415) 695-8777
Cathi Guntli (formerly of Zuni Cafe) combined a yellow and wedgewood blue decor and high-end all-American fare to make this neighborhood storefront a perfect place to meet your sister and her 2-year-old. A pile of lightly steamed asparagus comes with buttery crumbs and quail eggs; the chicken pot pie is organic comfort food extraordinaire.

Little City *Italian* $ - $$
North Beach 673 Union St. (Powell);
(415) 434-2900
This attractive but informal antipasti bar is the answer when you want to share a light meal with friends. The grilled portobello mushroom and ahi (or beef) carpaccio have rich flavors but won't weigh you down. Bruschetta and polenta round out a supper.

Lo Cocos *Italian* $ - $$
North Beach 510 Union St. (Grant);
(415) 296-9151
Residents of North Beach find refuge from the neighborhood frenzy within the red-brick interior of this quiet Sicilian restaurant. In addition to freshly prepared salads and pizzas, the menu offers spicy, robust pasta dishes not often found outside Sicily.

Lucky Creation *Chinese* $
Chinatown 854 Washington St. (Stockton); (415) 989-0818
Many locals come to this tidy, bright cafe for vegetarian dishes incorporating fresh produce and whole grains.

EXECUTIVE CHEF REED HEARON (LEFT) AT LULU

LuLu *Mediterranean/California* $$
South of Market 816 Folsom St. (4th St.)
(415) 495-5775
Under the impressive barrel-vaulted ceiling of this converted warehouse, diners share platters of chicken cooked on the open rotisserie, hot skillets full of mussels, and generous salads. Waiters in neckties and blue jeans sprint back and forth while chic San Franciscans sip cosmopolitans at the bar.

San Francisco Restaurants

Bookending LuLu are the more intimate **LuLu Bis ($$$)** a long narrow room where patrons often order from the prix-fixe menu (try the artichoke and fava bean salad), and the informal **LuLu Cafe ($$)**, which is open all day and offers oysters and light meals such as pizzettas.

MacArthur Park American $$
   Embarcadero South 607 Front St. (Jackson), (415) 398-5700
The ribs alone pack 'em in at this popular renovated warehouse near Jackson Square, but you can also order burgers, seafood, and salads. The best meats and fish are those cooked on the oakwood smoker.

Mandalay *Burmese* $
   Richmond 4348 California St.(6th Ave.); (415) 386-3895
The delicious food served in this attractive dining room may open your mouth to a few new taste sensations. Try *lap pat dok*—marinated tea leaves mixed with condiments—or ginger salad.

Marnee Thai *Thai* $ - $$
   Sunset 2225 Irving St. (23rd Ave.); (415) 665-9500
Almost always crowded, this Thai restaurant has earned its reputation for deep-fried items such as spicy angel wings. Also wonderful is the *chan pad poo,* a rice noodle dish with crabmeat, egg, and scallion.

Masa's *French/California* $$$$
   Union Square 648 Bush St. (Powell); (415) 989-7154
Invariably listed among the Bay Area's top restaurants, Masa's oozes indulgence. Each artfully presented course is complex and richly flavored—without making you feel the chef is screaming to be noticed. Service is attentive in the extreme: one diner claims that when she dropped her salad fork, a waiter caught it in mid-air with his left hand while placing a fresh utensil on the table with his right. A fantastic dining experience is guaranteed.

Mecca *Mediterranean/California* $$ - $$$
   Castro 2029 Market St. (Dolores); (415) 621-7000
Smack dab in bustling Duboce Triangle is the industrial exterior of this ultra-hip, velvety supper club. Dim, plush alcoves surround the central circular bar; on a small stage nearby, a jazz combo performs. Lynn Sheehan serves wonderful if rich dishes like grilled beef on melting onion potato tart, and lasagna with greens, roasted eggplant, and chèvre. Prices, especially for drinks, may be a tad high, but you might think of the extra cash as a cover charge. The food here is robust enough to grab your attention from the chanteuse's red silk dress. Do go to Mecca prepared for sensory overload.

The Meetinghouse *American* $$$
   Pacific Heights 1701 Octavia St. (Bush); (415) 922-6733
Husband and wife chef-owners John Bryant Snell and Joanna Karlinsky emphasize unpretentious, but complex American regional cuisine in this lovely 40-seat restaurant, sparely furnished with cherry wood in Shaker style. One recent menu featured hominy crusted catfish with black-eyed peas and smoked tomato stew, as well as roasted duck breast with wild rice and apple fritters.

Michelangelo Caffè *Italian* $ - $$
North Beach 579 Columbus (Union)
(415) 986-4058
The walls of this extremely popular corner cafe are covered in pastel portraits and paint-by-number pictures, but the decor only adds to the light-hearted atmosphere. The reasonably priced, basic Italian-American pastas and entrées are predictable but tasty. Everyone feels like family when the giant bowl of biscotti gets passed around.

Millennium *Vegetarian/Eclectic* $$
Civic Center 246 McAllister St. (Hyde); (415) 487-9800
If you're a vegan looking for a night out, a vegetarian tired of the sometimes impersonal service at Greens, or an omnivore looking for a change of pace, try this upmarket restaurant near the new library. Sophisticated vegan food like portobello mushrooms with Moroccan spice, as well as macrobiotic stews. Dairy items (parmesan for your Caesar) provided on request.

Miss Pearl's Jam House *Caribbean* $$
Tenderloin/Civic Center 601 Eddy St. (Larkin); (415) 775-5267
A tin roof, colorful kitsch, and a festive atmosphere make this place feel like a funky Caribbean party. Unusual salads, fresh fish dishes, and spicy jerked barbecues draw from Jamaican, Californian, and various island cuisines. You might catch a reggae band at night, or sit by the pool of the adjacent Phoenix Inn and drink a Red Stripe.

Moose's *Italian/California* $$
North Beach 1652 Stockton St. (Union)
(415) 989-7800

Frisco socialite/restaurateur Ed Moose has proved able to attract the famous and powerful to the white tablecloths of his Washington Square brasserie, where items like gnocchi and risotti are consistently good.

North Beach Pizza *Pizza* $
North Beach 1499 Grant Ave. (Union)
(415) 433-2444
Locations in North Beach and Mission take-outs in Haight/Cole Valley and Sunset
San Francisco's favorite pizza parlors—and we won't argue. Chewy crust and lots of cheese, with generous portions of artichoke, sausage, or whatever you desire.

North India *Indian* $$
Cow Hollow 3131 Webster St. (Lombard)
(415) 931-1556
Locals give this family-run eatery high marks for its tandooris. Breads and vegetarian paneers (matar, sag) are also excellent.

One Market *American/California* $$$
Financial District 1 Market St. (Steuart); (415) 777-5577
Former Aqua chef George Morrone works with the well-known Bradley Ogden at this huge, often noisy, two-tiered brasserie, where the accent is on updated American classics: from Morrone's grilled boneless quail with warm potato salad and white truffle to Ogden's signature Yankee pot roast with roasted winter vegetables.

Oritalia *Japanese/Italian* $$ - $$$
Japantown/Upper Fillmore 1915 Fillmore St. (Pine); (415) 346-1333
From the wood-paneled dining rooms patrons can watch the chefs in the open kitchen as they blend Asian and Italian

San Francisco Restaurants

San Francisco Restaurants

cuisines seemlessly in dishes like pappardelle with unagi, and tuna tartare on sticky rice.

Osome *Japanese* $$ - $$$
Pacific Heights 1923 Fillmore St. (Bush)
(415) 346-2311 (dinner only)
Cow Hollow 3145 Fillmore St. (Greenwich); 931-8898
Come to either one of these nicely appointed locations for impeccably fresh sushi, but you'll have to select from over 40 choices. These sushi chefs take pride in their creations. An unusual beef roll of sliced sirloin wrapped around Asian chives nicely complements sashimi.

Pacific *French/California* $$$
Union Square 500 Post St. (Mason);
(415) 771-8600
At the Pan Pacific Hotel's attractive restaurant, former Masa's sous-chef Takayoshi Kawai emphasizes local produce with his classically French, yet unpretentious cooking style. Reasonable prix-fixe dinners.

Paella La Movida *Spanish* $$
Mission 3228 16th St. (Guerrero);
(415) 552-3889
Sit at the counter of this eatery for awesome paella: chorizo, prawns, the works.

Palio D'Asti *Italian* $$$
Financial District 640 Sacramento St.
(Battery); (415) 395-9800
At lunchtime, this restaurant fills up with downtown professionals who come for the Italian regional cuisine of Gianni Fassio (former chef at the landmark Blue Fox). Try an antipasti of salmon cured in grappa, then Piedmontese braised duck.

Pancho Villa *Mexican* $
Mission 3071 16th St. (Valencia);
(415) 864-8840
The long line moves quickly here, so be ready to choose the filling for your burrito: grilled chicken and steak, prawn, vegetable, and spicy tofu (and more) are all available.

Pastis *French* $$ - $$$
Embarcadero North 1015 Battery St.
(Green); (415) 391-2555
When Fringale's chef-owner Gerald Hirigoyen opened this bright bistro near Levi Plaza, he met with instant success for his signature Basque-influenced French dishes, this time executed with a simpler and more summery touch. A starter of roasted piquillos (the red peppers native to Navarre, near Hirigoyen's birthplace) might come with chèvre, zucchini, and basil; crispy striped bass could sit atop shredded cucumber with lemon and coriander.

PASTIS

Phnom Penh *Cambodian* $
Civic Center/Tenderloin 631 Larkin St.;
(415) 775-5979
The location of this cafe may not be ideal, but the reasonably priced curries and juicy,

marinated charbroiled lamb and chicken have wowed many a customer.

Picaro *Spanish* $
Mission 3120 16th St. (Valencia)
(415) 431-4089
Under the same ownership of Esperpento —with exactly the same menu—Picaro boasts a long tapas bar, España-style, and the airy dining room feels less chatoic here.

PlumpJack Cafe *California/Eclectic* $$ - $$$
Marina 3127 Fillmore St. (Filbert);
(415) 563-4755
A warm, romantic atmosphere and fantastic food for the price make this bistro a local favorite. Mussels in lemongrass broth are subtle perfection; you'll also appreciate the ultra-reasonable wine prices (bottles come from the affiliated shop next door).

Postrio *California/Eclectic* $$$$
Union Square 545 Post St. (Taylor);
(415) 776-7825
Culinary star Wolfgang Puck's San Francisco venue is a three-level number frequented by local and visiting glitterati. Innovative chefs put an Asian spin on French, Italian, and American regional cuisines in dishes such as grilled squab with ginger plum sauce and parsnip hash browns. The bar serves pizzas and other appetizers past midnight.

Powell's Place *American/Barbecue* $
Civic Center 511 Hayes St. (Octavia);
(415) 863-1404
Owner Emmit Powell is well known as a gospel singer (and part-time dj) but his Hayes Valley soul food restaurant is popular too, especially for its fried chicken and sweet-potato pie. Befitting Powell's other jobs, he's got an impressive R&B/soul/gospel jukebox. Cash only.

Pozole *Mexican* $
Castro 2337 Market St. (Noe);
(415) 626-2666
Upper Market residents and their pals flock to this taqueria, where burritos are filled with nopale cactus or hominy and sweet chiles, the walls are covered in Dia de los Muertos paraphernalia, and the waiters might be Arnold Schwarzenegger's kid brothers. Cash only.

R&G Lounge *Chinese* $ - $$
Chinatown 631 Kearny St. (Clay);
(415) 982-7877
Incredible Cantonese food, authentically served on lazy susans: try stir-fried water spinach and any of the fresh seafood. Great for groups. A bit more expensive than your typical noodle shop but worth it.

Rasselas *Ethiopian* $ - $$
Western Addition 2801 California St. (Divisadero); (415) 567-5010
Enjoy tasty East African lentils and injera while listening to a local jazz combo or R&B group. Cash only.

Red Crane *Chinese/Vegetarian* $
Richmond 1115 Clement St. (12th Ave.);
(415) 751-7226
A must-go for vegetarians and Chinese-food lovers alike. Start with the veggie pot stickers, then try greens with black mushrooms. There's tasty seafood, too, as well as vegetarian "chicken."

San Francisco Restaurants

Restaurant at 2223 Market
California/Mediterranean $$ - $$$
Castro 2223 Market St. (Sanchez);
(415)431-0692
Also known as the "No Name Restaurant," this elegantly spare but comfortable eatery is a blessing to Castro residents, who've long missed a high-quality neighborhood restaurant. Entrees like roast pork are wonderful, and salads—field greens with candied pecans and Danish bleu cheese—are paid equal attention, a plus for those eating light. It's hard not to notice the volume of *GQ* types eating (and working) here.

RESTAURANT AT 2223 MARKET

Ristorante Ecco *Italian* $$
South of Market 101 South Park
(2nd St.); (415) 495-3291
Tucked into a storefront in the attractive South Park neighborhood, this Italian cafe lets diners select interesting variations on classic dishes: carpaccio here might mean slivers of salmon served with marscapone and red caviar.

Ritz-Carlton *California/Eclectic*
Nob Hill 600 Stockton St. (Pine);
(415) 296-7465

The exquisite **Dining Room** ($$$$) rates high for its opulent decor, superior service, and complex, memorable food. The kitchen transforms perfect produce, seafood, and meats into intriguing dishes redolent with flavor. Formulate your own prix-fixe meal from the seasonal menu. A little more casual is the **Terrace** ($$ - $$$) which offers one of the best brunches in town: on fair days you can sit on the patio and listen to live jazz while enjoying a salad of, say, warm scallops and prawns with spinach and avocado in a ginger-sesame dressing; or check out the buffet. Dinner is also served here.

Rooster *International* $$
Mission 1101 Valencia St. (22nd St.);
(415) 824-1222
Country fare from everywhere is served at this inviting, earth-toned corner eatery. Catalan zarzuela, gumbo from the bayou, even pot stickers and curries warm the soul.

Rose Pistola *Italian* $$ - $$$
North Beach 532 Columbus (Stockton);
(415) 399-0499
At this popular trattoria, chef Reed Hearon (of LuLu fame) serves what's best described as North Beachj cuisine. Like the cooking of early North Beach immigrants, the cuisine here is Ligurian or Genovese—which means that plenty of garlic, lemon, and olives are used. The menu also offers neighborhood classics such as a wonderful cioppino—the hearty seafood stew. Don't miss the cured fish (anchovies will never taste the same) or the rabbit. A real plus: the bright dining room, done in wood and colorful tile, is open past 12 on weekends.

Rosmarino *Mediterranean/California* $$$
Laurel Heights 3665 Sacramento St. (Locust); (415) 931-7710
This sunny courtyard restaurant is chic yet intimate and welcoming. Similarly, dishes here are sophisticated yet comforting. Try the ricotta gnocchi of the day: light as air, they might be served with squash blossoms or perhaps wild mushrooms. Brunch might be poached eggs with lentil cakes and grilled radicchio and endive.

Royal Thai *Thai* $ - $$
Richmond 951 Clement St. (11th Ave.); (415) 386-1795
One of the best restaurants along Clement's ethnic restaurant row is this second location of San Rafael's Royal Thai. Fresh, light salads can be downright incendiary, while other dishes such as spinach in peanut sauce or sweet-and-sour vegetables have distinct, subtle, and satisfying flavors.

Rubicon *California/Eclectic* $$$$
Financial District 558 Sacramento St. (Sansome); (415) 434-4100
Because it's owned by Robin Williams, Robert DeNiro, and Francis Ford Coppola (who named this spot for the red wine blend produced at his winery) some expected Rubicon to become an elitist Planet Hollywood when it opened. But chef Traci des Jardins stole the show: her roast chicken, lamb, and foie gras with caramelized onions are out of this world. (Prices are, too, but you pay to rub elbows with stars.)

Ruby's *Pizza/California* $$
South of Market 489 Third St. (Bryant); (415) 541-0795

You can't miss the giant tomato hanging outside this SoMa pizzeria/cafe, and if you step inside to sample the famous cornmeal-crust pizza, you won't be disappointed. Caesar salads and crabcakes are pretty outstanding as well.

Rumpus *American/California* $$ - $$$
Union Square 1 Tillman Pl. (Grant); (415) 421-2300
Excellent New American dishes like veal chops, lamb shanks, and roast chicken, presented with unintimidating sophistication. Great wine list and reasonable prices, especially for this neighborhood.

Sanppo Restaurant *Japanese* $
Japantown 702 Post St. (Buchanan); (415) 346-3486
The big draws in this unadorned eatery are Japanese lunch-counter dishes like donburi and udon; most outstanding are the nearly grease-free tempuras—including oysters.

Sapporo-Ya *Japanese* $
Japantown 1581 Webster St. (Fillmore); (415) 563-7400
Locals come here for homemade ramen, perfect for a light meal or after-movie snack.

Scott's Seafood Grill & Bar
American/Seafood $$ - $$$
Financial District 3 Embarcadero Center; (415) 981-0622
Marina 2400 Lombard St. (Scott); (415) 563-8988
With locations downtown, in the Marina, and Oakland, this restaurant has won many loyal customers with its fresh seafood, traditional preparations, comfortable dining rooms, and friendly service.

San Francisco Restaurants

San Francisco Restaurants

Silks *Pacific Rim* $$$$
Financial District 222 Sansome St.;
(415) 986-2020
The upholstered armchairs and well-spaced tables of the Mandarin Oriental Hotel's restaurant provide a luxurious setting for savoring exotic starters like seared scallops and foie gras shumai with Sauternes shallot broth. Expense account dining, to be sure.

The Slanted Door *Vietnamese* $
Mission 584 Valencia (17th St.);
(415) 861-8032
The high-ceilinged dining room here is spare but warm, thanks to color-stained wood, strategically placed crushed velvet cushioning, and a neo-French Colonial cast-iron balcony. All of the curries, full of sweet potatoes and other vegetables, and eggplant simmered in coconut are amazing, especially at these prices and in this setting.

Slow Club *California/Mediterranean* $ - $$
Potrero Hill 2501 Mariposa St.
(Hampshire); (415) 241-9390
At night, the neighborhood theater crowd shows up at this dimly lit, industrially decorated bar and cafe. Food is fresh and simple; best bets are the marinated and roasted items you'll spy on the counter as you come in. Service is, appropriately, a bit slow, but a Bombay martini and some people-watching will help the time pass.

South Park Café *French* $$ - $$$
South of Market 108 South Park; (415)
495-7275
In the green oasis of South Park, this bistro serves simple French country food in a casual, comfortable setting. On nice days, the rather hip clientèle sits outside to eat onion soup or sweetbreads with baby greens.

Spaghetti Western *American* $
Lower Haight 576 Haight St. (Steiner);
(415) 864-8461
The only spot really hopping on this block before 10 A.M., this colorfully painted joint features breakfasts ranging from the Country Boy—eggs with ham, hash browns, gravy, and biscuits—to more modest items like buckwheat pancakes and fresh fruit. On weekends come early to beat the crowds.

Splendido's *California/Mediterranean* $$$
Financial District Embarcadero 4;
(415) 986-3222
Hand-painted tiles and wood beams make this Pat Kuleto–designed restaurant feel like an Italian villa. Attentive servers bring hearty Mediterranean dishes ranging from ravioli with prosciutto and marscapone to curry with couscous.

Stars *California/Eclectic* $$$$
Civic Center 555 Golden Gate Ave.
(Polk); (415) 861-7827
Celebrity chef Jeremiah Tower heads this well-known eatery, where a piano bar in the middle of the bustling room entertains patrons, and the walls are covered with posters of French aperitif ads. Entrées and desserts can be rich and over the top; sitting at the bar for a snack may be the most fun: order a skewer of scallops and a Stars martini (made with melon liqueur), and look around for Frisco politicos. Sometimes Jeremiah himself tends bar. To avoid the sometimes overwhelming atmosphere

(and prices) of Stars proper, try its younger more relaxed brother **Stars Cafe** *($$ - $$$)* around the corner. *Civic Center* 500 Van Ness (McAllister); (415) 861-4344

Stoyanof's *Greek $ - $$*
Inner Sunset 1240 Ninth Ave. (Lincoln); (415) 664-3664
This bright, airy restaurant serves Greek salads and pastries cafeteria style for lunch and sit-down dinners of delicious Greek chicken and fish dishes. The friendly staff kindly accommodates small children.

Tadich Grill *American/Seafood $$*
Financial District 240 California St. (Battery); (415) 391-2373
To many second- or third-generation natives (and some tourists), this near 150-year-old restaurant, with its wooden booths and veteran waiters, defines old-time San Francisco. Straightforward, high-quality seafood, along with lots of sourdough bread and a heavy dose of Gilded Age nostalgia.

Thanh Long *Vietnamese $ - $$*
Sunset 4101 Judah St. (46th Ave.); (415) 665-1146
Local word-of-mouth recommendations for Vietnamese restaurants always include this family-run outpost (the An family also own Crustacean restaurant) not far from Ocean Beach. Dungeness crab, cooked with garlic and ginger, is the specialty here.

Thep Phanom *Thai $ - $$*
Lower Haight 400 Waller St. (Fillmore); (415) 431-2526
Those in the know come here for "Weeping Lady," a fantastic eggplant dish. It's the locals' favorite Thai eatery.

Ti Couz *French $ - $$*
Mission 3108 16th St. (Valencia); (415) 252-7373
In the vanguard of 16th Street's little boom, this airy Breton-style creperie quickly drew crowds for rich, savory buckwheat crepes filled with ratatouille or salmon and heavenly dessert crepes with poached pears. The high ceilings, white stucco and wood-beamed walls, and farm-style furniture will transport you to Brittany. Prepare to wait on weekend nights.

Tommy Toy's Haute Cuisine Chinoise
Chinese $$$$ Financial District
655 Montgomery St. (Washington); (415) 397-4888
This extremely upmarket Chinese restaurant is famous for entrées like whole lobster with peppercorn sauce on angel-hair pasta. The elegantly presented but rather straightforward food may not justify these prices, but the gleaming surfaces and attentive service exude luxury. Well-spaced tables allow plenty of privacy when you want to make a call from your mobile phone.

Universal Cafe *California/Eclectic $$ - $$$*
Potrero Hill 2814 19th St. (Florida); (415) 821-4608
Another in the dimly lit, industrial decor category, but this one's quieter and more intimate than its colleagues. Great attention is paid to every menu item: a recent salad mixed asparagus tips, pea shoots, arugula, and bocconcini. Snack on the flat bread appetizer with caramelized onions.

San Francisco Restaurants

VERTIGO

Vertigo *California/Eclectic* $$$ - $$$$
Financial District 600 Montgomery St.
(Clay); (415) 433-7250
This chic yet welcoming two-level restaurant at the base of the Transamerica Pyramid affords views *straight up* of the foreshortened skyscraper. Locals (and the occasional local celeb) come here for chef Jeffrey Inahara's Asian-accented eclectic cuisine: dishes like roast sea bass with onion confit and vegetables are perfection.

Vicolo *Pizza* $
Civic Center 201 Ivy St. (Franklin); (415) 863-2382
On a side street in Hayes Valley, this high-ceilinged cafe serves rich cornmeal-crust pizza; toppings are always perfect and well-balanced. For a few bucks, one piece of the artichoke pizza at lunch will keep you full until dinner. Or order a half-baked pizza to go, which you finish baking in your oven.

Woodward's Gardens *California/Eclectic* $$$
Mission 1700 Mission St. (Duboce);
(415) 621-7122
Despite an urban no-man's-land location, foodies and locals in-the-know flock to this

intimate and rather chic eatery, the creation of veteran chefs Dana Tomassino (Greens) and Margie Conrad (Postrio). In the shadow of the freeway at a busy intersection, Woodward's Gardens is named for the formal garden that was planted here in the 19th century (note archival images on wall). Dishes like broiled tangerine with gorgonzola and almost any fresh fish are beautifully presented, and less expensive than they'd be elsewhere in town. Make reservations: 9 tables and 4 seatings per night. No credit cards.

CHEF MARGIE CONRAD AT
WOODWARD'S GARDENS

Wu Kong *Chinese* $$ - $$$
Financial District/Embarcadero South
101 Spear St. (Mission); (415) 957-9300
At this swank Shanghai-cuisine restaurant, dishes are prepared with high style: "vegetable goose" is rich and satisfying, while chicken in wine sauce is light and subtle.

Yank Sing *Chinese* $ - $$
Financial District 427 Battery St.;
(415) 362-1640

South of Market 49 Stevenson St.;
(415) 495-4510
Both locations of this relatively upscale tea-house fill quickly at lunchtime with fans of this restaurant's house specialty, dim sum.

YaYa *Middle Eastern* $$ - $$$
Inner Sunset 1220 Ninth Ave. (Lincoln);
(415) 566-6966
Steps away from the Ninth Avenue Golden Gate Park entrance, this small, popular restaurant serves high-end "Mesopotamian" (Iraqi) dishes with a California/haute cuisine twist. Main courses of kuftas and kebabs are inventive and deceptively rich.

Yoshida-Ya *Japanese* $$ - $$$
Pacific Heights 2909 Webster St. (Union)
(415) 346-3431
Patrons can order both traditional and original Japanese dishes in this smart sushi bar and restaurant. For instance, you might start with classic yakitori (grilled chicken), or choose a sampler of mushrooms sauteed in a sake sauce. But service is not the best.

YoYo Bistro *Japanese/Eclectic* $$$
Japantown 1611 Post St. (Laguna)
(415) 922-7788
Elka Gilmore's nouvelle bistro features entrées such as crisp-skinned salmon with wild mushrooms and gingered parsnip puree, but the staff is most proud of its menu of "tsumami" (snacks to accompany cocktails): oysters come with wasabi vinaigrette or tomato lemongrass gelee. Housed in the Miyako Hotel.

Zazie *French* $$
Cole Valley 941 Cole (Parnassus);
(415) 564-5332

Roast chicken or salad on the patio of this cozy neighborhood bistro is a perfect brunch, but be prepared to wait.

Zarzuela's *Spanish* $$
Russian Hill 2000 Hyde St. (Union)
(415) 436-0800
More authentic (if pricier) than the city's other tapaterias, this attractive, popular storefront offers plates of octopus (thankfully less oily than you'd find in Madrid), marinated mushrooms, and Spanish tortilla. Plus a seafood-stocked paella.

Zuni Café *California/Mediterranean* $$ - $$$
Civic Center 1658 Market St. (Rose);
(415) 552-2522
Excellent service, moderate prices, terrific cocktails, and an informal yet tony atmosphere make this a favorite spot for San Franciscans. The expertly prepared food is never precious. Choose from an impressive list of oysters, then order Caesar salad or roast chicken with Tuscan bread salad.

ZUNI CAFE

San Francisco Restaurants

East Bay Restaurants

East Bay

Bay Wolf *California/Eclectic* $$$
Oakland 3853 Piedmont (Rio Vista)
(510) 655-6004
The talented kitchen staff at this quiet, un-pretentious restaurant do outstanding interpretations of various Mediterranean and regional American cuisines, changing their menu every few weeks to highlight a different cooking tradition. Some locals place it neck and neck with Chez Panisse, and at more reasonable prices, too. They might serve a duck liver flan with green peppercorns and marsala; another day may bring crabcakes with peanut slaw and black-eyed peas to the menu.

BAY WOLF

Blue Nile *African* $ - $$
Berkeley 2525 Telegraph Ave. (Dwight);
(510) 540-6777
As Berkeley's best Ethiopian restaurant, the low-key, comfortable spot attracts lots of students and locals who come to savor specialties like split-pea stew and pepper beef. Huge portions.

Bucci's *Italian/California* $$ - $$$
Emeryville 6121 Hollis St. (59th St.)
(510) 547-4725
The ur Emeryville restaurant experience: warehouse chic and excellent Cal-Italian cuisine—pizzas and antipasti are consistently delectable. Plastic columns lit from the inside add a sense of humor to an otherwise slightly attitudinous atmosphere.

Cafe at Chez Panisse *(see* **Chez Panisse***)*

The Cambodiana's *Cambodian* $ - $$
Berkeley 2156 University Ave. (Oxford)
(510) 843-4630
The French-accented Khmer cuisine by husband-wife chef team Lim Sue Ke and Bopha Pol impresses critics and patrons far and wide. Try grilled lamb marinated in ginger, chiles, and lemongrass.

Chez Panisse *California/Eclectic* $$$$
Berkeley 1517 Shattuck Ave. (Cedar);
(510) 548-5525
Alice Waters and a clowder of like-minded chefs re-invented American cuisine when they opened the doors of this shaded Craftsman-style former home in 1971 (named for a character in the French Marius film trilogy, as the many art deco movie posters will tell you). Using only the finest organic produce and free-range meats and poultry, the kitchen staff presents new dishes every day in their prix-fixe seasonal menus: some have included green asparagus and spring onion risotto with black trumpet mushrooms, and grilled striped bass with black olives, white bean puree, esca-

role, and spinach. Upstairs is the more affordable **Cafe at Chez Panisse** (548-5049 $$ - $$$), a simple but warm Mission oak-trimmed room where the pizzettas, salads, and grilled entrées are impeccable.

*IN THE KITCHEN AT
CHEZ PANISSE*

Citron *California/Eclectic* $$$
Oakland 5484 College Ave. (Lawton)
(510) 653-5484
Lemony yellow walls, flagstone floor, and wicker chairs make this Rockridge spot ideal to savor a range of brilliant dishes: Hangar steak with sweetpea anchoiade appears on the same menu as Caribbean crab in citrus sauce with Bhutan red rice and fennel-papaya salsa.

Everett & Jones Barbeque *Barbecue* $
Berkeley 1955 San Pablo Ave.
(University); (510) 548-8261
Oakland 3411 Telegraph Ave. (34th St.);
(510) 601-9377
After 20 years of 'cueing, E&J's has a large and loyal clientele.

Flint's Bar-B-Q *Barbecue* $
Oakland 6609 Shattuck Ave. (66th St.);
(510) 653-0593

Oakland 3114 San Pablo Ave. (Market);
(510) 658-9912
Flint's is the joint for spicy barbecue—ask for the hot sauce. After your wait in line, you'll get one of the many pork and beef options (there's chicken too), slathered in tingling sauce, wrapped in foil to take away with a side of potato salad.

Hong Kong East Ocean *Chinese* $$
Emeryville 3199 Powell St. (on marina)
(510) 655-4456
Looking out over San Francisco Bay, this is probably the most popular special-occasion restaurant for Oakland's Hong Kong expats. Excellent dim sum by day and Cantonese dishes by night.

Kirala Sushi *Japanese* $
Berkeley 2100 Ward St. (Shattuck);
(510) 549-3486
Not a lot of atmosphere, but the friendly chefs and servers deliver on fresh, good, inexpensive sushi. Perfect for a quick fix.

La Imperial *Mexican* $
Hayward 948 C St.; (510) 537-6227
Good food, hearty portions, and a relaxed atmosphere in this family-run restaurant attract a clientele that includes everyone from bikers to business executives.

Lalime's *Mediterranean/California* $$
Berkeley 1329 Gilman St. (Neilsen);
(510) 527-9838
A charming white stucco home houses this warmly lit, sophisticated restaurant where items like lamb medallions and ahi tuna are given creative treatment. Best values are prix-fixe dinners: sign onto the mailing list to know menus ahead of time.

East Bay Restaurants

Le Cheval *Vietnamese* $ - $$
Oakland 1007 Clay St.
(510) 763-8957/344 20th St.; (510) 763-3610
Authentic Vietnamese cooking; you'll notice a French accent in some dishes. Try the marinated "orange flavor" beef or the lemongrass prawns.

Nan Yang *Burmese* $
Oakland 301 8th St. (Harrison); (510) 465-6924/6048 College Ave. (Claremont); (510) 655-3298
California-influenced Burmese dishes allow you a change of pace: go for the fish soup, then share a shrimp and mango saute, as well as a filling noodle dish.

Oakland Grill *American* $
Oakland 301 S. Franklin St. (3rd St.)
(510) 835-1176
Housed in the Oakland Produce Market, this converted warehouse is great for families with rowdy tykes. Big breakfasts all day long, as well as burgers and steaks.

O Chame *Japanese/California* $$$
Berkeley 1830 Fourth St. (Hearst)
(510) 841-8783
Chef-owner David Vardy began his Japanese culinary career baking teacakes; now he and his wife Hiromi run a sophisticated restaurant whose stone floors, spare wood furniture, and dim lighting create a serene mood. California and Japanese cuisines balance and blend in such dishes as udon with smoked trout and wakame.

Oliveto's *Italian/California* $$$
Oakland 5655 College Ave. (Shafter)
(510) 547-5356

The second-floor dining room of this corner restaurant in the Rockridge Market Hall now offers top-notch northern Italian risotti and pastas thanks to an influx of chefs from Chez Panisse, Campton Place, and Stars. If you've any time or budget constraint, don't go upstairs for lunch (service is slow at best, portions tiny) although the room is pleasant at that time of day. Downstairs ($) you can order fresh pizza and tapas for a light, moderately priced lunch from the counter, then sit by the open French doors.

Omnivore *California/Eclectic* $$ - $$$
Berkeley 3015 Shattuck Ave. (Ashby)
(510) 848-4346
In a welcoming, almost homey setting, you can enjoy fresh, light California fare which draws from Asian and Mediterranean cuisines, but never seems self-conscious or overdone.

Petrouchka *Russian* $$
Berkeley 2930 College Ave. (Ashby); (510) 848-7860
In a relaxing and warm room decorated with Chagall posters, diners relish updated Russian favorites like pirogi, blintzes, and golubtzy. A string quartet plays some evenings.

Pho 84 *Vietnamese* $
Oakland 354 17th St. (Webster)
(510) 832-1429
Always crowded, this casual phö shop serves good low-priced standards like clay pots and chicken salad, as well as a very good phö (spiced beef noodle soup).

Plearn Thai *Thai* $ - $$
Berkeley 2050 University Ave. (Shattuck)
(510) 841-2148
More than likely, you'll have to wait to eat at this highly regarded Thai restaurant—but you'll be glad you did when you tuck into sauteed prawns or green mussels.

Red Sea *African* $ - $$
Oakland 5200 Claremont (Telegraph)
(510) 655-3757
Family-style restaurant full of East African patrons. Spicy dishes are served with injera.

Rick & Ann's Cafe *American/California* $
Berkeley 2922 Domingo Ave. (Ashby)
(510) 649-8538
"California rustic" may best describe the interior of this sunny cafe near the Claremont Resort. Come for a breakfast of lacy and light cornmeal pancakes, or eggs with salsa and turkey sausage. For dinner, order upscale renditions of American Mom foods like meatloaf and macaroni and cheese.

Rivoli *Mediterranean/California* $$
Berkeley 1539 Solano Ave. (Peralta)
(510) 526-2542
An instant hit, thanks to the creative Mediterranean and Italian regional cuisine offered by chef-owners (and husband and wife) Roscoe Skipper and Wendy Brucker. Try portobello fritters with lemon aioli and arugula, then perhaps Dungeness crab and saffron lasagna with leeks, bechamel, and tomato sauce. Desserts are American and dairy-intensive. Sit in the elegant back room, with its glass wall overlooking the garden and its (believe it or not) rather lovely resident skunks.

RIVOLI

Rustica *Italian/California* $$
Oakland 5422 College Ave. (Manila);
(510) 654-1601
Yet one more Rockridge gourmet spot, Rustica earns its address with darn good pizza. Choose peasant style, cornmeal-fennel, or wheat-free rice crust, and top it with feta, smoked chicken, artichokes, or any of the appetizing combinations listed.

Scott's Seafood & Grill
Seafood/American $$ - $$$
Oakland Jack London Square
(510) 444-3456
As at Scott's San Francisco locations, you're best off ordering basic seafood dishes: try the grilled salmon, served on a bed of greens. Locals flock to the Sunday jazz brunch and sip Ramos Gin Fizzes.

Skates *Seafood/Eclectic* $$ - $$$
Berkeley 100 Seawall Dr. (on marina);
(510) 549-1900
The crowd's energetic, the appetizers are delicious, and the view is splendid at this waterfront restaurant. Order fresh seafood or mesquite-grilled ribs for dinner, sashimi or chicken satay for a snack.

East Bay Restaurants

Tachibana *Japanese* $$ - $$$
Oakland 5812 College Ave. (Birch);
(510) 654-3668
Any of the sushi offerings in this spacious, appealing dining room reveals that these chefs are true perfectionists. Also impressive are the light tempura and robata grilled chicken.

Vi's *Vietnamese* $
Oakland 724 Webster St. (7th St.);
(510) 835-8375
Unassuming but attractive, this excellent Chinatown eatery is always packed with locals (Alice Waters stops by) who come for succulent beef stew, crisp chicken salad, and refreshing rice-paper rolls, for a song.

SOUTH BAY & PENINSULA

Blue Chalk Cafe *American* $$
Palo Alto 630 Ramona St. (Hamilton);
(415) 326-1020
Superb Southern-style cooking in Silicon Valley? Try the fried catfish here before answering. Enjoy the sun on the front patio, or shoot a game of pool. The crowd leans to the singles set.

Flea Street Cafe *California/Eclectic* $$$
Menlo Park 3607 Alameda de las Pulgas (Avy) (415) 854-1226
Freshly baked breads accompany Jesse Cool's imaginative dishes—try roasted Cornish hen with sage-jalapeño gravy and red onion cornbread stuffing. Victorian-inspired dining rooms make this a romantic restaurant; excellent for brunch.

Gordon Biersch Brewing Co. *American* $$
Palo Alto 640 Emerson St. (Hamilton)
(415) 323-7723/*San Jose* 33 E. San Fernando St. (1st St.) (408) 294-6785
Students and locals flock here, sometimes for basics like roast chicken or seafood stew, but most come for a pint brewed on site.

Hong Kong Flower Lounge *Chinese* $$$
Millbrae 51 Millbrae Ave. (El Camino);

(415) 592-6666
1671 El Camino Real (Park Blvd.); (415) 588-9972
Two more in Alice Wong's Flower Lounge group. Go to the Millbrae Avenue spot for dishes incorporating shark's fin and abalone as well as many other shellfish; go to El Camino (the original Flower Lounge) for dim sum at lunch, or hot pot at dinner.

Il Fornaio Cucina Italiana *Italian* $ - $$
Palo Alto 520 Cowper St. (Hamilton)
(415) 853-3888
Another in the Il Fornaio chain, this one serves delicious pizzas from the wood-burning oven. It's situated in a lovely Italianate setting at the Garden Court Hotel.

Left at Albuquerque *Mexican* $$
Palo Alto 445 Emerson St. (University)
(415) 326-1011
On weekends, this high-ceilinged room fills with high-spirited Silicon Valley thirty-somethings craving Southwest cuisine. Choose from over 100 tequilas while you await chef David Cox's grilled pork with chipotle mashed potatoes or roast corn and chicken tortilla soup.

Le Mouton Noir *French* $$$ - $$$$
  Saratoga 14560 Big Basin Way (5th St.)
  (408) 867-7017
Varied and perfectly presented lamb, duck, and game dishes are the specialties at this intimate restaurant. Vegetarians can choose from the seasonal fresh produce selection.

MacArthur Park *American* $$ - $$$
  Palo Alto 27 University Ave. (El Camino);
  (415) 321-9990
As at the SF location, this steakhouse is popular for mesquite-grilled steaks and oakwood-smoked ribs.

Peninsula Fountain & Grill *American* $
  Palo Alto 566 Emerson St. (Hamilton);
  (415) 323-3131
Come to this real soda fountain (ca. 1923) for malts, pancake breakfasts, and meatloaf.

Tavern Grill *American* $$$
  Burlingame 1448 Burlingame Ave.
  (El Camino); (415) 344-5692
Ben Davis (formerly of San Francisco's Cypress Club) presents fresh, seasonal produce in his "American bistro" menu—try a spicy oyster B.L.T. or a turkey Cobb salad accented with currants and spiced walnuts. Pretty patio; good live music, too.

231 Ellsworth *French* $$$
  San Mateo 231 S. Ellsworth St. (2nd St.);
  (415) 347-7231
It's worth the trip to this elegant restaurant, where chef Derek Burns turns out contemporary French haute cuisine. Co-owner Ken Ottoboni harvests mushrooms on the side, so many dishes feature fresh morels and chanterelles.

Vicolo Pizzeria *Pizza* $
  Palo Alto 473 University Ave. (Cowper);
  (415) 324-4877
With its faux-Italian decor, the Palo Alto location of the San Francisco pizzeria draws lots of Stanford students, who come for the cornmeal-crust pizza with toppings like sautéed vegetables and interesting cheeses.

The Village Pub *California/Eclectic* $$$
  Woodside 2967 Woodside Rd. (Whiskey Hill); (415) 851-1294
Hardly pub-like, this restaurant's understated interior—eggshell walls accented with contemporary prints—suits perfectly the haute California cuisine. Come here for roast duck with ancho chili and mango, perhaps after a trip to nearby Filoli.

South Bay Restaurants

North Bay & Wine Country Restaurants

North Bay & Wine Country

Marin County

Guaymas *Mexican* $$
Tiburon 5 Main St. (at ferry);
(415) 435-6300
A terrific dockside location and an action-packed bar scene make this trendy regional Mexican restaurant a festive place to eat, if a tad pricy. Flavors are generally mild, but the mesquite-grilled seafood and the many tamales go well with the reliable margarita.

Jennie Low's *Chinese* $
Mill Valley 38 Miller Ave.
(E. Blithedale); (415) 388-8868
Novato 120 Vintage Way
(Rowland Blvd.); (415) 892-8838
These very popular spots serve Hunan, Szechuan, Cantonese, and Mandarin cuisines (with a nod to California health and freshness standards). Jennie hovers in the tidy dining room while Marinites feast on spicy string beans and pot stickers.

Lark Creek Inn *American* $$$
Larkspur 234 Magnolia St. (William)
(415) 924-7766
Bradley Ogden's "rural sophisticate" cooking style is featured in this attractive clapboard house, nestled in a redwood grove. Best is brunch, when you can sit on the patio or in the skylit dining room and feast on eggs with smoked salmon or wild berry flapjacks with lemon butter.

Left Bank *French* $$
Larkspur 507 Magnolia St. (Ward);
(415) 927-3331
At this pretty, upbeat eatery, chef Roland Passot (of the city's La Folie) serves French brasserie classics like steak and frites, steamed mussels, and roast chicken. Have brunch on the sunny patio.

Napa County

Auberge du Soleil *California/Eclectic* $$$$
Rutherford 180 Rutherford Hill Rd.;
(707) 963-1211
With a Provençal decor and stunning views, the "Inn of the Sun" may be Napa's most romantic spot, but the kitchen can be inconsistent. But hearty dishes like grilled venison rack with huckleberries and sweet potatoes live up brilliantly to the lovely surroundings. (See picture page 286.)

Brava Terrace *California/Eclectic* $$ - $$$
St. Helena 3010 Hwy. 29 (Lodi Ln.);
(707) 963-9300
At this pretty bistro, diners relish chef-owner Fred Halpert's flavorful French provincial cassoulets and Italian risotti while seated in the maple-floored dining room or on the lovely back terrace overlooking a picturesque creek. Great service.

DOMAINE CHANDON

Domaine Chandon *French/California* $$$$
Yountville 1 California Dr. (Hwy. 29);
(707) 944-2892
Since its arrival 20 years ago as the region's
first fine restaurant, chef Philippe Jeanty
has maintained impeccable standards at
this sparkling-wine house. A California accent is used in French dishes such as roasted squab with wild mushrooms, fava beans,
foie gras, and black Mission fig sauce.

French Laundry *French/California* $$$$
Yountville 6640 Washington St. (Creek);
(707) 944-2380
Chef Thomas Keller showcases high-profile
ingredients such as caviar, duck confit, and
foie gras in delicious—if a bit overpriced
haute cuisine. Tasteful country French
decor and soft lighting are inviting.

MUSTARD'S GRILL

Mustard's Grill *American/California* $$$
Yountville 7399 Hwy. 29 (Yountville
Cross); (707) 944-2424
The black-and-white tile floor here has
been much trod upon: as at her Fog City
Diner, Cindy Pawlcyn's Mustard's is noisy
and lively. Food is American country fare

with a California twist: grilled rabbit,
mesquite-grilled seafood, and excellent sal-
ads and soups.

Terra *California/Eclectic* $$$
St. Helena 1345 Railroad (Hunt) (707)
963-8931
Critics and patrons rave about this place.
Chef-owner Hiro Sone combines French,
Italian, and Asian cuisines in dishes like
duck liver wontons with wild mushroom
sauce or salmon in miso. Sone's wife, Lissa
Doumani, handles the service, as well as the
fantastic desserts. The dining rooms' exposed wood beams and fieldstone walls create a casual, unpretentious atmosphere.

TRA VIGNE

Tra Vigne *Italian* $$$
St. Helena 1050 Charter Oak Ave. (Hwy.
29); (707) 967-4444
Inside this fieldstone former wine cellar,
you'll feel warmed by the sun; at night, by
the gilt trim, wood floor, and Italian tiles.
After considering the house-cured pancetta
and homemade mozzarella, breads, vine-
gars, sauces, and pastas, you might order
several antipasti and pastas, then share.

North Bay & Wine Country Restaurants

North Bay & Wine Country Restaurants

Sonoma County

Bistro Ralph *California/French* $$
Healdsburg 109 Plaza St. (Healdsburg);
(707) 433-1380
Friendly and fun, with a winemaker clientele, Ralph Tingle's place pleases with an array of well-executed tony bistro dishes: try Dungeness crab ravioli, Szechuan calamari, or lamb meatloaf. Great wine list, with unusual varieties like cinsault listed.

Cafe Lolo *American/California* $$
Santa Rosa 620 Fifth St. (D St.);
(707) 576-7822
This fun bistro is proof that Santa Rosa is acknowledging its Wine Country surroundings. Try the grilled chicken salad, with applewood smoked bacon, oranges, baby spinach, and crispy fried onions.

Kenwood Restaurant *French/California* $$$
Kenwood 9900 Hwy. 12 (Warm Springs)
(707) 833-6326
This low-key restaurant offers a wide array of simple country French/American regional dishes, from crabcakes with greens to rack of lamb with Bordelaise sauce. The kitchen consistently turns out excellent lunches and dinners.

KENWOOD RESTAURANT

Sonoma Mission Inn *California/Eclectic*
Sonoma 18140 Hwy. 12 (Boyes Blvd.);
(707) 938-9000
In the hotel's formal restaurant, the **Grille** ($$$), patrons can sit by French windows overlooking the inn's pool and gardens, or dine on the patio. "Wine Country" dishes include the signature roast leg of Sonoma lamb, as well as spa cuisine. Many prefer the more casual **Cafe** ($$), where an open kitchen turns out hearty breakfasts and regional Italian dishes from the wood-burning oven. Appetizers here are meal-sized.

San Francisco Restaurants by Cuisine

Refer to pages 289 - 311 for alphabetically listed reviews of the restaurants below.

African
Rasselas $ - $$

American
The Big Four $$$
Big Nate's Bar-B-Q $$
Bix $$$
Cafe Majestic $$$
California Cul. Acad. $$$
Campton Place $$$$
Flytrap $$ - $$$
Fog City Diner $$$
Fournou's Ovens $$$$
Harris's Steak House $$$
Hayes Street Grill $$ - $$$
Ivy's $$ - $$$
Kate's Kitchen $
Klein's Delicatessen $
Liberty Cafe $$
MacArthur Park $$
The Meetinghouse $$$
One Market $$$
Powell's Place $
Rumpus $$$
Scott's Seafood Grill $$ - $$$
Spaghetti Western $
Stars $$$$
Stars Cafe $$ - $$$
Tadich Grill $$

Austrian
Hyde Street Bistro $$

Basque
Des Alpes $

Barbecue
Big Nate's Bar-B-Q $$
Powell's Place $

Burmese
Mandalay $

California/Eclectic
Act IV $$$$
Alain Rondelli $$$ - $$$$
Aqua $$$ - $$$$
Big Four $$$$
Bistro M $$$
Bistro Rôti $$$
Boulevard $$ - $$$
Bruno's $$ - $$$
Cafe Majestic
California Cul. Acad. $$$
Campton Place $$$$
Carta $$
Cypress Club $$$
Delancey Street $$ - $$$
Eleven $$
Enrico's $$
Eos $$
Firefly $$$
Flying Saucer $$$ - $$$$
Fog City Diner $$$
42 Degrees $$$
Greens $$ - $$$
Hawthorne Lane $$$$
The Heights $$$$
Ivy's $$ - $$$
JT's Bistro $$$$
Julie's Supper Club $$
Liberty Cafe $$
LuLu $$
LuLu Bis $$$
LuLu Cafe $$
Masa's $$$$
Mecca $$$
Millennium $$
Moose's $$
One Market $$$
Oritalia $$ - $$$
Pacific $$$
PlumpJack Cafe $$ - $$$

Postrio $$$$
Rest. at 2223 Market $$ - $$$
Ritz-Carlton Din. Rm. $$$$
Ritz-Carlton Terrace $$ - $$$
Rooster $$
Rosmarino $$$
Rubicon $$$$
Ruby's $$
Rumpus $$$
Slow Club $ - $$
Splendido's $$
Universal Cafe $$ - $$$
Vertigo $$$ - $$$$
Woodward's Gardens $$$
YoYo Bistro $$$
Zuni Café $$ - $$$

Cambodian
Angkor Wat $
Phnom Penh $

Caribbean
Cha Cha Cha $ - $$
Geva's $$
Miss Pearl's Jam House $$

Central American
Cha Cha Cha $ - $$
El Nuevo Frutilandia $ - $$

Chinese
China Moon Cafe $$$
Eric's $
Gourmet Carousel $
Happy Immortal $
Harbor Village $$ - $$$
Hong Kong Flower $$
House of Nanking $
Kowloon Vegetarian $
Lucky Creation $
R&G Lounge $ - $$
Red Crane $

San Francisco Restaurants by Cuisine

Tommy Toy's $$$$
Wu Kong $$ - $$$
Yank Sing $ - $$

Deli
Klein's Delicatessen $

French
Alain Rondelli $$$$
Amelio's $$$ - $$$$
Baker Street Bistro $$
Bistro M $$$
Bistro Rôti $$ - $$$
Bizou $$
Café Bastille $
Café Claude $ - $$
California Cul. Acad. $$$
Des Alpes *(Basque)* $
Fleur de Lys $$$$
Flying Saucer $$$ - $$$$
Fringale $$$
The Heights $$$$
JT's Bistro $$$$
La Folie $$$$
Le Trou $$ - $$$
Masa's $$$$
Pastis $$ - $$$
Pacific $$ - $$$
South Park Café $$ - $$$
Ti Couz $ - $$
Zazie $$

Greek
Stoyanof's $ - $$

Indian
Ganges $
North India $$

International
Carta $$
Eos $$
Rooster $$

Italian
Acquerello $$$$
Buca Giovanni $$$

Caffe Delle Stelle $ - $$
Caffe Macaroni $$
Eleven $$
Enrico's $$
Hyde Street Bistro $$
Il Fornaio $$
Kuleto's $$ - $$$
Laghi $$$
Little City $ - $$
Lo Cocos $$
Michelangelo Caffè $ - $$
Moose's $$
Oritalia $$ - $$$
Palio D'Asti $$
Ristorante Ecco $$
Rose Pistola
Ruby's $$

Japanese
Ebisu $$
Kabuto Sushi $$ - $$$
Oritalia $$ - $$$
Osome $$ - $$$
Sapporo-Ya $
Yoshida-Ya $$ - $$$
Yoyo Bistro $$$

Mediterranean
Act IV $$$$
Bruno's $$ - $$$
LuLu $$
LuLu Bis $$$
LuLu Cafe $$
Mecca $$ - $$$
Rest. at 2223 Market $$ - $$$
Rosmarino $$$
Slow Club $ - $$
Splendido's $$
Vertigo $$$ - $$$$
Zuni Café $$ - $$$

Mexican
Cadillac Bar $$ - $$$
Chevy's $$
La Cumbre $

Pancho Villa $
Pozole $

Middle Eastern
YaYa $$ - $$$

Pacific Rim
Betelnut Peiji Wu $$
China Moon Cafe $$$
Pacific $$ - $$$
Silks $$$$
YoYo Bistro $$$

Pizza
North Beach Pizza $
Ruby's $$
Vicolo $

Seafood
Aqua $$$ - $$$$
Hayes Street Grill $$ - $$$
Scott's Seafood Grill $$ - $$$
Tadich Grill $$

Spanish
Alejandro's $$
Esperpento $
Paella La Movida $$
Picaro $
Zarzuela's $$

Thai
Khan Toke Thai House $$
Marnee Thai $ - $$
Royal Thai $ - $$
Thep Phanom $ - $$

Vegetarian
Greens $$ - $$$
Kowloon Vegetarian $
Millennium $$
Red Crane $

Vietnamese
Crustacean $$ - $$$
Golden Turtle $$
The Slanted Door $
Thanh Long $ - $$

PIPE DREAMS ON AN EMPTY STOMACH

*M*y feet tingled. I thought I was going to die the very next moment. But I didn't die, and walked four miles and picked up ten long butts and took them back to Marylou's hotel room and poured their tobacco in my old pipe and lit up. I was too young to know what had happened. In the window I smelled all the food of San Francisco. There were seafood places out there where the buns were hot, and the baskets were good enough to eat too; where the menus themselves were soft with food esculence as though dipped in hot broths and roasted dry and good enough to eat too. Just show me the bluefish spangle on a seafood menu and I'd eat it; let me smell the drawn butter and lobster claws. There were places where they specialized in thick red roast beef au jus, or roast chicken basted in wine. There were places where hamburgs sizzled on grills and the coffee was only a nickel. And oh, that pan-fried chowmein flavored air that blew into my room from Chinatown, vying with the spaghetti sauces of North Beach, the soft-shell crab of fisherman's Wharf—nay, the ribs of Fillmore turning on spits! Throw in the Market Street chili beans, redhot, and french-fried potatoes of the Embarcadero wino night, and steamed clams from Sausalito across the bay, and that's my ah-dream of San Francisco. Add fog, hunger-making fog, and the throb of neons in the soft night, the clack of high-heeled beauties, white doves in a Chinese grocery window . . .

—Jack Kerouac, *On the Road*, 1957

East Bay Restaurant Index

East Bay Restaurant Index

Refer to pages 312 - 316 for alphabetically listed reviews of the restaurants below.

By Cuisine

African
Blue Nile $ - $$
Red Sea $ - $$

American
Oakland Grill $
Rick & Ann's Cafe $
Scott's Seafood $$ - $$$

Barbecue
Everett & Jones Barbeque $
Flint's Bar-B-Q $

Burmese
Nan Yang $

California/Eclectic
Bay Wolf $$$
Bucci's $$ - $$$
Cafe at Chez Panisse $$ - $$$
Chez Panisse $$$$
Citron $$$
Lalime's $$
O Chame $$$
Oliveto's $$$
Omnivore $$ - $$$
Rick & Ann's Cafe $
Rivoli $$
Skates $$ - $$$

Cambodian
The Cambodiana's $ - $$

Chinese
Hong Kong East Ocean $$

Italian
Bucci's $$ - $$$
Oliveto's $$$
Rustica $$

Japanese
Kirala Sushi $
O Chame $$$
Tachibana $$ - $$$

Mediterranean
Lalime's $$
Rivoli $$

Mexican
La Imperial $

Russian
Petrouchka $$

Seafood
Scott's Seafood $$ - $$$
Skates $$ - $$$

Thai
Plearn Thai $ - $$

Vietnamese
Le Cheval $ - $$
Pho 84 $
Vi's $

By Town

Berkeley
Blue Nile $ - $$
Cafe at Chez Panisse $$ - $$$
The Cambodiana's $ - $$
Chez Panisse $$$$
Everett & Jones $
Flint's Bar-B-Q $
Kirala Sushi $
Lalime's $$
O Chame $$$
Omnivore $$ - $$$
Petrouchka $$
Plearn Thai $ - $$
Rick & Ann's Cafe $
Rivoli $$
Skates $$ - $$$

Emeryville
Bucci's $$ - $$$
Hong Kong East Ocean $$

Hayward
La Imperial $

Oakland
Bay Wolf $$$
Citron $$$
Everett & Jones $
Flint's Bar-B-Q $
Le Cheval $ - $$
Nan Yang $
Oakland Grill $
Oliveto's $$$
Pho 84 $
Red Sea $ - $$
Rustica $$
Scott's Seafood $$ - $$$
Tachibana $$ - $$$
Vi's $

South Bay Restaurant Index

Refer to pages 316 - 317 for alphabetically listed reviews of the restaurants below.

By Cuisine

American
Blue Chalk Cafe $$
Gordon Biersch Brewing $$
MacArthur Park $$ - $$$
Peninsula Fountain & Grill $
Tavern Grill $$$

California/Eclectic
Flea Street Cafe $$$
Tavern Grill $$$
The Village Pub $$$

Chinese
Hong K ong Flower Lng. $$$

French
Le Mouton Noir $$$ - $$$$

231 Ellsworth $$$

Italian
Il Fornaio $ - $$
Vicolo Pizzeria $

Mexican
Left at Albuquerque $$

By Town

Burlingame
Tavern Grill $$$

Menlo Park
Flea Street Cafe $$$

Millbrae
Hong Kong Flower Lng. $$$

Palo Alto
Blue Chalk Cafe $$
Gordon Biersch Brewing $$
Il Fornaio $ - $$
Left at Albuquerque $$
MacArthur Park $$ - $$$
Peninsula Fountain & Grill $
Vicolo Pizzeria $

San Mateo
231 Ellsworth $$$

Saratoga
Le Mouton Noir $$$ - $$$$

Woodside
The Village Pub $$$

North Bay Restaurant Index

Refer to pages 318 - 320 for alphabetically listed reviews of the restaurants below.

By Cuisine

American
Cafe Lolo $$
Lark Creek Inn $$$
Mustard's Grill $$$

California/Eclectic
Auberge du Soleil $$$$
Bistro Ralph $$
Brava Terrace $$ $$$
Cafe Lolo $$
Domaine Chandon $$$$
French Laundry $$$$
Kenwood $$$
Lark Creek Inn $$$
Mustard's Grill $$$
Sonoma Mission Cafe $$
Sonoma Mission Grille $$$
Terra $$$

Chinese
Jennie Low $

French
Bistro Ralph $$
Domaine Chandon $$$$
French Laundry $$$$
Kenwood $$$
Left Bank $$

Italian
Tra Vigne $$$

Mexican
Guaymas $$

By Town

Healdsburg
Bistro Ralph $$

Kenwood
Kenwood $$$

Larkspur
Lark Creek Inn $$$
Left Bank $$

Mill Valley
Jennie Low $

Rutherford
Auberge du Soleil $$$$

St. Helena
Brava Terrace $$ $$$
Terra $$$
Tra Vigne $$$

Santa Rosa
Cafe Lolo $$

Sonoma
Sonoma Mission Cafe $$
Sonoma Mission Grille $$$

Tiburon
Guaymas $$

Yountville
Domaine Chandon $$$$
French Laundry $$$$
Mustard's Grill $$$

Nightlife

SWINGING, SIPPING, AND SLACKING IN SAN FRANCISCO

OK, so it's Thursday night, the best night to go out in the city, and you're jonesing for a martini. Maybe a little people-watching is in order. Where to go? For a massive top-shelf martini in a one-of-a-kind setting, step inside the **Red Room**, a small, moody lounge burning with magenta lighting, scarlet upholstery, and a wall of bottles filled with a mysterious crimson liquid (827 Sutter). A bit of inferno, in lower Nob Hill. South into the Tenderloin, the larger, swanky **Club 181** served decades ago as a gangster hangout (rumor has it that before it reopened in 1992, sheetrock hangers found a skeleton in the ceiling), but today it's a groovy-roovy wannabe model hangout where only the cosmopolitans might kill you (181 Eddy).

A less atittudinous scene can be found near Duboce Triangle: down a staircase carpeted in red and black swirls, retro **Cafe du Nord** offers cocktails and live music ranging from swing to salsa to acid jazz (2170 Market). A block away, **Mecca** (2029 Market) is a see-and-be-seen supper club for the next century: half post-industrial, half brown velvet, the spacious room is comprised of small niche areas which surround a circular bar. Singers entertain the well-dressed patrons, many of whom hail from the nearby Castro. Over in the Mission District, **Bruno's** (2389 Mission, 415-550-7455) is a supper club with the decor of a New Jersey Italian restaurant. If you

The Red Room glows red-hot in the evening. (Kerrick James)

Nightlife

The Fillmore's Poster Room is an archive of rock and roll. (Kerrick James)

can, reserve a naugahyde booth for a fantastic dinner (see page 292) or join the cigar-smoking crowd in the bar room next door. Bands play on the tiny stage in the room past the the bar; some folks even try to dance. The ultimate 1940s lounge experience can be found at the corner of Haight and Ashbury, believe it or not, at **Club Deluxe**, home to Brylcreemed bartenders and serious swing dancers. Newcomers are always amazed by the jitterbugging couples spinning and tossing each other between tables and booths. You might catch owner Jay Johnson crooning a Sinatra-esque tune, or Vise Grip and his band; in any event do order a perfectly sugar-rimmed sidecar.

Rock or jazz concerts in the city are pretty swell, too. Most major shows take place in ornate, historic theaters with chandeliers and curtained balconies. Recently reno-vated to its 1920s movie palace glory, the **Warfield** usually hosts big-name folk, rock, and rap bands such as the Foo Fighters and Ice Cube (982 Market St., 415-775-7722). The **Fillmore**, the Warfield's sister concert venue, also has its share of chande-liers and balconies, and while it became famous in hippie days, it's still one of the best places to see shows, which are frequent and varied—the Funky Meters, Garbage, D'Angelo—and the staff is the friendliest in town. Be sure to chill a few minutes in the Poster Room, and check out the historic psychedelia. 1805 Geary, 415-346-6000). Perhaps the most eclectic bookings happen at the exuberantly decorated **Great American Music Hall**, built as a bordello in 1907; you'll find folk, rock, jazz,

Nightlife

and rap here (859 O'Farrell, 415-885-0570). A wonderful old club offering both style and fantastic live music, family-run **Bimbo's** was founded in 1931 by Agostino "Bimbo" Giuntoli. It's easy to picture Ricky Ricardo playing here. These days, the club hosts hot swing bands like Royal Crown Revue and Combustible Edison, as well as rock and jazz acts ranging from Pulp to Cassandra Wilson. (1025 Columbus, 415-474-0365). Since you're in North Beach, stop by stylin' **Enrico's** (504 Broadway). Grab a table outside and sip a Sweetart-like aviation cocktail.

By now it's approaching midnight, and you need a break from the plucked eyebrows and Bombay Sapphire gin. All you want is a good pint of beer, a well-worn barstool, and a decent jukebox. Historic favorites can be found around the corner, especially at **Vesuvio's** (255 Columbus), with its kaleidoscope exterior and Beatnik interior. Across the street are **Spec's**, a dim and smoky joint, and swankier **Tosca**, with its comfy red booths and opera jukebox. All have somehow escaped tourist and yuppie takeover. If you're near the Mission, check out the row of bars on 16th Street between Valencia and Guerrero, all of which offer a solid range of microbrews, good music, and secondhand smoke. If you sign your name to the chalkboard, be warned that pool is serious business in these parts. Around the corner, the appropriately named **Elbo Room** (17th at Valencia) is a hotspot for local acid jazz.

Now it's 1:00 A.M. You've rested up, and the dance clubs are just getting going. Most of the dance-oriented, house-music playing clubs can be found South of Market, and they usually host different theme nights during the week. Pick up a *Bay Guardian* or *SF Weekly* to see what's happening when. The largest clubs, **DV8** (540 Howard), **Sound Factory** (525 Harrison), and **1015 Folsom**, are cool spaces with solid house and hip-hop, but they tend to attract huge hordes on weekends. Local artsy types and bike messengers prefer the **Covered Wagon Saloon** (917 Folsom) and the **Stud** (399 Ninth St.), both of which also host some raucous queer nights. A similar crowd hangs at Potrero Hill's insider favorite **Bottom of the Hill** (1233 17th St.), where edgy bands play for skate rats and diehard rock fans. On Thursdays, there's nothing better for pure dancing than the gay-oriented **Box**.

After-hours clubs in the the city include the **DNA Lounge** (375 11th St.), with its second-floor couches and "VIP Lounge," and the **Cat's Alley** (1190 Folsom), a smaller and trendier spot. If you're gay and male and it's Saturday, there's no other place but **Club Universe** (177 Townsend). It's now 4 A.M., and your hungry club-hopper pals toddle off to **Baghdad Cafe** (2295 Market), where they'll wait a half-hour for a table. You wisely go home, and plan your next morning. I recommend a bloody mary at **Zeitgeist** (199 Valencia) or the **Orbit Room** (1900 Market), then . . .

—Julia Dillon

HOTELS & INNS

SAN FRANCISCO'S MAIN HOTEL DISTRICT lies north and west of Union Square, a good location for shopping, theater, and restaurants. Cheaper hotels can be found in the neighboring Tenderloin, and though the hotels themselves may be quite good, the neighborhood usually is not. Nob Hill is famed for grand and historic hotels, while the large hotels in the Financial District cater to executives on large business accounts. A few family-style motels congregate on Lombard Street, along Van Ness, and around Fisherman's Wharf. San Francisco and environs have some of the most charming bed-and-breakfasts, many occupying older Victorian buildings in interesting neighborhoods. Budget-minded travelers might search out a Spartan, European-style pensione in areas like North Beach and Chinatown.

The East Bay offers B&Bs, while in the South Bay, larger corporate-style hotels are the norm. The North Bay and Wine Country offer many lovely resorts and historic inns.

> *Room Rates:*
> *Per night, double occupancy, before tax:*
> $ = under $85; $$ = $85 - 130; $$$; $130 - 180; $$$$ = over $180

San Francisco

Archbishops Mansion *Western Addition*
$$$ 1000 Fulton St. (Stcincr);
(415) 563-7872
Once the official home of local Catholic prelates, this opulent B&B on Alamo Square is decorated in Belle Epoque style and is topped with a 16-foot-wide leaded glass dome. Some fireplaces, Jacuzzis.

Bed and Breakfast Inn *Cow Hollow*
$ - $$$ 4 Charlton Ct. (Union);
(415) 921-9784
An Italianate Victorian built in 1885, this English country-style B&B stands along a quiet mews just off Union Street. Rooms range from affordable doubles with shared baths to a large suites. The Mayfair Suite has a balcony and a spiral staircase to a loft.

Campton Place *Union Square* $$$$
340 Stockton St. (Post);
(415)781-5555/(800) 235-4300
Excellent personal service and lavish decor make this one of the city's most highly rated hotels. Rooms from the ninth floor up overlook an atrium. Campton Place is the hotel's restaurant (See "RESTAURANTS").

Clarion Bedford Hotel *Union Square* $$
761 Post St. (Jones);
(415) 673-6040/(800) 227-5642
A mid-sized hotel with many business services, the Bedford is a reasonably priced option for executives on a budget.

Donatello *Theater District* $$$
501 Post St. (Mason);
(415) 441-7100/(800) 227-3184

San Francisco Hotels & Inns

Modern amenities here include in-room modem links, meeting rooms, exercise room, and sauna, but the antique decor helps this 94-room hotel maintain a classic, elegant feel. Guests appreciate little extras such as thick bathrobes left on the beds.

Fairmont Hotel *Nob Hill* $$$ - $$$$
950 Mason St. (California);
(415) 772-5000/(800) 527-4727
The grand Nob Hill classic, with a huge red-carpeted, faux-marbled lobby replete with chandeliers, as well as the (in)famous Tonga Room, famous for its waterfall and tropical drinks. Corporate travelers like the large meeting rooms (once ballrooms), transport to downtown, and health club.

Four Seasons Clift Hotel *Theater District* $$$$ 495 Geary St. (Taylor);
(415) 775-4700/(800) 65-CLIFT
First choice for many seasoned travelers; known for its exceptional personal service. Patrons admire the subdued urban contemporary style of the guest rooms, and swoon over the beautiful Art Deco Redwood Room lounge. Exercise and meeting rooms.

Grant Plaza *Chinatown* $
465 Grant St. (Pine);
(415) 434-3883/(800) 472-6899
A convenient location, 24-hour restaurant, and business services make this a good no-nonsense option for corporate travelers (or Chinese food lovers) on a budget.

Handlery Union Square *Union Square* $$$
351 Geary St. (Powell); (415) 781-7800/(800)843-4343
Business travelers often prefer the relatively personal feel of this well-appointed hotel.

Holiday Inn *Chinatown* $
750 Kearny St. (Washington);
(415) 433-6600
This reasonably priced, standard chain hotel is very convenient to Financial District, Union Square, and North Beach. Pool.

Hotel Majestic *Cathedral Hill* $$
1500 Sutter St. (Gough);
(415) 441-1100/(800) 869-8966
This restored Edwardian inn features romantic rooms, many with fireplaces, claw-foot tubs, four-poster beds, and restored woodwork. Business services and downtown transport, too. The Cafe Majestic is the hotel restaurant. (See "RESTAURANTS").

Hotel Monaco *Theater District* $$$
501 Geary St. (Taylor);
(415) 292-0100/(800) 214-4220
With its playful, technicolor decor and chic atmosphere, the new hotspot in town attracts stylish out-of-towners; meanwhile, locals frequent the hyper Art Nouveau–style Grand Cafe restaurant and bar. Impressive sauna and gym; in-room fax and modem.

Hotel Nikko *Union Square* $$$$
222 Mason St. (O'Farrell);
(415) 394-1111/(800) NIKKO-US
This elegant hotel offers both Western and Japanese-style rooms; efficient service, Japanese garden atrium, and indoor pool.

Hotel Triton *Union Square* $$
342 Grant Ave. (Bush);
(415) 394-0500/(800) 433-6611
The whimsically decorated lobby of this hotel might have been inspired by Dr. Seuss. Rooms are small, but are also extremely comfortable and stylishly decorated.

The Hotel Monaco has won many design awards for its imaginative decor. (Kerrick James)

A favorite among art directors, designers, and the like.

Hotel Vintage Court *Union Square* $$
650 Bush St. (Powell);
(415) 392-4666/(800) 654-1100
Housing the renowned Masa's restaurant (see "RESTAURANTS"), this 100-room hotel offers reasonably priced yet lovely rooms furnished in a Wine Country theme.

Huntington Hotel *Nob Hill* $$$$
1075 California St. (Taylor); (415) 474-5400/(800) 227-4683
Renowned for highly attentive service and exclusive clientele, this 100-room brick-and-ivy hotel features plush rooms done in inviting leather and velvet. The Huntington's Big Four restaurant is one of the best in town.

Hyatt Regency *Financial District* $$$
5 Embarcadero Ctr. (Market at Drumm);
(415) 788-1234
The 800 large, stylishly appointed rooms here are arranged around a dramatic sunlit atrium lobby. Revolving rooftop restaurant, large fitness center, business center as well as in-room modem links.

Inn at the Opera *Civic Center* $$$
333 Fulton St. (Franklin);
(415) 863-8400/(800) 325-2708
This small, elegant hotel frequently hosts divas, primas, and jazz musicians. The well-connected staff can often provide its other guests with access to seats at the opera, ballet, and symphony. Rooms are furnished with half-canopy beds, antiques, and lots of pillows. Voice mail, in-room fax hook-ups.

Inn at Union Square *Union Square* $$ - $$$ 440 Post St. (Mason); (415) 397-3510/(800) 288-4346
An alternative to the large downtown hotels, this small inn offers guestrooms furnished in Chippendale reproductions and floral printed upholstery, as well as shared sitting rooms with wood-burning fireplaces on each floor; 24-hour concierge.

Jackson Court Bed & Breakfast Inn *Pacific Heights* $$ 2198 Jackson St. (Buchanan); (415) 929-7670
This turn-of-the-century brownstone features tastefully furnished rooms, a sunny library, wood-beamed ceilings, and a private garden.

Mandarin Oriental *Financial District* $$$$
222 Sansome St. (California);
(415) 885-0999/(800) 622-0404
Occupying the top 11 floors in one of downtown's tallest buildings, this luxury hotel boasts terrific views of the bay, in addition to a business center, health club privileges, lots of conveniences, and Silks restaurant (see "RESTAURANTS").

Mansions Hotel *Pacific Heights* $$
2220 Sacramento St. (Laguna);
(415) 929-9444
At this lovely Victorian, built in 1887 and supposedly haunted, quirky theme rooms are named after famous San Franciscans: there's a "Huntington Room" and a "Tom Thumb Room." The flamboyant innkeeper hosts weekend "magic extravaganzas."

Marina Inn *Marina* $
3110 Octavia St. (Lombard);
(415) 928-1000/(800) 274-1420

This restored 1928 building offers English country ambiance, light breakfast, and airport transportation, all at reasonable rates.

Mark Hopkins Inter-Continental Hotel *Nob Hill* $$$ 1 Nob Hill (Mason); (415) 392-3434/(800) 327-0200
Capped by the famous Top of the Mark bar, this Nob Hill landmark features a sun-filled grand lobby, resplendent with crystal chandeliers and marble floors. Rooms are sleekly yet comfortably decorated.

Miyako Hotel *Japantown* $$ - $$$ 1625 Post St. (Laguna); (415) 922-3200/(800) 333-3333
Both Western-style rooms and traditional Japanese suites with tatamis and furo tubs.

Monticello Inn *Financial District* $$ 127 Ellis St. (Powell); (415) 392-8800/(800) 669-7777
Standing amid the downtown giant hotels, this intimate hotel is decorated in American Colonial style.

Obrero Hotel *Chinatown* $ 1208 Stockton St. (Broadway); (415) 989-3960
The Basque owners of this B&B offer budget lodgings in a European-style pensione.

Pan Pacific Hotel *Theater District* $$$ 500 Post St. (Mason); (415) 771-8600/(800) 533-6465
A perfect hotel for business executives, this luxurious hotel pampers its guests with lovely rooms and a highly attentive staff.

Park Hyatt. *Financial District* $$$ 333 Battery St. (Sacramento); (415) 392-1234/(800) 323-7275

Plush rooms, excellent service, and little extras like gourmet chocolates and imported soaps appeal to business travelers. Best are the rooms with balconies and bay views.

Phoenix Inn *Van Ness/Civic Center* $$ 601 Eddy St. (Larkin); (415) 776-1380/(800) 248-9466
This funky, revitalized 1950s motel overlooks a colorfully painted swimming pool, where diners from the adjacent Miss Pearl's Jam House can eat (see "RESTAURANTS"). The first choice for touring rock musicians.

Prescott Hotel *Union Square* $$$ 545 Post St. (Taylor); (415) 563-0303/(800) 283-7322
Perhaps best known as the site of Wolfgang Puck's Postrio restaurant (see "RESTAURANTS"), this renovated old hotel has plush, handsome guest rooms decorated in rich colors and cherry wood. The capable staff provides personal service.

Queen Anne Hotel *Western Addition/ Japantown* 1590 Sutter St.; (415) 441-2828/(800) 227-3930 $$
Originally a posh girls' school, this lovely "painted lady" on Cathedral Hill offers 49 rooms, all differently decorated; many have fireplaces. The breakfast buffet is served in the large lobby, which is replete with gorgeous cedar and oak woodwork.

Red Victorian *Haight/Golden Gate Park* $$ 1665 Haight St. (Cole); (415) 864-1978
Famous for theme rooms—like the "Japanese Tea Garden" and the "Summer of Love" —and situated on a bustling block of the Upper Haight, this very popular spot is perfect for young hipsters.

San Francisco Hotels & Inns

San Francisco Hotels & Inns

Renaissance Stanford Court *Nob Hill* $$$$
905 California St. (Powell);
(415) 989-3500/(800) 227-4736
With the well-known Fournou's Ovens (see
"RESTAURANTS") under its roof, this Nob
Hill grandee features a beautiful stained
glass dome over its central court. The generously sized rooms are decorated in 19th-
century reproductions.

Ritz-Carlton *Nob Hill* $$$
600 Stockton St. (Pine);
(415) 296-7465/(800) 241-3333
Actually a renovation of the neoclassical
Metropolitan Life building, this superb
hotel impresses visitors with a splendid
lobby replete with crystal chandeliers and
museum-quality oil paintings. Legendary
afternoon teas, and excellent sports facili-
ties to boot. (See "RESTAURANTS")

San Francisco Airport Hilton *SFO* $$
(415) 589-0770/(800) HILTONS
The only hotel really at the airport. Pool,
fitness center, business services.

San Francisco Marriott *Financial District*
$$$ 55 Fourth St. (Market);
(415) 896-1600/(800) 228-9290
The huge, arched windows at the top of
this hotel near SoMa's Moscone Center
have earned it the sobriquet of the Jukebox
Hotel among San Franciscans. The 1,500
rooms are large and nicely decorated, and
the View Lounge on the 39th floor is ver-
tiginously spectacular.

San Remo Hotel *North Beach* $
2237 Mason St. (Francisco);
(415) 776-8688/(800) 352-REMO

At this charming yet affordable European-
style pensione, the management is helpful
and the bright, cozy rooms are decorated
with plants and redwood antiques.

Sheraton Palace Hotel *Financial District*
$$$ 2 New Montgomery (Market);
(415) 392-8600/(800) 325-3535
Built on the site of the old Palace Hotel,
this elegantly renovated version features the
spectacular, glass-ceilinged Garden Court
restaurant, a pool with a skylight, a health
club, and Maxfield's Restaurant, home of
Maxfield Parrish's Pied Piper painting.

Sir Francis Drake *Union Square* $$$
450 Powell St. (Post); (415) 392-7755/
(800) 268-7245
Recently updated (yet still plush), this hotel
has regained popularity—thanks also to the
swank Starlite Room at the top

Spencer House *Middle Haight* $$$
1080 Haight St. (Baker);
(415) 626-9205
The hospitable proprietors of this B&B
across from Buena Vista Park have lavishly
appointed their Queen Anne Victorian with
silk wallcovering and Louis XVI antiques.

Stanyan Park Hotel *Haight/Golden Gate
Park* $$ 750 Stanyan St. (Waller);
(415) 751-1000
The very reasonable rates here include
breakfast as well as accommodation in a
charming room; the larger suites feel like
real San Francisco apartments—some
opening to the outdoors, allowing for a
great sense of privacy.

The San Francisco Marriott (a.k.a. the Jukebox Hotel) appears to rise above Grant Avenue.

San Francisco Hotels & Inns

Tuscan Inn *Fisherman's Wharf* $$$
425 Northpoint St. (Mason);
(415) 561-1100/(800) 648-4626
A European flavor permeates this classic "boutique" hotel. Business services; room service provides good Italian food.

Union Street Inn *Cow Hollow* $$ - $$$
2229 Union St. (Fillmore);
(415) 346-0424
Run by a former schoolteacher, this quaint Edwardian-era B&B has a redwood patio in the back that overlooks a lovely English garden. For extra privacy, book the carriage house with its whirlpool bathtub.

Victorian Inn on the Park *Middle Haight*
$$ - $$$ 301 Lyon St. (Fell);
(415) 931-1830/(800) 435-1967
This inn on Golden Gate Park's Panhandle is splendid with period furnishings, lots of pillows, and William Morris reproductions.

Villa Florence *Union Square* $$$
225 Powell St. (Geary); (415) 397-7700/
(800) 553-4411
Rooms here are warm and quiet, despite the bustling locale. The marble-appointed lobby contains Kuleto's (see "RESTAURANTS").

Washington Square Inn *North Beach* $$
1660 Stockton St. (Filbert); (415) 981-
4220/(800) 388-0220
This beautifully appointed B&B on Washington Square recalls a country home, and the complimentary wine, high tea, and hors d'oeuvres served in the afternoon add to an air of relaxed luxury.

Westin St. Francis *Union Square* $$ - $$$
335 Powell St. (Geary);
(415) 397-7000/(800) 228-3000
This grand dame was renovated in 1991, when three giant trompe l'oeil murals were added to the lobby; many rooms retain their original 1904 woodwork.

White Swan Inn *Union Square* $$$
845 Bush St. (Mason);
(415) 775-1755/(800) 999-9570
In addition to the fireplaces, Laura Ashley-style decor, and four-poster beds which grace every guest room are conveniences such as hair dryers and TVs. Homemade breakfast dishes and afternoon refreshments are so delightful that the proprietors have published their own cookbook.

East Bay Hotels & Inns

Claremont Resort and Spa *Berkeley* $$$$
41 Tunnel Rd. (Ashby); (510) 843-3000
Covering 22 acres, this historic resort hotel (ca. 1915) offers uniquely decorated rooms, two pools, a workout center, 10 tennis courts, and restaurants offering standard as well as spa cuisine. The vast chateau-like structure, with its surrounding woodland, is visible even from the city.

French Hotel *Berkeley* $ 1538 Shattuck
Ave. (Cedar); (510) 548-9930
This narrow, red-brick hotel faces Berkeley's well-known Chez Panisse. The reasonably priced rooms are decorated in high-tech style. Cafe downstairs.

Gramma's Rose Garden Inn *Berkeley*
$$ - $$$ 2740 Telegraph Ave. (Ward);
(510) 549-2145
This B&B comprises a beautiful Tudor-style mansion (ca. 1900) and three smaller houses behind it. Rooms are furnished with antiques; some have fireplaces and balconies. Sunny courtyard in back.

Hotel Durant *Berkeley* $$ 2600 Durant Ave. (Bowditch); (510) 845-8981
A small European-style hotel close to U.C. Berkeley; lovely restaurant and bar.

Marriott Inn *Berkeley* $$$ Berkeley Marina (510) 548-7920/(800) 228-9290
Modern and attractively decorated, Berkeley's largest hostelry has waterfront views, but is just two miles from downtown Berkeley. Two indoor pools; fitness room.

Oakland Marriott *Oakland* $$ 1001 Broadway (10th St.); (510) 451-4000
This full-service luxury hotel caters to executives and professionals doing business in downtown Oakland.

Washington Inn *Oakland* $$ 495 10th St. (Broadway); (510) 452-1776
Turn-of-the-century charm and elegance, convenient to downtown Oakland.

Waterfront Plaza Hotel *Oakland* $$ - $$$ 10 Washington St. (Embarcadero); (510) 836-3800
Situated on Jack London Square, this large hotel offers 144 luxury guest rooms, fireplaces, and health facilities including a pool and indoor sauna.

South Bay Hotels & Inns

Garden Court Hotel *Palo Alto* $$$$
520 Cowper St. (University); (415) 322-9000/(800) 824-9028
Situated downtown, this elegant hotel offers 62 lovely, comfortable rooms—some with whirlpools and fireplaces. There's also the appeal of ordering room service from Il Fornaio Cucina (see "RESTAURANTS").

Hyatt St. Claire *San Jose* $ - $$$
302 S. Market St. (San Carlos); (408) 295-2000/(800) 824-6835
With its original Spanish tile courtyard, fountain, and wood-beamed ceiling restored in 1992, this impressive downtown hotel (ca. 1926) is today a national historic landmark. Business travelers can expect the full range of amenities.

Mill Rose Inn *Half Moon Bay* $$$ - $$$$
615 Mill St. (Church); (415) 726-9794/(800) 900-ROSE
This small, charming B&B has six plush rooms, each with a private entrance and a garden view. Half Moon Bay's stunning coastline is a few yards away.

Stanford Park Hotel *Menlo Park* $$$
100 El Camino Real (Cambridge); (415) 322-1234/(800) 368-2468
A short walk from Stanford University and the Stanford Shopping Center is this cedar-shingled and red-brick hotel. Nicely furnished rooms come in varying shapes and sizes, some with fireplaces and sitting rooms. Pool, sauna, and fitness room.

East Bay/South Bay Hotels & Inns

North Bay Hotels & Inns

Marin County

Casa Madrona *Sausalito* $$ - $$$
  8015 Bridgeway ; (415) 332-0502
With the warmth of a B&B, this small hotel offers 39 rooms—some with contemporary and some with Victorian decor—most of which have stunning views of the Sausalito harbor and San Francisco. Hot tub and stylish restaurant.

Manka's Inverness Lodge *Inverness*
  $$ - $$$$ Callendar Way (Argyle);
  (415) 669-1034
Just uphill from the tiny hamlet of Inverness is this former hunting lodge, with eight rooms and four cottages, as well as an enchantingly rustic dining room where fresh-caught fish and wild game dishes are served. Perfect for an idyllic weekend.

Pelican Inn *Muir Beach* $$$
  Hwy. 1 (Pacific Way); (415) 383-6000
A little piece of Old England in Marin, this whitewashed Tudor features seven rooms with leaded windows, hanging tapestries, and Oriental scatter rugs. You can sample any number of stouts, ales, ports, and sherries in the hotel pub, and the hearty breakfast includes eggs, toasted breads, and, of course, sausages and bacon.

Ten Inverness Way *Inverness* $$ - $$$
  10 Inverness Way; (415) 669-1648
The redwood living room of this homey B&B features a large stone hearth and lots of bookshelves, and the simple but pretty guest rooms have hand-sewn quilts. Delicious breakfast items.

Napa County

Ambrose Bierce House *St. Helena* $$
  1515 Main St. (Pine); (707) 963-3003
Yes, America's favorite literary curmudgeon did indeed live here—until 1913, when he became bored with the peaceful wine valley and vanished into Pancho Villa's Mexico. The two suites have private baths.

Auberge du Soleil *Rutherford* $$$$
  180 Rutherford Hill Rd., ; (707) 963-1211
This deluxe French country inn is the valley's most famous lodging. Set in an old olive grove and overlooking the valley, the Auberge has stunning views. Guest rooms have French doors, terra-cotta tiles, and a private terrace. The more deluxe rooms have fireplaces and whirlpool baths.

Brannan Cottage Inn *Calistoga* $$ - $$$
  109 Wapoo Ave. (Lincoln);
  (707) 942-4200
The last cottage remaining from Sam Brannan's 1860 Calistoga Hot Springs Resort which is still on its original site. Six rooms with private entrances and baths.

Fanny's *Calistoga* $
  1206 Spring St.; (707) 942-9491
This simple, quiet, Craftsman-style cottage (ca. 1915) is a quiet retreat just off Calistoga's busy main street. Private baths and window seats, with spacious living room and dining room. Sumptuous breakfast.

La Residence *Napa* $$-$$$
  4066 St. Helena Hwy.; (707) 253-0337
Thise ultra-comfortable hotel is comprised

of an ornate mansion built in 1870 and Cabernet Hall, which is supposed to resemble a French barn. Heated swimming pool and rose gardens separate the two buildings. Excellent wine and cheese repasts and delicious breakfasts. Rates are about two thirds of what they are at lesser lodgings up-valley.

Meadowood Resort *St. Helena* $$$$
900 Meadowood Ln., ; (707) 963-3646
A truly great resort and a cozy place to hide out in. The spacious, well-insulated, and perfectly quiet guest rooms are spaced over the property in small clusters, touching the nine-hole golf course on one side and the oak woods on the other. Croquet grounds, tennis courts, pool, and spa.

Silverado Country Club & Resort *Napa*
$$$ 1600 Atlas Peak Rd. (Hwy. 121);
(707) 257-0200
With two 18-hole golf courses, 9 swimming pools, 20 tennis courts, and hundreds of condos, this 1,200-acre resort may not be intimate, but it's perfect for weekend athletes. The two- to three-room condos also work well for families.

White Sulphur Springs Resort & Spa
St. Helena $ -$$$ 3100 White Sulphur Springs Rd.; (707) 963-8588
The oldest hot springs resort, established in 1852, is still going strong.

Sonoma County

Applewood–An Estate Inn *Guerneville* $$$
13555 Hwy. 116; (707) 869-9093
This pink Mediterranean-style villa some-

how fits right into the redwoods and apple trees. A truly great place, with splendidly comfortable rooms, inviolate privacy, and some of the best breakfasts in the Wine Country—all within walking distance of Guerneville.

Camellia Inn *Healdsburg* $$ - $$$
211 North St. (East); (707) 433-8182
This quiet, very homey old building dates to 1869, and the more than 50 varieties of camellias on the property go all the way back to horticulturist Luther Burbank, who was a family friend. Innkeeper Ray Lewand is an accomplished amateur winemaker—happy hour on the swimming pool is an education. Huge breakfast and private baths. Just a few blocks from the Healdsburg Plaza.

El Dorado Hotel *Sonoma* $$ 405 First St. W. (Spain); (707) 996-3030
Built as the home of Gen. Mariano Vallejo's never-quite-respectable brother Salvador, the El Dorado has been extensively restored, and the newer ground-level suites beyond the patio and pool are luxurious. Enjoy breakfast under the courtyard fig tree. Since it faces the Plaza, the El Dorado is convenient to everything in town.

Gaige House Inn *Glen Ellen* $$ - $$$
13540 Arnold Dr.; (707) 935-0237
A very quiet, though very lively, B&B housed in an 1890 Queen Anne and run by Ardath Rouas, founder of Auberge du Soleil. The hammock hanging from the trees just invites you to snooze under the stars. Breakfasts are outrageously good.

Kenwood Inn & Spa *Kenwood* $$$$
10400 Sonoma Hwy.; (707) 833-1293
A Mediterranean feel pervades this compound of yellow buildings, which surround the quiet, flowery courtyard. Oak woods rise to one side of the road, vineyards to the other. A substantial breakfast is served from the large dining room's open kitchen.

Raford House *Healdsburg* $$
10630 Wohler Rd. (River);
(707) 887-9573
Built in the 1880s in Russian River Wine Country, the Raford House is surrounded by vines as well as tall palms that were planted as status symbols in the 19th century. Very comfortable and down-to-earth. Delicious breakfast, and generous afternoon wine and appetizers.

Sonoma Hotel *Sonoma* $$$
110 W. Spain St. (First St. W.);
(707) 996-2996
Conveniently located on the Sonoma Plaza, this beautiful historic 17-room hotel—a former dry goods store and meeting hall—is accented with old oak and stained glass. The hotel bar is usually hopping.

Sonoma Mission Inn *Boyes Hot Springs* $$$ 18149 Hwy. 12 (Boyes Blvd.);
(707) 938-9000/(800) 862-4945
Established as a health spa in the mid-1800s, the 170-room Sonoma Mission Inn offers packages structured around your choice of physical regimen: there are tennis courts, an Olympic-sized pool—and two restaurants (see "RESTAURANTS").

Timberhill Ranch *Cazadero* $$$$
35755 Hauser Bridge Rd.;
(707) 847-3258
Truly an incredible retreat, just a short drive from the Russian River: it's like a summer camp for adults. The ultra-plush cabins stand on extensive grounds which lie at the edge of wilderness. A private chef offers delicious multi-course dinners every night in the grand dining room; the wine list is laudable, too.

San Francisco Hotels by District

Refer to pages 329 - 336 for alphabetically listed reviews of the hotels below.

Chinatown
Grant Plaza $
Holiday Inn $
Obrero Hotel $

Civic Center
Inn at the Opera $$$
Phoenix Inn $$

Cow Hollow/Marina
Bed and Breakfast Inn $ - $$$
Marina Inn $
Union Street Inn $$ - $$$

Financial District
Hyatt Regency *Financial District* $$$
Mandarin Oriental $$$$
Monticello Inn $$
Park Hyatt $$$
San Francisco Marriott $$$
Sheraton Palace Hotel $$$

Fisherman's Wharf
Tuscan Inn $$$

Haight
Red Victorian $$
Spencer House $$$
Stanyan Park Hotel *Park* $$
Victorian Inn on the Park $$ - $$$

Japantown/Cathedral Hill
Hotel Majestic $$
Miyako Hotel $$ - $$$
Queen Anne Hotel $$

Marina/Pacific Heights
Jackson Court Bed & Breakfast Inn $$
Mansions Hotel $$
Marina Inn $

Nob Hill
Fairmont Hotel $$$ - $$$$
Huntington Hotel *Nob Hill* $$$$
Mark Hopkins Inter-Continental $$$
Renaissance Stanford Court $$$$
Ritz-Carlton $$$

North Beach
San Remo Hotel $
Washington Square Inn $$

San Francisco Airport
San Francisco Airport Hilton $$

Union Square/ Theater District
Campton Place $$$$
Clarion Bedford Hotel $$
Donatello $$$
Four Seasons Clift Hotel $$$$
Handlery Union Square $$$
Hotel Monaco $$$
Hotel Nikko $$$$
Hotel Triton $$
Hotel Vintage Court $$
Inn at Union Square $$ - $$$
Pan Pacific Hotel $$$
Prescott Hotel $$$
Sir Francis Drake $$$
Villa Florence $$$
Westin St. Francis $$ - $$$
White Swan Inn $$$

Western Addition
Archbishops Mansion $$$
Queen Anne Hotel $$

Hotels & Inns by Town

East Bay Hotels by Town*

Berkeley
Claremont Resort and Spa $$$$
French Hotel $
Gramma's Rose Garden Inn $$ - $$$
Hotel Durant $$

Marriott Inn $$$
Oakland
Oakland Marriott $$
Washington Inn $$
Waterfront Plaza Hotel $$ - $$$

South Bay Hotels by Town*

Half Moon Bay
Mill Rose Inn $$$ - $$$$

Menlo Park
Stanford Park Hotel $$$

Palo Alto
Garden Court Hotel

San Jose
Hyatt St. Claire $ - $$$

North Bay Hotels by Town*

Boyes Hot Springs
Sonoma Mission Inn $$$

Calistoga
Brannan Cottage Inn $$ - $$$
Fanny's *Calistoga* $

Cazadero
Timberhill Ranch $$$$

Glen Ellen
Gaige House Inn $$ - $$$

Guerneville
Applewood–An Estate Inn $$$

Healdsburg
Camellia Inn $$ - $$$
Raford House $$

Inverness
Manka's Inverness Lodge $$ - $$$$
Ten Inverness Way *Inverness* $$ - $$$

Kenwood
Kenwood Inn & Spa $$$$

Muir Beach
Pelican Inn $$$

Napa
La Residence $$-$$$
Silverado Country Club & Resort $$$

Rutherford
Auberge du Soleil $$$$

Sausalito
Casa Madrona $$ - $$$

St. Helena
Ambrose Bierce House $$
Meadowood Resort $$$$
White Sulphur Springs Resort $ -$$$

Sonoma
El Dorado Hotel $$
Sonoma Hotel $$$

* Refer to pages 333 - 337 for alphabetically listed reviews of the Bay Area hotels above.
***East Bay Hotels:** 336 - 337; **South Bay Hotels:** 337; **North Bay Hotels:** 338 - 340.*

PRACTICALITIES

Public Transportation

■ TOURIST INFORMATION

Compass American Guides makes every effort to ensure the accuracy of its information; however, as conditions and prices change frequently, we recommend that readers also contact the local visitors bureaus listed. In San Francisco, contact:

San Francisco Convention & Visitors Bureau. (415) 974-6900. Daily Events Line: (415) 391-2001. Visit the lower level of Hallidie Plaza at Powell and Market.

For information outside the city, contact:

Oakland Convention & Visitors Bureau. (510) 839-9000.

Napa Valley Conference & Visitors Bureau. (707) 226-7459.

San Jose Convention & Visitors Bureau. (800) SAN JOSE.

Sonoma County Convention & Visitors Bureau. (707) 586-8100

■ PUBLIC TRANSPORTATION

TO & FROM AIRPORTS

San Francisco International Airport (SFO) is just east of U.S. 101 about 14 miles south of downtown San Francisco, in San Mateo County. The terminals are built in a partial circle around a parking garage, making it easy to find your way around once you understand the layout. For the benefit of travelers caught between flights, SFO maintains a hall in the north terminal for art and museum exhibits. Call (415) 761-0800 for airport information.

For general information regarding ground transportation to and from the airport, call the **Transportation Hotline** at (800) SFO-2008. Buses run frequently to the city from dawn until midnight. The downtown airport bus terminal is located in the Tenderloin (one of the rougher sections of town, but close to Union Square); the bus also stops at the Transbay Terminal, Stonestown, and Daly City BART. Every 20 minutes from 5 A.M. to 10 P.M., the SFO Airporter bus service makes the round of downtown hotels to take passengers to the airport. Taxis and door-to-door shuttle service are also available. Check the telephone book yellow pages under "Airport Transport" for companies.

Public Transportation

Oakland International (OAK) and San Jose International (SJC) airports offer less stressful alternatives. Oakland is handy for passengers using BART to San Francisco. San Jose is convenient for visiting Silicon Valley. Train connections from SJC to San Francisco's railroad depot are available on CalTrain. For airport information, call Oakland International at (510) 577-4000, and San Jose International at (408) 277-4759.

AROUND TOWN

San Francisco's public bus and streetcar system is called MUNI. It's cheap, convenient, and relatively safe (relative to New York, for example). Exact fares are required, and passes are available. Call (415) 673-MUNI for information.

BART (Bay Area Rapid Transit) is San Francisco's small and tidy subway system, whisking commuters from downtown San Francisco to Colma along the city's southern border, and under the bay to North Concord, Richmond, and Fremont in the East Bay. You are better off riding BART than driving if your destination lies near a BART station and you're not traveling between midnight and 4 A.M. (or 6 A.M. on Saturdays, 8 A.M. onSundays). All stations have neighborhood street maps posted. Call (415) 788-BART for information.

MUNI streetcars share four downtown stations with BART, making Embarcadero, Montgomery, Powell, and Civic Center stations the four key transfer points between intra-city and inter-city transport systems. The streetcar is a particularly interesting and easy way to ride to Golden Gate Park (the N-Judah to 9th Ave.) or the San Francisco Zoo (the L-Taraval to the end of the line). MUNI sells "Passports" to ride all streetcars, buses, and cable cars for one, three, or seven days. Passports also entitle you to discounts at the zoo and city museums. Buy them from cable car terminals at Fisherman's Wharf, Ghirardelli Square, and Hallidie Plaza; or from the Cable Car Barn or the visitors center at Hallidie Plaza.

The commercial coach terminal is south of Market in the Transbay Terminal, on Mission between First and Fremont. **CalTrain**, a commuter rail line, connects San Francisco's Townsend Street station (at Fourth) with San Jose and points between; call (800) 228-4661. **Amtrak** pulls into Oakland Station (corner of 17th and Wood streets), and runs passenges across the bay by bus; call (800) 872-7245.

FERRIES

Ferries, a most civilized means of transport, are limited to a few commuter routes. Golden Gate Transit ferries run to Larkspur and Sausalito in Marin County from the downtown Ferry Building. Red and White Ferries go to Angel Island, Sausalito, and Vallejo from Fisherman's Wharf. Ferry service also connects Oakland's Jack London Square and Alameda with the Ferry Building. For schedules and information, call **Golden Gate Transit** at (415) 332-6600, **Red and White** at (415) 546-2815, and the **Oakland-Alameda** ferry at (510) 522-3300.

CABLE CARS

The three operational lines are as follows: the **Powell-Mason Line** between Hallidie Plaza and Bay Street, near Fisherman's Wharf; the **Powell-Hyde Line** runs from Hallidie Plaza to Ghirardelli Square, via the thrilling 21.3 percent Hyde Street grade; and the **California Street Line** runs 17 blocks in a straight line along California Street from Embarcadero Center (Frost Plaza) to Van Ness Avenue. To avoid long lines boarding at any terminus, catch a car somewhere along its route, if there's room.

For a coordinated, comprehensive explanation of all the transport systems of the Bay Area, buy a copy of the San Francisco Bay Area Regional Transit Guide, published by the Metropolitan Transportation Commission. The book is available in downtown BART stations, among other places.

■ FESTIVALS & EVENTS

Late January to March (depending on lunar calendar): Chinese New Year. Firecrackers, the Miss Chinatown pageant, and the famous Chinatown parade; (415) 982-3000.

March 17: Saint Patrick's Day. Be Irish for a day: join the big parade (call 415-661-2700 for date), or hoist a few with the merrymakers at the bars.

April: Cherry Blossom Festival. Japantown celebrates the new blooms with a fair featuring traditional arts and crafts; (415) 922-6776.

Late April to May: San Francisco International Film Festival. The city's biggest cinematic event, based at the Kabuki Theater and Berkeley's Pacific Archive; (415) 931-FILM.

Easter: Easter Sunday. Sunrise service is held at dawn on Mount Davidson. Russian Orthodox Easter is colorfully celebrated at the Cathedral of the Holy Virgin, in the Richmond District.

May: Cinco de Mayo. Anniversary of the Mexican defeat of the French army at Puebla, celebrated in the Mission District around May 5 with a colorful parade and festivities; (415) 826-1401.

Late May: *San Francisco Examiner* Bay to Breakers. Over 100,000 runners (from international athletes to costumed joggers) participate in a $7^1/_2$-mile road race that begins at the Embarcadero and ends at Ocean Beach; (415) 777-7770.

Late May: Carnaval. Over Memorial Day weekend, the Mission District hosts San Francisco's version of Brazil's Carnaval; (415) 826-1401.

June: Ethnic Dance Festival. At the Palace of Fine Arts; (415) 474-3916.

June: Street Fairs. Neighborhood celebrations with food and arts and crafts. Haight Street's hosts big-name music acts. **Haight Street,** (415) 661-8025; **North Beach,** (415) 403-0666; **Union Street,** (415) 346-4561.

Festivals & Events

Late June: Lesbian and Gay Freedom Day. Marked by a parade down Market from Civic Center to Justin Herman Plaza, where a huge street party takes place; (415) 864-3733.

June - August: Stern Grove Midsummer Music Festival. Outdoor concerts at Sigmund Stern Grove; (415) 252-6252.

Fourth of July. Fireworks over the bay (fired from San Francisco's Aquatic Park), though the fog layer is often too low for viewers to see much.

July: San Francisco Marathon. (800) 722-3466.

July through September: San Francisco Shakespeare Festival. One play showing weekends at Golden Gate Park, San Jose's St. James Park, and Oakland's Duck Pond Meadow; (415) 666-2221.

August: Nihonmachi Street Fair. Japantown festival, with taiko drummers, arts, and crafts; (415) 922-8700.

Labor Day Weekend: À la Carte, À la Park. Fine restaurants sell samples of their wares to benefit the Shakespeare Festival; live music; (415) 383-9378.

September: Opera Season Opening. The city's premier gala event, with the opera glitterati; (415) 864-3330.

Late September: San Francisco Blues Festival. Concerts at Justin Herman Plaza and Fort Mason; (415) 979-5588.

October: Castro Street Fair. Neighborhood celebration with booths, arts, and crafts; (415) 467-3354.

October: Columbus Day. A city holiday, especially honored in the Italian community. Festivities include the blessing of the fleet, Columbus landing pageant, and parade; (415) 434-1492.

Late October to November: San Francisco Jazz Festival. Concerts throughout the city; (415) 864-5449.

November 2: Dia de los Muertos (Day of the Dead). Latino festival honoring dead ancestors, marked by dances, ethnic foods, costumes, and a parade in the Mission District; (415) 647-0224.

■ PROFESSIONAL SPORTS

San Francisco sports fans cheer the 49ers (the "Niners") in football and the Giants in baseball. Both teams play at Candlestick Park. The Oakland Athletics (the "A's") play baseball in the Oakland Coliseum across the bay. The Golden State Warriors basketball team also bangs the boards in Oakland, but draws support from both sides of the bay.

Golden State Warriors: (510) 638-6300
Oakland Athletics: (510) 638-0500
San Francisco 49ers: (415) 486-2249
San Francisco Giants: (415) 467-8000
San Jose Sharks: (408) 287-7070

■ TOURS

BUS TOURS

Gray Line Tours. Bay Area tours; (415) 558-9400.

MUNI Tours. Public transport tours available on request; (415) 673-MUNI.

Near Escapes. Behind-the-scenes tour of San Francisco Zoo, shopping tours of SoMa, backstage theater tours, cemetery tours, etc.; (415) 386-8687.

WATER TOURS

Blue & Gold Fleet. Bay cruises; (415) 781-7890.

Golden Gate Ferry Service. Ferry service to Sausalito, Larkspur; (415) 332-6600.

Oceanic Society Expeditions. Boats leave the city and Half Moon Bay for whale watches (several hours long) during migration season (January to April); (415) 474-3385.

Red & White Fleet. Bay tours and scheduled service to Sausalito, Alcatraz, Wine Country, Tiburon, Angel Island; (415) 546-2896.

WALKING TOURS

Chinatown Adventure Tours with the Wok Wiz. Culinary and historical strolls with cookbook author and television chef Shirley Fong-Torres, with lunch or dinner. (415) 355-9657.

Chinese Culture Foundation. Culinary tour and heritage walk; (415) 986-1822.

City Guides. Architectural, cultural, and historical walking tours of City Hall, Civic Center, Coit Tower, Market Street, North Beach, Pacific Heights, fire houses, Mission District murals, Cathedral Hill, Japantown, Presidio, Jackson Square, Golden Gate Bridge, etc.; (415) 557-4266.

East Bay Regional Parks. (510) 635-0135. Ranger-led tours and activities in the parks are geared for all ages.

Frisco Tours. Film, fiction, and witty crime tours by bus or on foot with author Mark Gordon; (415) 681-5555.

Golden Gate National Recreation Area. Ranger-led interpretive walks through the parks, including Sutro Baths, Marin Headlands, Muir Woods, Tennessee Valley; tours of the Maritime Museum ships, gun batteries, tide pools; Indian folklore walks, photography walks, sunset walks, etc.; (415) 556-0560.

Helen's Walk Tours. (510) 524-4544. San Francisco neighborhood tours in English, French, Spanish, or Arabic.

Heritage Walks. (415) 441-3000. Architectural tours of Pacific Heights on Sunday afternoons.

Literary Tours. Don Herron leads a tour of Dashiell Hammett's haunts in the city, sometimes in period costume; other literary tours (e.g., Russian Hill) can be arranged (707) 939-1214.

Oakland Heritage Alliance. (510) 763-9218. Architectural and historical tours of Oakland's neighborhoods and Mountain View Cemetery.

Performing Arts

■ PERFORMING ARTS

The Bay Area is a big center of the performing arts. Some, like the San Francisco Opera (415-864-3330), ACT (American Conservatory Theater; 415-749-2228), and the Berkeley Repertory (510-845-4700), have national reputations, but there are scores of innovative smaller companies, like the Eureka Theater, the Magic Theater, the Asian American Theater, Theater Rhinoceros, George Coates Performance Works, and the San Francisco Mime Troupe, scattered throughout the city and beyond. *Beach Blanket Babylon,* a campy, long-running musical revue, continues to play to packed houses at **Club Fugazi** in North Beach, call (415) 421-4222. If you're in the mood for a laugh, San Francisco is also famed for its comedy clubs, which nursed such national figures as Lenny Bruce, Bill Cosby, the Smothers Brothers, and Robin Williams. **Josie's Cabaret & Juice Joint** is well known for its gay-oriented comedians and performers.

San Francisco's dance aficionados like to follow the **San Francisco Ballet,** which performs at the War Memorial Opera House (415-703-9400). (While the War Memorial undergoes renovation, the ballet performs at the Yerba Buena Center for the Arts, 415-978-2787.) Other companies to follow include ODC Dance Company, Lines Contemporary Ballet, Margaret Jenkins Dance Company, Zaccho, and the Joe Goode Performance Group. These and other local companies perform at Theater Artaud, the Yerba Buena Center for the Arts, the Cowell Theater, ODC Performance Gallery, and Oakland's Laney College. Every summer, San Francisco State University hosts the **Ethnic Dance Festival,** where audiences are treated to a taste of capoeira, Balinese dance, traditional Scots folk dance, and In Berkeley, prominent national names in dance as well as music can be found at the University of California's **Zellerbach Hall;** call Cal Performances (510) 642-9988.

The **San Francisco Symphony** (415-431-5400) season runs from September through May. The **California Palace of the Legion of Honor** arranges regular concerts of classical music, including demonstrations of antique forms and instruments, as well as lectures. In the fall, **Jazz in the City** asks jazz musicians of every stripe—bebop, Latin, fusion—to play at venues throughout San Francisco. The Asian Art Museum hosts an annual **Asian American Jazz Festival.** Blues, jazz, folk, country and ethnic music, including Irish bands and Beijing opera, spice the mix.

New releases play nightly in the city's cinemas, and seldom-seen classic films and independent releases can be found at theaters including the Castro, Embarcadero, Lumiere, Gateway, Roxie, Vogue, and Clay theaters. Film lovers should keep an eye on the universities, especially Berkeley, where the **Pacific Film Archive** serves as the Bay Area's film gallery. The **San Francisco International Film Festival,** based in Japantown's Kabuki Theatre, brings works from around the world to San Francisco every spring. Call (415) 931-FILM.

In October, **Artists' Open Studios** offers a peek into artists' studios around San Francisco; call (415) 861-9838. In the East Bay, Artists' Open Studios takes place in June; call (510) 763-4361. You can pick up a free quarterly pamphlet called "Bay Area Gallery Guide" at many galleries around town, with a map and artist listings.

Complete listings of cinema, dance, music, clubs, and other happenings appear weekly in the *Sunday Chronicle* "Datebook" section, also called the "Pink Sheet." For the current word on concerts, festivals, and clubs, check out the *Bay Guardian* or *SF Weekly.*

■ MUSEUMS, AMUSEMENTS & CULTURAL CENTERS

The four big fine arts museums of San Francisco are the Museum of Modern Art, the M. H. de Young Museum, the Asian Art Museum, and the California Palace of the Legion of Honor. The city also has two large science museums: the Exploratorium and the California Academy of Sciences. (The latter houses an aquarium and a planetarium.) In addition, San Francisco supports a zoo, botanical gardens, the National Maritime Museum, and a surprising number of small, sometimes eccentric museums. Most large museums in San Francisco grant free entry on the first Wednesday of every month.

Beyond San Francisco are the Oakland Museum, the Lawrence Hall of Science and the University Art Museum in Berkeley, and the Egyptian Museum, the San Jose Museum of Art, and the Technical Museum of Innovation in San Jose.

The following institutions are described in the text; check the index.

SAN FRANCISCO

African-American Museum. Building C, Fort Mason; (415) 441-0640.

Alcatraz. Ferry leaves from Pier 41, near Fisherman's Wharf; (415) 546-2896.

American Indian Contemporary Arts. 685 Market St.; (415) 495-7600.

Ansel Adams Center. 250 Fourth St.; (415) 495-7000.

Asian Art Museum. Music Concourse, Golden Gate Park; (415) 668-8921.

Cable Car Barn. Mason and Washington; (415) 474-1887.

California Academy of Sciences. Music Concourse, Golden Gate Park; (415) 750-7145.

California Palace of the Legion of Honor. Lincoln Park; (415) 750-3600.

Cartoon Art Museum. 814 Mission St.; (415) 546-3922.

Chevron Oil Museum. 555 Market St.; (415) 555-6697.

Chinese Historical Society. 650 Commercial St.; (415) 391-1188.

Coit Tower. Telegraph Hill; (415) 362-0808.

Craft and Folk Art Museum. Building A, Fort Mason; (415) 775-0990.

De Young Museum. *See M. H. de Young Museum.*

Diego Rivera Gallery, San Francisco Art Institute. 800 Chestnut St.; (415) 771-7020.

Museums, Amusements & Cultural Centers

Museums, Amusements & Cultural Centers

Exploratorium. 3601 Lyon St.; (415) 561-0360.

Federal Reserve Bank. 101 Market St.; (415) 974-2000

Fire Department Museum. *See San Francisco Fire Department Museum.*

Fort Point. End of Marine Dr., under the Golden Gate Bridge; (415) 921-8193.

Haas-Lilienthal House. 2007 Franklin St.; (415) 441-3004.

Jewish Community Museum. 121 Steuart St.; (415) 543-8880.

Josephine Randall Junior Museum. 199 Museum Way (near Corona Heights Park); (415) 554-9600.

Laserium. In Morrison Planetarium at the California Academy of Sciences, Golden Gate Park; (415) 750-7138.

M. H. de Young Museum. Music Concourse, Golden Gate Park; (415) 750-3600.

Mexican Museum. Building D, Fort Mason; (415) 441-0404.

Mission Dolores. Dolores (16th St.); (415) 621-8203.

Morrison Planetarium. California Academy of Sciences, Golden Gate Park; (415) 750-7141

Museo Italo Americano. Building C, Fort Mason; (415) 673-2200.

Musée Mécanique. Cliff House, 1066 Point Lobos; (415) 386-1170

Museum of Russian Culture. 2450 Sutter; (415) 921-4082.

Museum of the Money of the American West. Basement, Bank of California, 400 California St.; (415) 765-0400.

National Maritime Museum. Beach St. at Polk; (415) 556-8177.

North Beach Museum. 1435 Stockton St.; (415) 391-6210.

Octagon House. 2645 Gough St.; (415) 441-7512.

Old U.S. Mint. Fifth St. (Mission); (415) 556-6704

Pacific Heritage Museum. 608 Commercial St.; (415) 399-1124

Presidio Army Museum. Funston at Lincoln Blvd. in Presidio; (415) 561-4331

SS *Jeremiah O'Brien.* Pier 32, foot of Brannan St.; (415) 441-3101

San Francisco Craft and Folk Art Museum. Building A, Fort Mason; (415) 775-0990.

San Francisco Fire Department Museum. 655 Presidio Ave.; (415) 861-8000.

San Francisco History Room. Main Library, Larkin at Grove; (415) 857-4567.

San Francisco Museum of Modern Art. 151 Third St.; (415) 357-4000.

San Francisco Performing Arts Library and Museum. 399 Grove St. (Gough); (415) 255-4800.

San Francisco Zoo. Sloat Blvd. at 45th Ave.; (415) 753-7080

Steinhart Aquarium. California Academy of Sciences, Golden Gate Park; (415) 750-7145.

Telephone Pioneer Communications Museum. 140 New Montgomery; (415) 542-0182.

USS *Pampanito. See National Maritime Museum.*

Wax Museum at Fisherman's Wharf. 145 Jefferson St.; (415) 885-4975.

Wells Fargo History Room. 420 Montgomery St.; (415) 396-2619.

EAST BAY

Ardenwood Historic Farm. Hwy. 84 and Ardenwood Blvd., Fremont; (510) 796-0663.

Bancroft Library. East side of Doe Library, U.C. Berkeley; (510) 642-3781.

Benicia Camel Barns. 2060 Camel Rd., Benicia; (707) 745-5435.

Benicia Old State Capitol Building. First St. (G St.), Benicia; (707) 745-3385.

Chabot Observatory. 4917 Mountain Blvd., Oakland; (510) 530-5225

Children's Fairyland. Lakeside Park, north shore of Lake Merritt, Oakland; (510) 452-2259.

Ebony Museum. Jack London Square, Oakland; (510) 763-0745.

Jack London Museum. Jack London Square, Oakland; (510) 451-8218.

John Muir House. 4202 Alhambra Ave., Martinez; (510) 228-8860.

Knowland State Park and Oakland Zoo. 9777 Golf Links Rd., Oakland; (510) 632-9523.

Lawrence Hall of Science. Centennial Dr.

(Grizzly Peak Blvd.); U.C. Berkeley; (510) 642-5133.

Judah L. Magnes Memorial Museum. 2911 Russell St., Berkeley; (510) 849-2710.

Marine World Africa USA. 1000 Fairgrounds Ave. (US 80/CA37), Vallejo; (707) 643-6722.

Mission San Jose. Mission Blvd. (Washington), Fremont; (510) 657-1797.

Oakland Museum. 1000 Oak St., Oakland; (510) 238-2200.

P. A. Hearst Museum of Anthropology. Kroeber Hall, U.C. Berkeley, Bancroft Way; (510) 643-7648.

Paleontology Museum. Earth Sciences Bldg., U.C. Berkeley; (510) 642-1821.

University Art Museum. 2626 Bancroft Way, Berkeley; (510) 642-1207.

University Botanical Gardens. Centennial Dr., U.C. Berkeley; (510) 642-3343.

Western Aerospace Museum. North Field, Oakland Airport, 8260 Boeing St., Bldg. 621; (510) 638-7100.

SOUTH BAY

Barbie Hall of Fame. 433 Waverley St., Palo Alto; (415) 326-5841.

Children's Discovery Museum. Corner of West San Carlos St. and Woz Way, San Jose; (408) 298-5437

Filoli Estate. Canada Rd. off US280, near Woodside; (415) 364-2880.

NASA/Ames Research Center. Moffett Field, near Mountain View; (415) 604-5000.

Museums, Amusements & Cultural Centers

Roaring Camp & Big Trees Railway. Felton; (408) 335-4484.

Rosicrucian Egyptian Museum. Park Ave. (Naglee); San Jose; (408) 287-9171.

San Jose Museum of Art. 110 S. Market St., San Jose; (408) 294-2787.

Stanford University Museum of Art. Museum Way, Stanford University, Palo Alto; (415) 723-4177.

Technical Museum of Innovation. 145 W. San Carlos, San Jose; (408) 279-7150.

Villa Montalvo. 15400 Montalvo Rd. off CA 9, Saratoga; (408) 741-3421.

Winchester Mystery House. 525 South Winchester Blvd. (near US 280 and CA 17), San Jose; (408) 247-2101.

NORTH BAY

Bay Area Discovery Museum. 557 East Fort Baker (GGNRA, near Sausalito); (415) 332-9646.

Bay Model. 2100 Bridgeway, Sausalito. (415) 332-3870.

California Marine Mammal Center. Near Rodeo Beach, GGNRA; (415) 927-3394.

Jack London State Park. 24000 London Ranch Rd., Glen Ellen; (707) 938-5216.

Lachryma Montis. Spain and Third St. West, Sonoma; (707) 938-1519.

Marin County Historical Museum. The Gatehouse, Mission St. (B St.), San Rafael; (415) 454-8538.

Marin Museum of the American Indian. 2200 Novato Blvd., Novato; (415) 897-4064

Napa Valley Wine Train. 1275 McKinstry St., Napa; (800) 427-4124 or (707) 253-2111.

Point Reyes Visitors' Center. Bear Valley, Point Reyes National Seashore; (415) 663-1092.

San Francisco Bay Model. *See Bay Model.*

San Quentin Museum. Building 106, San Quentin Prison; (415) 454-1460.

Sharpsteen Museum. 1311 Washington St., Calistoga; (707) 942-5911.

Silverado Museum. 1490 Library Ln., St. Helena; (707) 963-3757.

Sonoma State Historical Park. 20 E. Spain St., Sonoma Plaza, Sonoma; (707) 938-1519.

Vallejo's House. *See Lachryma Montis.*

RECOMMENDED READING

■ HISTORY

Ashbury, Herbert. *The Barbary Coast*. New York: Alfred A. Knopf, Inc., 1933. An entertaining jaunt through some of San Francisco's shadier byways.

Bronson, William. *The Earth Shook, the Sky Burned*. New York: Doubleday, 1959. Pictures and reporting from the 1906 earthquake.

Chinn, Thomas Wo. *Bridging the Pacific*. San Francisco: Chinese Historical Society, 1989. The most complete history of Chinatown.

Cole, Tom. *A Short History of San Francisco*. San Francisco: Lexikos, 1981. A succinct and entertaining account, widely available in museums and bookstores.

Dillon, Richard H. *The Hatchet Men*. New York: Ballantine, 1972. A somewhat lurid, if entertaining, account of the tong wars.

Hansen, Jim. *The Other Guide to San Francisco*. San Francisco; Chronicle Books, 1980. Written with humor, this guide is particularly informative for persons tracking down such fading memories as Haight-Ashbury hippie haunts and North Beach beatnik rendezvous.

Margolin, Malcolm. *The Ohlone Way*. Berkeley: Heyday Books, 1978. History of the major Bay Area tribe. The history and culture of other pre-European Bay Area residents are treated in *The Way We Lived: California Indian Reminiscences, Stories, and Songs* (Berkeley: Heyday Books, 1993).

Muir, John. *The Mountains of California*. 1977. Berkeley: Ten Speed Press, 1977. World-renowned conservationist's earliest book about the Sierras, cradle of the conservation movement. *The Yosemite* (New York: The Century Co., 1912) is a description of the Sierra's most famous scenery.

■ GUIDEBOOKS

Bakalinsky, Adah. *Stairway Walks in San Francisco*. San Francisco: Lexikos, 1984. Illustrated. Pokes around some of the city's most enchanting stairways and obscure neighborhoods, territory unknown even to most natives.

Delehanty, Randolph. *The Ultimate Guide: San Francisco*. San Francisco: Chronicle Books, 1989. Delehanty's pleasant style, excellent maps, and rich observation of architecture, history, and city planning makes this a self-contained education in the humanities.

Doss, Margot Patterson. *Golden Gate Park at Your Feet.* San Francisco: Chronicle Books, 1970. One of a series of light-hearted walking books by the author. Other titles include: *Paths of Gold* (San Francisco: Chronicle Books, 1974), covering walks in the Golden Gate National Recreation Area; *San Francisco at Your Feet* (New York: Grove Press, 1970) describes idiosyncratic walks through San Francisco's neighborhoods. *The Bay Area at Your Feet* (San Francisco: Chronicle Books, 1970) suggests walks around the Bay Area, and *There, There* (San Rafael: Presidio Press, 1978) does the same for the East Bay.

Edwards, Don. *Making the Most of Sonoma County.* Alameda: Valley of the Moon, 1986. A thourough guide to this northern county, one of the main regions of the Wine Country.

Ferlinghetti, Lawrence, and Nancy J. Peters. *Literary San Francisco.* San Francisco: City Lights, 1980. The literary sites of the city, with terrific portraits and group photos.

Fodor's San Francisco. New York: Fodor's Travel Publications, Inc., 1996. Practical info for the whole Bay Area, with coverage of the Wine Country.

Fong-Torres, Shirley. *San Francisco Chinatown—A Walking Tour.* San Francisco: China Books & Periodicals, 1991. An intimate guide to the city's most populous quarter.

Graham, Jerry and Catherine. *Bay Area Backroads.* New York: Harper & Row, 1988. Discover out-of-the-way destinations with the hosts of the popular television show.

Guide to California's Wine Country. Menlo Park, CA: Lane Publishing Co., 1982. Lists virtually all the wineries by locale, with detailed maps and tour information.

Herron, Don. *The Literary World of San Francisco & Environs.* San Francisco: City Lights Books, 1985. Geared for literary tours of specific neighborhoods, and written by the man who gives the Dashiell Hammett walking tours.

Magary, Alan, and Kerstin Fraser Magary. *Across the Golden Gate.* New York: Harper & Row, 1980. A guide to the North Bay, with visits to the wineries.

Olmsted, Nancy. *To Walk with a Quiet Mind.* San Francisco: Sierra Club Books, 1975. A good companion on the Point Reyes and Mount Tamalpais trails.

Pitcher, Don. *Berkeley Inside/Out.* Berkeley: Heyday Books, 1989. The authority on Berkeley, and an entertaining read in its own right.

San Francisco and the Bay Area On the Loose. Berkeley, CA: Berkeley Guides,

Fodor's Travel Publications Inc., 1996. Written by U.C. Berkeley students, this guide gives a casual, insider's look at the Bay Area, with savvy advice and humorous commentary for the budget traveler.

Socolich, Sally. *Bargain Hunting in the Bay Area.* Berkeley: Wingbow Press, 1980. The definitive shopping guide, arranged by item.

Thollander, Earl. *Earl Thollander's San Francisco, 30 Walking Tours from the Embarcadero to the Golden Gate.* New York: Clarkson N. Potter, 1987. Charmingly illustrated.

Unterman, Patricia. *Restaurants of San Francisco.* Written with Stan Sesser. San Francisco: Chronicle Books, 1988. One of the city's best restaurants critics gives her advice.

Whitnah, Dorothy L. *Outdoor Guide to the San Francisco Bay Area.* Berkeley: Wilderness Press, 1989. The best of the great outdoors.

Woodbridge, Sally and John. *San Francisco—the Guide.* San Francisco: American Institute of Architects, 1982. A serious guide to city architecture.

The voice of the Beat generation lives on at City Lights bookstore in North Beach. (Kerrick James)

■ FICTION

Bierce, Ambrose. *The Devil's Dictionary.* Owings Mills, MD: Slemmer House, 1978. A devilishly clever list of bitingly cynical definitions. Arguably the most vitriolic book ever written. Published in part in 1906 under the title *The Cynic's Word Book.*

Coolbrith, Ina. *California.* San Francisco: Book Club of California, 1918. First poet laureate of California, longtime resident of San Francisco, and inspiring friend to many other literary lights.

Duane, Daniel. *Lighting Out, A Vision of California and the Mountains.* St. Paul, MN: Graywolf Press, 1994. A spiritual exploration of California landscape in the late twentieth century by the Berkeley-raised author and mountain climber.

Ferlinghetti, Lawrence. *These Are My Rivers: New & Selected Poems, 1955–1993.* New York: New Directions, 1993. The city's resident poet of the Beat generation.

Ginsberg, Allen. *Howl and Other Poems.* San Francisco: City Lights, 1959. The harbinger of the Beat movement in San Francisco.

Hammett, Dashiell. *Continental Op. Stories.* New York: Random House, 1974. Stories of the San Francisco-based detective with many colorful episode and characters around town. *The Maltese Falcon.* S. Yarmouth, MA: J. Curley, 1929. The most famous mystery story set in San Francisco, made into the classic film starring Humphrey Bogart.

Harte, Bret. *The Luck of Roaring Camp.* Oakland: Star Rover House, 1983. Written in San Francisco's Golden Era Building.

Kerouac, Jack. *On the Road.* New York: Viking Press, 1957. The book that defined the Beat Generation.

Kingston, Maxine Hong. *The Monkey King.* New York: Alfred A. Knopf, 1989. Novel with a Bay Area setting by the author of *China Men* (New York: Alfred A. Knopf, 1980) and *Woman Warrior* (S. Yarmouth, MA: J. Curley, 1978).

London, Jack. *Martin Eden.* New York: Macmillan, 1957. This semi-autobiographical novel describes the life of a struggling writer, and includes fictionalized characters of Bay Area literary figures like George Sterling.

Maupin, Armistead. *Tales of the City.* New York: Harper & Row, 1989. The serialized tales of contermporary city life collected in several volumes. Catch the television adaptation if you can.

Miller, Joaquin. *Selected Writings.* Eugene, OR: Orion Press, 1977. Poetry and "history" by the colorful frontiersman who lived in Oakland.

Norris, Frank. *The Octopus.* Cambridge, MA: R. Bentley, 1971. A scathing indictment of powerful nineteenth-century railroad corporations in California's Central Valley.

Seth, Vikram. *The Golden Gate.* New York, Random House: 1986. A contemporary novel of San Francisco life and manners in rhymed verse.

Sterling, George. *A Wine of Wizardry and Other Poems.* A. M. Robertson, San Francisco: 1909. Weird and wonderful, the poet at his best. *The Testimony of the Suns.* A. M. Robertson, San Francisco: 1907. Intensely beautiful language.

Stevenson, Robert Louis. *The Silverado Squatters.* Cutchogue, NY: Buccaneer Books, 1989. A pleasant jaunt with charming companions (Stevenson and bride Fanny on their honeymoon) through nineteenth-century Napa Valley.

Twain, Mark. *Roughing It.* Chicago: Gilman & Co., 1872. The funniest description of the nineteenth-century American West includes the author's colorful pictures of early San Francisco.

Wolfe, Tom. *The Electric Kool-Aid Acid Test.* New York: Farrar, Straus & Giroux, 1969. Recounting some of the local lore of the Merry Pranksters and the hippie years.

I N D E X

Muir, John   87, 244
Muir Beach   270-271
Muir Woods   269
museums   *also see* "Museums, Amusements, and Cultural Centers, in "PRACTICALITIES," 349-352
African-American Historical & Cultural Society 143, 164;   Ansel Adams Center 76
Asian Art Museum 188-189;   Bank of America History Room 60;   Barbie Hall of Fame 253
Bay Area Discovery Museum 268;   Behring Auto Museum 244;   Cable Car Barn 98-99;   California Palace of the Legion of Honor 173, 175-176;
Cartoon Art Museum 77;   Chevron Oil Museum 69;   Children's Discovery Museum 254;
Chinese Cultural Center 105;   Chinese Historical Society 104;   de Saisset Museum, University of Santa Clara 253;   Exploratorium 147, 148, 150;
Federal Reserve Bank 69;   Fire Department Museum 169;   Guinness Museum of World Records 138;   Jack London Museum 221;   Jewish Community Museum 68-69;   Josephine Randall Junior Museum 195;   Judah L. Magnes Memorial Museum 231;   Lawrence Hall of Science 238;
Lindsay Museum, Walnut Creek 244;   M. H. de Young Memorial Museum 188;   Main Library 86;   Marin Museum of the American Indian 265;   Mexican Museum 143;   Museo Italo Americano 143;   Museum of Russian Culture 168;   Museum of the History of San Francisco 138;   Museum of the Money of the American West 58;   North Beach Museum 118;   Oakland Museum of California 221-223;
Pacific Film Archives, Berkeley 236
Pacific Heritage Museum 62;   Paleontology Museum, Berkeley 234;   Phoebe Apperson Hearst Museum of Anthropology 235;
Presidio Army Museum 151;   Ripley's Believe it or Not Museum 138;   Rosicrucian Egyptian Museum 255;   San Francisco Craft and Folk Art Museum 143;   San Francisco Museum of Modern Art 75, 76, 78;   San Francisco National Maritime Museum 139;   San Francisco Performing Arts Library and Museum 87;   San Jose Historical Museum 254;   San Jose Museum of Art 254;   San Quentin Museum 265;
Sharpsteen Museum 287;   Silverado Museum 284;   Sonoma County Museum 277, 279;

Steinhart Aquarium 186, 188;   Tech Museum of Innovation 254;   Telephone Pioneer Communications Museum 77;   Treasure Island Museum 213;   University Art Museum, Berkeley 236;   University of California at Berkeley Museum, Blackhawk 244;   USS *Pampanito* 135, 137;   Wax Museum at Fisherman's Wharf 138;   Wells Fargo History Room 60;   Western Aerospace Museum 230

Napa, town of   278, 283
Napa County   281-287
Napa Valley wineries   282, 284, 285
NASA Ames Research Center   252
National Military Cemetery   151
Native Americans   21
Nevada   32
New Chinatown   172
nightlife   326-328
Nob Hill   36, 91-98
Noe Valley   204-206
Nordstrom   79
Norras Temple   106
Norris, Frank   15, 97-98
North Bay   261-287
North Beach   112-121
North Beach Museum   118
North Berkeley   239
Norton, Joshua A. *see* Emperor Norton
Nova Albion   22

O'Farrell, Jasper   25, 65, 68
O'Neill, Eugene   241
Oakland   215-231;   Chabot Observatory 230;   Children's Fairyland 223;   Chinatown 220;   Claremont Resort 231;   downtown 215-220;   estuary 220-221;   Grand Lake Theater 224;   Heinold's First and Last Chance saloon 221;   Housewives Market 217;   Jack London Museum 221;   Jack London Square 220-221;   Jack London Village 221;   Joaquin Miller Park 227;   John B. Williams Plaza 216;   Knowland State Park 230;   Lake Chabot 227;   Lake Merritt 221-224;   Lakeside Park 223;   Oakland Museum of California 221-223;   Outdoor Market 217;   Paramount Theater 216-217;   Redwood Regional Park 224, 227;   Rockridge 230;

COMPASS AMERICAN GUIDES

Critics, Booksellers, and Travelers All Agree You're Lost Without a Compass.

Arizona (3rd Edition)
1-878-86772-5
$18.95 ($26.50 Can)

Chicago (2nd Edition)
1-878-86780-6
$18.95 ($26.50 Can)

Colorado (3rd Edition)
1-878-86781-4
$18.95 ($26.50 Can)

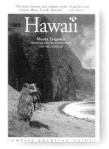

Hawaii (3rd Edition)
1-878-86791-1
$18.95 ($26.50 Can)

Wine Country (1st Edition)
1-878-86784-9
$18.95 ($26.50 Can)

Montana (2nd Edition)
1-878-86743-1
$17.95 ($25.00 Can)

Oregon (2nd Edition)
1-878-86788-1
$18.95 ($26.50 Can)

New Orleans (2nd Edition)
1-878-86786-5
$18.95 ($26.50 Can)

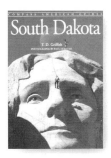

South Dakota (1st Edition)
1-878-86726-1
$16.95 ($22.95 Can)

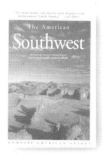

Southwest (1st Edition)
1-87866779-2
$18.95 ($26.50 Can)

Texas (1st Edition)
1-878-86764-4
$17.95 ($25.00 Can)

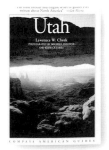

Utah (3rd Edition)
1-878-86773-3
$17.95 ($25.00 Can)

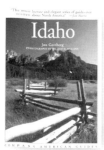

Idaho (1st Edition)
1-878-86778-4
$18.95 ($26.50 Can)

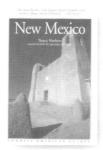

New Mexico (2nd Edition)
1-878-86783-0
$18.95 ($26.50 Can)

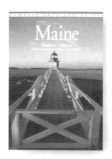

Maine (1st Edition)
1-878-86751-2
$16.95 ($22.95 Can)

Manhattan (2nd Edition)
1-878-86794-6
$18.95 ($26.50 Can)

Las Vegas (4th Edition)
1-878-86782-2
$18.95 ($26.50 Can)

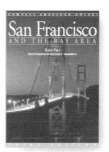

San Francisco (4th Edition)
1-878-86792-X
$18.95 ($26.50 Can)

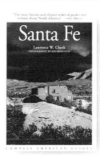

Santa Fe (1st Edition)
1-878-86775-X
$18.95 ($26.50 Can)

South Carolina (1st Edition)
1-878-86766-0
$16.95 ($23.50 Can)

Virginia (2nd Edition)
1-878-86795-4
$18.95 ($26.50 Can)

Washington (1st Edition)
1-878-86758-X
$17.95 ($25.00 Can)

Wisconsin (1st Edition)
1-878-86744-X
$16.95 ($22.95 Can)

Wyoming (2nd Edition)
1-878-86750-4
$18.95 ($26.50 Can)

KELLY DUANE

■ ABOUT THE AUTHOR

Born and raised in the San Francisco Bay Area, writer and editor Barry Parr brings to this guide a native's first-hand knowledge of the city and the perspective of a world traveler. Mr. Parr earned degrees in English literature from the University of California at Berkeley and from Cambridge University in England. He has lived for several years in England and Hong Kong, where he worked as a magazine editor and writer. He has contributed articles to *Travel & Leisure, Discover, Mandarin, Asiaweek,* and other publications. Currently he resides in the Bay Area with his wife and two children.

■ ABOUT THE PHOTOGRAPHERS

San Francisco-born photographer **Michael S. Yamashita** has been shooting pictures for National Geographic Society magazines and books since 1979. He is a frequent contributor to *Travel & Leisure* and *Portfolio,* and his many corporate clients include the Mexican Tourist Board, Singapore Airlines, and Nikon Cameras. Mr. Yamashita's work has been exhibited at the Smithsonian Institution's Museum of American History, the National Gallery in Washington, and Kodak's Professional Photographer's Showcase at EPCOT center in Florida.

Kerrick James grew up in the San Francisco Bay Area, and credits its cosmopolitan atmosphere and cultural variety in enriching his photography. His work often appears in travel and inflight magazines, as well as in other Compass titles including *Arizona, Las Vegas,* and *The American Southwest.* He lives in Mesa, Arizona with his wife Theresa and son Shane.